INTERNATIONAL
AND
COMPARATIVE
CRIMINAL
LAW
SERIES

A Guide to Documents on the Arab-Palestinian/Israeli Conflict: 1897–2008

M. Cherif Bassiouni

Shlomo Ben Ami

MARTINUS NIJHOFF PUBLISHERS

2009

Library of Congress Cataloging-in-Publication Data

A guide to documents on the Arab-Palestinian/Israeli conflict : 1897–2008 / [compiled by] M. Cherif Bassiouni and Shlomo Ben Ami.—[Rev. ed.]
p. cm.
Rev. ed. of: Documents on the Arab-Israeli conflict / edited by M. Cherif Bassiouni.
ISBN 978-90-04-17534-1
1. Arab-Israeli conflict—Law and legislation—History—Sources. 2. Palestine—International status—History—Sources. 3. Arab-Israeli conflict—History—Sources. I. Bassiouni, M. Cherif, 1937– II. Ben-Ami, Shlomo. III. Documents on the Arab-Israeli conflict.
KZ6795.A72D63 2009
956.04—dc22

2009009922

Koninklijke Brill NV incorporates the imprints Brill, Hotei Publishers, IDC Publishers, Martinus Nijhoff Publishers, and VSP.

Manufactured in the United States of America

To three men whose roles as beacons of peace in the Middle East should inspire other leaders and never be forgotten—

Anwar al-Sadat

Jimmy Carter

Menachem Begin

"Blessed are the peacemakers." (Matthew 5:9)

*Facsimile of the Original Signature Page of the 1979 Egypt-Israel Peace Treaty**

- 7 -

DONE at Washington, D.C. this 26th day of March, 1979, in triplicate in the English, Arabic, and Hebrew languages, each text being equally authentic. In case of any divergence of interpretation, the English text shall prevail.

حررت فى واشنطن دى . سى . فى ٢٦ مارس ١٩٧٩م ، ٢٧ ربيع الاول ١٣٩٩ هـ
من ثلاث نسخ باللغات الانجليزية والعربية والعبرية وتعتبر جميعها متساوية
الحجية ، وفى حالة الخلاف حول التفسير فيكون النص الانجليزى هو الذى يعتد به .

נעשה בוושינגטון, די.סי. ביום זה כ"ז באדר לשנת תשל"ט, 26 במרץ 1979, בשלושה
עותקים בשפות האנגלית, הערבית והעברית וכל נוסח אמין במידה שווה. במקרה של הבדלי
פרשנות, יכריע הנוסח האנגלי .

For the Government of the Arab Republic of Egypt:

من حكومة
جمهورية مصر العربية :

בשם ממשלת הרפובליקה הערבית
של מצרים :

For the Government of Israel:

من حكومة
اسرائيل :

בשם ממשלת ישראל :

Witnessed by:
شهد التوقيع :
הועד על-ידי :

Jimmy Carter, President
of the United States of America

جيمى كارتر ، رئيس
الولايات المتحدة الامريكية

ג'ימי קארטר, נשיא
ארצות הברית של אמריקה

* *See infra* Doc. 310.

Excepts of Speeches Made on the White House Lawn on March 26, 1979

Let there be no more wars or bloodshed between Arabs and Israelis. Let there be no more wars or bloodshed between Arabs and Israelis. Let there be no more suffering or denial of rights. Let there be no more despair or loss of faith. Let no mother lament the loss of her child. Let no young man waste his life on a conflict from which no one benefits. Let us work together until the day comes when they beat their swords into plowshares and their spears into pruninghooks. And God does call to the abode of peace. He does guide whom He pleases to His way.

The President of the Arab Republic of Egypt
Anwar al-Sadat

Two prophets, Yishayahu Ben Amotz and Micah Manorashti, having foreseen the spiritual unity of man under God, with these words coming froth from Jerusalem, gave the nations of the world the following vision—expressed in identical terms—"And they shall beat their swords into plowshares and their spears into pruninghooks: nation shall not lift up sword against nation, neither shall they learn war any more."

Despite the tragedies and disappointments of the past, we must never forsake that vision, that human dream, that unshakable faith.

Peace is the beauty of life. It is sunshine. It is the smile of a child, the love of a mother, the joy of a father, the togetherness of a family. It is the advancement of man, the victory of a just cause, the triumph of truth. Peace is all of these and more, and more.

The Prime Minister of the State of Israel
Menachem Begin

All our religious doctrines give us hope. In the Koran, we read: "But if the enemy incline towards peace, do thou also incline towards peace, and trust in God; for He is the One that heareth and knoweth all things."

And the prophet Isaiah: "Nations shall beat their swords into plowshares and their spears into pruninghooks: nation shall not lift up sword against nation, neither shall they learn war any more."

So let us now lay aside war. Let us now reward all the children of Abraham who hunger for a comprehensive peace in the Middle East. Let us now enjoy the adventure of becoming fully human, fully neighbors, even brothers and sisters. We pray God, we pray God together, that these dreams will come true. I believe they will.

The President of the United States
Jimmy Carter

Table of Contents

Author's Preface

The Arab-Israeli conflict has been referred to in different terms over the last sixty years, namely, the Palestine Question, the Palestine-Jewish Question, the Arab-Israeli Conflict, the Palestinian-Israeli Conflict, the Arab-Zionist Conflict. Lack of consensus as to what to call this conflict reveals only the tip of its complexities. These are made up of a mixture of ideological, religious, and political factors. Combined, they have led to more than a half-century of inter-community violence, several wars, and regional instability. More significantly, they have caused an estimated 100,000 casualties, the disintegration of Palestinian society, billions in economic costs, and the loss of opportunities to millions of people for a better life.[1] All parties concerned are to blame, as is the international community, which has all too frequently failed to bite the bullet and impose a fair peace with which all sides could live.[2] In early 2008 the hope was that the worst has occurred and that the prospects for peace are better now than in the past few years. But as experience painfully reveals, every time a new depth has been reached, leading to the belief that the conflict has reached bottom, another lower level is reached. This was the case with Israel's invasion of Gaza on December 27, 2008, and the harm that it caused the Palestinians during that attack.[3] The accumulation of human, material, and moral harm has led to bitter harvests. Recent events might suggest to some that no worse can happen, but it can.

A more rational approach based on mutual understanding and an appreciation of the conflict's complex dimensions is indispensable to advancing the goals of peace and reconciliation. Yet, the protagonists are so polarized that even a description of the conflict raises claims of partisanship by one side or the other.[4] This extends to comprehensive

[1] For figures, see for example the Jewish Virtual Library Web site, "Casualties of the Arab-Israeli Wars," http://www.jewishvirtuallibrary.org/jsource/History/casualties.html.

[2] In 1947, the British decided against imposing upon Palestine the United Nations Partition Plan outlined in Security Council Resolution 181 given Arabs' rejection of it.

[3] The Gaza Crisis resulting in between 1,100 and 1,300 dead in Gaza, 5,300 injured, destruction of infrastructure and personal property; rocket fire from Gaza during the crisis killed thirteen Israelis as roughly 560 rockets were fired by Palestinian Militants.

[4] For example, Ilan Pappe, a member of Israel's Communist Hadash party (whose writings are discounted by most mainstream academics) won praise for *A History of Modern Palestine: One Land, Two Peoples*. *Library Journal's* review cited the "increasingly harsh conditions imposed by the realities of Israeli policies in the Occupied Territories." Reviewing the book for *The New Republic*, Benny Morris, the most prominent of the so-called "new" Israeli historians, claims that Pappe has a fierce anti-Israel agenda. In turn, Benny Morris's book *1948: A History of the First Arab-Israeli War* was critically reviewed by one of these writers, Shlomo Ben Ami, in the September/October 2008 issue of Foreign Affairs.

analytical works that evidence shared experiences and the commonality of values between Palestinians and Israelis. Indeed, no scholar on either side has ever presented an account of the two peoples' history which has satisfied both Arabs and Jews. Perhaps it is because Arabs and Jews share such a momentous history that everything in this conflict is perceived as being larger than life and that even slight disagreement raises fundamental issues central to the culture, identity, and self-esteem of each side. The divisiveness of the conflict has conditioned the protagonists' perceptions of each other and of themselves. This has in part shaped their actions, which have been characterized by an evolving cycle of violence that has so far proven difficult to arrest.

At the risk of over-simplification, the conflict can be summed up in the following formulation: two groups of people—related by race, ancestry, belief, and culture—find themselves competing over the same territory and are driven by different nationalistic and religious goals.

For those on both sides who are willing to share the land and accept the concept of two states living in peace with each other, conflict is not inevitable. For them the possibility of peace and reconciliation is not hopeless. However, for those who seek exclusive control over land, the conflict is intractable and peace only attainable when one side triumphs over the other. Because the forces of division are stronger than those of rapprochement, they represent the more visible aspect of the conflict. These forces of division have so far successfully managed to thwart peace efforts through their strategies of polarization and radicalization.

In its sixtieth anniversary Israel stands at a most vital crossroads. Never has this cliché been more appropriate. The fate of the state, no less, is at stake. It was after all none other than Israel's prime minister, Ehud Olmert, who warned that if Israel remained bogged down in the Occupied Territories and a Palestinian state is not established this might be "the end of the Jewish state." Israel must assume that the territorial phase of Zionism is over, and that its victory in the 1948 war can be sealed only when the national dignity of the Palestinians is restored, and their right to live in dignity in their own independent state is implemented on a territory that is geographically contiguous and economically viable.

This is not impossible, and the dismantling by Israel of the settlements in the Gaza Strip in 2005 proves that the march of folly of settlements' expansion is not irreversible. For, against the ominous predictions of those who saw the spectre of civil war looming over Israel if a massive dismantling of settlements was carried out, in Gaza, the disengagement proved to be an anti-climax. It showed that Israel is a society mature enough to face the challenge of defining its permanent borders without internal political and social upheavals. The task remains of course laden with difficulties, for it would be wrong to draw an automatic analogy between the Gaza experience and the case of the more sensitive lands of Eretz-Israel, as Israelis and Jews call Judea and Samaria, and which the Palestinians call "the West Bank"—not to speak of Jerusalem which the Palestinians call, with religious reverence, al-Quds, the holy city. But the precedent has been established and, for the first time in its history, the State of Israel challenged the Eretz-Israel taboo and survived and similar steps in furtherance of place are possible.

For the Israelis, it is vital to assume that no change in the international system, however radical it may be, will spare them the hard and painful choices that they have to make. They will also hopefully learn the lesson from their attempts to quell the *Intifada* or dismantle the Hamas regime in Gaza. In this respect, they are not the first in history to learn that states, however strong, do not really have a deterrent power against national uprisings. Internationally legitimized borders will offer Israel more deterrence power than F-16 raids on targets, however legitimate, that end up killing innocent civilians, without really deterring attackers. For Israel, the capacity to deter its enemies remains vital. But, as the United States has learned the hard way in Iraq, this is an era where power without legitimacy only breeds chaos, and military supremacy without international consent for the use of force does not offer security. Israel's respect for its international border with Lebanon has given more security to its northern villages than twenty years of military occupation of that country. Only when a free and independent Palestinian state will acquire a vested interest in preserving regional order and have a democratic government based on the Rule of Law, can real peace prevail.

Peace with the Palestinians will, sooner or later have to be complemented with a peace agreement between Israel and Syria, whose parameters are only too well known. Only then might the conditions be created for an accommodation between Israel and the Arab and Muslim worlds, and a regional system of security with the elimination of weapons of mass destruction be possible. Any attempt to develop such a regional system before the Arab-Israeli conflict has been solved is doomed to failure.

One would also expect that the Palestinian national movement would reshape itself to allow for an end to the latent civil war in their midst between secular and religious nationalists. This is not going to be a smooth or easy affair. For, not all these trends of national disintegration have to do with the failure of the peace process, nor is the decline of secular nationalism a strictly Palestinian phenomenon. Throughout the entire Arab world the incumbent regimes have failed to address vital issues of social, economic, and cultural alienation. Loyalty to the state and to the nation is being superseded everywhere by alternative loyalties, such as the family, the tribe, but first and foremost by loyalty to Islam as a form of government. Seen from a wider regional perspective, the Palestinian problem in the last twenty years has mirrored the broader Middle East where we can see a growing challenge to state institutions representing regimes which failed to provide their part of the bargain in the social contract. Alienation has brought about the emergence of powerful non-state actors whose goals include enmity toward Israel and the United States, as well as against the American-led peace process.

The sixty years of war and conflict that we have witnessed in that small part of the Middle East, reveal, if anything, how little human consideration each side has given the other. Efforts at peacemaking have invariably been of a state-centric nature, ignoring the human dimension of what peace is really about. Peace, if it is not to be a mere cease-fire, can only occur when the protagonists to a given conflict have embarked on a process of reconciliation. It is when people reach out to understand each other, to have compassion for one another, and translate that into action that peace does occur. A piece of paper on which the word agreement is written is worth no more than the value of the paper it is written on.

For sure, old grievances must be settled; wounds must be healed, victims must be satisfied, truthful history must be written, memorials have to be established, and the lessons of the past must be learned in order to avoid repeating the previous mistakes. In short, justice in the broadest human and material sense must be part of the peace process. And contrary to what many believe, it is not as difficult a course to embark upon once the will to do so has been marshaled.

Peace is not only a matter of assuaging the feelings of the opponent. It is about providing security and confidence in the future. The former, however, should not overshadow the latter. It is mostly confidence in the future that provides assurances for security. Confidence in the future requires hope for sustained economic development with integration of the economies of those who were once enemies. As they become economically dependent on one another, no matter what their respective economic strengths may be, and as they come to share reciprocal concerns for their security, they can achieve conditions of peace that no document, no matter how well drafted, can ever match.

What has been lacking in the last decades of peace process efforts is not only such a broad vision of the future, but a detailed blueprint of how to achieve it. If only, as a matter of academic exercise, authorities on the Israeli and Palestinian sides convened a group of experts covering various aspects of economic and social develop as well as security, the group of experts would likely produce such a blueprint. This would include a common system for utilities, sharing of natural resources, a common transportation system, free movement of goods and people, a common banking and financial system with convertible currencies, an urban development plan, harmonization of laws and enhancement of legal capabilities, and so on. There is just so much that can and should be done, and that in itself would establish confidence in the future.

At this point, there is little for the Israelis to look forward to, other than maybe a lull or stoppage in violent interaction, but even less for the Palestinians, whose economy has been devastated, their national unity shattered, and the good will that came from their victimization at the hands of Israel wasted by their in-fighting and by suicide bombings which have killed innocent Israeli civilians. Neither side has much to offer the other if things stay as they are. But they have much to offer to one another if they have a shared vision of their future relations and economic development.

The Israeli-Palestinian vision should not stop with them. It can and should expand to include a regional security system that would encompass Israel, Palestine, Jordan, Egypt, Syria, and Lebanon. That could lead to a regional economic union that would thrust that part of the world into a new era similar to the one that Europe experienced when it first founded the Common Market and then the European Union. There is no reason why a regional vision cannot transform the economies and well-being of all of the states mentioned above and establish a strong foundation for peace and security.

What must be stated, however, is that none of that can take place without the marginalization of those who believe in the exclusivity of their survival or of the hegemony of their relationship with the other. If peace is to occur it will be because those in Israel who seek territorial expansion and hegemony over the Palestinians will have been politically marginalized, and violent and intolerant extremists among the Palestinians will have also been marginalized.

The Holy Places in Palestine and Israel, represent that which most links the three Abrahamic faiths of Judaism, Christianity, and Islam. More particularly, the monotheistic concept that exists in Judaism and Islam constitutes a significant commonality between these two religions. Yet, notwithstanding that which links the Abrahamic faiths, we have witnessed throughout times devastating conflicts between Jews, Christians, and Muslims. At times these conflicts have taken on a religious characteristic, at others a political one. No matter the reason, in the end, it has always resulted in human tragedy and material destruction.

For three religions who acknowledge the existence of one God, who has created a single humanity and who has communicated to that single humanity through a succession of prophets and messengers, it is hard to understand why there is not greater harmony in that part of the world between people who are, after all, cousins.

War is not inevitable and peaceful co-existence and cooperation is possible. Leaders with vision must emerge on both sides, supported by their respective external constituencies to frame the new discourse of peace in terms with which the people in question can identify.

It may be self-evident to state that people can walk into the future while looking exclusively at the past. Admittedly, it is not easy to turn one's back to the past without breaking faith with it, and that is not what is suggested.

Each community, Palestinian and Israeli, will have to forge their new identities in view of the future that they will seek to chart for themselves. Israelis will have to see themselves as something more than emanations of the holocaust, and Palestinians will have to see themselves as more than victims of Zionism.[5]

M. Cherif Bassiouni and Shlomo Ben Ami
done respectively in Chicago and Toledo,
February 2009.

[5] "These days Israel has no guide for the perplexed; values have been blurred, mutual support is disintegrating and becoming riddled with holes, the diplomatic road to peace is blocked and gloomy. From the outside, Iran, Gaza, and the realities of demographics and population loom, and a public debate on the future of our tormented state barely exists. The political system is fatigued and remains outside the piercing discussion on the fundamental question of our lives and of the quest for new answers."—Avraham Burg, The Holocaust Is Over We Must Rise From Its Ashes XIV (2007).

Acknowledgements

This book is a shorter and modified version of the two volumes entitled *Documents on the Arab-Israeli Conflict,* which I compiled and which were published by Transnational Publishers in 2005. Shlomo Ben Ami joined me, and his contribution to the section of additional documents has given this book a valuable dimension.

In preparing this edition, I was assisted by Ryan Carey (J.D. cand. 2009, DePaul University) whose help in updating the documents from 2005 to 2008, as well as securing additional new documents that were not in the previous compilation, is highly appreciated.

M. Cherif Bassiouni

Introduction

This straightforward, comprehensive, and non-partisan compilation is designed to provide the reader with relevant source material on the history and evolution of the Arab-Israeli conflict. Its goal is to further our understanding of the conflict.

The book consists of three parts. Part I provides a chronology of events in the Arab-Israeli conflict. Part II puts the conflict into perspective by providing the historical background and discussing the various conflicts, military strategies, prospects for peace, and more. Part III includes summaries and cites to 690 documents on the Arab-Israeli conflict covering the period from 1897 to 2008, as well as key texts on Jerusalem going back to 636 C.E.

The documents begin with the Program of the First World Zionist Congress, held in Basle, Switzerland, in 1897, and conclude with the Security Council resolution on the conflict in Gaza in the beginning of 2009.

What sets this compilation apart from others is its comprehensive inclusion of documents from diverse civil, religious, national, and international bodies, including the League of Nations; United Nations agencies; the governments of Britain, Egypt, Israel, Jordan, the Palestinian Authority, and the United States; the European Union; the League of Arab States; the Jewish Agency; and the Holy See.[6]

Part III is organized according to the conflict's major topic areas, with introductory notes for each part and section, as well as a summary of each document. It is divided into nine main section, with documents therein presented in chronological order. The division of the sections reflects both a historical and topical approach, and, thus, some of the documents contained in one section are necessarily relevant to other sections. In such cases, they are cross-referenced and should be jointly consulted.

---

[6] Walid Khalidi's *From Haven to Conquest: Readings in Zionism and the Palestine Problem Until 1948* (1971); John Norton Moore's *The Arab-Israeli Conflict* (1975); The Institute for Palestine Studies' *United Nations Resolutions on Palestine and the Arab-Israeli Conflict, Vols. 1–4,* and an electronic compilation by Yale University's Avalon Project. Walter Laquer and Barry Rubin have compiled *The Israel-Arab Reader: A Documentary History of the Middle East.* There are also various Web sites that contain compilations of many relevant documents. The following Web sites are extremely useful and have been relied upon as electronic document sources in this work: United Nations Information System on the Question of Palestine (UNISPAL), *available at* http://domino.un.org UNISPAL.NSF?OpenDatabase; United Nations General Assembly, *available at* http://www.un.org/ ga/59/; United Nations Security Council, *available at* http://www.un.org/Docs/sc/; Official Document System of the United Nations, *available at* http://ods-dds-ny.un.org/doc/RESOLUTION/GEN/NR0/435/33/IMG/NR043533.pdf?OpenElement; Israeli Ministry of Foreign Affairs, *available at* http:// www.mfa.gov.il/mfa/; Yale University Avalon Project, *available at* http://www.yale.edu/lawweb/ avalon/avalon.htm.

Section 1 covers World War I, the fall and dismemberment of the Turkish Ottoman Empire, the British occupation of Jerusalem, and the general period that preceded the League of Nations Mandate for Palestine. It contains documents that reflect the views of leading political figures of the time, such as Sharif Hussein of Mecca, Winston Churchill, Theodor Herzl, and Chaim Weizman. Their influence helped shape policy and future events in Palestine.

Section 2 covers the period of the League of Nations Mandate for Palestine from 1922 to 1948, when Britain held administrative authority in Palestine. Documents in this section include the text of the 1922 mandate,[7] which gave Britain formal and internationally recognized control over Palestine, and United Nations General Assembly Resolution 181 (1947),[8] which if implemented would have divided Palestine into two states—one Arab and one Jewish, with Jerusalem reserved as a *corpus separatum.*

Section 3 covers the five major Arab-Israeli Wars of 1948, 1956, 1967, 1973, and 1982. It should be read alongside relevant documents from Section 6, Jerusalem and the Holy Sites, and Section 8, Status of the Palestinians.

Section 4 includes documents on the Arab-Israeli peace process. Although the actual peace process did not gain real momentum until Egyptian President Anwar al-Sadat's speech before the Israeli Knesset in 1977,[9] United Nations Security Council Resolutions 242 (1967)[10] and 338 (1973)[11] lead this section because of their integral role in establishing a legal basis for peace in the region.

Section 5 includes documents on pressing security concerns in the Middle East—demilitarization, disarmament, and the regulation and control of nuclear capabilities and weapons of mass destruction. It begins with a series of documents on the demilitarization of Mount Scopus in Jerusalem during the 1948 war[12] and includes United Nations General Assembly Resolution 3263 (1974),[13] the first United Nations resolution calling for the establishment of a nuclear-weapons-free zone in the Middle East.

Section 6 contains documents pertaining to the City of Jerusalem and the Holy Sites. It includes historical documents from 636 to 2008 that outline the unique legal regimes that have been specially established

---

[7] *See* Doc. 24.

[8] *See* Doc. 60.

[9] *See* Doc. 299.

[10] *See* Doc. 242.

[11] *See* Doc. 198.

[12] *See* Docs. 327.

[13] *See* Doc. 329.

for Jerusalem during the last fourteen centuries—including the Turkish Ottoman *Status Quo* Decree of 1852, which protects the rights of worshippers and grants religious denominations the right to manage their respective Holy Sites, and the 1948 United Nations Draft Statute for the City of Jerusalem.[14] Because of the central importance of Jerusalem to the conflict and to its protagonists, this section should be referenced in connection with all other sections.

Section 7 contains documents from the Israeli-Palestinian peace process. It includes groundbreaking agreements such as the Declaration of Principles on Interim Self-Government between Israel and the Palestine Liberation Organization (PLO),[15] the Interim Agreement on the West Bank and Gaza Strip between Israel and the PLO,[16] the Amendment to the PLO Charter,[17] the Wye River Memorandum,[18] the Road Map,[19] and Israeli Prime Minister Ariel Sharon's Disengagement Plan.[20]

Section 8 includes documents on the legal status of the Palestinians since 1948. Divided into four sub-sections, it reveals the evolving nature of their conflict with Israel: as refugees from 1948–2008 (Section A); under occupation from 1967–2008 (Section B); as an emerging national entity, 1964–2008 (Section C); and as a minority group in Israel (Section D).[21] Section 8 also provides the reader with a systematic examination of Palestinian legal rights and claims in the Occupied Palestinian Territories and Israel.

Section 9 covers the escalation of violence during the two Palestinian *Intifadas* (or uprisings) of 1987 and 2000. International humanitarian law defines these military conflicts as different from the major Arab-Israeli wars because they are not of an international character. The reader is invited to examine these sections alongside documents in Section 8, Status of the Palestinians.

Most of the documents contained in this compilation are of a legal nature. The majority are United Nations documents, international treaties, and other agreements. Redundant United Nations resolutions have not been included, but whenever relevant, they are referred to in a footnote. Also included are a number of reports issued by investigatory

---

[14] *See* Doc. 346.

[15] *See* Doc. 432.

[16] *See* Doc. 442.

[17] *See* Doc. 450.

[18] *See* Doc. 458.

[19] *See* Doc. 484.

[20] *See* Doc. 494.

[21] In this volume, the term "Palestinian Israelis" is used to refer to those Arabs currently residing within the State of Israel. This term is used with an understanding of the complexity of identity distinctions within the region.

commissions at key points in the conflict, as well as political documents, such as letters and memoranda from heads of state. Several laws, decrees, and commission reports from the State of Israel are included because of their relevant subject matter—as are Arab summit declarations and resolutions that contribute to an understanding of position of the Arab states. The dates of issue or publication and citations for the documents are also provided.

Glossary of Terms

The documents summarized in this volume are mainly resolutions and reports issued and adopted by the various United Nations bodies and agencies, as well as treaties and agreements relating to conflict and peace. The names and titles of some of these documents may be less familiar to the reader than others, and their connotation may not be readily understandable. Thus, some of these terms are described below. It should be noted, however, that they are not always uniformly applied or interpreted as this depends on the intentions of the source or body that produced the document or that subsequently interprets it. The explanations of terms that follow are the authors' and are intended exclusively for this publication.

ACCORD: An agreement or arrangement between two or more governments and/or other quasi-public entities that may or may not have legal status under international law. If it is between states, it has the same status as a treaty, convention, agreement, and pact (see also *Covenant* below). The term *accord* is, however, occasionally used to give the impression that the nature of the agreement is more "soft" than a treaty in terms of legal obligations. See, for example, the OSLO ACCORDS (1993).[22]

ADVISORY OPINION: Opinion issued by the International Court of Justice at the request of a United Nations body. It is not an adjudication of a case or controversy and has no binding legal effect on states as does an opinion in a contentious case. It has, however, a strong indicative legal character and, thus, carries significant moral and/or legal authority if it reflects or declares customary international law. See, for example, the INTERNATIONAL COURT OF JUSTICE DECISION: LEGAL CONSEQUENCES OF THE CONSTRUCTION OF A WALL IN THE OCCUPIED PALESTINIAN TERRITORY (2004).[23]

AIDE-MEMOIRE: A diplomatic document that records what a state, acting through its diplomatic channels, means or understands about a specific obligation, including a treaty obligation. Sometimes such a document allows the parties to a treaty whose terminology is ambiguous to explain their separate understandings. See, for example, AIDE MEMOIRE PREPARED BY UNITED NATIONS SECRETARY-GENERAL DAG HAMMARSKJOLD, ON CONDITIONS FOR THE WITHDRAWAL OF UNEF (1957).[24]

ARMISTICE AGREEMENT: A suspension or cessation of hostilities by agreement between belligerent powers or combatants that is equivalent to a truce, cease-fire, or suspension of hostilities. Such an agreement is a binding treaty if made between states. If made between a state and an insurgent group, it is also binding under international humanitarian law. While its duration is usually temporary, in the case of the 1949 Armistice

[22] Doc. 432.

[23] Doc. 589.

[24] Doc. 144.

Agreements between Israel and certain Arab states, these agreements have become almost permanent.[25] (See also *Separation of Forces Agreement.*)

BASIC LAW OF THE STATE OF ISRAEL: Israel has no written Constitution; however, certain laws enacted by the Knesset constitute a core body, which the Supreme Court of Israel has deemed equivalent to a constitution. See, for example, BASIC LAW: HUMAN DIGNITY AND LIBERTY (1992).[26]

COMMUNIQUÉ: An official pronouncement expressing public policy or a statement issued after a meeting or conference that constitutes the participants' public expression of that meeting or conference's outcome. Unlike a treaty, it is non-binding, but it could be considered a manifestation of a state's position or intention. The same applies to a communiqué issued by a group of states or by an international organization. See, for example, COMMUNIQUÉ ISSUED BY THE QUARTET (2002).[27]

COVENANT: A formal agreement between two parties, such as states or quasi-public entities, or a unilateral promise contained in a treaty or other document expressing the binding intention of the state or state official making the undertaking. See, for example, the COVENANT OF UMAR (636 or 638 CE).[28]

DECLARATION: A unilateral formal statement or a proclamation by a government that may be legally binding on that state. A declaration is not predicated on reciprocal promises and undertakings by another state. Sometimes it is intended to reflect state policy or a state's intentions as to future policy. (See also *Proclamation.*) See, for example, the BALFOUR DECLARATION (1917).[29]

DECREE: The term may refer to a law adopted by a duly constituted legal authority that is not a legislative authority. It usually applies to the issuance of orders by heads of state, governmental bodies, or quasi-public bodies exercising administrative functions. In some legal systems, the term refers to a judicial decision or to an executive order. In this volume, the first of these two meanings applies. See, for example, DECREE OF SURRENDER OF JERUSALEM INTO BRITISH CONTROL (1917).[30]

LETTERS OF EXCHANGE: A formal letter of transmission from a state to another state or international organization that conveys a formal diplomatic text, such as a treaty or instrument of ratification. Sometimes it contains legal positions intended to bind the issuing authority, or it may reflect something agreed upon that the parties do not want to formally include

[25] Docs. 93–96.
[26] Doc. 631.
[27] Doc. 483.
[28] Doc. 344.
[29] Doc. 8.
[30] Doc. 394.

in a treaty. (See also *Note Verbale* below.) See, for example, EXCHANGE OF LETTERS BETWEEN UNITED STATES PRESIDENT JIMMY CARTER, ISRAELI PRIME MINISTER MENACHEM BEGIN, AND EGYPTIAN PRESIDENT ANWAR AL-SADAT (1978).[31]

FIRMAN OR FARAMAN: An edict or order issued by the Sultan of the Turkish Ottoman Empire, similar to a *Decree* (see above). Usually provides a grant, license, or permission to a person, group of persons, or a community (*e.g.*, religious). See, for example, IMPERIAL FIRMAN CONCERNING THE CHRISTIAN HOLY PLACES (1852).[32]

INTERIM AGREEMENT: A temporary or provisional agreement entered into for a limited period of time deemed to be an intervening time, prior to a permanent agreement. It is legally binding upon its parties. See, for example, INTERIM AGREEMENT ON THE WEST BANK AND GAZA STRIP BETWEEN ISRAEL AND THE PLO (1995).[33]

MEMORANDUM OF UNDERSTANDING: It may be an expression of "best efforts" or "intentions" between parties and thus non-binding. Good faith performance is, however, expected. Sometimes it is a legally binding agreement. The United States and Israel have a number of such agreements, particularly in the area of military cooperation. This type of document is used to avoid the necessity of having the agreement go through a parliamentary process that is constitutionally or legally required. This applies to the United States, where a treaty is constitutionally required to obtain the U.S. Senate's "advice and consent." See, for example, MEMORANDUM OF UNDERSTANDING BETWEEN ISRAEL AND THE UNITED STATES (1975).[34]

NON-PAPER: Term of art for a written document intended to express a state's position without, however, committing that state thereto. It is not intended to be an expression of a final position. Usually employed as a diplomatic method for testing ideas and generating discussion. Frequently used in multilateral negotiations and within international organizations. (See also *Working Paper.*) See, for example, EUROPEAN UNION NON-PAPER ON THE TABA CONFERENCE (2001).[35]

NOTE VERBALE: A French term meaning a diplomatic note containing a state's assertion of a position. Also used to express a protest. See, for example, NOTE VERBALE FROM THE PERMANENT MISSION OF ISRAEL TO THE SECRETARIAT OF THE COMMISSION ON HUMAN RIGHTS (2004).[36]

---

[31] Doc. 309.
[32] Doc. 346.
[33] Doc. 442.
[34] Doc. 215.
[35] Doc. 472.
[36] Doc. 585.

EXECUTIVE ORDER: An order issued by the president of the United States pursuant to his constitutional powers that directs or instructs the executive agencies or government officials or sets policies for the executive branch to follow. It has become equivalent to decrees issued by other heads of states. (See *Decree.*) See, for example, U.S. EXECUTIVE ORDER 12947: PROHIBITING TRANSACTIONS WITH TERRORISTS WHO THREATEN TO DISRUPT THE MIDDLE EAST PEACE PROCESS (1995).[37]

ORDINANCE: Derives from the French term *ordonnance*, which is equivalent to a law or decree. Common law systems, however, use the term for official acts adopted by municipal governments to regulate local administration. See, for example, Israel's AREA OF JURISDICTION AND POWERS ORDINANCE (1948).[38]

PEACE INITIATIVE: It may be anything from a a call for a conference to a formal peace proposal produced by an entity or by an individual of standing that is aimed at furthering the peace process. More frequently, it refers to a specific idea or a substantive or procedural proposal. See, for example, ARAB PEACE INITIATIVE ESTABLISHED AT THE ARAB LEAGUE SUMMIT (2002).[39]

PROCLAMATION: A formal public announcement made by a government or head of state or by an entity such as a quasi-public body, similar to a *Declaration* (see above). See, for example, PROCLAMATION OF THE ESTABLISHMENT OF THE PALESTINE LIBERATION ORGANIZATION (1964).[40]

PROTOCOL: An amendment to an existing treaty. It is also a term used for a document containing the formal record of the proceedings of a conference or negotiations. In this case, it is equivalent to what is called in diplomatic parlance, a *procés-verbal.* See, for example, PROTOCOL ON ECONOMIC RELATIONS BETWEEN THE GOVERNMENT OF ISRAEL AND THE PLO (1994).[41]

SEPARATION OF FORCES AGREEMENT: An agreement similar to an *Armistice* (see above), but of a more temporary and limited nature. Sometimes, however, it can be considered a binding treaty. It usually precedes an armistice or a more permanent peace agreement. See, for example, SEPARATION OF FORCES AGREEMENT BETWEEN ISRAEL AND EGYPT (1974).[42]

WHITE PAPER: A statement of policy usually issued by a government to express a position on a given matter or present a report on a past incident or describing a previous situation. The British Government issued several such papers during the period of the League of Nations Mandate for

---

[37] Doc. 441.
[38] Doc. 79.
[39] Doc. 479.
[40] Doc. 604.
[41] Doc. 435.
[42] Doc. 205.

Palestine. See, for example, STATEMENT OF BRITISH POLICY IN PALESTINE (CHURCHILL WHITE PAPER) (1922).[43]

WORKING PAPER: A document reflecting a non-binding work in progress or describing ongoing negotiations. (See also *Non-Paper.*) See, for example, WORKING PAPER PREPARED BY THE SECRETARIAT, UN CONCILIATION COMMISSION FOR PALESTINE: THE FUTURE OF ARAB PALESTINE AND THE QUESTION OF PARTITION (1949).[44]

[43] Doc. 21.

[44] Doc. 101.

Table of Documents

1. Antecedents to the Mandate for Palestine: 1897–1922

B. Suez War: 1956

i. Pre-War Developments

ii. 1956 War (October 29, 1956–March 6, 1957)

ii. 1967 War (June 5–11, 1967)

iii. Post-War Developments

B. Status of the Palestinians under Occupation: 1967–2008

List of Abbreviations and Acronyms

AIPAC	America Israel Public Affairs Committee
DMI	Director of Military Intelligence
GSS	General Security Service (Israel)
HAMAS	Islamic Resistance Movement
IAEA	International Atomic Energy Agency
ICCPR	International Covenant on Civil and Political Rights
ICJ	International Court of Justice
ICRC	International Committee of the Red Cross
IDF	Israeli Defence Force
LHY	Lochamei Heruth Israel (or Stern Group)
NGO	non-governmental organization
NPT	Treaty on the Non-Proliferation of Nuclear Weapons
OAPEC	Organization of Arab Petroleum Exporting Countries
PNA	Palestinian National Authority
PFLP	Popular Front for the Liberation of Palestine
PLO	Palestine Liberation Organization
TIPH	Temporary International Presence in Hebron
U.N.	United Nations
U.S.	United States
UNEF	United Nations Emergency Force
UNESCO	United Nations Educational, Scientific and Cultural Organization
UNIFIL	United Nations Interim Force in Lebanon
UNSCOP	United Nations Special Committee on Palestine
UNTSO	United Nations Truce Supervision Organization (Palestine)
UNRWA	United Nations Relief and Works Agency for Palestinian Refugees
USSR or Soviet Union	Union of Soviet Socialist Republics
WMD	weapons of mass destruction

Part I

Chronology*

B.C.

1004	Approximate date of the founding of the ancient State of Israel.
586	Destruction of the first Jewish temple, built by Solomon, by King Nebuchadnezzar of Babylonia and the "Babylonian Captivity" of the Jews.
538	Jews released from captivity by Cyrus the Great of the Achaemenian Empire of Persia. Cyrus assists Jews in reconstruction of the temple.
520–516	Completion of second temple.
168	Temple either completely destroyed or seriously damaged by earthquake.
37–34	Construction of third temple, or reconstruction of second temple, by Herod the Great.

A.D.

71–72	Temple and entire city of Jerusalem destroyed by order of Roman Emperor Titus. Construction of an entirely new city that is forbidden to the Jews. Beginning of the "diaspora."
638	Surrender of Jerusalem to Muslims completes the conquest of Palestine.
683	Construction of the Dome of the Rock on Mount Zion ("Temple Mount") by Umayyad Caliph 'Abd al-Malik.
1071	Saljuk Turks take Jerusalem and Holy Land.
1099	Capture of Jerusalem by the Crusaders and establishment of the "Kingdom of Jerusalem."
1516	Ottoman Turkish conquest of Syria and Palestine by Selim the Grim. Entire Fertile Crescent absorbed into Ottoman Empire. Palestine created as "Sanjak of Jerusalem."
1881	Assassination of Alexander II, "Tsar of all the Russians." Organized riots (*pogroms*) break out against the Jews on behalf of the Russian Orthodox Church. Pogroms spread westward into Central Europe.

* *See* Charles L. Geddes, A Documentary History of the Arab-Israeli Conflict XI (1991); Bernard Reich, Arab-Israeli Conflict and Conciliation 7 (1995)

1882	Leo Pinsker publishes pamphlet *Auto-emancipation*, calling for the creation of a "Jewish state somewhere on earth." Beginning of first aliyah to Palestine.
1896	Publication of *Der Judenstaat* ("The Jewish State") by Theodor Herzl.
1897	World Zionist Organization is created.
1897	First Zionist Congress held Basel, Switzerland, August 29–31. Adoption of the "Basel Program." Until his death seven years later Herzl attempts to obtain land in Palestine for Jews from Ottoman Sultan.
1903	Seventh Zionist Congress held in Basel. Great Britain offers huge tract of land in highlands of British East Africa for Jewish national home, which is refused.
1904	Death of Theodor Herzl. Leadership of Zionist Organization passes into hands of David Wolffsohn.
1908	"Committee of Union and Progress" effects revolution against the Ottoman Government. Extreme Turkish nationalism and Ottomanism eliminates any possibility of Zionists obtaining land in Palestine by legal means.
1914	Outbreak of World War I in Europe in August. Ottoman Empire enters conflict on side of Central Powers (Germany and the Austro-Hungarian Empire) in November.
1915	July 4–March 10, 1916, exchange of ten letters between Sharif of Two Holy Cities of Mecca and Medina and British Government—"Hussein—McMahon Correspondence." Arabs promise military assistance to Great Britain in return for recognition of their independence.
1916	Exchange of notes between British, French, and Russian governments leads to "Sykes-Picot Agreement" May 6–9, in which the three states agree to divide Fertile Crescent among themselves. On November 2, Sharif Hussein proclaims himself "King of the Arab Countries." Great Britain and France officially recognize him as "King of the Hijaz."
1917	British war cabinet, hoping that rallying American Jews to Britain's cause would help bring the United States into the war, and probably also keep Russia in the war, issues to Baron Rothschild a letter on November 2, known as the "Balfour Declaration." Previously accepted by Prime Minister Georges Clemenceau of France and President Woodrow Wilson of United States.

1918 President Wilson delivers "Fourteen Points" speech before U.S. Congress on January 8. States that self-determination of peoples is one of the objectives of the war. Three days previously, on January 5, Prime Minister David Lloyd George of Great Britain makes a similar declaration. On October 1, Arabs under command of Prince Feisal, son of King Hussein, enter Damascus Proclamation of "Arab Constitutional Government" over Syria and Palestine. Ottoman Turks surrender in the Near East on October 30. Publication of "Anglo-French Declaration on November 7.

1919 Feisal-Weizmann correspondence. King-Crane Commission delivers its final recommendation concerning the Near East to President Wilson on August 28. Not published until 1922.

1920 San Remo Conference of Entente Powers (Great Britain, France, Italy, and Japan) establishes mandates for Great Britain over Palestine and Iraq, and France over Syria on April 25.

1921 Transjordan becomes separate entity; Abdullah established as emir, March.

1922 Issuance of "Churchill White Paper" in June as official British position regarding virtually unlimited Jewish immigration into Palestine. On July 24, Palestine Mandate "officially as signed to Great Britain by Council of the League of Nations. U.S. Congress endorses "Balfour Declaration" by Public Resolution on September 21. Beginning of U.S. involvement in coming dispute.

1924 By Anglo-American Convention United States accept British mandate over Palestine.

1930 Issuance of "Passfield White Paper." Publication of public letter from British Prime Minister Ramsay McDonald to Chaim Weizmann in *The Times* to elucidate "White Paper" ("McDonald Letter"). Shaw Commission Report. Hope-Simpson Report. British issue Passfield White Paper limiting Jewish immigration into and Jewish land purchases in Palestine.

1936 General strike by Palestinian Arabs against British mandate and Zionist program from April to October.

1937 June 22—publication of Peel Commission Report recommending partitioning of Palestine. Woodhead Commission appointed January in 1938 to put partition into effect. Government finds partitioning "impracticable."

1939 London Conference in attempt to find solution fails. Publication of "1939 White Paper" on May 17, recognizing impossibility of partition and placing limit on further Jewish immigration and land purchases and proposing establish men of independent Palestinian state at end of ten years. Rejected by both Jews and Arabs as not going far enough to meet their respective, and opposing, demands. Outbreak of World War II on September 3.

1942 Biltmore Program promulgated, May.

1945 Formation of League of Arab States on March 22. Germany and Austria surrender on May 7.

1946 Recommendations of the Anglo-American Commission of Inquiry signed on April 20 call for future single state in Palestine. Until hostilities cease, territory is to remain under mandate or given over in trusteeship to United Nations. Joint six-member committee formed by United States and Great Britain to examine recommendations of Commission results in "Grady-Morrison Plan," which supports the concept of a single state. Conference on Palestine convened in London on September 10 between British, Arab, and Zionist leaders.

1947 London talks recognized as complete failure, February 14. In letter to secretary-general of United Nations, April 2, Britain announces decision to surrender mandate over Palestine. On November 29, U.N. General Assembly passes Resolution 181 (II) calling for partitioning of Palestine into three states: Jewish, Arab, and an internationalized Jerusalem by a vote of thirty-three to thirteen with ten abstentions.

1948 Proclamation of State of Israel May 14, immediately recognized by President Harry Truman. British mandate over Palestine officially ends on May 15 with withdrawal of troops. May 15 outbreak of first Arab-Israeli war lasting until July 1949. Israel occupies new section of Jerusalem. Beginning of Palestine refugee problem with hundreds of thousands fleeing conflict.

1949 Israel admitted into membership of United Nations. General Assembly establishes United Nations Relief and Works Agency to assist destitute Arab Palestinian refugees. King Abdallah of Jordan annexes the West Bank and East Jerusalem in December. Ratified by Jordanian Parliament in April 1950.

1956 President Jamal 'abd al-Nasir of Egypt nationalizes Suez Canal on July 26. Israel, France, and Great Britain attack Egypt leading to "Suez War."

1964 Palestine Liberation Organization (PLO) founded in Jerusalem on June 2 with adoption of Palestinian National Covenant and

Constitution. Israel's National Water carrier begins operation; crisis erupts over Jordan waters.

1965 Fatah is established and launches its first attack against Israel on January 1.

1967 "Six Day War" of June leads to Israeli capture of old city of Jerusalem and territories in West Bank. U.N. Security Council passes Resolution 242.

1973 "Yom Kippur War," October, leads to Israeli capture of Syrian Golan Heights, West Bank from Jordan and Gaza Strip from Egypt.

1974 PLO granted "Observer Status" in U.N. General Assembly.

1975 Israeli-Egyptian Agreement signed in September for withdrawal of forces from Sinai Peninsula and establishment of American observers along the cease-fire line ("Sinai I" and "Sinai II").

1978 "Camp David Accord" signed September 17 between President Jimmy Carter of the United States, President Anwar al-Sadat of Egypt, and Prime Minister Menachem Begin of Israel. Arab summit in Baghdad on November 5 denounces Camp David Accords and criticizes Egypt.

1979 Peace treaty between Egypt and Israel signed in Washington, D.C., on March 26. March 31 "Baghdad Resolution" of Islamic Conference leads to isolation of Egypt from most other Arab countries. President al-Sadat assassinated.

1980 European Community leaders issue "Venice Declaration" as basis for peace.

1981 Crown Prince Fahd of Saudi Arabia enunciates "Fahd Peace Plan" on August 8. Adopted by other Arab states as "Fez Declaration."

1982 Israeli invasion and occupation of southern Lebanon begins June 5. PLO withdraws from Lebanon under U.S. sponsorship.

1987 Uprising *(Intifada)* of Palestinians in West Bank and Gaza Strip, which Israeli army attempts to suppress with "iron fist" policy without success.

1988 HAMAS is created in the Gaza Strip, February. Palestinian National Council declares independent State of Palestine in West Bank and Gaza Strip on November 15. In statement issued December 15, Yasser Arafat, Chairman of the PLO Executive Committee, explicitly recognizes Israel's right to exist. By Resolution 43/177, December 15, U.N. General Assembly acknowledges the proclamation of the State of Palestine. On December 16, United States opens talks with PLO at its headquarters in Tunis.

1989 Egypt readmitted to the Arab League on May 22. European Community issues Madrid statement on June 27. U.S. Secretary of State James Baker suggests five-point plan in October.

1990 President Bush calls off talks with PLO on June 20. On August 2, Iraqi troops invade neighboring Kuwait. That evening, in an emergency session, the Security Council passes the first of a series of twelve resolutions calling for withdrawal of Iraq and establishing an international military force to implement decisions. PLO leader Yasser Arafat and large numbers of Palestinians declare support for Saddam Hussein, president of Iraq. On October 8, a Jewish fundamentalist group, "Faithful of the Temple Mount," marches on al-Aqsa Mosque to symbolically place a stone for rebuilding of Jewish Temple, although forbidden by Israeli Supreme Court. Muslims gathered to prevent action begin throwing stones at marchers. Israeli police shoot at demonstrators with live ammunition, killing seventeen to twenty, wounding approximately 150. Security Council, October 12, passes Resolution 672 condemning Israel for use of excessive force. Resolution denounced by Israeli government.

1991 International force of twenty-eight nations begins action against Iraq to force withdrawal from Kuwait, January 16. On February 28, truce implemented when Iraq agrees to comply with all Security Council resolutions. President Bush announces time propitious to settle disputes in Near East, including Arab-Israeli conflict. On March 5, Secretary of State James Baker begins lengthy series of talks with leaders. During summit meeting in Moscow Presidents Bush and Gorbachev of Union of Soviet Socialist Republics (USSR) announce on July 31 to jointly sponsor Arab-Israeli peace conference to begin October 10. Israeli government and PLO agree to participate, August 4.

1992 Yitzhak Rabin forms coalition government in Israel, July.

1993 Secret negotiations between Israel and PLO in Oslo, Norway, in the spring. Israel launches Operation Accountability in Lebanon, July. Israel-PLO Declaration of Principles (DOP) signed in Washington, D.C., on September 13. Israel and Jordan sign a Common Agenda for negotiations on September 14. The Conference to Support Middle East Peace (the Donors Conference) meets in Washington on October 1. Israel and the PLO open talks in Egypt on implementation of the DOP on October 13.

1994 Oslo Declaration issued in Oslo, Norway, on September 13. In December, at the end of a two-day summit meeting in Alexandria, Egypt, Egyptian President Hosni Mubarak, Saudi Arabia's King Fahd, and Syrian President Hafez al-Assad issue a joint statement expressing support for "Syria's valid demand for a full Israeli withdrawal from the Golan Heights as a condition to a peace treaty with Israel."

1996 Palestinian National Authority is established on January 20, and Yasser Arafat becomes its first president.

1997 Hebron Accords are signed by Israel and Palestine. The agreement calls for Israelis withdrawal from Hebron and the West Bank while Palestine commits to revise the Palestinian national charter and fight terrorism.

2000 On May 22, Israel withdraws all troops from Lebanon under Ehud Barak's orders. On July 25, President Bill Clinton, Ehud Barak, and Yasser Arafat meet for Camp David II Summit. In September, Ariel Sharon visits Haram al-Sharif, sparking protests and riots. This marks the beginning of the second *Intifada.*

2002 Israel implements Operation Defensive Shield wherein the Israeli Defence Forces entered into the West Bank and Gaza in search of weapons and terrorists. At the same time, Israel surrounded Ramallah and sieged Arafat's compound for five weeks.

The Arab League's Peace Initiative.

2006 Following the January 25 election for the Palestinian National Auth-ority's legislature, Hamas won a majority of the seats in the government. The outbreak of the July War between Lebanon and Israel begins after Hezbollah fires rockets into Israel and Israel responds.

2007 Tensions that had been building between Fatah and Hamas since the 2006 elections turns into armed conflict in June. The fighting results in Hamas taking control of Gaza and the dissolution of the Unity party that had been formed between Fatah and Hamas.

2008 Launching of the Annapolis Initiative.

The attack on Gaza.

Part II

Arab-Israeli Conflict in Perspective

1. Historical Background

The Middle East conflict has been shaped by an array of complex historic events. Some are the product of circumstances external to the will of the protagonists, while others are the result of specific choices and purposeful strategic decisions. Cumulatively, these and other factors add to the complexity of the conflict and the difficulties of Israelis and Arabs to find the common ground necessary for a peaceful accommodation that links their futures in mutually beneficial ways. Admittedly, progress was made with the signing of the Israeli-Egyptian peace agreement and the more recent peace settlement between Jordan and the Jewish state. The all-Arab peace initiative of 2002 should also be seen as a defining moment whereby the parameters for an end to the conflict were for the first time agreed upon by the entire Arab world. Alas, the core of the Arab-Israeli conflict, that is the question of Palestine, remains an open wound, and the main obstacle to a comprehensive Arab-Israeli peace. Regardless of the progress that might have been made, some of the most essential traits of the Israeli-Palestinian conflict, and the yet unsolved dispute between Israel and its northern neighbors, Syria and Lebanon, have not changed over the last sixty years, except for the relative positions of the parties. In fact, one can say that the conflict has been a constant variation of the same.

Much depends on the sovereign decisions of the parties to the conflict, yet the Middle East has been and continues to be an elastic description of a region whose countries are too frequently shaped by the changing geopolitical and economic interests of major powers. In the late nineteenth century, the region was commonly referred to as the Orient or the Middle East because that was its location on a world map as viewed from London.[45] If that same map had been viewed from New Delhi, however, instead, the same region would have been called the Middle West. But geography has only loosely defined this region because the areas it has been deemed to include have changed frequently to accommodate the West's shifting strategic interests.

[45] The term "Middle East" came into prominence in place of the more historical notion of the "Orient," which was originally used with reference to countries lying immediately to the east of the Mediterranean or Southern Europe (*i.e.*, east of the Roman Empire).

Since the nineteenth century, the region was defined and molded mostly by Great Britain and then the United States.[46] To a lesser degree, France had an influence on the region, as did Czarist Russia and then the Soviet Union.[47] The motivations of these major powers have been strategic, but their vision of the region has been narrow, rarely focusing on its long-term interests or its inhabitants. Not surprisingly, Western policies have bred considerable conflict in the region that, with few exceptions, they have been able to manage.

A. *Pre-Mandate Palestine*

At first, the region was seen primarily from the perspective of its access to India, Britain's richest and most important colony. This made Egypt and the Suez Canal—conduits for trade with India—Britain's colonial centerpiece.[48] With events leading to WWI and during that war, Britain's perceptions of the region's geopolitical significance changed, as did its purported boundaries. The Turkish Ottoman Empire became the focus of British attention when it allied itself with the Central Powers, Germany and Austria-Hungary, against the Entente Powers. Germany's support for the Ottoman Abrogation of the Capitulations, a Turkish law that granted economic privileges to the subjects of friendly non-Muslim states. The capitulations were abolished in 1914 when Turkey joined the war on the side of the Central Powers, influenced the Turkish Ottoman Empire's decision to side with the Central Powers in the war.[49] (Britain, France, and Russia rejected the terms.) The Middle East then became a secondary military theater, with an importance that grew only in light of the harm that could be imposed on the Turks. Thus, it was essential the region was defined as the area from the Suez Canal east to include Palestine, Syria, Lebanon, and Mesopotamia and southeast to include the Arabian Peninsula from the Red Sea to the Persian Gulf and south to the Indian Ocean. Thus, it excluded all of North Africa, including Algeria, Tunisia, and most of Morocco, which were under French control.[50]

---

[46] By the end of WWI, few Middle Eastern states had yet gained their independence, with the exception of Northern Yemen 1918.

[47] The Middle East was an important region for Soviet foreign policy and national security. The Soviet Union shared boundaries with both Iran and Turkey, and some of those states' ethnic, religious, and language groups were represented within the Soviet borders. The region's oil resources and shipping lanes were of significant interest to the Soviet Union and to the West. After WWII, the main Soviet goal in the region was to minimize the influence of the United States.

[48] The canal allows two-way north-south water transport and trade from Europe to Asia without circumnavigating Africa. Before the opening of the canal on November 17, 1869, transport was conducted by offloading ships and carrying the goods overland between the Mediterranean and the Red Sea.

[49] The text of the Abrogation is available in PALESTINE AND THE ARAB-ISRAELI CONFLICT: A HISTORY WITH DOCUMENTS 94–95 (Charles Smith ed., 4th ed. 2001).

[50] The French also expanded their influence in North Africa, establishing a pro-

France and Czarist Russia had different interests in the region. In the period prior to WWI, Russia had designs on Turkey, the Trans-Caucus area, and, more particularly, on the Dardanelles, which link the Black Sea to the warm waters of the Mediterranean.[51] At the time, Britain, of course, also had designs on this sea passage, but for different reasons. But after the 1917 Revolution, Russia pulled out of the war by signing a treaty with the Turkish Ottoman Empire—thus ending their rivalry.[52]

Since the Crusades, France had maintained a cultural and religious interest in the Levant (today's Syria and Lebanon) and considered itself the protector of Christians in that part of the world. Its alliance with Britain in WWI gave it the opportunity in 1916 to carve out the Levant from Britain's zone of influence after the dismemberment of the Ottoman Empire. France held fast to the area from 1916–43, but with its independence, France traded military occupation for cultural influence. France also spread its influence in Egypt, knowing that it could not regain a foothold there after Napoleon's 1798 campaign ended in failure and Britain began occupation of the country in 1882.[53]

Algeria, Tunisia, and most of Morocco were also occupied by France in the 1800s for almost a century. Spain occupied a smaller part of Morocco for vital strategic reasons, being the other side of Gibraltar, a tiny enclave occupied by the British to control passage between the Mediterranean Sea and the Atlantic Ocean. At this time, the Dardanelles, Gibraltar, and the Suez Canal were all of significant strategic importance to Britain.

In November 1914, when Turkey entered WWI on the side of the Central Powers, Britain began to maneuver for Arab support in the region through the Sharif Hussein ibn Ali, Sharif of Mecca and King of the Hejaz.[54] The correspondence between the British high commissioner in Cairo, Sir A. Henry McMahon, and Sharif Hussein provided assurance to the Arab leadership of Britain's support for Arab independence in the region. McMahon's assurance can be read as a strategic move on the part of

---

tectorate on Tunisia in 1881. Gradually, French control was established over much of Northern, Western, and Central Africa by the turn of the century (including the modern nations of Mauritania, Senegal, Guinea, Mali, Côte d'Ivoire, Benin, Niger, Chad, Central African Republic, Republic of Congo), as well as the east African coastal enclave of Djibouti (French Sornaliland). In 1911, Morocco became a protectorate.

[51] The passageway remains strategically important to Russia, Europe, and the United States.

[52] On March 3, 1918, Soviet government officials signed the Treaty of Brest-Litovsk, relinquishing Poland, the Baltic lands, Finland, and Ukraine to German control and giving up a portion of the Caucasus region to Turkey.

[53] Britain occupied Egypt in 1881, but left formal sovereignty to the Turkish Ottoman Empire.

[54] Correspondence between Sir Henry McMahon, G.C.M.G., G.C.V.O., K.C.I.E., C.S.I., His Majesty's High Commissioner at Cairo, and Sharif Hussein of Mecca, 1939, Cmd. 5957, at 3–18.

Great Britain to gain Arab support against Constantinople. Consequently, Hussein sided politically with Britain, hoping for an independent Kingdom of Hejaz at the end of the war. An interesting aspect of this correspondence is McMahon's insistence that some Western parts of the territories, first and foremost Palestine, were not purely Arab and, thus, should be treated uniquely—a clear nod to Zionist interests in Palestine.

During the war, Britain also declared Egypt, then a formal Ottoman territory, a British protectorate, bringing it formally into the British Empire. This was followed by the deposition of the ruling khedive, King Fouad, the sixth son of Khedive Ismail, as well as the transformation of his flag into an Egyptian national flag.

In 1916, Britain and France under a secret plan known as the Sykes-Picot Agreement allotted themselves parts of the Turkish Ottoman Empire.[55] In this agreement, signed by and named for Sir Mark Sykes of Britain and Charles Georges-Picot of France, Britain and France divide the provinces into zones of influence, intending to eventually grant independence to some future Arab states. According to the plan, Palestine would be subject to an international administration, to be settled in consultation with the Allies, Russia, and Sharif Hussein of Mecca. Later, British policy makers decided that internationalization was not in line with British interests and that aspect of the agreement was never implemented.

Partially in fulfillment of this plan, British forces captured Jerusalem and Baghdad in 1917, and France took Damascus by force in 1920.[56] This entailed the removal of Emir Feisal, the third son of Sharif Hussein of Mecca, from his newly elected position as King of Greater Syria, following the General Syrian Congress.[57] In 1921, Britain separated the land-mass east of the Jordan River from Palestine to create the Emirate of Transjordan

---

[55] Sykes-Picot Agreement, May 16, 1916, IV DOCUMENTS ON BRITISH FOREIGN POLICY, FIRST SERIES, 1919–1939 245–47 (1952). In 1917, the Soviet government published this agreement along with other secret treaties made by imperial Russia to scandalize Western governments.

[56] British General Allenby attacked the Ottomans in Palestine. The high point in the British assault was the capture of Jerusalem in December 1917. Notably and in seeming contrast to the Balfour Declaration, Allenby issued a proclamation declaring that the object of the war in the East was to liberate all peoples formerly oppressed by the Turks and to establish national governments deriving from the initiative of the people themselves.

[57] The General Syrian Congress was an assembly of leaders from the Arab World who met in Damascus to decide the fate of former Ottoman territories after the break-up of the Ottoman Empire. In its resolutions, it calls for the complete independence of Greater Syria, which included Palestine and the area that would soon become Transjordan, argues for Lebanon's absorption into Syria, and rejects the Sykes-Picot Agreement, the Balfour Declaration, and the League of Nations' mandatory system.

and installed a Hashemite monarch, Emir Abdullah, the elder son of Sharif Hussein of Mecca.[58]

That same year, Britain created the Hashemite Kingdom of Iraq out of Mesopotamia and installed the recently ousted Emir Feisal as its king. Thus, the defeat and dismemberment of the Turkish Ottoman Empire resulted in the creation of four new states in the region—Iraq, Lebanon, Syria, and Transjordan, with Palestine as a quasi-state—which were each immediately placed under the tutelage of either Britain or France.

During this time, Zionism and Arab nationalism in Palestine were on the rise. Arab and Jewish groups sought to gain British favor to advance their respective nationalistic goals. The defining document to bolster Zionist claims to Palestine was the 1917 Balfour Declaration, which expressed Britain's support for the creation of a Jewish Homeland in Palestine.[59] The declaration was a private letter from British Foreign Secretary Arthur James Balfour to Baron Lionel Walter Rothschild, outlining British policy on Palestine. The first paragraph expressed support for the establishment of a "national Jewish homeland in Palestine," and the second paragraph contained a caveat that the promissory clause should not affect the civil, religious, or political rights of the Palestinian Arab majority. The Balfour Declaration was never intended to be a precursor to the partition of Palestine into two separate states—one Jewish and one Arab—but events overtook it. The letter marked a watershed in the development of World Zionism. In particular, as it came on the heels of *Der Judenstaat* and the first World Zionist Congress.

Theodor Hertzel, in 1896, published a pamphlet entitled *Der Judenstaat* promoting the establishment of a Jewish state, though not necessarily one in Palestine.[60] Hertzel's vision of the state was more than a refuge from persecution: it was to be a model of tolerance to set an example for all of humanity, echoing the words in Isaiah, "a light unto the nations."[61] The first World Zionist Congress, organized and led by Chaim Weissman, was held in

[58] STATEMENT OF BRITISH POLICY IN PALESTINE FROM MR. CHURCHILL TO THE ZIONIST ORGANIZATION (THE CHURCHILL WHITE PAPER), 1922, Cmd. 1700, at 17–21. The Churchill White Paper, presented by Sir Winston Churchill to the British government in 1922, declares British support for the establishment of Arab sovereign independence in Palestine. It asserts that Britain's plan is not for Palestine as a whole to be converted into a Jewish national home, and identifies territories on the east bank of the Jordan River as a distinct territory. This White Paper states that territories west of the Jordan River are excluded from Sir Henry McMahon's pledge of Arab independence. The Palestinian Arab community rejected it.

[59] THE BALFOUR DECLARATION, 1940, Cmd. 5957, at 1–16.

[60] Published in 1896, Theodor Herzl's *Der Judenstaat* had generated considerable interest among Jewish intellectuals in the establishment of an independent Jewish state as a possible solution to the "Jewish Question."

[61] Isaiah 42:6;49:6

Basel, Switzerland, in 1897.[62] Consensus within the Congress was enough to produce a final pronouncement, the Basle Program, which publicly declared the Zionist ambition to create a homeland for the Jewish people in Palestine. This text set the institutional framework for all subsequent Zionist policy, which included securing a homeland according to public law and procuring the assent of all necessary governments. The following year, the Second Zionist Congress established the Jewish Colonial Trust, a financial institution that would serve the political and economic needs for the establishment of a Jewish national home.[63]

The return of the Jews to the "promised land" has long formed part of the daily Jewish prayer, although for some Orthodox Jews it did not comport the necessity of actual physical transfer to Jerusalem or Palestine. In time, this expectation turned into a political program.

In 1901, one of Hertzel's early attempts to achieve this political program was to persuade the Grand Vizier and Sultan of the Ottoman Empire to allow the establishment of a Jewish colony.[64] In the following years, Zionists would try alternative methods of achieving a homeland in Palestine. The Jewish National Fund, established at the fifth Zionist Congress, served a non-political method of acquiring land in Palestine. Despite resistance by the Ottoman Empire, the Jewish National Fund served as a method for purchasing and developing land for Jews in Palestine.

At the time of the Balfour Declaration, there was a great deal of uncertainty as to whether the modern Zionist movement would gain much strength in Europe. Early on, many involved in the movement were more concerned with anti-Semitism in Europe, particularly in France after the infamous trial of Alfred Dreyfus, a Jewish captain in the French army. In 1894, Dreyfus came under suspicion of providing classified information to the German government. Though claiming innocence, he was found guilty of treason in a secret military court-martial, during which he was denied the right to examine the evidence against him. The French writer Emile Zola, made the case a not only French, but also a European *cause célèbre,* publishing in a daily newspaper his denunciation of the cover-up.

Certainly, European anti-Semitism was not new. While attention in the first twenty years of the 1900s symbolically focused on the Dreyfus case, Jews also recalled their historic persecution in Russia and in Eastern European countries. Many Jews linked European anti-Semitism to the long-standing Jewish history of persecution, from their slavery under the Egyptian

---

[62] Israel Cohen, The Zionist Movement 77(1946), *reprinted in* The Arab Israeli Conflict (John Norton Moore ed., 1974).

[63] *See* Victor Kattan, International Law and the Origins of the Arab-Israeli Conflict 1891–1949 13 (2008).

[64] *Id.,* 14.

Pharaohs and exodus out of Egypt to their expulsion from Jerusalem by the Romans in 70 C.E. following the destruction of the Second Temple. The Jews of the twentieth century actively began to link their historical Diaspora with expectations of return. This expectation and the political circumstances spurred immigration to Palestine, providing the historic opportunity for the fulfillment of these hopes.

But, the Arab indigenous population of Palestine could not be indifferent to the presence of the new Jewish settlers. From 1891 and onward, tensions existed between Jewish settlements and Arab residents and these tensions came to a boil in 1920 when riots broke out in Jerusalem during the Nabi Musa pilgrimage.[65] The protesting during the riots was targeted specifically against establishment of a Jewish national home in Palestine.[66] In response to the riots, the British military instituted a court of inquiry to establish the causes of the protests. In the initially unpublished inquiry, the court found the causes to be from disappointment at the non-fulfillment of British promises, conflicts between the Balfour Declaration and promises to the Palestinian people, and fear of Jewish competition and domination. Continued riots in the following year lead to the Haycraft Commission of Enquiry. The commissioner's report found similar frustration with Jewish immigration and influence on government policies. These tensions would only increase as British influence in the region supplanted that of the Ottoman Empire in the years following World War I.

Three British reports were released in 1930 (the Shaw Commission of Inquiry, the Hope-Simpson report, and the Passfield White Paper of 1930, which before it could come into effect was abrogated by the MacDonald letter thanks to Chaim Weizmann's skillful lobbying) in response to demonstrations and protests in 1928–1929. The disturbances were precipitated by disputes over rights to worship in front of the Western Wall in Jerusalem which occurred after police removed a dividing curtain during Jewish prayers.[67] The reports, however, delved further into the underlying causes for the protests. In addition to the Shaw Commission's stipulations to worship at the Western Wall, the White Paper concluded that continued Jewish immigration would encroach upon Arab villagers and, as such, implemented limits on further Jewish immigration.

Despite these limitations, Jewish immigration markedly increased in the early 1930s, in part due to the rise of the National Socialist party in Germany. Resentment against the incoming Jewish population and the British presence in Palestine resulted in general strikes by the Arab population and eventually the outbreak of the Great Arab Revolt which

---

65 *Id.*, 38.
66 *Id.*, 40.
67 *Id.*, 44.

lasted from 1936 to 1939. As attacks on Jewish settlements and British authorities increased to levels much more intense than that of the riots in the preceding decade, the British authorities called for additional reinforcements and appointed a Royal Commission of Inquiry to investigate the causes of the insurgency. The Peel Commission of Inquiry determined the revolt, much like riots of the past, was caused by the Arab opposition to the Jews getting any part of the country they viewed as rightfully theirs, and as sacred Muslim soil, and by concern over the ever increasing Jewish presence. Additionally, the commission suggested an end to the British mandate and a partition of Palestine between the Jewish and Arab population. The Zionists accepted the commission's recommendations, and they were especially happy with the recommendation that called for the transfer, forcefully if needed, of Arabs from the proposed Jewish state. The Arabs rejected all the commission's recommendations.[68]

B. Western Imperialism

In 1919, following WWI and the break up of the Turkish Ottoman Empire, the League of Nations established a system of mandates that allowed certain Western governments to administer former colonies and territories in Africa and Asia as "trusteeships." This mandatory system was predicated on the idea that developed Europeans nations should assist less-developed African and Asian communities in governing their populations and in advancing toward national independence.

The mandatory system was built into the League of Nations from its inception and features in its 1919 covenant.[69] Article 22 of the covenant defines the national status of all former colonial territories in Asia and Africa and organizes territories according to three hierarchical categories: (1) Class A Mandate—those closest to achieving national independence (*i.e.*, "certain communities formerly belonging to the Turkish Empire"); (2) Class B Mandate—those requiring near-complete administration from a mandatory power (*i.e.*, territories in Central Africa); and (3) Class C Mandate—those to be permanently administered by a mandatory power (*i.e.*, Southwest Africa and certain of the South Pacific Islands). The mandatory system was unprecedented in the history of international relations. It was a new form of colonialism that had the appearance of international legitimacy.

The League of Nations established mandates for three former Ottoman provinces in the Middle East: Palestine, Lebanon, and Syria. On July 24, 1922, Britain was handed formal control over Palestine as a Class A Mandate. This meant that Palestine was deemed close to achieving

---

[68] *Id.*, 48.

[69] League of Nations Covenant, June 28, 1919, art. 22, 2 Bevans 48, 55–57 (1969), *reprinted in* U.N. GAOR, U.N. Doc. A/297 (1947).

independence and that all attempts should be made to "encourage local autonomy" in the territory. The mandate also included a clear commitment to Zionist goals in Palestine as its preamble reproduced passages of the Balfour Declaration.

In a memorandum submitted by Emir Feisal to the Conference of Allied Powers at the House of Commons, March 10, 1921, he expressed deep concern over decisions by the European powers to carve up the region into separate states irrespective of their cultural homogeneity and economic interdependence.[70] He explained that Arabs joined the war on the side of the Allies out of the promise from Britain of independence in return for their support. After fighting alongside the Allies, tutelage under European powers was not what Arabs had in mind.

The territory along the eastern and western banks of the Jordan River had been part of the historic land of Palestine for two millennia of recorded history. The distinct nature of Palestine as a cohesive political entity was a function of its historically recognized territorial and population characteristics. The Turkish Ottoman Empire administered this region for four centuries as an integral, yet distinct unit of their territorial holdings. From 1517 to 1917, the lands of the eastern Mediterranean and Egypt formed part of the Ottoman Empire. Arab territories such as the Sanjak of Jerusalem and the Vilayet of Beirut were ruled as separate administrative districts from the Ottoman seat of power in Constantinople. Following the Ottoman conquest in 1517, the land was divided into four districts, attached administratively to the province of Damascus and ruled from Istanbul. Thus, while it is correct to say that Palestine was not a sovereign state under the Turkish Ottoman Empire, it is nonetheless true that distinct territories of that far-flung empire maintained their own territorial, demographic, and administrative characteristics, as was true, for example, for Egypt. The Ottoman Empire ruled these territories as separate units, permitting them some local autonomy, though denying them the ability to exercise national sovereignty.

It is for this reason of autonomy that the League of Nations Mandate designated Palestine as a provisionally independent territory, categorized as a Class A Mandate. While the British Mandatory Administration subsequently divided the territory along the Jordan River, forming Transjordan (later the Hashemite Kingdom of Jordan), residents in the western portion of the land flew a Palestinian flag and utilized Palestinian passports issued by the British administrative authorities.

---

[70] Memorandum Submitted by Emir Feisal to the Conference of Allied Powers at the House of Commons, *available at* http://domino.un.org/UNISPAL.NSF/9a798adbf322aff38525617b006d88d7/93f6acc76ad42d2285256ced006997d3!Opendocument. This memorandum was submitted by General Hoddad Pasha (Hejaz Army).

The 1922 correspondence conducted by the British Colonial Office and the two main representative bodies in Palestine—the Palestine Arab Delegation and the Zionist Organisation—before the implementation of the League of Nations Mandate for Palestine is revealing. Letters from the Palestine Arab Delegation emphasize the need for a representative government in Palestine and are a meticulous line-by-line criticism of Britain's Palestine Order in Council, which stated that territories west of the Jordan River were excluded from Sir Henry McMahon's pledge of Arab in dependence.[71] Palestinian delegation letters also complain that promises to establish a Jewish homeland in Palestine and the influx of "alien Jews" to the territory were threatening the prosperity of Palestinian national life. In contrast, the Zionist Organisation, under Chaim Weizmann, expressed satisfaction with Britain's reiteration of the commitment to establish a Jewish homeland.

In 1936, Saudi Arabia was made out of the Hejaz and other tribal areas in the Arabian Peninsula, but did not include the entire peninsula. In the process, Britain sacrificed Sharif Hussein, the ruler of the Hejaz, in favor of Abdul Aziz ibn el-Seoud, who founded the Kingdom of Saudi Arabia. The territories not incorporated by King el-Seoud into Saudi Arabia became Kuwait, United Arab Emirates, Qatar, Oman, and Bahrain, a series of sheikhdoms based on the tribes that inhabited them. Britain carved Kuwait out of a small territory that could have easily been claimed by Iraq or Saudi Arabia. Only because the British favored the leader of the small fishing tribe who controlled a small seaport on the Persian Gulf was it separately apportioned.[72] Only Yemen remained geographically within the region as it had been for centuries.

C. League of Nations Mandate for Palestine

The goal of the mandate authority was to lead the Palestinian territory to full independence within a relatively short period of time. But the double promise of a Jewish homeland on the one hand and the preservation of the rights of the Palestinians proved eventually to be inconsistent, thus causing the British Mandatory Power to play a numbers game with regard to Jewish immigration. In 1922, when the mandate began, approximately nine out of every ten residents in Palestine were Arab.[73] With immigration

---

[71] Correspondence between the Palestine Arab Delegation and the Zionist Organisation (Feb.-June 1922), *available at* http://doniino.un.org/UNISPALNSF/9a798ad bf322aff38525617b006d88d7/48a7e5584ee1403485256cd8006c3f be!Open Document.

[72] In 1990, Iraq's Ba'athist regime claimed Kuwait as a province of Iraq during the period of the Turkish Ottoman Empire. This led to the United States' first Gulf War in 1991, which was surely motivated by the strategic oil interests it had in Kuwait, Saudi Arabia, and the other Gulf States.

[73] British 1922 Census.

during the successive waves of *Aliyah,* the number of Jewish residents from Eastern and Central Europe steadily increased, contributing to vast social and economic changes in the area. This was the result of agreed-upon quotas designed to fulfill the promissory clause of the Balfour Declaration and to meet the needs and expectations of the world Zionist movement. The resistance and the protest, frequently violent, by the indigenous Arab population would force the British to impose limitations on Jewish immigration.

Subsequently, there was extensive correspondence between Feisal and the British government with respect to the future administration of Palestine, what was to become of the Kingdom of Transjordan, and British interests in the area. It reveals Prince Feisal's vision of a peaceful co-existence with the Jews, as contemplated in the Balfour Declaration. As history has shown, this was not to be the case—angry protests and violent demonstrations erupted recurrently on a large scale throughout the mandate period, making such an arrangement impossible.

Intensifying conditions, the British Mandatory Power issued conflicting and inconsistent policy statements (or White Papers) during this period, exacerbating tensions between Arab and Jewish communities. White Papers regularly favored one side over the other depending on Britain's immediate political interests. This approach naturally caused alarm and frustration among the newly disfavored group. Britain, thus, managed to alienate both sides of the conflict in Palestine. In 1936, Palestinian Arabs, dissatisfied with British policy and trying to stop further Jewish immigration, began a three-year struggle to effect governmental change in Palestine. In response, Britain expelled the Palestinian leadership, leaving the primary Arab political role in Palestine to the Hashemites of Transjordan.

Between 1922, when the mandate began, and 1947, when the United Nations approved the Partition Plan, there was room for reconciling the Zionist claim with indigenous Palestinian rights by providing for a "national Jewish homeland in Palestine." At the time of the Balfour Declaration and for almost two decades after, there was not much expectation that large numbers of Jews would be interested in exercising a right to immigrate to Palestine. Early on, the assumption was that the limited number of immigrant Jews who would want to return to Palestine could be absorbed without disrupting the civil, political, and religious rights of the Palestinian Muslims, Christians, and others already there.

Jewish immigration to Palestine, however, was accelerated by tragic events taking place on the world stage. The Russian pogroms of the 1880s and the Holocaust prompted hundreds of thousands of European Jews to flee hostile states in search of a safe haven.[74] When the Nazi regime

---

[74] *See The "Final Solution." Nazi Extermination of European Jewry, in* PALESTINE AND THE

expanded its autocratic character, particularly after it passed the anti-Semitic laws of 1936, the numbers of Jews seeking to migrate increased significantly. Some settled in Western Europe, others crossed the Atlantic to the United States and South America (predominantly Argentina), and still others settled in Palestine. The years 1936–1947 witnessed especially large waves of Jewish immigrants from Europe, a continent that was rapidly becoming a mass grave for its Jews. By the time the declaration of independence of the State of Israel was made in May 1948, the Jewish population of Palestine stood at 650,000. Some of these immigrants had entry visas, but most of those escaping the Holocaust did not.

It is worth noting that until Nazi repression gained considerable force, Zionists did not have an easy time recruiting immigrants to Palestine, particularly among German and Austrian Jews who were deeply attached to their countries, only later to be brutally repressed by them. But the meaning and value of a Jewish homeland changed considerably during the period of Nazi repression in the late 1930s and more significantly after the war ended in 1945, when the world took cognizance of the horrors of the Jewish Holocaust. And in the late 1930s and early 1940s, it was difficult for European Jews to gain visas for resettlement in European countries and the United States, often the direct expression of anti-Semitic quotas and immigration policies. In this sense, it was a combination of brutal Nazi repression and international neglect that spurred the immigration movement of European Jews to Palestine between 1936 and 1947.

After WWII ended and the horrors of the Jewish Holocaust became known, the United States and the liberated countries of Europe found themselves confronted with what was then euphemistically called the "displaced persons" problem. From the perspective of many European governments, the easy solution was resettlement in Palestine. In part, Palestine was appealing because it relieved these governments from absorbing these populations and in part because it responded to the aspirations of some elements of the Jewish population. As a result of these circumstances, a large number of Jewish refugees sought to enter Palestine between 1945–47, most of whom lacked legal immigration visas and thus entered the country illegally.

The British Mandatory Authority sought to stem the wave of illegal Jewish immigrants by denying them entry into Palestine. However, these policies were broadly criticized in Europe and America because of the terrible destruction wrought by the Holocaust. The plight of Holocaust survivors presented the international community with serious and pressing human demands.

Arab-Israeli Conflict: A History With Documents 213 (Charles D. Smith ed., 4th ed. 2001).

Notwithstanding the special relations of the Mufti Haj Amin al-Husseini, the leader of the Palestinians, with Nazi Germany and with Hitler personally, the Palestinian Arabs and other Arab states' populations had little knowledge or understanding of what had happened in Europe and in particular the extraordinarily brutal destruction of the Holocaust. For almost all Arabs, what they vaguely heard of the Nazi policies towards the Jews seemed to them unbelievable. In general, people in the Arab world could not fathom that such atrocities had been carried out on such a large scale. Even today, many Arabs do not believe that the Holocaust was real, and it is common to hear that it is an exaggeration designed to gain sympathy for the Zionist cause and for Israel. Still, the Holocaust was a catalyst for advancing the goals of an independent Jewish state, though many Arabs saw it only as an excuse for Zionists to lay claim to Palestine and they still fail to see its significance.

It is worth noting that, between 1937 and 1939, several commissions issued recommendations to end Jewish immigration to Palestine as a way of reducing the severity of the internal conflict brimming between the two communities. Considering what the Jews were facing in Nazi Germany, these recommendations were seen by the Palestinian Jews and the Zionist movement as a warning that they had no alternative but to bolster their political efforts and for some to resort to violence in order to keep open Jewish immigration to Palestine. This gave rise to negative reactions on both sides that brought about a wave of violence between the two communities.

Palestine could hardly accommodate the influx of post-WWII Jewish settlers in compliance with the Balfour Declaration's offer to the Jews of a "national home" while keeping the promise that "nothing should be done which may prejudice the civil and religious rights of existing non-Jewish communities in Palestine." This inconsistency lay at the root of the Arabs vehement opposition to the Balfour Declaration. A major flaw of the declaration was that, while endorsing the political aspirations of the Jews, it did not acknowledge the political rights of the Palestinian Arabs; theirs were "civil and religious rights," not political. However, an immigration process of that scope required significant economic and social development programs necessary to aid in the absorption of so many immigrants from many different countries in fewer than five years. There were certainly tensions between Jews and Arabs in their struggle for the control of resources, but the mandate years were generally a time of economic prosperity with some of the British high commissioners leading a Keynessian policy of considerable investment in the country's infrastructure. Understandably, historians have focused on Jewish immigration—and there is no doubt that the Jews benefited from the economic policies of the mandatory power more than the Arabs—but there was also considerable immigration of Arabs from the surrounding countries precisely because of the opportunities offered by the Palestinian economy.

As large numbers of immigrants continued to arrive in Palestine without external economic support, the clash between Jewish settlers and indigenous Palestinian Jews on one side and Palestinian Arabs on the other became inevitable. Solidarity between Palestinian Jews and Jewish settlers was stronger than that between Palestinian Jews and Palestinian Arabs.

Jewish employers were known to fire Arab employees to replace them with Jewish immigrants. There were campaigns by the Jewish Agency and other funds to buy Arab lands for use by Jewish immigrants. This period saw many violent demonstrations and the gradual emergence of hard-line positions on both sides, prefiguring the divisions that characterize the conflict today.

The Jewish community in Palestine (the Yishuv) was deeply divided over what strategy to follow. Those led by David Ben Gurion initially believed that a political solution could be found, while those led by Jabotinsky and groups such as the Irgun and the Lochamei Heruth Israel (LHY or so-called Stern Group) believed that violent conflict was inevitable. As violence commenced, it did not take much to escalate, and the spiraling process fed itself. There was a sense among the Arabs that their living space, not only economically but also politically and nationally speaking, was being reduced by Jewish immigration and land acquisition. And though the Arabs were more than willing to sell land to the Jewish settlers, the problem was essentially that of an alien people coming to Palestine. The Arabs would have opposed this growing Jewish presence even if it would not have had any adverse economic consequences on them. Notwithstanding the intensive efforts at social reconciliation, the demographic, economic, social, and political situation that developed from 1936–47 led to an escalation of violence, inevitably paving the way to a greater conflict that eventually involved all neighboring Arab states.

Israel Zangwill, one of the Zionist leaders in Britain in the early years of the movement, coined the slogan, "A land without people for a people without a land." For those in Europe and America who knew little of the history of Palestine, a statement of this type seemed reasonable. However, for the Palestinian Arabs who had inhabited the land for centuries, along with a Jewish minority, the slogan was factually incorrect and roundly insulting. A wall mounting in the U.S. Holocaust Memorial Museum in

Washington still prominently displays this motto attesting to the fact that significant historical misunderstandings continue to define this conflict to this day.

D. Partition Plan

In the short period of time between 1917 and 1947, the promissory clause of the Balfour Declaration of a "national Jewish homeland" without prejudice to the Palestinian Arab majority's civil, religious, and political rights was transformed into the recognition of Jewish aspirations for an independent Jewish state on part of the territory of Palestine. With the strong political support of the United States, driven by the emerging Jewish lobby, the General Assembly of the United Nations adopted in November 1947 a resolution partitioning Palestine into more or less two geographically equal states. This occurred notwithstanding the fact that the proportion of Jews in Palestine was estimated at about 10 percent at the start of WWI. The 1931 census of Palestine showed the number of Jews to be 18 percent. By 1947, estimates of the percentage of Jews fluctuate between 20 percent and 30 percent, depending on whether that percentage includes illegal immigrants. Nevertheless, the territory allocated to the prospective Jewish state by the Partition Plan consisted of approximately half of the total territory of Palestine. Thus, 80 percent of the Arab population of Palestine, who owned 90 percent of the land, received approximately half of the overall territory. The plan was viewed by Arab Palestinians and by the neighboring Arab states as fundamentally unfair, and they rejected it. They also saw such a plan as lacking legitimacy because it violated the Palestinian's right to self-determination, a right enshrined in the United Nations Charter. This, and the fact that hundreds of thousand of Palestinians were expelled or driven to leave during the 1948 war, is why Palestinians today claim a "right of return." The conflict of narratives in this tragic dispute is such that, the Jews also claimed the "right of return" to ensure their right to immigrate to Palestine.

British attempts to reign in the Arab and Jewish communities and to stabilize Palestine had little or no lasting effect. With Britain's economy drained by the war, and its presence in Palestine becoming more and more unpopular at home, the government no longer wanted to assume the responsibility for Palestine by itself. In November 1947, thirty years after taking control of Palestine and after making no headway toward the creation of an independent state in Palestine as the Mandate for Palestine had required, Britain announced its decision to withdraw from Palestine and to leave the "Question of Palestine" to the United Nations Trusteeship Council.

2. Open Conflict

A. *1948 War*

In 1948, disputes over how to resolve the crisis of who would control Palestine after the withdrawal of the British Mandatory Power led to the first of five major wars between the State of Israel and the forces of Arab states in the region and the Palestinians. With no plans in place for a post-mandate government, due in part to Britain's unwillingness to enforce the United Nations Partition Plan without popular support, the British withdrawal abandoned the country to a state of virtual anarchy.

The first Arab-Israeli war started in November 1947, as an immediate response of the local Palestinians to the Partition Plan decided by the General Assembly (Resolution 181), which they violently opposed. This immediately developed into a civil war between the two communities in Palestine. The second phase of the war started in mid-May 1948 with the invasion of the Arab armies on the morrow of Israel's Declaration of Independence by David Ben-Gurion, head of the provisional government, before a twenty-four-member Provisional Council (later to become the Knesset). U.S. President Harry S. Truman gave *de facto* recognition of the state eleven minutes later. The Soviet Union quickly followed suit. Egypt, Iraq, Lebanon, Syria, and Transjordan responded by sending their armies into Palestine.

Israeli forces, despite their limited numbers and lack of military equipment, gained an early and decisive advantage in the war, with Arab military forces being comparatively disorganized and largely ineffective. Israeli forces reopened the road to Jerusalem, gained control of the Coastal Plain, secured the Upper Galilee, and made headway into the Negev. By the end of the war, Israel held 23 percent more land than was allotted to it under the 1947 Partition Plan. The remainder of the Palestinian territory was occupied by Egypt and Jordan, with Egypt gaining the Gaza Strip and Transjordan gaining the West Bank and East Jerusalem.

After occupying part of Jerusalem in 1948, Jordan wrongfully closed access to the Western Wall and other Holy Sites to Jews, thus increasing Israel's motivation to occupy the city once King Hussein committed the blunder of joining the war against Israel in 1967. The armistice agreements of 1949 left Transjordan in control of the West Bank and "East Jerusalem," and King Abdallah of Transjordan arranged for Palestinian elders to offer him leadership through a process called *bai'*a, a pledge of allegiance. As a result, he annexed the West Bank and what is known as "Arab Jerusalem" to Transjordan, transforming that state into the Hashemite Kingdom of Jordan. The illegal annexation of what was to be the territory of a Palestinian state was *accepted* by Israel, which favored dealing with the Hashemite monarchs rather than with the Palestinians. No independent

Arab Palestinian state could thus be established in the area, as envisioned by the Partition Plan.

B. Palestinian Refugees

The major losers in this war were the Arab Palestinians, 700,000 of whom were displaced during fighting and reduced to refugee status. On Israel's side, the argument is that they left voluntarily, yet the Israelis never allowed them back, in violation of international law. The Israelis claimed that the Palestinians' return would not only destabilize Israel, but would also constitute an internal threat insofar as Palestinians do not recognize the legitimacy of Israel. The Palestinians claimed that they have an inalienable right of return which is guaranteed by the United Nations Charter and the International Covenant on Civil and Political Rights.

A debate has arisen as to whether the Palestinians left of their own accord, were encouraged to leave by the Arab states who were waging war with Israel, were purposefully driven out by the Israelis, or were simply fleeing violence, as is the case with most civilian populations caught in the midst of war. The issue is highly divisive since different interpretations of what took place serve to legitimize divergent understandings of the conflict. The Israeli claim suggests that the mass exodus of Palestinians was a purposeful strategy of a hostile population and was based on statements by Arab leaders that the civilian population should move out to allow Arab armies to enter and defeat the Jews. Some Palestinians, Arabs, and researchers in Israel support the position that the advancing Jewish forces sought to purge the territory of as many Palestinians as possible. Many among the civilian population feared acts of extreme violence, as evidenced by the Deir Yasin Massacre in 1948, in which approximately 256 Palestinians, men, women, and children, were slaughtered by the LHY. Other repressive actions and policies by Jewish forces were designed to intimidate Palestinians in order to create a climate of terror and thus force these groups to flee. Additionally, following the 1948 war, Israel enacted several national laws that blocked the return of Palestinian refugees, including the Emergency Land Requisition (Regulation) Law (1949), the Law of Return (1950), the Absentees' Property Law (1950), the Land Acquisition (Validation of Acts and Compensation) Law (1953), and the Prevention of Infiltration (Offences and Jurisdiction) Law (1954). Under these laws, Israel legalized the expropriation of Arab land and property. Contemporaneously, however, the Palestinians also engaged in violence against Jews in Palestine. Whatever the reason why the Palestinians left, they have under international law the right to return.[75]

---

[75] The government of Prime Minister Barak agreed to the concept of family reunification already in the secret negotiations which Minister Shlomo Ben-Ami led with Palestinian Chief Negotiator Abu-Ala in the spring of 2000 in Sweden. . But, the proposal could not be seen by the Palestinians as a recognition by Israel of the principle of the

The Palestinian refugees of 1948 lived, to the shame of Arab states, in the squalor of segregated camps guarded with suspicion by the governments that hosted them. These refugee camps were set up in Lebanon, Syria, and Jordan, as well as in the Gaza Strip, which was administered by Egypt. Generations of Palestinians were brought up in these squalid camps under conditions of significant deprivation. As refugees, their residence in these communities was understood to be temporary, and their collective hope was directed toward returning to their homeland. In fact, they were ghettoized. Jordan was the only Arab state that absorbed Palestinian refugees into its population, many of whom are now second- and third-generation Jordanians. However, in 1970, Jordan feared the growing political power and autonomy of the refugee camps and the emergence of Arafat's Palestine Liberation Organization (PLO) as a formidable political and military challenge to the Hashemite monarchy, and unleashed its army against these communities, killing 3,000 to 15,000 Palestinians. This event is known by Palestinians as "Black September."

A similar situation developed in Lebanon in 1982 when the PLO challenged the national government and ignited a civil war that lasted with varying degrees of intensity for two decades, dividing the nation, and ultimately resulting in the death of over 170,000 Lebanese. The Palestinians' control of parts of Lebanon and their attacks on Israel was the key reason that Israel invaded the country, illegally occupying parts of its territory, and creating a dependent Lebanese militia under the name Southern Lebanese Army (SLA). The Lebanese civil war illustrates the profound destabilizing effect that the Palestine Question has had on other states in the region. The civil war that ensued in Lebanon caused Syria to enter the country initially as a peacekeeping force authorized by the League of Arab States, and to then continue its presence as a *de facto* foreign occupying force until it was forced to withdraw in 2006. This situation allowed Syria to extend its control over the *Shi*'a-Hezbollah party and its armed faction, which carried out attacks against Israel from southern Lebanon.

From 1949 until 1969, the United Nations defined all non-Israeli Palestinians as legal refugees. Characterization changed with General Assembly Resolution 2535 (1969), which recognized Palestinians for the first time as a people with a national identity and collective rights. However, Palestinians still retain a special status in refugee law and fall partially outside the protection of the 1951 convention.[76] The recognition of Palestinian national identity was strengthened in 1974 when the United

---

right of return for it was not addressed to all the Palestinians that could prove family links; rather, it mentioned numbers, limited quotas.

[76] United Nations Convention Relating to the Status of Refugees, *opened for signature* July 28, 1951, 19 U.S.T. 6259, 189 U.N.T.S. 137 (entered into force Apr. 22, 1954), *available at* http://www.ufsia.ac.be/'-dvanheul/migrationigenconv.html. *See also* Protocol Relating to the Status of Refugees, Jan. 31, 1967, 19 U.S.T. 6223, 606 U.N.T.S. 267.

Nations granted observer status to the PLO and invited PLO Chairman Yasser Arafat to address the General Assembly as if he were a head of state.

Although armistice agreements were signed in 1949, legally the state of war persisted and the absence of peace treaties contributed to four subsequent Arab-Israeli wars from 1956 to 1982: the Suez War (1956), the Six-Day War (1967), the October/Yom Kippur War (1973), and the War in Lebanon (1982).

C. 1956 War

After WWII, renewed colonial domination of the new Arab states by France and Britain was impossible, and both held on dearly to whatever was left of their former colonial empire. On July 26, 1956, Egyptian President Gamal Abdel Nasser announced the nationalization of the Suez Canal. This was an important act that represented the close of the last stage of Western colonialism in Egypt.

Britain and France, however, were determined not to lose control of the Suez Canal. A plan was devised at a secret meeting in Sèvres, France, that involved Israel attacking Egypt and then Britain and France, after delivering a twelve-hour ultimatum to the two parties to end the fighting, occupying the Suez Canal. Britain and France were to invoke their rights under the 1888 Constantinople Convention, which established the international right of freedom of navigation through the Suez Canal.[77] Israel cooperated with the plan in part out of frustration over the blockade of the Suez Canal and the Gulf of Aqaba to Israeli and Israel-bound shipping and in part in response to *Fedayeen* attacks against Israeli citizens originating from the Gaza Strip. Palestinian *Fedayeen* incursions into Israeli territory had resulted in the killing of Israeli citizens in the Negev. These incursions started in the early 1950s, but it was only from 1955 that they had Egyptian support. In addition, Egypt had obtained arms from Czechoslovakia and Russia and could have soon been in a position to militarily overwhelm Israel. Considering the constant stream of bellicosity by the Nasser regime, Israel assessed the prospective threats to its security as real and their occurrence in the near future as likely. The international community did nothing to alleviate Israel's legitimate concerns.

Israel launched the initial attack against Egypt on October 29, 1956, under the leadership of then Chief of Staff Moshe Dayan. The Israeli campaign was swift and effective. Within days of its first assault, the Gaza Strip and the entire Sinai Peninsula fell to Israel. As planned, on November 5, 1956, British and French forces began their invasion. British

---

[77] *See* The Constantinople Convention Respecting the Free Navigation of the Suez Maritime Canal, Oct. 29, 888, *reprinted in* 171 The Consolidated Treaty Series 241–46 (Clive Parry ed., 1979). *See also* http://www.mfa.gov.eg/EnglishlTreaties/ConstantinopleConventionOfTheSuezCanal.aspx?ph=43. Great Britain, Germany, Austria-Hungary, Spain, France, Italy, the Netherlands, Russia, and Turkey were parties to this treaty.

troops captured Port Said and sought to advance south in the direction of Suez City—but a United Nations cease-fire stopped them.

In a rare display of political unity, the United States and the Soviet Union condemned the attacks and demanded that Israel return to its previous borders. They also demanded that British and French forces withdraw from all Egyptian territory. After extensive negotiations, Israel complied with the demands, but only on the condition that the United Nations place a U.N. Emergency Force (UNEF) in the Sinai and at Sharm el-Sheikh to guarantee the free passage of Israeli ships through the Gulf of Aqaba. Israeli withdrawal was carried out in phases from November 1956 to March 1957.

The unprecedented common stance of the United States and the Soviet Union during the 1956 war, at the height of the Cold War, happened due to President Eisenhower's sense of betrayal at not having been informed by Britain or France of their planned joint attack and the Soviet Union's ties to Egypt.

One of the simmering issues that remains from that conflict is Israel's alleged killing Egyptian POW's and Palestinian civilians in the Gaza Strip, which constitute war crimes under international humanitarian law. These facts are documented and deeply felt in Egypt but remain unaddressed by both the Israeli and Egyptian governments.

Between 1956 and 1967, Egypt replenished its Soviet-made military arsenal and continued its public bellicosity against Israel. Then, in 1967, Egypt provoked Israel by closing access to the Port of Eilat in the Red Sea and also preventing passage of any shipping headed toward Israel through the Suez Canal, as guaranteed by the 1956 war settlement. Egypt's actions were publicly presented as a response to a Syrian request to discourage an Israeli attack on that country, but the justification lacked substance. The crisis escalated as the United States failed to respond to the situation and Egypt sought the withdrawal of UNEF, which had been posted on its borders since the 1956 war as part of the disengagement agreement between Egypt and Israel. Regrettably, the United Nations did not hold fast to the maintenance of its peacekeeping forces, and Israel refused to have these forces on its side of the Sinai borders. These events made war imminent, though Nasser thought he could avert a war and achieve a major political victory, as in the aftermath of the 1956 war. But the circumstances of 1967 were different. Israel responded by attacking Egypt, an act of aggression under international law that defines pre-emptive attacks as outside the scope of self-defense.

D. 1967 War

Israel launched a preemptive attack against Egypt on June 6, 1967, destroying the Egyptian air force and crippling Egypt militarily. Egypt called on Jordan and Syria to join in fighting on the basis of the 1950 Treaty of Joint Defense and Economic Cooperation of the Arab League, which commit contracting states to consider any act of armed aggression made against any one or more of the members or their armed forces to be directed against all the members.[78] Yet, the military coordination between the Egyptians and the Jordanians started before Israel attacked. On May 30, King Hussein flew to Cairo and signed a mutual defense pact with President Nasser. An Egyptian general, 'Abd al-Mun'im Riad, was appointed overall commander of the Jordanian army. The war engulfed Israel, Egypt, Syria, and Jordan—though Israel secretly urged Jordan not to be drawn into the war.

Between June 6 and 12, the Security Council passed multiple resolutions calling for an immediate cease-fire. Israel did not stop its offensive until it had secured all of its military objectives. At the end of fighting, it controlled the Sinai Peninsula, the Golan Heights, the Gaza Strip, the West Bank, and, arguably the most important acquisition of all, East Jerusalem. This was an extraordinary victory for Israel, and a devastating defeat for the Arabs, who were deeply humiliated by their twin losses of territory and perceived military power. Admittedly, the Israeli cabinet proposed on June 19 a peace deal based on a return to the 1967 borders with Syria and Egypt (the West bank and Jerusalem were left out of the initiative), but Israel never actively pursued these ideas. Its policy, especially in the wake of the Arab League's Khartoum Summit of October 1967, was to let the Arabs take the initiative towards peace.

E. 1973 War

From 1967 to 1973, the military situation remained unchanged on the Egyptian-Israeli front during a "war of attrition" that involved intermittent artillery exchanges between Egyptian and Israeli forces across the Suez Canal. These artillery battles destroyed portions of three Egyptian cities along the canal, namely, Ismailia, Port Said, and Suez. The situation's untenability increased, portending new war.

The 1973 war began on October 6, 1973, the Jewish high holiday of Yom Kippur,[79] with Egypt and Syria launching a surprise attack against Israel. The holiday was strategically chosen to catch Israeli forces off guard with most soldiers engaged in religious observance and/or on leave from military positions. In messages to the United States, Egyptian President

---

[78] Treaty of Joint Defense and Economic Cooperation, June 17, 1950, 1 American Foreign Policy 1950–1955, Basic Documents (U.S. State Dep't ed., 1957). Oct. 31, 1951, by Egypt, Rev. 22, 1951; by Jordan, Mar. 31, 1952, by Iraq, Aug. 7, 1952, by Saudi Arabia, Aug. 19, 1952; by Lebanon, Dee. 24, 1952; and by Yemen, Oct. 11, 1953; entered into force Aug. 22, 1952.

[79] Yom Kippur, "the Day of Atonement," is the holiest day of the Jewish year. Most of the holiday is spent in the synagogue in prayer.

Anwar al-Sadat explained that this war was not aimed at destroying Israel itself, but at driving Israel back to its pre-1967 position.

The bulk of combat occurred in the Suez Canal in the south and in the Golan Heights in the north between Israeli and Egyptian-Syrian forces, with at least ten other Arab states symbolically aiding in the war effort with personnel, military equipment, and/or financial support.[80] Some Palestinian Arabs fought with the Egyptian-Syrian forces and shelled Israeli towns from Lebanon.

Initially, Israeli aircraft and tanks were destroyed at a high rate. By October 9, Israel grew increasingly concerned that the Arab armies would cross the 1967 borders in an attempt to destroy the state. Fearing that Israel might resort to using nuclear weapons to end the war, U.S. President Richard M. Nixon and Secretary of State Henry Kissinger decided to accommodate Israeli requests for defense assistance. On October 14, the first American Galaxy transport aircraft arrived with supplies for Israel; other U.S. planes delivered military material and ammunition in the Sinai.[81] This turned the tide of the war, as Israel broke through Egyptian positions in the south.

On October 16, Israeli forces under the command of General Ariel Sharon crossed the Canal and advanced south toward the City of Suez. That operation, in an area of the Suez Canal called the *"Deversoir"* (spillway), cut the supply line to Egypt's Third Army, which was east of the canal, while Sharon's division was behind it, west of the canal. This untenable situation precipitated Egypt's acceptance of a cease-fire agreement mediated by Kissinger whereby both Egypt and Israel could claim victory.

On the economic front, the Organization of Arab Petroleum Exporting Countries (OAPEC) announced on October 17 that it would reduce its oil production until Israel withdrew from the Arab territories it occupied during the 1967 war. This was followed by a total oil embargo on the United States and the Netherlands. The prevailing Cold War atmosphere also complicated the war because the Soviets backed the Arab states and the United States backed Israel; it became increasingly possible that the two superpowers could clash over the Middle East.

Both Israel and Egypt accepted the United Nations cease-fire agreement laid out in Security Council Resolution 338 on October 22, but it was soon broken. On October 23, the Security Council adopted Resolution 339, which confirmed Resolution 338 and called for the dispatch of United Nations observers to supervise a cease-fire. Within two days, the Security

---

[80] Arab states included Algeria, Iraq, Jordan, Kuwait, Lebanon, Libya, Morocco, Saudi Arabia, Sudan, and Tunisia.

[81] *See* T.G. Fraser, The Arab-Israeli Conflict 99–101 (T.G. Fraser & J.O. Springhall eds., 1995).

Council established a UNEF, and, on October 27, fighting officially ended. Egypt's success in crossing the Suez Canal and briefly defeating Israeli forces became the primary lesson of the war for Israel.

It is important to note that the United Nations issued virtually no formal resolutions or reports on the situation during the course of hostilities. The first United Nations decision addressing the war, Security Council Resolution 338, was passed only when it was apparent that Egypt's offensive was stopped and Israel had moved its military from the defensive to the offensive. In adopting this strategy, the United Nations tacitly confirmed Egypt and Syria's right to reclaim their territories from Israel. Israel's military gains allowed for the public representation that neither side lost face, thus opening the door for step-by-step negotiations under U.S. auspices and two disengagement agreements in 1974 and 1975. These two disengagement agreements paved the way for Egyptian President Anwar al-Sadat's 1977 visit to Jerusalem, which led to subsequent developments, namely, the 1978 Camp David Accords and the 1979 peace treaty, which both sides have upheld to date.

It should be noted that from 1948 to 1977, Arab states offered no political option to Israel other than war. Palestinian and Arab rhetoric heralded the extinction of Israel, and Arab slogans included "throwing them back into the sea." Israel's past experiences and potential military vulnerability were such that it could not ignore these threats. Given this embattled position, Israel resolved towards constructing a society firmly oriented towards national defense at all costs. Israel invested its resources and political influence to encourage the large-scale immigration of Jews into the territory, the creation of a diverse, sustainable economy, and the significant power its defense.

With the occupation of Arab territory after the war came the transformation of Israeli society. Security was always a sacred cow in Israel, even before 1967. But, the tragic dichotomy that developed after 1967, one that persists to this very day, is that of a supposedly democratic Israeli society that applies norms of military and police repression against an occupied people next door. Policies enforced by Israel in the territories it occupied following the 1967 war included collective punishment, the deportation and relocation of civilians, the destruction of villages and homes, the denial of the right of return to refugees, and torture. The issues arising out of occupational policies and practices relate to the legal status of Palestinians in accordance with, *inter alia,* international humanitarian law and more particularly the Fourth Geneva Convention of August 12, 1949, and the Hague Convention of 1907.[82] Israel, however, has claimed the

[82] Hague Convention 1907 (IV), 36 Stat. 2277 (entered into force Jan. 26, 1910). Geneva Convention Relative to the Protection of Civilian Persons in Time of War (Fourth Geneva Convention), Aug. 12, 1949, 6 U.S.T. 3516, 75 U.N.T.S. 287. There

inapplicability of these conventions to the Occupied Territories after the 1967 war because it considers the conflict between it and the Palestinian people is of a non-international character. Moreover, Israel justifies its repressive practices on the basis of its inherent right to self-defense and by reason of military necessity. Israel has further discounted allegations of excessive use of force by labeling their occurrences as anomalous and unsanctioned. To date, Israel has not complied with many of the decisions of the various United Nations bodies aimed at improving living conditions for Palestinians in the Occupied Territories.

Moreover, Israel has placed settlers in the post-1967 Occupied Territories, a practice which is illegal under the Fourth Geneva Convention. Recently, it was revealed that some of these settlements are also illegal under Israeli law. According to the first official Israeli report on the illegal settlements in the Occupied Territories, which was prepared for submission in March 2005 by former chief state prosecutor and attorney Talia Sasson of the State Attorney's Office at the request of the state, Israeli governments have for years allowed illegal settlements to be established by turning a blind eye and by using a variety of unofficial and even illegal methods to support them. Sasson's report, which examines such activities during the past ten years, when more than 120 illegal settlements were established, uncovers the long-standing method by which services and maintenance were supplied by the state to outposts that were never approved by the state, despite orders from the attorneys general to stop the transfers. According to the report, officials in the local authorities of various settlements disregarded the requirements of the law when they budgeted projects for putting up mobile homes, connecting to the waste and electricity infrastructure, establishing kindergartens, etc., for illegal neighborhoods and settlements. The report inculcates: the Defence Ministry, the Israeli Defence Force (IDF), the Civil Administration, the Police, and the Ministries of Infrastructure, Education, Industry and Trade, Finance, Housing, and Religious Affairs. While Israel has agreed to withdraw its settlements from Gaza under Ariel Sharon's Disengagement Plan, it anticipates maintaining some territories in the West Bank under a final settlement peace agreement with the Palestinian Authority. Under such an arrangement, Palestinians might cede to Israel large, heavily populated settlements located near the 1967 border and receive corresponding land elsewhere.

---

were three other Geneva Conventions since 1949. *See* Geneva Convention for the Amelioration of the Condition of the Wounded and Sick in Armed Forces in the Field (First Geneva Convention), Aug. 12, 1949, 6 U.S.T. 3114, 75 U.N.T.S. 31; Geneva Convention for the Amelioration of the Condition of Wounded, Sick and Shipwrecked Members of Armed Forces at Sea (Second Geneva Convention), Aug. 12, 1949, 6 U.S.T. 3217, 75 U.N.T.S. 85; Geneva Convention Relative to the Treatment of Prisoners of War (Third Geneva Convention), Aug. 12, 1949, 6 U.S.T. 3316, 75 U.N.T.S. 135.

Israel's victory over Arab forces in the 1967 war dramatically changed the landscape of Palestinian politics, as control of the West Bank, the Gaza Strip, and East Jerusalem shifted from the Hashemite Kingdom of Jordan to the State of Israel. Subsequently, groups like the PLO that emphasized Palestinian identity over Pan-Arabism gained strength. This period also saw the formation of the Popular Front for the Liberation of Palestine (PFLP), which was among the first of the Palestinian organizations to use terrorism as a means to win attention to its cause, carrying out numerous terrorist attacks in the international arena, particularly hijackings of civilian airliners.

In 1974, the question of Palestine and the right of the Palestinian people to self-determination was reintroduced in the General Assembly following PLO Chairman Yasser Arafat's speech to the General Assembly on November 13, 1974. Soon, United Nations General Assembly Resolution 3236, which reaffirmed the inalienable rights of the Palestinian people, and Resolution 3237, which granted the PLO observer status, were passed.

F. Lebanon War

A terrorist attack against two Israeli buses near Tel-Aviv by Palestinian groups based in Lebanon in March 1978 killed thirty-seven Israelis and injured an additional seventy-six. In response, the IDF launched a major military incursion into southern Lebanon, called "Operation Litani," seeking to eliminate the bases of these groups. Once Israel had moved into Lebanese territory and attacked its acknowledged targets, it did not immediately withdraw, however. The U.N. Security Council, backed by the United States, responded to the incursion with Resolution 425, which secured an Israeli withdrawal by June and the creation of a United Nations Interim Force in Lebanon (UNIFIL). Thereafter, attacks by PLO units from Lebanon against Israeli towns continued, frustrating any chances of a resumption of peaceful relations between the two states.

The conflict persisted with Israeli townships along the border bearing the brunt of Palestinian attacks and Israel retaliating in kind. In June 1982, following an attempt by a Palestinian splinter group (the Abu-Nidal group) to assassinate Israel's ambassador in London, Israel launched "Operation Peace for Galilee" under the direction of Defense Minister Ariel Sharon. Its declared purpose was the creation of a forty-kilometer security zone in southern Lebanon, but soon Israeli forces had passed the forty-kilometer line and laid siege to the city of Beirut.

After intervention on the part of the United States, a cease-fire was accepted. Subsequently, United States Ambassador Phillip Habib negotiated a peaceful PLO withdrawal from Lebanon that was supervised by a multinational force. By September 9, over 8,000 PLO fighters had left by sea and over 6,000 had evacuated overland to Damascus.

A multinational force was to supervise the process. Complicating the fragile situation, however, the newly elected Lebanese president, Bashir Gemayel, was assassinated before he could take office, prompting Israeli troops to reenter west Beirut under the pretense of maintaining order. Defense Minister Sharon then allowed the militias of the Phalange, Bashir Gemayel's loyals, to enter the Palestinian refugee camps of Sabra and Shatila presumably in order to "clean out" the terrorists still lurking there. That was an irresponsible, fatal decision, for the revenge-thirsty Phalangists massacred hundreds of defenseless Palestinians.

Lebanon continued for years to come to be the playground of foreign forces. On October 23, suicide car bombers attacked the multinational bases inside Lebanon, killing seventy-eight French troops and 241 U.S. marines. On February 8, 1984, President Reagan announced his plan to withdraw the marines from Lebanon.

In June 1985, Israeli Prime Minister Shimon Peres ordered a unilateral withdrawal of most of Israel's troops from Lebanon, leaving only a small residual Israeli force and an Israeli-supported Lebanese militia in a "security zone." On May 22, 2000, Israeli Prime Minister Ehud Barak decided unilaterally to withdraw all Israeli troops from Lebanon, ending Israel's twenty-two-year military presence.

3. Palestinian Popular Uprisings or *Intifadas*

A. *First* Intifada

With major political and military setbacks in the 1970s and 1980s that sent the Palestinian political leadership into exile in Jordan, Lebanon, then Tunisia, popular support for the resistance movement waned until the spontaneous outbreak of the *Intifada* in December 1987. From a legal perspective, the two Palestinian *Intifadas* (the second broke out in September 2000) differ from the Arab-Israeli wars in that the law defines the Wars of 1948, 1956, 1967 1973, and 1982 as international in character, that is, they are conflicts conducted between states. The conflict between the Palestinians and Israeli occupying forces is of a non-international character, but invokes the laws of occupation, including the right of a people to resist a belligerent occupation. Many of the primary contentions over issues of sovereignty and self-determination that initially led to war in 1948 remain unresolved.

On December 8, 1987, an Israeli army vehicle crashed into a truck carrying Palestinian workers in the Gaza Strip, causing the death of four passengers. The incident sparked protests in the West Bank and Gaza Strip that escalated into a popular uprising that involved massive demonstrations, economic boycotts, tax resistance, and strikes.[83] These efforts were aimed

---

[83] Rumors had circulated that the incident was a deliberate retaliation for the fatal stabbing of an Israeli in Gaza two days before.

at ending the military occupation of the West Bank and Gaza Strip and achieving national independence for Palestinians.

The *Intifada* was not headed by the established Palestinian leadership, but by a new generation who had been born and raised under Israeli occupation. These new groups took command of the local resistance.[84] During this period, the PLO's political leadership came under threat from rival groups that often stressed Islam, such as the Islamic Resistance Movement *(Hamas)* and Islamic Jihad.

As the violence escalated, the United Nations followed the situation closely, primarily through the Committee on the Exercise of the Inalienable Rights of the Palestinian People and the Special Committee to Investigate Israeli Practices Affecting the Human Rights of the Palestinian People and Other Arabs of the Occupied Territories. The United Nations Committee on the Exercise of the Inalienable Rights of the Palestinian People submitted reports on the measures used by the Israeli armed forces to end protests, such as the use of live ammunition against demonstrators and punitive beatings. Israel also resorted to various forms of collective punishment, such as the demolition of houses, the imposition of prolonged curfews, and restrictive economic measures. These policies intensified the already difficult living conditions inside the Occupied Territories.

The Israeli government then approved a plan to build a tunnel adjacent to the *Haram al-Sharif* the most holy Muslim site in Jerusalem. Fighting then spread throughout the Occupied Territories and Israel declared a state of emergency. Around this time, King Hussein of Jordan relinquished Jordanian responsibility for the West Bank, enabling the PLO to declare the establishment of an independent Palestinian state in the West Bank and Gaza Strip in November 1988.[85]

The human, social, and economic costs of the *Intifada* were high. In the first two years of fighting, approximately 50,000 Palestinians were arrested (about half of whom were under the age of eighteen), 7,000 were wounded, and 500 were killed.[86] For Israel, the political fallout was significant as images of the IDF's often aggressive responses to Palestinian protests were broadcast across Israel and around the world. The *Intifada's* most salient images were of Arab children throwing stones at Israeli tanks and soldiers. After the Oslo Accords, the *Intifada* waned as Palestinians began to build hope for a better future.[87]

---

[84] *See, e.g., Communiqué No. 1 of the Intifada Issued by the Unified National Leadership, reprinted in* CHARLES D. SMITH, PALESTINE AND THE ARAB-ISRAELI CONFLICT: A HISTORY WITH DOCUMENTS 296 (4th ed. 2001).

[85] On July 31, 1988, King Hussein announced the severance of all administrative and legal ties with the occupied West Bank.

[86] PETER MANSFIELD, A HISTORY OF THE MIDDLE EAST 317 (1991)

[87] In 1996, the Palestinian National Authority (PNA) was established and, on Jan-

B. Intifadet al-Aqsa

On September 28, 2000, violent protests again erupted on the *Haram al-Sharif* following a visit to the site by Ariel Sharon. Palestinians, who recalled Sharon's role in the massacre of Palestinians in the Sabra and Shatila camps in Beirut (1982), regarded the visit as a deliberate provocation and an attempt to assert Israeli sovereignty over the site. A twelve-year-old Palestinian boy, Muhammad al-Dura, became a symbol of the new *Intifada* after he was shot to death at Netzarim Junction in Gaza by Israeli bullets as he hid beside his father. The incident was filmed and broadcast worldwide. Between September 28 and October 6, 2000, more than seventy Palestinians were killed and 1,900 injured in clashes with Israeli police. By mid-October, the unrest was being referred to as *"Intifadet al-Aqsa,"* the al-Aqsa Uprising.

Many observers of the Palestinian-Israeli conflict viewed these events as the logical outcome of the floundering peace process. The Sharm El-Sheikh Fact-Finding Commission, known as the "Mitchell Commission," established at the Sharm el-Sheikh Conference was called on to determine the cause of the unrest. The committee, headed by former U.S. Senator George Mitchell, spent five months in the region before releasing a report in April 2001 citing Israel's settlement activity in Palestinian territories as a root cause of the violence. Israel did not reject the report. It had its reservations just as the Palestinians had theirs. The Israelis were obviously happy with the report's conclusion that Sharon's visit to the Temple Mount was not the reason for the outbreak of violence, a conclusion the Palestinians were understandably not happy about. The Mitchell report was a carefully balanced document that more than dealing with the root causes of the problem tried to establish the premises for a return to negotiations. Indeed, the Mitchell report was later endorsed by both the Palestinians and the Sharon government, together with the Tenet Plan, as the basis for a possible shift from violence to political negotiations.

The situation escalated in March 2002 when, in a reaction to a series of massive suicide attacks by Palestinians, the last on Passover's eve leaving more than twenty people dead in the lobby of a Natanyah hotel, Israel launched Operation Defensive Shield, during which Israeli forces made incursions into the West Bank and the Gaza Strip to arrest terrorists, find and confiscate weapons, and destroy facilities where explosives were manufactured. Simultaneously, Israeli troops occupied and surrounded the West Bank city of Ramallah and laid siege to Palestinian Authority Chairman Yasser Arafat's compound for five weeks with Arafat inside.[88]

---

uary 20, 1996, its first general elections were held, bringing Arafat to the presidency. Arafat's name has since become synonymous with the PLO and the PNA and is symbolic of the Palestinian nationalist movement.

[88] Israel and the United States had formed a hard-line position against Arafat after

After fighting broke out in Bethlehem, Israeli forces laid siege to the Church of the Nativity, the traditional site of Jesus' birth, with more than 100 armed Palestinians inside. The siege lasted five weeks, until a deal was brokered that allowed remaining fighters to be evacuated from the church unharmed. On April 4, Israeli forces reoccupied all but two of the major West Bank towns and, on April 17, Israeli forces reoccupied sections of the Gaza Strip, undoing much of the work of the peace process.

After concluding the operation, the government of Israel, authorized a plan to build a "Security Wall" running the full length of the West Bank at an estimated cost of $lm per kilometer. Since that time, the Security Council and General Assembly have passed resolutions condemning the construction of the wall inside the pre-1967 borders (the Green Line). International criticism of the wall was bolstered by the International Court of Justice (ICJ) Advisory Opinion of July 9, 2004, which found Israel's wall in violation of international law.[89]

4. Palestinian-Israeli Peace Process

Not every plan for a settlement is a peace plan. Some initiatives were intended to serve only as a basis for a peace plan or a method of arriving at a peace plan, but were not complete solutions and were not intended to be viewed as such.

The majority of initiatives are based on either the binational state model or the two-state solution. The binational state model, first formally presented by the Anglo-American Commission in 1946, envisioned a democratic one-state system open to members of both communities.[90] It failed to garner the support of the Palestinian leadership or Arab states, however. Since then, progressive thinkers and many among the Palestinian intelligentsia have called for a revival of the binational state model.[91]

The two-state solution, formally outlined in United Nations General Assembly Resolution 181 (1947), called for the creation of two sovereign states in Palestine, one Jewish and one Arab. This proposal has become

---

talks at Camp David 11(2000) failed to produce a peace settlement. Many blamed him for shirking his role as peacemaker and not doing enough to stop Palestinian armed resistance groups from attacking Israeli civilians inside Israel.

[89] Legal Consequences of the Construction of a Wall in the Occupied Palestinian Territory, 2004 I.C.J. 131, *available at* http://www.icj-cij.org/icjwww/idocket/imwp/imwpframe.htm. The International Court of Justice rendered this advisory opinion pursuant to a request by General Assembly Resolution ES-10/14. The court decides that the construction of the Wall is contrary to international law, and, accordingly, Israel is obligated to stop its construction and dismantle already existing portions. Further, Israel is obligated to pay reparations for any damage caused by its construction.

[90] This model was first favored by Mapam, the second largest Jewish political body in Palestine, and by the USSR.

[91] Modern proponents of the binational system have included Noam Chomsky, Tony Judt, and Edward Said.

the prevailing model and serves as the basis for the present Palestinian-Israeli peace process.

Thus far, no proposal based on either of these two models has proved acceptable to both sides for the fundamental issue of peace goes beyond the well-known issues of borders, security, arms control, right of return, compensation, Jerusalem, and water. Fundamentally, there can be no reasonable expectation of peace without reconciliation between the two communities. This in part may require the establishment of a truth and reconciliation commission, payment of compensation, and other mechanisms that are usually addressed in the context of confidence-building measures. Surprisingly, however, throughout the lengthy history of negotiations between Palestinians and Israelis, issues of justice, truth, and reconciliation have seldom been addressed. There is a lack of articulation of a vision of the future that is likely to provide a common basis of hope for the two communities' future co-existence. There is no doubt that without a final status peace agreement between the State of Israel and the putative State of Palestine, instability will continue to prevail in the region with significant impact beyond the region.

5. Protagonists

The conflict's history and how it is perceived by its protagonists and their external constituencies has a deep and abiding impact on its significance and its evolving outcomes.

The protagonists may be grouped into two forces powerfully divided by ideology, politics, and divergent interpretations of history. Each side, however, includes external parties and constituencies whose involvement in the conflict and whose objectives vary considerably.

From 1922–47, the primary protagonists were Palestinian Arabs, both Muslims and Christians, and Palestinian Jews, as well as Jewish immigrants, who subsequently became Israelis. Since 1948, the primary protagonists are the Israelis and the Palestinians. The identification of these primary protagonists is not, however, without complicating factors. Both have external constituencies whose allegiance is either divided or multiplied.

There are Palestinian Arabs who remained in Israel after that state declared its independence in 1948 and who became Israeli citizens. They generally consider themselves Palestinians, and Israel treats them in some respects as such, but they are nonetheless Israelis. There are also large numbers of Palestinian Arabs who left Palestine between October 1947 and May 1948 and who became part of a Palestinian diaspora. They have since spread out throughout the world and have acquired different nationalities.

There is also a large population of Jews who have experienced their own diaspora, both as understood as a key element of Jewish identity and history and as being directly bound to recent history and the terrible experience of the Holocaust and who have different nationalities. They, too, have divided or multiple allegiances.

For many Jews who are nationals of different countries, Israel is a nation of enormous symbolic and political import. For Palestinians in and outside Palestine, and for Jews in and outside of Israel, there exists a similar link between these two respective communities. But the strength of these respective links is not the same, and the result is an asymmetry of forces between them, which is overwhelmingly weighted in favor of the Jews and against the Palestinians. The latter's tragedy is that there is no force and no system of law to redress this imbalance.

The external constituencies for both sides have varied over the conflict's evolution. As the conflict between the Palestinian Arab and Jewish communities in Palestine evolved during the British mandate period (1922–47), its external constituencies played a significant role. On the Palestinian side, the external constituency consisted of some Arab states characterized by varying degrees of interest and involvement. Ultimately, the Arab states were of no help to the Palestinians. They were divided between those nations known as "the confrontation states"—Egypt, Jordan, Syria, and Lebanon, and to some extent Iraq—and other states that are members of the League of Arab States and whose support for the Palestinians has generally been marginal. During each military conflict, these states have been defeated by Israel, and at all times, they were politically outmaneuvered by it. Thus, they were ineffective in their support for Palestinians. Even this marginal support ended with peace treaties being signed between Egypt and Israel in 1979 and Jordan and Israel in 1994, and the *de facto* state of peace, or at least a state of no war, between Syria and Lebanon and Israel.

The external constituency for the Palestinian Jews consisted originally of the world Zionist movement whose effectiveness grew over the years, especially after WWII. The degree of Zionist and other international Jewish community support for, at first, the Yishuv (the organized Jewish community in Palestine), and then for the State of Israel, varied from country to country, and it also varied as to the type and quality of involvement and support provided by these international Jewish communities to Israel.

But it was in the United States that support for the political aspirations of the Jewish nation grew significantly. It started at the end of WWII and was exhibited in the United States' support for the 1947 United Nations General Assembly Partition Plan and its near-immediate recognition of the State of Israel. Over time, the involvement and support of the American Jewish community and its ability to marshal political support for Israel through a powerful pro-Israel lobby became an important factor that helped transform the United States into an external constituency of

Israel. Geo-strategic considerations played a role in America's support for the Jewish state. That was clearly the case during the Cold War and in the wake of the 1967 war when Israel was perceived as a central ally in America's drive to dismantle the Soviet influence in the Middle East.

Since 1948, the imbalance between the interests of the Palestinians and the State of Israel has been heightened by the general exclusion of the Palestinians from the political arenas where their fate has been decided. Responsibility for representing Palestinian interests originally fell on relatively ineffective Arab states. When Palestinians assumed their proper role in representing their own interests, they lacked the force and capability of effectively achieving their goals. This situation was exacerbated by the absence of an Arab lobby in the United States capable of balancing the Israeli lobby. While Arab states have only themselves to blame for this lack of symmetry, they instead criticize Israel and its supporters for being so effective.

The United States has always been an indispensable party to the peace process, even while remaining a staunch ally and supporter of Israel. It was an honest broker in the 1978 Camp David Accords, the 1979 Egypt-Israel Peace Treaty, the Madrid Conference of 1991, and the 1994 Jordan-Israel Peace Treaty. However, with respect to the Palestinians, the United States has consistently been less than even-handed.

Since 1967, there has been a new and growing external constituency in this conflict, namely, the global Muslim community. In general, Muslims identify with and support the Palestinian cause, and view Israel as a threat to Muslim Holy Sites in Jerusalem. The Palestinian-Israeli conflict has come to condition inter-Arab and intra-Arab politics and is extending to almost all Muslim countries of the world, feeding into the growing populist Islamic nationalism.

The Muslims' antagonism toward Israel is sometimes traced to the days of Prophet Muhammad and historical conflicts with the Jewish tribes of Yathrib (near Medina, now in Saudi Arabia). These tribes had signed a peace treaty with the Muslims who had migrated from Mecca to Medina, and then betrayed the Muslims at a time of high vulnerability. This story provides a powerful textual support for a common perception among Muslims that Jews are untrustworthy. While Jews and Muslims have a long history of mutual acceptance, classic tales of this type are commonly overlaid onto the nationalistic conflict between Zionist Jews and Palestinian Arabs and are used to interpret Israel's treatment of the Palestinians. These and other factors help fuel religious antagonism between Muslims and Jews. The role and influence of Muslim fundamentalists have exacerbated the situation by introducing an intransigent religious dimension into the conflict, matched only by that of extremist fundamentalists among Jews in Israel and elsewhere.

Islamic nationalism brings into the region countries historically outside of it, like Iran, Afghanistan, and Pakistan. The latter two have respectively fallen under the control and influence of the United States, but there exists military resistance in Afghanistan and popular opposition in Pakistan. Iran is a target of U.S. regime-change policy, but that is not likely to occur, and it would be folly for the United States to try to do there what it did in Iraq. Both Iran's army and people would fail to be easy conquests, and the United States knows that.

A. *Islamic Nationalism*

Both Israel and the United States have throughout failed to see how the widespread perception that their strategic alliance is aimed at controlling the Middle East is affecting the peoples of the region. A strong radicalization has occurred among the estimated 300 million Arabs. And while there is still a strong traditional nationalistic streak among Arabs, they are driven to Islamic nationalism, both for the reasons stated above, and as a response to the failures of the incumbent Arab regimes, at a speed that is beyond assessment. The growth in influence of underground ideological movements is never easy to assess, and this one is more difficult than others.

If there are cycles to history, or at least stages evolving with some predictability, then it can be said that the Middle East, its diversity notwithstanding, may find its new identity and maybe even its unity in the rising Islamic nationalism.

Unlike Arab secular nationalism, which sprang from the top, Islamic nationalism rises from a popular base. Grounded in traditional Islamic values which strongly bind all Muslims irrespective of national characteristics, Islamic nationalism is stimulated by the failure of secular regimes to govern properly and to produce the necessities of their respective societies. The movement is also stimulated by the Israeli-American treatment of the Palestine Question, and more recently by the Palestinians' treatment under Israeli occupation. Lastly, American arrogance and misguided approach has driven the movement's rise.

It is hard to predict how Islamic nationalism will unfold and affect the region, but its impact is, in many respects, already evident. Islamic nationalism is, at this stage, more nationalistic than worldwide Islamicism. This is evident in the cases of Iran and Afghanistan, where an Islamic revolution seized power, and almost the case with Pakistan, Sudan, and Algeria, where the same result did not occur. Only one of these five experiments—Iran—showed some success, though it is now undergoing secular Western transformation.

Even though it is hard to predict the success or failure of Islamic nationalism in the region, it is easier to predict its continued efforts at seizing power for at least the next decade. For sure, their resort to violence will increase in this decade. If Afghanistan and Iraq are an indication of how the United States will react to it, Islamic nationalism will gain ground. But it is mainly the way in which Israel and the United States deal with the Palestinians that will be the driving engine of Islamic nationalism in the region and beyond it. Thus, it is the Palestinian-Israeli conflict, which started as the Palestinian-Jewish conflict over sharing/dividing Palestine and which has reverted to that, that is critical to peace in the region. Just as Britain underestimated Arab and Jewish nationalism between 1914 and 1945 and thought it could control it, the United States is underestimating Islamic nationalism.

It should be noted, however, that all the region's ills are not derived from the Palestinian-Israeli conflict, nor for that matter, from Israel. For if that conflict were resolved tomorrow and Israel disappeared from the world map, the Arab world would remain in turmoil and the Islamic national revolution would continue to gain ground. The conditions within each and every Arab state are only marginally caused by Israel or by the Palestinian-Israeli conflict, even when these countries are politically impacted by that conflict. Surely corrupt and inefficient regimes, growing populations, lack of productivity, weak economies, and lack of national purpose and social discipline cannot be blamed on Israel. Other countries facing conflict situations have managed to progress and develop—suffice it to recall Taiwan in the face of China, and South Korea in the face of North Korea.

Countries which faced almost insurmountable difficulties in the aftermath of WWII, like India and Malaysia, have overcome them and are now developed societies. Even populous Muslim societies like Indonesia have managed to made progress. And Turkey, dismembered after WWI, is now a developed European country. To blame Israel for the woes of Arab states is demagoguery. To blame it for the plight of the Palestinians is valid, but to absolve the Palestinian and Arab leadership from blame is historic fallacy.

B. Third-Party Politics

Since 1948, the United States has had an increasingly influential role in the affairs of the region, which it now dominates. Essentially, it inherited Britain's Middle East imperial mantle in the 1940s. Israel, whose existence was threatened by neighboring Arab states since its inception, is now capable of militarily challenging all surrounding Arab states simultaneously. Its strategic alliance with the United States has become superior to any strategic arrangements the latter has with any Arab country.

Between the 1950s and the 1970s, the Soviet Union rekindled its interest in the region, and it wanted to wrest control of the Arab Middle East from the West for much the same reasons as the West had for controlling it—oil, its strategic location, and the large population base. But without Egypt, it could not do so, as that state had, since the mid-1970s, entered the American zone of influence.

Much as Britain did between 1882 and 1945, the United States consistently changed its perceptions and goals in the region. Also, like Britain before it, the United States has no vision for the region. Even now after Iraq's conquest in March 2003, the United States claims to have an overall strategic view of the region, but that view is limited and misguided. This is probably due to the fact that for both Britain and the United States, there has been a callous disregard of peoples' interests. During WWI, Britain played on the Arab expectation of independence, while substantially disregarding the populace, except when it suited its imperial purposes. Since the end of WWII, the United States has manipulated Arab leaders often as political vassals, without regard for the system of government that was imposed on people. This should help explain why throughout the Arab world the leaders are mostly pro-American while the masses deeply resent America. More recently, the brazen military occupation of Iraq, following that of Afghanistan, evidences a United States policy reminiscent of Britain's military dominance from 1882 to 1945. But just as the latter elicited nationalistic resistance, so will the former.

Libya, which was once an Italian colony, passed to American control. Then under its present regime, it subtracted itself from that position, but the United States still expects to regain control of that country.

Iraq was under direct U.S. military occupation and control, and no one can predict the outcome of the clumsy occupation. The Gulf States, including Saudi Arabia, are dependent upon U.S. military protection, but the future of the Saudi monarchy rests uneasy. Egypt and Jordan are clearly under U.S. influence, and the former is feeling the strong influence of Islamic nationalism, in light of the growing armed resistance.

Now that Israel is perceived by the peoples of the region as part of the United States' strategic power, regional hegemony by the United States and Israel looks to them as interchangeable. Israel should therefore look for ways to reconcile itself with the surrounding Arab world. However vital the alliance with a global superpower might be, the power relationship in the region can change, and Israel needs to develop a long-term strategy that dos not rely exclusively on the military and political backing of the United States.

The political standing of countries within the region has also been changing in light of their respective power-relationship to the region's imperial and neo-imperial suzerains. Egypt, which was once the dominant country within and outside the region, receded in its regional importance when it no longer was at the forefront of Arab nationalism and became a vassal to the United States. Saudi Arabia, which was once so influential with the United States, also receded to a secondary role when it became a suspect ally because of its Wahabi-leaning population, which is moving closer to Islamic nationalism. Paradoxically, the United States' unbridled support for Israel, and its inability or unwillingness to press its friendly regimes in the region to achieve needed political, social, and economic reforms, is leading to the destabilization of these regimes.

C. Protagonists' "Perceptions"

The protagonists' self-perceptions and their perceptions of each other add an additional dimension to the conflict's complexity and divisive nature. To explain these perceptions is not easy, yet understanding them is essential to unraveling some of the conflict's complexity.

Palestinians see the State of Israel as a usurper of their national identity and territory. They generally view the establishment of Israel as illegitimate and sustained by the rule of force. Moreover, they see their suffering at the hands of Israelis as the ongoing manifestation of injustice imposed by raw power. The Palestinian community perceives this situation as a product of the unbridled support given to Israel by the United States, owing to the political influence of American Jews, and more recently, by neo-conservatives—with the particularly strong support of the Christian Right. Palestinians also perceive a lack of adequate support from Arab states as a key factor in the power disparity. Arab and Muslim communities around the world share these perceptions.

Israelis tend to perceive the Palestinians as hostile to their existence and opposed to the legitimacy of their state. They also view Palestinians as representing a distinct and oppositional culture that encourages anti-Jewish ideas and actions. Members of Jewish communities outside of Israel and non-Jewish supporters of Israel often share these views. In addition, Israelis see themselves as an island in the midst of an Arab-Islamic sea of hostility. They tend to view their future as linked to the West, and thereby distinct from the region. In general, Israelis do not entertain the idea that their country forms part of the Arab world, or that their society might openly embrace Palestinian society. At best, Israelis envision themselves as co-existing side by side with a Palestinian state that is devoid of any means of endangering their security. As to the rest of the Arab world, though Israelis see themselves as related to that world only by an accident of geography, they aspire to have normal economic and political relations with it.

These combined perceptions have led to the proposition that this conflict is the fuel for a clash of civilizations, namely a clash between Judeo-Christian Western civilization and the Muslim civilization.

Throughout the conflict, peace efforts have seldom taken these complex social and cultural factors into consideration. Consequently, over the last half century, there have been limited attempts to bridge these differences. Rather than seeking to mitigate these differences, the divisiveness that characterizes the Middle East conflict has aggravated them, thus deepening the gulf of separation and reducing the opportunities for reconciliation. In the era of globalization, however, there are new means for bridging these social and political differences and new strategies for developing improved understanding between these divided protagonists.

The protagonists' perceptions of each other, their self-perceptions, as well as those of their external constituencies, have played a major part in shaping and defining this conflict.

As with every conflict, the protagonists psychologically prepare themselves and their broader audiences by representing their opponents in particularly negative terms. This representational process ranges from mild exaggeration of the opponents' threatening intentions to the complete fabrication of aggressive intent. Moreover, throughout that process, a variety of agents actively construct propaganda that serves to motivate fear and engender hatred in the psyches of their respective constituencies. At times, this process involves representing opponents as dangerous enemies with no legitimate political objective, and at times it demonizes or dehumanizes opponents, making it easier to inflict violence upon them, against the likes of which the better instincts of human nature would usually have rebelled.

Propaganda typically portrays one's own conduct as reasonable and legitimate and the opponent's actions as unreasonable and illegitimate. Words and symbols play an important role in this endeavor, and those with greater sophistication and access to the media can better achieve their goals. There are few international questions that present a greater global division regarding the competing legitimacy of two sides than the Israeli-Palestinian conflict. Around the world, political actors tend to side strongly with one side or the other. The Palestinian plight and the evils of Israeli occupation are now part of a commonly acknowledged narrative. But, so is also that which Israel and its supporters have been highly successful in divulging, a portrait of the Palestinians as "terrorists" and themselves as "victims."

Because of the incredible divisiveness of the conflict, conspiracy theories are commonly utilized, a clear means of undermining the possibility of rational dialogue. Conspiracy theories respond to fear and uncertainty and present simple explanatory narratives to make sense of complex socio-political situations. One classic example that continues to influence the Middle East conflict is the late Nineteenth Century Czarist Secret Police-fabricated conspiracy against the Jewish people known as

"The Protocol of the Elders of Zion." Borrowed from an anti-Semitic German novel, the text presents a "plan" of an international Jewish conspiracy to dominate the world. It was a fabrication by Russian Czar Nicholas II's police to blame Jews for problems in Russia. Even though it was authoritatively demonstrated to be pure propaganda in the 1920s and 1930s, it received wide acceptance during the Nazi regime and repeatedly resurfaces in white racist literature, as well as in Arab popular beliefs.

In recent times, the government of Ariel Sharon and Israel's friends in the United States have capitalized upon the events of 9/11 to depict Palestinians, and for that matter Arabs and Muslims in general, as terrorists, supporters of terrorism, or sympathetic to terrorism. Palestinian suicide bombers have provided great fuel for that campaign.

The demonization of the enemy by both sides has been a consistent feature of this conflict. This process serves the interests of extremists on both sides. On the Arab side, the popular representation of Jews as a racist domineering force, often seen as conspiring with the United States, and the West more generally, has entrenched feelings of hatred against Israelis and Jews in general and against the West. On the Israeli-Jewish side, the representation of Arabs as fundamentally untrustworthy and Islam as a backward and violent religion generated similar effects as those deriving from Arab perceptions and portrayals.

The image of Israelis as victims, however, is a certain cultural historical legacy. It plays off powerful historical feelings of dispossession, oppression, and marginalization in the modern period, and is thus linked to the Holocaust. The victimization of Israelis through suicide bombings to a more general historical oppression within which Palestinians, Arabs, and Muslims are represented as the latest in a long line of repressive political actors. This generates enormous support for Israel. It also engenders a strong aggressive/defensive attitude among Israelis.

To the degree that these perceptions gain ground among the protagonists and their external constituencies, they reinforce each other, increasing negative perceptions and enhancing the conflict's intensity. In the American media, there is seldom a portrayal of Israeli abuses against Palestinians or their degradation and humiliation. This is due to the fact that the pro-Israel lobby has turned the debate over the conflict into a zero-sum game. Thus, Israel can do no wrong, and the Palestinians can do no right. Moreover, support for Israel must be absolute, as is condemnation of the Palestinians. Those who question Israel's policies and practices are all too frequently branded as anti-Israel and even anti-Semitic. In contrast, the Israeli media is far more open to criticism of its government and more descriptive of the dehumanizing measures taken by its governments against Palestinians.

On the Arab side, it is perceived, of course, as a reflection of the double standards applied by Israel and the United States because Palestinians are deemed less worthy of humane consideration than Israelis. More than anything else, the treatment of Palestinians—its rationalization and lack of compassion—is the most significant factor stimulating Palestinian suicide bombings. The self-evident nature of this observation leads many in the Arab world and beyond to believe that this is a conscious part of the present Israeli government's plan to further radicalize and polarize Israelis and Palestinians in the hope of preventing any effective plans for peace. Under such conditions, Israel could make Palestinian lives so intolerable that they would leave *en masse,* as happened in 1948, and thus achieve "ethnic cleansing" by more subtle means. This then would give Israel more opportunity to expand settlements and take over more Palestinian territories, as has been the case since 1948. This is why the treatment of the Palestinians and the escalating violence is a threat to peace. The threat extends not only to the Palestinians, but to the whole region and the Muslim world. Avoiding the self-fulfilling prophecy of a clash of civilizations should be the primary concern.

The Palestinians' policy from 1967 to date has been a two-prong approach, political action and armed resistance. But the very nature of this duality created uncertainty about the Palestinian leadership's genuine desire for peace. Because armed resistance had to be internal and the Palestinians did not have the means to fight the Israelis in a conventional war, they resorted to guerilla tactics and terrorist practices. Some of these are permissible under international humanitarian law, namely, attacking military forces and military installations. Others are not—such as attacking innocent civilians and civilian facilities. The military asymmetry between Palestinians and Israelis and the civilian retaliatory targeting of Palestinians by Israelis led Palestinians to escalate their violence against Israeli civilians, even though these acts contravene international humanitarian law. This, in turn, led Israel to escalate its violence against the Palestinians, which in some cases also involved violations of international humanitarian law. The marked difference between the two is that the Israelis, especially now that Jihadist organizations terrorism became a global concern, have managed to convince world public that Palestinian violations are "terrorism," while theirs are justifiable.

While Palestinian vulnerability to Israel's forces was obvious, Israeli vulnerability to suicide bombing attacks against innocent civilians was not contemplated. Thus, Israel faced a new security phenomenon that it was not prepared for, and this impacted its political/military strategy.

D. Socio-Psychological Dimensions

It is difficult to understand this conflict without some insight into the ethos and pathos of the protagonists. There is in this respect much to be said, and what follows only scratches the surface. But it is an important complement to the preceding discussion, even at the risk of being too general.

Who is an Arab and who is a Jew? Both questions are far more complicated than one may imagine.

An Arab is someone who lives in a country whose official language is Arabic. Such countries, now twenty-two by their membership in the League of Arab States, vary culturally. They range from Morocco on the Atlantic to the Gulf States on the Indian Ocean to sub-Saharan Arab states, from Mauritania on the Atlantic to Djibouti on the Red Sea. These countries are essentially linked by their having been at one time part of the world of Islam dominated by Arabs from the Arabian Peninsula. Thus, the Arab identity and its cultural characteristics merged with the values of Islam and were propagated in tandem with that religion. In time, as the Arabo-Islamic cultural characteristics were assimilated into local cultures, they produced a set of linked, though culturally unique, groups. The overlapping of these three circles and their interaction in different societies makes for real distinctions among Arab states and much more so between Arab Muslim states and non-Arab Muslim states. This is one of the challenges faced by Islamic nationalism.

As stated above, the three circles encompassing the Arab world are dominated by a shared Arabo-Islamic culture. The first is linked to the values and social characteristics of Arab Bedouin tribes. The second is linked to the earlier period of Islam under the Prophet and the four righteous Khalifas, and the values that they represented. But there is also a stratum of Western influence, which is in part European and in part American. It offers the attractiveness of modernity, and yet at the same time it causes tension with the tradition of Arab Bedouin society and the Islamic values of its earlier ascetic days.

The Arab-Bedouin culture values hospitality, generosity, courage, honor, self-respect, formality, and face. These social values are reflected in the Arabic language, which holds an almost spellbinding effect on its people. Its rhetoric is made of exaggeration, over-assertion, and the evocation of poetic historical and mystical imagery. In this rhetoric, there is no necessary connection between words and reality. Promises and threats are as good as accomplished, and with the mere assertion of the word, the deed becomes almost superfluous.

The Arab personality has other characteristics which derive from the divergent national experiences of these groups. The pre-Islamic Bedouin tribal society of the Arabian Peninsula had anarchical traits by which it expressed its rejection of external authority. Consequently, Arab Bedouins did not form a cohesive society that pursued the same endeavors as sedentary civilizations. Instead, they were a collection of individualists with warrior qualities, craving conquest but with little social discipline. The early Islamic period changed the Arab-Bedouin society—and an Arabo-Islamic civilization blossomed from which Western civilization benefited extensively from the ninth to the twelfth century C.E.

Contemporary Arab societies, notwithstanding the influence of Islam, retained the characteristics of individuality, indecisiveness, inaction, and indolence. These characteristics however, in the modern period, have to be to preserve face and maintain the appearance of dignity, honor, courage, and wisdom. Thus, the word provides the necessary cover. The literature and public and private discourse exalt the virtues and character that these societies lack. Verbal expressions are a substitute for facts, and this negates opportunities for change.

The basic Arab ethics of virtue—courage, bravery, hospitality, generosity, honor, and dignity—are blunted by the absence of pragmatism. The inability to achieve or live up to these values requires face-saving, and Arabs go to great lengths to protect themselves from shame, even at the cost of denying reality.

Muslim beliefs may also feed some of these negative Arab characteristics. To accept the will of God becomes easily transformed into a sense of fatalism that weakens the will to change one's destiny. This is also why the Arab mind often accepts words as equivalent to reality. If the willed reality does not manifest itself it is then turned into the unavoidable acceptance of reality as is the will of God.

While these and other traits make Arabs individualistic, sentimental, and appealing in their persona, it also makes them less capable of social solidarity and group discipline. The sentimental aspects overwhelmingly overtake the pragmatic aspects in individual action. In short, the endearing and engaging individual character traits of the Arabs are also their negative social and group characteristics.

In contemporary political dynamics, it is easy for Israel and its supporters to play on these personality characteristics, showing Arabs as unreliable, unable to meet the challenges of modernity, and essentially possessing contradictory values. Conversely, Jewish/Israeli's characteristics of social organization, cohesion, group discipline, determination, and pragmatism reveal a closer affinity to present-day characteristics of Western societies. As Israelis identify themselves more and more with the West and the gap between the West and the Arabs increases, political consequences translate into greater support for the former and a lack of support for the latter.

While Israelis enhance their closeness to the Western world, Arabs merely express their resentment of it and do nothing to counteract it. In fact, throughout the conflict, Israel's military, political, and public relations successes were resented by the Arabs and, in a perverse way, they blamed Israel and the Jews for their failures without admitting to them. Yet, Arabs have seldom, if ever, acknowledged the success of the Israelis if, for no other reason, than to learn from these successes or to learn from their own failures. The only time this was done was in the period 1971–73 when Egypt prepared for the crossing of the Suez Canal. Its strategy and tactics took into account the successful strategy and tactics that had worked for the Israeli armed forces. Following that, Anwar al-Sadat also learned from Israel and the American pro-Israel lobby approaches to public opinion in America and embarked on a most successful public relations campaign that convinced the world of Egypt's peaceful intentions. This was made dramatically vivid in Sadat's trip to Jerusalem in 1977, his speech to the Knesset, the Camp David negotiations of 1978, and the ensuing peace treaty with Israel of 1979. But during that entire three-year period, the message was consistent and on point—Egypt was a country seeking peace and capable of honoring its commitments. Thus, during the 1973 war and in its aftermath, Egypt, under Sadat and later under Hosni Mubarak, learned from the Israelis and, in a sense, beat them at their own game, though ultimately for the benefit of both sides.

The Arab personality is at once complex and ambivalent. At times, it is the Arab factor that becomes more characteristic as in the era of Pan-Arabism from the 1920s to the 1970s, when it embraced the Post-WWII anti-colonial movement of these different countries. Since the 1970s, however, the Pan-Arab movement has waned, and the Islamic circle has become more prominent. The latter has worldwide reach, but in the Arab world, the Pan-Islamic movements also have nationalistic overtones.

Whereas Pan-Arabism is secular, Pan-Islamism aims at establishing Islamic national societies within the context of a broader Islamic *umma.* These movements, however, also oppose various Arab secular nationalistic movements seeking to establish Western-style democratic systems. Thus, the fact that the Arab nationalist movement and the Pan-Islamic movement decry corrupt Arab regimes in the Arab world does not, however, make them likely allies.

In the 1970s, Arab regimes saw secular nationalistic and pro-democracy movements as a threat, and to counteract them, these regimes reinforced the Islamic fundamentalist movements, only to face them later as even greater threats.

As the Islamic movement increased in popularity and political influence in the Arab states and made Israeli treatment of Palestinians and anti-Jewish sentiment among their primary concerns, Israel perceived it as a greater threat than Arab nationalism. It was joined in these perceptions by those in America who see themselves in a clash of civilizations, with the world of Islam. In turn, this reinforced the Islamic movement in its belief that Jews were agitating Christians against Muslims in order to instigate another era of crusades, pointing to Afghanistan and Iraq as evidence.

Who is a Jew is as difficult a question to answer as who is an Arab. According to Jewish Law, a Jew is a person who belongs to the Jewish faith and whose mother is Jewish or who has converted to Judaism. Conversion to Judaism is deemed by the dominant orthodox as only valid when done in accordance with orthodox practice. But Jewishness is a broader concept than being a member of the Judaic faith.

Jews since the Diaspora are generally considered part of either of two distinct Jewish cultural traditions: the Ashkenazim and the Sephardim. Both Ashkenazi and Sephardi Jews share the same beliefs, but they are also affected by different cultural experiences, as is even evident in contemporary Israeli society. Like their Arab cousins, rhetoric and debate is very much part of Jewish life, as is their history. Unlike the Arabs, however, they look at the mirror of history to remember the tragedies that have befallen them as a way of reminding themselves that they should never be lulled into complacency, lest the same fate befalls them again. Thus, they are hardnosed realists. They look to the future as a constant challenge and make themselves ready to face tomorrow's obstacles. More significantly, through the accumulated experiences of time, Jews have learned the lessons of cohesiveness, group discipline, and the necessity of pragmatism in facing their collective problems.

Judaism binds its followers in the belief that they are the "chosen people," sharing a unique covenant with God. This, in their own perception, distinguishes them from other groups. To many Jews, the appeal to Palestine is not only a form of nationalism, but the fulfillment of a Biblical promise by which the Creator bestowed the lands of Canaan upon the people of Israel. Thus, there is a dual perception of nationalism in the sense of the desire for a secular Jewish state, a safe haven, and a belief system that transcends pure nationalism.

The ethnic identity and religious beliefs of Jews constitute two overlapping circles. The difficulty in achieving a complete overlap of these two circles owes to the cultural diversity of Jews, as well as the religious distinctions within Judaism. But the most significant social link between Jews is their more recent experience of European anti-Semitism from the Russian Pogroms of 1881 to the Nazi Holocaust of 1933–45.

Ashkenazi Jews in particular have embodied certain Western characteristics, placing a premium on achievement and work. As they have been discriminated against in Europe, they learned how to excel in order to be tolerated and accepted, if not to survive, in their respective societies. Thus, the contributions of Jews to science, technology, music, art, philosophy, and other subjects of learning have been extraordinary and far disproportionate to their numbers than any other ethnic or social group in the world. In a sense, the accomplishments of the Jews between the 1800s and 2000 are comparable to the accomplishment of the Muslims between 1200 and 1500. By then, the latter had settled in Spain, Southern France and Italy, all of North Africa, part of coastal East and West Africa, the Arabian Peninsula, the Fertile Crescent and Mesopotamia, Persia, and the Indian sub-continent, extending into parts of China, the Trans-Caucuses and Russia. The Arabs who brought Islam to these societies, like the Jews who found themselves in the midst of many other cultures, were challenged by these different environments, and many successfully rose to that challenge. But as the Arabs benefited from their earlier advances, they fell into complacency until they were overcome by Western civilization and conquered by it, ultimately becoming colonial vassals, themselves, mostly of France or England.

Probably because Jews have been discriminated against for so long, they have developed such an insular culture, a mindset of us against the world or against whomever it may be that is the enemy of the day. This has produced an enduring sense of persecution or, at least, a high threshold of sensitivity to threats and the perception of threats. Thus, Arab rhetoric heightens Israeli threat perceptions. But, as the saying goes, even paranoids have real enemies, and certainly Israel has its share of enemies among the Arabs and the Muslims. Irrespective of whether it has helped this hatred, or whether it is the product of their opponents' reactions, the fact remains that it is there. Contrary to Israeli perceptions, Arab moderates believe that this hatred is not so deep-rooted, that it is linked to the treatment of Palestinians and the arrogance of the power Israel has come to possess in the region.

As a result of their historic experiences, Jews have double standards with respect to their perceptions of "anti-Semitism" and their own conduct towards Arabs and Muslims. This is particularly evident since 9/11 in the United States with the pro-Israel lobby's alliance with the Christian Right and with their support and encouragement of discriminatory governmental practices against Arabs and Muslims in America, as well as against Arabs and Muslims in general. In Israel, the same syndrome is evident. The discrimination that Israelis exercise against Palestinian Arabs, including those who are Israeli citizens, is tolerated by the Jewish body politic. Furthermore, the constant degrading and humiliating treatment inflicted on the Palestinians is something no Jew in the world would have tolerated had it been inflicted by any group of people against Jews. Thus, Israel can target Palestinians for assassination and purport such action to be legitimate. There is no other country in the world that legitimates governmental assassinations (extrajudicial execution). Moreover, it is a violation of international human rights law.

The near perception of Jews that they are the only people who have suffered oppression throughout time leads to the conviction that the world still owes them and that no matter what they do to others, they are justified because of their past experience of persecution. Consequently, there is very little Israeli compassion for the plight of the Palestinian people and very little remorse for the harm they have inflicted. Since 1948, the only Israeli leader who has ever publicly expressed compassion toward the Palestinians was Prime Minister Ehud Barak in a 1999 speech to the Knesset.[92]

The Palestinian Arabs and other Arabs see their conflict with Israel as an extension of European colonialism. Jewish immigrants who settled in Palestine in the early years of the last century were, after all, mostly European, and they arrived in Palestine as a result of the support of America and Europe. As is common among colonized people, Arabs have admired, and have even been submissive to, European and American economic and military superiority, while also harboring feelings of resentment against it. These feelings have been heightened by the wide disparity between some characteristics of contemporary Arab society and key elements of Western modernity. At times, these disparities produce a simmering anger that is compounded by a sense of pride in a glorious past.

To the degree that Arabs interpret the failures of their societies to fully embrace the positive elements of modernity's transformative potential, they often adopt the position of victimhood, asking "Who did this to us?" Thereby, they reaffirm the notion that whatever is wrong with Arab society is the result of foreign conspiracies. Thus, they doom themselves to helplessness, while paradoxically hoping that some external power will extricate them from their predicaments. Blaming foreign powers, and yet seeking these foreign powers to save them, is a continuing paradox of

---

[92] "Here, today, I call upon all the leaders of the region to extend their hands to meet our outstretched hand, and toward a 'peace of the brave,' in a region which has known so much war, blood and suffering. To our neighbors the Palestinians, I wish to say: the bitter conflict between us has brought great suffering to both our peoples. Now, there is no reason to settle accounts over historical mistakes. Perhaps things could have been otherwise, but we cannot change the past; we can only make the future better. I am not only cognizant of the sufferings of my people, but I also recognize the sufferings of the Palestinian people. My ambition and desire is to bring an end to violence and suffering, and to work with the elected Palestinian leadership, under Chairman Yasser Arafat, in partnership and respect, in order to jointly arrive at a fair and agreed settlement for co-existence in freedom, prosperity and good neighborliness in this beloved land where the two peoples will always live." Speech by Prime Minister Ehud Barak on the Presentation of the Government to the Knesset, Jerusalem, July 6, 1999, *available at* http://www.israel-mfa.gov.il/mfa/government/speeches%20by%20israeli%20leaders/1999/pm%20barak-%20presentation%20of%20government%20-%20july%206-%20199.

Arab politics. It is easier to blame the outside world and to await relief than to bring about the necessary changes on the inside in order to bring about positive changes in their reality.

At different times in history a resurgence of Arab pride, inventiveness, initiative and action have brought about brief interludes of success. This has occurred throughout Arab modern history: Egypt and Algeria's successful struggles for independence, the spread of Nasser's Arabism in the 1950s, and Egypt's 1973 crossing of the Canal, to mention only a few examples. But these successes were all too often heralded in Arabic rhetoric as momentous and long-lasting accomplishments, overshadowing the challenges that lay ahead. This led them to be comforted, if not lulled into complacency, by their few newly acquired laurels. This perception of reality became repeatedly distorted, as the mirror they looked at reflected the images of the past, not the challenges of the future.

In their military confrontations with Israel, Arab armies were frequently poorly equipped and trained because they were dependent on foreign military weapons, technology, and methods that suppliers could turn on or off at will to suit their own political needs. Conversely, Israel developed its own military technologies and capabilities, as well as their own tactics, which fit their needs. But, it is the Arab social structure that placed the most limitations on their military capabilities. The class distinctions, absence of leadership accountability, lack of social organization and personal discipline, and above all, the loss of the historic values of Islam's early days are among the relevant factors for the Arabs' poor performance.

The Arab struggle for independence from European colonialism gave way to American neo-imperialism in the region, and most Arab regimes have since then owed their existence to American support. Long gone are the heady days of Gamal Abdel-Nasser's pan-Arabism, which Sadat supposedly redeemed in 1973. While Nasser remained defiant and inactive in defeat, Sadat was resilient and decisive about peace. But the Arabs also lost the historic opportunity between WWII and now to modernize, develop democratic institutions, and govern themselves in accordance with the rule of law. Instead, their regimes are characterized by dictatorships, corruption, and inefficiency. This resulted in the frustration of Arab masses who found it easier to blame Israel than blame themselves for their failures.

Divisions within the Arab world brought on by the signings of the Egyptian-Israeli and Jordanian-Israeli peace agreements and the failure of Syrian and Iraqi Ba'athism transformed Arab nationalism into a sentimental illusion, leaving Arab countries each with their respective brand of nationalism. But these too failed as a result of corrupt and inefficient governments. The brief emergence of Marxist ideology among some Arabs was short-lived, and that too dissipated into thin air after the end of the Cold War. Only one path was left to the Arab masses—Islamicism. In some countries, like the Sudan and Algeria, and among Palestinians, Islamicism had strong nationalistic overtones; thus combining nationalist aspirations with an appeal to values deeply ingrained in Arab Muslims. The call for a new *jihad* became inexorable, and many among the hopeless and downtrodden heeded the call. The emergence of Pan-Islamism united Palestinian Muslims and other Muslims in the struggle against Israel.

Unfulfilled expectations, repressed pride, and deepening humiliation are the ingredients that lead Palestinians to violence. Israel exploited this situation by branding the Palestinians as terrorists. For sure, suicide bombing is an act of terrorism, but for those who have no other military option, fighting an asymmetric war, it is perceived as an act of heroism. Repressive reactions by the Israelis have left the Palestinians with the belief that these acts of violence are no different than those of the Israelis. Thus, both sides accuse each other of terrorism, while seeing themselves as victims and heroes.

As the cycle of violence has increased in the last few years, so has the gap in perceptions about peace. Security has become the overwhelming concern for Israel, thus leading to the conclusion that peace and security can only come through a separation from the Palestinians.

Extremists on both sides see the only tangible solution as the elimination of one another. For Israeli extremists, it includes the removal of Palestinians from their ancestral lands and fulfilling the biblical promise of "Eretz Israel," the land of Israel that once stretched from al-Arish in the Sinai to the Euphrates. But even extremist Israelis do not go that far, extending their claims only to what they call "Judea and Samaria" *(i.e.,* the West Bank) and some parts of the Gaza Strip. Arabs see these claims as part of the creeping expropriation of Palestinian lands, and their total expulsion from Palestine, except for those willing to remain in an enlarged Israel as second-class citizens. The claim by some extreme right wing Israelis to remove Palestinians from "Judea and Samaria" reinforces these threat-perceptions. Paradoxically, the Sharon government's separation wall allays some of these fears while reinforcing those of the Palestinians.

6. Israel's Political/Military Strategy

Israel's perception of its security needs dominates its foreign and domestic policy. While Israel clearly has the strongest military in the region, its policies towards the Arab states and relations with the Palestinians are driven by security considerations. At first, Israel's concerns were its immediate Arab neighbors. Of late, its greater concerns are Iran's nuclear ambitions and the country's internal security, which is constantly under threat from Palestinian armed resistance. While so far the latter has been limited to suicide bombings, and more recently to barrages of homemade

Qassam rockets launched at Israeli townships around the Gaza Strip, it nonetheless has the potential of expanding into an all-out war, reminiscent of the Algerian War of Independence against France.

Israeli military strategy after the 1948 war was essentially defensive, but the country took on an essentially offensive strategy with the 1956 war. This was possible with French military assistance in tanks, armored personnel carriers, and aircrafts. During that war, the predominance of air force was matched in strategic thinking by the innovative use of rapid moving armor and supporting infantry devised by the late General Moshe Dayan, the architect of the 1956 and 1967 Israeli victories over the Arab states.

After the 1956 war, Israel's military strategy was reshaped to conduct operations outside Israel, preferably in the open desert, where air and armor superiority, as well as tactical planning, would favor Israel. The 1967 war confirmed these military assumptions. In fact, Israel's strategy and tactics in that war were almost a carbon copy of those used in the 1956 war. In 1967, within hours of the conflict's opening, Israel had destroyed over 70 percent of Egypt's air force on the ground, quickly rendering the rest ineffective. The rapid advances on the ground in the Sinai in 1967 were also almost identical to those of 1956.

The 1982 war in Lebanon reflected the strategy of occasional incursion outside Israel and the development of a controlled military buffer zone in Lebanese territory. Twenty years later, the strategy was recognized as a failure, and Israel under Prime Minister Ehud Barak withdrew its forces from Lebanon in 2000.

The 1973 war had a significant impact on Israel's future strategy, which took into account the need to overwhelm all of its enemies simultaneously on multiple fronts. This meant that Israel's military had to be able to simultaneously defeat all four surrounding Arab states: Egypt, Lebanon, Syria, and Jordan. As a result, the Israeli military significantly increased its ground troop capabilities, air force, and motorized units of tanks and armored personnel carriers.

The strength of the Israeli military rests upon a longstanding strategic alliance with the United States, which was enhanced during the Clinton administration, when Israel started to assemble and manufacture components of Abrams M-4 tanks and aircrafts and work on joint projects with the United States in arms technology. As a result, Israel's military capabilities have reached the point where its forces can simultaneously confront all Arab countries at once.

Israel's militarized society arises out of legitimate security concerns, as well as complex psychological factors bound to the experience of the Holocaust. One aspect of Israeli military policy is to defend the promise of "never again" by ensuring that Israel has the capacity to defend itself against virtually any conceivable threat. It is with this mindset that Israel embarked in the 1950s on the development of nuclear weapons and the capacity to deliver them.

Nuclear weapons cannot have a strategic utility in a conflict in the region, particularly because of the close proximity of possible enemy targets to Israel's own civilian population. But Israel's nuclear strategy satisfies two needs: it provides a "security blanket" for the Israeli population, and it represents the ultimate deterrent if an Arab state or a coalition of Arab states manages to seriously threaten Israel's existence. In fact, it is hard to see how such a scenario could occur. Even if an Arab state or a coalition of states could prevail in a series of battles and occupy some parts of Israel, it is almost inevitable that the United States, other countries, and the United Nations Security Council would intervene and impose a cease-fire. To contemplate the possibility that Israel could drop a nuclear weapon on Amman, Cairo, or the Aswan Dam is unthinkable. Yet for Israel, the possibility represents an effective deterrent, even as Egypt and other Arab states regard the idea as unacceptable nuclear blackmail.

Removing Israel's nuclear deterrent from its line of defense would require an effective regional security regime and the development of a culture of trust and cooperation. It would also require eliminating all weapons of mass destruction from the region. These goals can only be considered after bilateral peace treaties are signed between Israel and respectively, Syria, Lebanon, and Iraq, and after a final settlement of the Palestine Question. Israel's contemporary strategy is based on a *de facto* military alliance with the United States. America did not launch the first and second Gulf Wars because of its alliance with Israel, but the concern for Israel's security is always a factor in U.S. policy in the region, and Iraq definitely represented the only Arab country that could have threatened Israel militarily. And, although a nuclear Iran might be a threat to the Arab world as much as it is a threat to Israel, it is America's overriding concern with Israel's security that is a major driving motive in U.S. pressure on Iran to reduce its military capabilities, and in particular, to make sure that it does not acquire the capacity to develop and/or deliver nuclear weapons. The joint military-political strategies of Israel and the United States are also aimed against Islamic Fundamentalists. This strategic alliance was reinforced after the events of 9/11, and in response the Arab and Muslim masses tend to view Israel and the United States as allied against them, thus fueling joint anti-American and anti-Israel sentiments.

Among Arabs and Muslims, there are those who believe that Israel and the pro-Israel lobby in the United States was purposely driving the Bush administration's anti-Arab and anti-Islamic positions in order to radicalize Arabs and Muslim against the United States, leaving Israel the only United

States ally in the region. Israel's alliance with American-Christian Zionists (the Religious Right in the United States) brings credence to this belief.

The unforeseen alliance between American-Christian Zionists and the pro-Israel lobby in the United States is an alliance of convenience. The Christian fundamentalists believe that the Messiah will mean the return of Jesus Christ on earth once the Jews of the world have accomplished the possession of Eretz-Israel and the ingathering of the exiles, the consequences of which are bound to be the removal of the Palestinians from Jerusalem and Judea and Samaria. The America Israel Public Affairs Committee (AIPAC), the powerful Jewish lobby in Washington, might not share the same eschatological vision of America's evangelists, but it uses the alliance with them to promote what they view as Israel's political and strategic interests. AIPAC has definitely developed a position on the peace process that is frequently counterproductive and reprehensible.

Contemporary Israeli political strategy consists of a double-edged drive to consolidate its alliance with the United States while preventing too intimate a relationship between America and its Arab allies in the region. In that sense, the radicalization of Arabs and Muslims serves as a message to the United States that Israel is, after all, the most reliable ally America can expect to have in the region. At the same time, the alliance of Saudi Arabia and Egypt with the United States. is an Israeli interest so long as America keeps its pledge of maintaining Israel's military edge on its Arab neighbors. After all, it is Saudi Arabia's alliance with the United States that brought it to conceive the so-called Arab peace initiative, and it is Egypt's alliance with the United States that made Egypt into a regional peace broker that serves well Israel's interest. The recent cease-fire agreement between Israel and Hamas that was brokered by Egypt is a case in point. Israel certainly expects U.S. economic and military support to secure its conventional military superiority over all combined Arab states and its monopoly of nuclear weapons in the region.

Israel's internal security strategy is to reduce the eventual Palestinian state to a demilitarized one and to surround it militarily so as to isolate it from Jordan, with a militarized wall separating it from Israel.

This Israeli strategic vision is one of the factors contributing to the difficulties of peace. The strategic policy of Israel is very much a reflection of its self-perception and the perception of its Arab neighbors, Palestinians, and Muslims in general. In short, if Israel perceives itself as an island in the midst of a hostile Arab sea and of growing Muslim hostility around the world, it can only react by fortifying its island militarily and turn more toward the West for its political, economic, and social links. Paradoxically, this attitude reinforces Israel's separation and alienation from its surroundings and from its neighbors.

Only a new perspective by Israel of its place in the region can change its strategic orientation. This can only be accomplished by considering Israel's security in terms of regional security and by Israel's joining its Arab neighbors in developing a regional security regime that includes the elimination of weapons of mass destruction. This approach would essentially turn enemies into allies, much as Europe was able to achieve after WWII.

7. Israeli Territorial Settlements

After the 1967 war, Israel found itself in control of the West Bank, East Jerusalem, and the Gaza Strip. The Israeli government that same year extended its authority over East Jerusalem and expanded the city's boundaries, populating the new areas with Jewish settlements. In 1969, a "Basic Law" was adopted by Israel's Knesset, confirming the *de facto* annexation. Succeeding governments consistently expanded Israeli settlements in Jerusalem and in the post-1967 Occupied Territories and developed policies designed to depopulate Jerusalem of its Palestinian inhabitants and prevent other Palestinians from returning to Jerusalem.

The West Bank has been settled with what is now estimated at 250,000 Jewish settlers (not including East Jerusalem). In Gaza, succeeding Israeli governments allowed settlements to be built that brought some 8,000 settlers to the area. Some of these settlers were Jewish immigrants from the United States; many others are Israeli religious nationalists whose orthodox views make them intransigent and unwilling to abandon these settlements in the event of a peace agreement. The bulk of the settlers are, however, "real estate" settlers who came to the Occupied Territories in search of cheap land and an affordable quality of life. These can be removed with due compensation. The main problem lies with the religious, ideologically driven settlers. It is they who pose a challenge to any Israeli government negotiating a "Final Settlement" with the Palestinians.

The construction of settlements inside the "Occupied Territories" violates the Third Geneva Convention and the customary international law applicable to armed conflicts. Thus, they are illegal under international law—but with the support of the United States, Israel has managed to avoid strong international condemnation. The various U.S. administrations have, however, condemned or opposed these settlements. Consistently, U.S. administrations have held the position that such settlements are an impediment to peace and have also publicly expressed disapproval of settlements and their expansion. This was also the position of the Bush administration.

Since 1967, these settlements have cost Israel billions of dollars. That the funds are overwhelmingly Israeli funds that come from the government's budget does not make this Israeli match of folly of settlements building and expansion any more benign. America's sin lies in its political incapacity to stop this, not in financing it. In 1990 and again in September, 2003, the U.S. administration threatened to withhold loan guarantees to Israel if it persisted in its policy of settlement expansion, but eventually the loan guarantees were given and settlements continued to expand.

Succeeding Israeli governments since 1967 have been faced with right-wing demands for more settlements, with the center and left-wing arguing against them, but frequently themselves engaging in settlements expansion. Rabin and Barak, the former the martyr of peace and the latter the negotiator in Camp David and Taba, expanded settlement no less, and probably more, than any other Israeli "enemy of the peace process." Contrary to the perception in the Arab world, the Israelis do not work on the basis of master plans, they exploit opportunities, and more frequently their governments are dragged to wrong policies out of weakness and incapacity to resist the pressure of local lobbies, that of the settlers for example. The only Israeli politician who really had a master plan in the question of settlements was Sharon who wanted to prevent the creation of a contiguous Palestinian state by planting settlements all over the place. But even he came at the end to the conclusion that settlements had to be dismantled if Israel was to reach a modicum of stability and security.

As part of the 1978 Camp David Accords, the Likud government under Menachem Begin agreed to halt settlements. But when the Palestinians failed to seize the opportunity to negotiate a final settlement based on a "two-state" solution, the settlements grew in number and expanded in population.

Some of these settlements had a strategic purpose, and others were probably established to serve as bargaining chips in future negotiations. Only the Jerusalem settlements were deemed non-negotiable, though some in the West Bank also gradually became part of an irreversible fact.

The Israeli body-politic and non-Israeli Zionists see the settlements in Biblical terms as they consider them part of the area the Bible calls "Eretz Israel." Palestinians see the settlements as a manifestation of the creeping expropriation of their lands.

The international community sees the settlements as a violation of international law, and an impediment to peace with the Palestinians. But the inability to apply pressure that would put an end to them has exacerbated animosity by Arabs and Muslims all over the world against Israel and against the United States for allowing them and for directly and indirectly funding them.

At the 2000 Camp David Summit, and later through the December 23 Clinton Peace Parameters, Prime Minister Ehud Barak offered to dismantle some of these settlements and to negotiate the status of others, but the

Palestinians deemed his proposals either too vague or unsatisfactory. The loss of that historic opportunity and the policies of the succeeding Likud government under Prime Minister Sharon mooted the issue, and settlement population was increased.

It is hard to see how Israel can hold on to these settlements and yet achieve a "final settlement" with the Palestinians. The settlement map in the West Bank reveals that a prospective Palestinian state would be dotted with Jewish settlements that would partly break up its territorial contiguity. The settlements also ring the Palestinian state, making it a series of territorial enclaves wholly surrounded by Israeli territory.

8. Jerusalem

The key protagonists, who are the descendants and followers of the Abrahamic faiths of Judaism, Christianity, and Islam share the same essential moral values. Yet, they have been unable to transcend their political differences to find common ground in their shared values. Thus, what should have been a basis for understanding has turned into grounds for antagonism and enmity. Nowhere is this conflict more evident than with respect to Jerusalem. This is ironic considering Jerusalem could be the basis of the creation of a sense of cooperation between these three faith-based communities.

Jerusalem and other areas of Palestine contain many Holy Sites of the highest religious significance to Judaism, Christianity, and Islam. Consequently, freedom of access to these Holy Sites and freedom of religious exercise by adherents to these three faiths must be guaranteed along with the rights of the faith-based communities living in and around these areas. To avoid religious-based conflict over Jerusalem, the United Nations in 1947 called for the internationalization of the city and again in the 1950, as the Statute for Jerusalem.

Holy Sites in Jerusalem, Bethlehem, and other parts of Israel-Palestine, are of immeasurable significance to all three faiths, and competition for control over these sites helps explain why relations between the respective religious communities have often been marked by periods of intense violence. However, religious understanding and compassion have also played an important historical role in enabling positive relations among the faiths.

Jerusalem was home to the central Jewish temple until 70 C.E., when Roman forces destroyed the structure and expelled the Jews. Roman domination of the area and the continual repression of the remaining Jews continued until 638 C.E., when Arab Muslims defeated the Romans. On that occasion, Umar ibn el-Khattab, the second *Khalzfa* of the Muslim nation after the death of Prophet Muhammad, issued an edict that abrogated the Roman decree of banishment of Jews and guaranteed freedom of access and freedom of religious exercise by Jews and Christians in Jerusalem. The edict also provided that each religious community be able to freely exercise its own rights over its Holy Sites and over its respective faith communities. Interfaith violence continued to produce enormous suffering in the region, however, as evidenced by the Crusades and numerous other acts linking religious fervor and political domination. Still, Umar ibn el-Khattab's edict was reinstated by the Turkish Empire, under the so-called *Status Quo* Decree, which recognizes and defines a legacy of tolerant religious co-existence.

The 1947 United Nations Partition Plan provided for the internationalization of Jerusalem as a means of allowing members of all faiths to fully enjoy their rights of access to all the Holy Sites in the city. After the 1948 war, the Hashemite Kingdom of Jordan occupied parts of Jerusalem, including the Old City, where the Western Wall *(Kotel)*, which is believed to be a remnant of the Second Jewish Temple, is situated. During this period, Jews were denied access to the site, in violation of their basic rights, a situation that lasted until 1967, when Israel occupied East Jerusalem, including the Old City, and made Jerusalem a *de facto* part of its territory.

While Muslim Holy Sites have remained under Palestinian control, Israel has continually restricted Palestinian Muslims' access to Jerusalem and established settlements around these Muslim and Christian Holy Sites to alter the demographic, social, religious, and political character of these areas. These restrictions have increased since the start of the 2000 *Intifada (Intifadet al-Aqsa)* and more particularly as of 2002 with the wave of suicide bombings.

Some Muslim Holy Sites in the Occupied Palestinian Territories have been taken over by Israeli settlers, who consider the sites theirs. This includes the tombs of Abraham in Hebron where, admittedly, the compound has been divided between Jews and Moslems, those of Joseph in Napleth and Samuel just outside Jerusalem. These Holy Sites were Muslim mosques before Israeli settlers took possession of them. They have since been converted into synagogues.

Under the Oslo Accords, Israel retained control of several religious sites, including Rachel's Tomb in Bethlehem and the Cave of the Patriarchs in Hebron. These sites brought both a settler and military presence to the heart of these predominantly Arab cities and have consistently been a source of friction and conflict. The problems in Hebron became particularly well known in 1994 after an Israeli extremist from the United States entered a Mosque during prayers and killed thirty-nine worshippers.

These practices have been interpreted by Muslims all over the world as a concerted policy designed to deny religious rights of access, and possibly endanger the physical integrity of Muslim Holy Sites. These threats add a serious international religious dimension to the conflict, leading to the involvement of Muslim masses and particularly Muslim fundamentalist organizations as external protagonists to this conflict.

One of the most controversial issues in the settlement of this conflict is whether Israel will allow the prospective Palestinian state to use a portion of Jerusalem as its capital. Similarly, it remains unclear whether what is called "East Jerusalem" or "Arab Jerusalem," including the Muslim Holy Sites there, will be part of the Palestinian state or part of an internationalized regime.

9. Prospects for Peace

Following the 1949 Armistice Agreements, feeble efforts were made by the West to find a permanent solution to the state of conflict and particularly to the plight of the Palestinian people who had become refugees in neighboring Arab countries. For sure, the Arab states bear the burden of responsibility for not having provided for the needs of these refugees or their development, but so did Israel by refusing them their right to return.

The humiliation of the Arabs after the 1967 war did not bring them to the peace table, but rather increased their public defiance. This attitude was manifested in what became known as the "three no's" of the 1967 Arab Summit in Khartoum: no peace with Israel, no negotiations with Israel, and no recognition of Israel. The *status quo* remained until the 1973 war and the events that ensued from it. After the 1973 war, Saudi Arabia and the Gulf States stood up for Arab solidarity when they declared an oil embargo that quadrupled world oil prices. This position represented both a global economic threat, as well as a powerful symbolic expression of the profound divisions that had come to characterize the conflict, extending far beyond the territory of what was once Palestine to become a key component of international affairs.

After the 1967 war, the United Nations Security Council adopted two major resolutions, Resolution 242 (1967) and Resolution 338 (1973), which provided for Israel's return of territories occupied in the 1967 war in exchange for peace. The fact that the resolution did not call explicitly for the return of "the" territories and spoke only of "territories" was by no means meant to imply that Israel was given a green light to expand its overall territory. The resolution's language meant that negotiations might lead to minor border adjustments, not to major territorial changes. Palestinian Arabs and Arab states still cling to these resolutions, which reiterate the international law principle of "non-acquisition of territory by force." To a large degree, the United Nations' position on the Israeli-Palestinian conflict was understood by Israelis as an expression of their isolation from the world community and their need to rely on a handful of key allies, most notably, the United States. Similarly, the broad support for the Palestinian cause within the Arab world and among post-colonial states in general helped define the conflict as indicative of general inequities of power within a deeply divided world. This tension is evidenced by United Nations Security Council Resolution 3379 (1975), which defined Zionism as equivalent to racism and described Israel as a racially exclusivist state. This position was strongly criticized by the Europe and the United States, which finally succeeded in having the resolution revoked in 1991.

From 1948, Israel, with the support of the West, has consistently treated the Palestinians as a question of "refugees," not as a political dispute over the Palestinians right of self-determination (Resolution 242, for example still treats the Palestinians as refugees and does not call for the creation of a Palestinian state in the lands occupied by Israel), that is to be resolved by their resettlement, but not necessarily in Israel proper.

Israel's military victory over Egypt, Jordan, and Syria in 1967 left these countries' leaders and people stunned. Military victory brought with it the unexpected consequences of administering territories three times as large as the State of Israel and an alien population almost equal in number to its own citizens. In Israel, agreement was found at the political and popular level for the reunification of Jerusalem and its annexation to the State of Israel. But the debate about what to do with territories inhabited by the Palestinians, namely, the West Bank and the Gaza Strip, were highly controversial. The right wing of the political spectrum favored annexing these territories to Israel, as a fulfillment of the Zionist goal of reconstituting Eretz Israel. Others in the center and left saw this as dangerous to Israel's very existence, as it would not only tend to generate greater Arab animosity, but pose the many problems associated with turning Israel essentially into a police state and absorbing over 3.5 million Palestinians into Israeli society. To do so would mean either to give this population Israeli citizenship and thus dilute the Jewish character of the State or to deny them rights of citizenship and make them an occupied people, with all of the consequences this would generate in terms of resistance, as well as international opposition. As a compromise, both the Likud and Labor governments, in varying degrees, allowed for the creeping annexation of some Palestinian territories by means of settlements, while holding out the promise of a Palestinian state on territory and with conditions to be negotiated.

The prospects of peace have all been based on the formula of "land for peace." That formula was first accepted by Israel's national unity government after the 1967 war. It remains the basis for the peaceful resolution of the conflict.

The 1973 war ushered in a new era of peace efforts. It started with two disengagement agreements between Egypt and Israel between 1974 and 1975, followed by the 1977 visit to Jerusalem by Egyptian President Anwar al-Sadat.

The Camp David Accords represented a historic opportunity for the Palestinians to establish a framework for a solution to the conflict. However, the Palestinian leadership failed to grasp that opportunity and rejected the two-state solution that was presented. Had they seized this opportunity, there might now exist a Palestinian state in its twenty-fifth year that would be larger than the territory offered by Prime Minister Ehud Barak at the 2000 Camp David Summit. This and other missed opportunities led the late Israeli statesman Abba Eban to coin the catchy phrase that the Palestinian leadership "never missed the opportunity to miss an opportunity." Still, this analysis is only partly true. Every time the Palestinians accepted Israel's terms, the latter came up with new terms, claiming that the situation had changed and that the previous terms were no longer operative. Thus, the Israelis presented steady incremental increases in their demands, which the Palestinians perceived to be unacceptable. So, as the Palestinians were always late in grasping opportunities, Israel exploited a situation of mistrust and uncertainty for its own political advantage.

Under the Carter administration, the United States vigorously expanded its efforts to solve the Palestinian-Israeli conflict, but to no avail. The first Bush administration, through the efforts of Secretary of State James Baker, continued these efforts, which produced the Madrid Conference in 1991. The Madrid efforts had two components, the Palestinian and multilateral Arab states and the Israel component. The latter included regional security, including the elimination of weapons of mass destruction. This was a laudable goal that came to a stalemate, however, when the Arab side insisted on an *a priori* Israeli commitment to the elimination of its nuclear military capabilities. That effort was preserved on an informal Track II basis between 1995–2003 by a group of experts from Israel, Jordan, Egypt and the United States, chaired by this writer. Under the Clinton administration, the Madrid process for all practical purposes came to an end, though that administration pursued the same goals. Clinton administration efforts evolved mostly during the second term, after early success brokering a peace treaty between Israel and the Hashemite Kingdom of Jordan, and culminated in the July 2000 Camp David II Summit between Barak and Arafat, and in President Clinton's peace parameters of December 2000.

Camp David was the natural follow up of the separate peace track that had developed directly between Israelis and Palestinians through

Norway and ushered eventually in the 1993 Oslo Accords, an agreement subsequently formalized under the auspices of the Clinton administration in a White House lawn ceremony involving Prime Minister Yitzhak Rabin, Minister of Foreign Affairs Shimon Peres, and PLO Chairman Yasser Arafat.

The accords allowed Arafat to establish a Palestinian Authority on the Gaza Strip and most of the West Bank. In January 1996, Arafat was elected as president in the Palestinian Authority's first elections, receiving 88 percent of votes.

In July 2000, Clinton sought to emulate President Carter's efforts at Camp David with a summit between Arafat and Barak. With the collapse of the talks into the al-Aqsa *Intifada*, efforts undertaken by President Clinton and President Hosni Mubarak at another summit at Sharm el-Sheikh in 2000, whose aim was to reach an end to the violence and bring back the parties to the negotiating table, ended in failure. Israel and the United States blamed the failure on Yasser Arafat's inability or unwillingness to seize the opportunity for peace. There are various explanations of that failure, which had been so close to success. Among them is the proposition that Yasser Arafat failed to grasp the opportunity offered by Barak, that Barak's proposal was not as generous as portrayed, and that Clinton lacked the patience and focus on detail to bring about successful closure.

The failure to capture the propitious opportunity at the 2000 Camp David Summit was followed by Ariel Sharon's provocative visit to the "Temple Mount" for the Jews and the "Haram el-Sharif" for the Muslims, after the Friday Muslim prayers. Accompanied by 1,000 members of Israel's security forces, Sharon provoked a riot that led to an unprecedented escalation of violence between Israelis and Palestinians. Between September 2000 and July 2003 an estimated 3,000 Palestinians were killed and over 25,000 were injured, and an estimated 800 Israelis were killed and 5,000 injured. The Palestinians resorted to suicide bombings which spread terror among the Israelis, and the Israelis resorted to excessive and indiscriminate force as retaliation, destroying Palestinian public and private property, and crippling that society's economy. As the violence escalated, each side blamed the other.

Efforts toward a peace treaty between Israel and Syria were undertaken during the Clinton administration based on Israel's return of the Golan Heights, but nothing came of it. The reasons for that failure are uncertain, but they most likely have to do with Syria's unwillingness to follow Egypt's lead in entering into a comprehensive peace treaty with Israel, including full normalization of relations. But, it may also be due to Israel's refusal to give up unconditionally the totality of the Syrian Golan Heights, as it did with Egypt with respect to the Sinai. The Israeli settlements in the Occupied Territories are definitely a major obstacle to a peace settlement.

To the right wing in Israel, these settlements are irreversible, but to others, throughout the Israeli political spectrum, it is not so. In fact, for many of the settlers, except for ultra-Orthodox ones, the prospects of compensation and relocation are acceptable. As the settlement process expanded, particularly around Jerusalem, the Palestinians became more and more concerned about forever losing these territories.

As the territorial issue of the West Bank and "East Jerusalem" shifted from Jordan to the Palestinians when Jordan gave up in 1988 its claim to these territories, the Palestinians found themselves without much leverage to induce Israel to return all the territories occupied in the 1967 war to a Palestinian state to be established on these territories with parts of Jerusalem as its capital. The Palestinian Authority established pursuant to the Oslo Accords of 1993 was given the administration of the Gaza Strip and a substantial portion of the "West Bank," but not including the territories illegally settled by Israelis.

Foreign occupation is always fraught with dangers. Only those occupiers in history who have been most ruthless have succeeded in keeping foreign occupied populations in check. Israel learned that lesson when it found itself more and more enmeshed into repressive tactics against the Palestinians which were in fundamental opposition to their values. IDF and security forces engaged in massive arbitrary arrests and detention, torture, and other forms of physical mistreatment of prisoners, blowing up houses in retaliation, cutting down productive groves of trees, restricting people's freedom of movement, and above all, engaging in conduct which constituted constant humiliation of the Palestinian people.

The Palestinians have felt these injustices, which have bred anger and despair. This in turn has led to violence, first intermittent, and then to the first full-fledged *Intifada* of 1987, and the *Intifada* of 2000, whose effects are still unfolding. The process of escalation of violence was inevitable, as each side blamed the other, and responded in kind. Israel, having the greater military strength, has been able to inflict the most harm. The Palestinians ultimately resorted to suicide bombings as the weapon of last resort.

Over the years, Israel has realized that it could not be a foreign military occupier engaging in repressive violent action against another people without feeling the consequences in its own society. This led to the realization by those in the center and left of the political spectrum that the West Bank and Gaza Strip should be part of a separate Palestinian state. Thus, Israel made the choice not favored by its right wing, to proactively engage in the process that would bring about a two-state solution to the Palestinian problem. This was, of course, the approach of the 1947 Partition Plan, as well as the 1978 Camp David Accords, which the Palestinians rejected. But as Israel grew stronger and inflicted greater punishment on the Palestinians, and the latter grew weaker with Arab states encouraging them to accept a two-state solution, that outcome appeared inevitable. Within Palestinian society, opposition remained strong, particularly among Hamas and other Islamic nationalistic movements, though many political observers of the Arab scene see this as political posturing, and as a way of strengthening the hand of Yasser Arafat and others in negotiating with Israel.

Within Israel, the political tensions between right and left are still present. The right still hopes either to gain more territory in the West Bank and Gaza Strip by denying it to the Palestinians, or by keeping the *status quo* festering in the hope that the Palestinians would despair and leave in large numbers, thus in effect achieving a subtle population removal. The balance is so precarious that on occasion, a single suicide bombing incident is capable of tipping the scales against the progress of peace.

Throughout this violent and humanly degrading occupation, the values of both communities have been sorely tested. As history is likely to point out, neither side will be very proud of that period in its history.

After the 9/11 attack upon the United States, Israel managed to marshal United States public opinion and the Bush administration to support its policy of retaliatory violence against the Palestinians. Israeli responses to Palestinian suicide bombers have wrought significant harm to the Palestinian people, and the cycle of violence has increased unabated.

The Bush Administration in the aftermath of the Iraq war opened the way for a new phase in the on-again, off-again peace process, based on the "Quartet Road-Map," named after its preparation by the United States, Russia, the United Nations, and the European Union. This present phase led to yet another dual summit in 2003 in Aqaba, with President Bush, King Abdallah of Jordan, Prime Minister Sharon, and then Palestinian Prime Minister Mahmoud Abbas. This was then followed by another summit in Sharm el-Sheikh, with President Bush, King Abdallah, President Mubarak, and Prime Minister Abbas. But issues pertaining to the territory of the future State of Palestine, the Israeli settlements, Israeli and Palestinian security, the sovereignty of a Palestinian state and the Palestinian's "right of return" remain to be solved.

By 2007, the Bush Administration decided to sponsor an initiative whose name came from the locaton of the meeting between Israelis, Palestinians, Arab states and others at Annapolis. No new ideas were presented. The initiative was essentially for the Administration's window-dressing purposes, though it also had a positive influence on all concerned.

The problem lies elsewhere. It lies in the poverty of the leadership and in the fragmentation of the Palestinian political system. The tragedy of this conflict is that the only man, Yasser Arafat, whose signature on a peace agreement based on a two-state solution could have been legitimate in the eyes of his people took this legitimacy with him to the grave.

President Mahmoud Abbas was never an inspiring authority for his people, and with the loss of Gaza to Hamas, his political clout has been diminished even further. In fact, Mr. Abbas does not even control the militias of his own party, Fatah, that have been even more active than Hamas in launching terrorist attacks against Israel. The Palestinian Authority's rule over the West Bank would have collapsed long ago if it were not for the Israelis' daily incursions against Hamas and Fatah territories in areas under Mr. Abbas' Fatah "control."

Frequently throughout history, national movements, almost invariably consisting of a radical and a pragmatic wing, had to split in order to reach the promised land. Consensus is the negation of leadership and frequently a recipe for political paralysis. Zionism is a case in point. Had Menachem Begin's ultra nationalist Irgun been in coalition with Ben-Gurion's pragmatic Mapai in 1947, the Zionists would have rejected the partition of Palestine, and Ben-Gurion would not have been allowed to declare the Jewish state in May 1948.

But, the concept should not be elevated to the level of a dogma. In the Palestinian case, and with the lack of the kind of strong leadership that Arafat could provide, there is no way that the radical wing, Hamas, can be discarded from the process leading to Palestinian statehood. Moreover, unlike in the Israeli case, in Palestine the radical wing represents the democratic majority as it emerged from the polls two years ago.

It is a self-deceiving fantasy to assume that the highly unpopular craftsmen of the Palestinian peace industry, those who had been there throughout all the stages of the discredited Oslo process can still muster the necessary popular legitimacy in order to mobilize their nation in favor of a historic compromise with the Jewish state that would require painful concessions on issues so central to the Palestinian national ethos such as refugees, Jerusalem and territory.

To invade or not to invade Hamas-controlled Gaza, that is the Hamletian dilemma that dominates the Israeli discourse in these days. Locked in a self-imposed conceptual paralysis that does not allow for a solution outside the box of a military answer whose unrealistic objective is to bring about the collapse of the Hamas regime, the Israeli system refuses to see that Hamas' attacks on Israeli territory are not intended to draw Israel into an invasion; they are rather an attempt to establish a new deterrent against Israel that would secure Hamas regime in the Gaza Strip.

Nor is it at all clear that a major invasion of the Gaza Strip can bring about the end of the rocket attacks on Israeli territory. Hamas has been undergoing a process of Hizballahization with the help of the Iranians. Its units are no longer simple terrorist cells; they are highly trained and well-equipped combat units, and its rockets, just like in southern Lebanon, are launched with the help of timers from crude underground silos. The traumatic experience of the Lebanon War has definitely made the Israeli leadership weary of yet another asymmetric war where a clear cut victory can never be claimed, and where the arithmetic of blood is always bound to turn the casualties of the supposedly superior force, Israel, into a severe domestic crisis.

Israel should therefore change its strategic objective in Gaza from that of toppling Hamas to that of rescuing the Annapolis process, and with it the last chance for a two-state solution, from inevitable perdition. This requires not only a cease-fire with Hamas, an important achievement of Egypt's diplomacy, but also a return to a Palestinian national unity government that should offer the peace process the vital legitimacy that it lacks today. Without the resurrection of the Mecca agreement (an agreement that was brokered two years ago by the Saudis, and allowed the creation of a Fatah-Hamas unity government that later collapsed) neither can Hamas expect to secure its control of Gaza, nor the PLO deliver on the peace process.

The notion so dear to the architects of the Annapolis process that peace can be achieved only when a wedge is driven between the "moderates" and the "extremists" is in the Palestinian case a misconception. National unity would not be an impediment to a settlement for the simple reason that the moderates that are now negotiating with Israel would anyway strive for an agreement that the extremists could not label as a treacherous sell-out. Hence, the difference between the Palestinian positions in the current negotiations and those they might hold when a unity government is restored can only be very minor.

It has been a tragic trait of the Israeli-Palestinian conflict that there has been little compassion from either side towards the other, but more so by Israelis toward Palestinians, since they are, after all, the ones suffering the greatest brunt of the harm. Nevertheless, there are many on both sides who have reached out to one another. It should be noted that there are many Jews throughout the world and in Israel who have been vocal in support of peace, and in support of the rights of the Palestinians. Their voices have been submerged by the sounds of violence, and more so by the tragedies of suicide bombings. As violence on both sides decreases, it is expected that supporters of peace within Israel and within the Palestinian community will transcend their mutual distrust and allow them to move in the direction of peace and reconciliation.

10. Conclusion

Peace and reconciliation are anathema to those on both sides who wish the conflict to continue until either side dominates or eliminates the other. However, there are many on both sides who genuinely desire peace, reconciliation, security, and mutual respect. Surprisingly, among the proponents of this hopeful perspective, there has been a remarkable lack of vision as to what the future should portend and how to achieve a more balanced understanding of equitable relations between Israelis and Palestinians.

At the governmental level, Israel has consistently failed to appreciate that by having the upper hand, it has an obligation to lead the way to peace with the Palestinians, and to be the prime sustainers of future Palestinian economic development. Unfortunately, Israeli governments have also failed to display the necessary openness towards a productive future. Motivated by the fear of a demographic doomsday if the two-state solution is not implemented, and in their desperate attempt to stop suicide terrorist attacks, Israel was driven to a policy of separation. Rather than building bridges between the two communities, Israeli governments built walls and barbed wires to enforce the two communities' separation. Instead of planning for an economically viable Palestinian state, the trend appears oriented towards a South African-style model of dependent, subservient Bantustans in Palestine.

Despite its reservations about the "road-map" and its security concerns, Israel must articulate a vision of peace that is based not only on security, but also on long-term cooperation for the benefit of both countries. The limited, contiguous space of Israel and Palestine and the projected population increase in the next thirty years compel co-existence and cooperation between these two communities. Understandably, the political climate in Israel and among Palestinians is characterized by distrust and limited confidence, but the respective governments have an obligation to create improved understanding, at least by eliminating the rhetoric of fear and anger.

History has repeatedly proven that a people whose human dignity is trampled and whose social and economic life is destroyed will fight to the bitter end with whatever means they have. No amount of military strength can prevent that reaction or ensure the security of those using such force.

The dehumanization and demonization of the Palestinian people, the excessive use of force used either as self-defense or as retaliation, and the destruction of the Palestinian economy and its social structure have bred extraordinary despair. These feelings leave Palestinians with armed struggle as the only means of asserting their human dignity. Violence reaps violence, and because the Palestinians do not have F-16s, Apache helicopters, and Abrams tanks, they are left with assassinations and suicide bombing.

Israel cannot have peace while taking over Palestinian land that it has occupied since 1967. This is contrary not only to international law, but also to justice and fairness. Israel has been very adept in gradually taking over more and more of the Palestinian areas, and that is an impediment to peace.

The Palestinian leadership has also failed to articulate a vision of peace and how future co-existence with Israel should be shaped. The Palestinians must lay to rest once and for all their claim to reconstitute what was once Palestine. Israel's existence and legitimacy to exist must be unequivocally recognized.

It is not naïve to believe in the goodness of human nature, nor to reach out for the better instincts of Palestinians and Israelis. There are enough people of good will on both sides to make peace workable. But peace is not only a signed agreement between leaders. If that were the case, it would only be worth the paper it is written on. Israel must understand, just as the Palestinians must also understand, that peace requires reconciliation between the peoples of both communities. Thus, their respective governments must work at establishing confidence based on a vision of a future of reciprocal respect and mutual understanding.

There is much to be done to rebuild mutual confidence. Admittedly, this will take time and effort on both sides, but it is easier than most skeptics claim. This is the time when the tide in the affairs of Israelis and Palestinians has come, and they must jointly seize the opportunities that it brings with it.

There is no more fitting conclusion than the Talmud's wise words:

The world rests on three pillars: on truth, on justice, and on peace. (Rabban Simeon Ben Gamaliel, Abot 1, 18).

A Talmudic commentary adds to this saying:

The three are really one, if justice is realized, truth is vindicated and peace results.

Part III

The Documents

1. Antecedents to the League of Nations Mandate for Palestine: 1897–1922

The twenty-three documents contained in this chapter cover the period directly preceding the League of Nations Mandate for Palestine. They derive from a variety of sources, including: the World Zionist Organization; the British government; and leading political figures of the period, such as Sharif Hussein of Mecca, Emir Feisal, Lord Rothschild, and Chaim Weizmann. These documents reflect an era of uncertainty in the Middle East, when the Turkish Ottoman Empire and European powers struggled for predominance in the region.[93]

From 1517 to 1917, the lands of the eastern Mediterranean and Egypt formed part of the Ottoman Empire, with Arab territories, such as the Sanjak of Jerusalem and the Vilayet of Beirut, being ruled as separate administrative districts from the Ottoman seat of power in Constantinople. When Turkey entered World War I in November 1914 on the side of the Central Powers against the Entente Powers,[94] Britain began to maneuver for Arab support in the region through the Sharif of Mecca.[95] Britain also declared Egypt—then a formal Ottoman territory—a British Protectorate.[96]

In 1916, Britain and France allotted to themselves parts of the Turkish Ottoman Empire under a secret plan known as the Sykes-Picot Agreement.[97] Partially in fulfillment of this plan, British forces captured

---

[93] Few Middle Eastern states had yet gained their independence, with the exception of Northern Yemen in 1918.

[94] Austria-Hungary and Germany formed the core of the Central Powers. Britain, France, and Russia formed the core of the Entente Powers. The United States eventually joined the war on the side of the Entente Powers as an Associate Power on April 6, 1917. Probably the best book on the history and politics of World War I's Mid-East implication is David Fromkin's *A Peace to End All Peace: The Fall of the Ottoman Empire and the Creation of the Modern Middle East.*

[95] On August 2, 1914, the Porte concluded a secret treaty of alliance with Germany. In the following weeks concessions granted to foreign powers under the capitulations, *i.e.*, extraterritorial privileges to foreign merchants conducting business in lands under Islamic law, were canceled in a document known as the Ottoman Abrogation of the Capitulations. Germany's support for it over Britain, France, and Russia's rejection of it influenced the Porte's decision to side with the Central Powers in the War. The text of the Abrogation is available in Palestine and the Arab-Israeli Conflict: A History with Documents 94–95 (Charles Smith ed., 4th ed. 2001).

[96] Britain occupied Egypt in 1882, but left formal sovereignty to the Turkish Ottoman Empire.

[97] *See* Doc. 5.

Jerusalem and Baghdad in 1917, and France took Damascus by force in 1920. In 1921, Britain separated the land-mass east of the Jordan River from Palestine to create the Emirate of Transjordan and installed a Hashemite monarch, Emir Abdullah, the elder son of Sharif Hussein of Mecca. That same year, Britain created the Hashemite Kingdom of Iraq out of Mesopotamia and installed Emir Feisal, the third son of Sharif Hussein of Mecca, as its king. Thus, the defeat and dismemberment of the Turkish Ottoman Empire resulted in the creation of five new states in the region—Iraq, Lebanon, Transjordan, and Syria, with Palestine in a status of a quasi-state—which were immediately placed under the tutelage of either Britain or France.

During this time, Arab nationalism and Zionism were on the rise, and Arab and Jewish groups in Palestine sought Britain's favor in advancing their respective nationalist goals. The defining document to bolster Zionist claims was the Balfour Declaration of 1917, which expresses Britain's support for the creation of a Jewish State in Palestine.[98] Much of the text of the Balfour Declaration was later incorporated into the League of Nation Mandate for Palestine, emphasizing Britain's commitment to establishing a Jewish homeland in the area.[99]

Many of the documents collected in this chapter can be characterized as attempts to resolve pressing questions of how to establish an independent Jewish state in the region and how to regulate Jewish immigration from Eastern Europe to Palestine given the rise of anti-Semitism in Europe.

Many of the pre-mandate documents contained in Section 6, Jerusalem and the Holy Sites, should be consulted in connection with these documents.

Document 1: Der Judenstaat (February 14, 1896). This document establishes the concepts Theodor Herzl envisioned for *Der Judenstaat* ("The Jewish State"). Herzl played a large role in both creating and pushing the political ideology of this worldwide movement. His pamphlet's importance lies in the influence it had over European statesmen on the Zionist Cause.

In the pamphlet, Herzl developed the old idea of the restoration of the Jewish state. He notes that although he believes in the practicality of this idea, he does not know how it will be carried out. Until the problem of creating a Jewish is solved, Jews will continue to be persecuted in all countries they occupy. He defines the Jewish question as a national, rather than social or religious, issue. Herzl proposes that sovereignty be granted to his people over a portion of the globe, preferably Palestine, as it is their memorable and historic home and will attract Jews who would be strong enough to form a model state once this land is attained.

Document 2: Basle Program of the First World Zionist Congress (August 29, 1897) [Israel Cohen, *The Zionist Movement* 77 (1946), *reprinted in* 3 The Arab Israeli Conflict 4 (John Norton Moore ed., 1974)]. The First World Zionist Congress, convened by

---

[98] *See* Doc. 8.

[99] *See* Doc. 24.

famed Jewish leader Theodor Herzl, in Basle, Switzerland, was the first international meeting of its kind. It produced the Basle Program, which publicly declares the Zionist ambition to create a homeland for the Jewish people in Palestine. It set the institutional framework for all subsequent Zionist policy, including measures such as following public law and procuring the assent of all necessary governments.

Document 3: Letter from Dr. Theodor Herzl to M. Yousef Zia Al-Khalidi (March 19, 1899) [Report of the Special Committee on Palestine, U.N. GAOR, Supp. No 11, at 39–40, U.N. Doc. A/364 (1947)]. Theodor Herzl, the founder of the World Zionist Organization, wrote this letter to M. Yousef Zia Al-Khalidi, the mayor of Jerusalem, after learning that Al-Khalidi did not support Jewish immigration to Palestine due to the opposition of Turkish rulers and the local population. In his letter, Herzl addresses these concerns and enumerates the benefits of Jewish migration to the area. In particular, he contends that development produced by Jewish settlers would increase the value of land in Palestine.

Document 4: Correspondence between Sir Henry McMahon and Sharif Hussein of Mecca (July 14, 1915–October 24, 1915) [His Majesty's High Commissioner at Cairo, and Sherif Hussein of Mecca, 1939, Cmd. 5957, at 3–18]. The correspondence between Sir A. Henry McMahon, British high commissioner in Cairo, and Hussein ibn Ali, Sharif of Mecca, provides assurance to the Arab leadership of Britain's support for Arab independence in the region. Given the backdrop of World War I, which placed Great Britain as an Allied power in opposition to the Ottoman Empire, Sir Henry McMahon's assurance can be read as a strategic move on the part of Great Britain to gain the support of oil-rich Arab countries against Constantinople. (Mid-East oil was first discovered in 1908 at Masjid-I-Sulaiman in Southwestern Persia, and the supply immediately became of critical interest to Britain.) Consequently, Hussein sides politically with Britain, hoping for an independent Kingdom of Hejaz (Hedjaz) at the end of the war. An interesting aspect of this correspondence is McMahon's insistence that some Western parts of the territories are not purely Arab and, thus, should be treated uniquely. This is a nod to Zionist interests in Palestine.

Document 5: Sykes-Picot Agreement (May 16, 1916) [IV DOCUMENTS ON BRITISH FOREIGN POLICY, FIRST SERIES, 1919–1939 245–47 (1952)]. In this agreement signed by and named for Sir Mark Sykes of Britain and Charles Georges-Picot of France, Britain and France plan to take control over Arab provinces of the former Ottoman Empire in the Middle East. The agreement divides the provinces into zones of influence, with the intention of eventually granting independence to some future states. According to the plan, Palestine would be subject to an international administration to be settled after consultation with Russia, the other Allies, and Sharif Hussein of Mecca. Later, British policymakers decide that internationalization was not in line with British interests, and the agreement is never implemented. Notably, this agreement conflicts with pledges of Arab Independence made by the British government to Sharif Hussein of Mecca. In 1917, the Soviet government published this agreement along with other secret treaties made by imperial Russia to scandalize Western governments.

Document 6: Excerpts from the Memorandum of Edwin Montagu on the Anti-Semitism of the Present (British) Government (August 23, 1917) [Great Britain Public Record Office,

Parl. Deb., Cab. 24/24 (Aug. 23, 1917)]. Lord Edwin Samuel Montagu, a Jewish minister of government, submitted this memorandum to the British cabinet, arguing that Zionism and the formation of a Jewish homeland in Palestine are not in the interest of Britain or its Jewish population as they will prevent Jewish citizens from being properly absorbed and nationalized into Britain. He writes that the formation of a Jewish Homeland in Palestine would marginalize Turks, "Mahommedans," and Christians living in the area.

Document 7: Letter from M.P.A. Hankey Containing a Draft of the Balfour Declaration (October 6, 1917) [British Library Manuscript No. Add.41178f]. In this letter, Sir Maurice Hankey, secretary to the war cabinet, requests the opinion of prominent Jewish leaders on the establishment of a Jewish homeland in Palestine. Copies of the letter were sent to: Sir Stuart Samuel, chairman of the Jewish Board of Deputies; Mr. Leonard L. Cohen, chairman of the Jewish Board of Guardians; Mr. Claud Monteflore; Sir Phillip Magnus, MP; Dr. Herz, the chief rabbi of England; Mr. N. Sokolov, chief representative in England of the International Zionist Executive; Dr. Weizmann, president of the English Zionist Federation. The letter contains a draft of the Balfour Declaration.

Document 8: Balfour Declaration (November 2, 1917) [The Balfour Declaration, 1940, Cmd. 5957, at 1–16]. The famous Balfour Declaration was written as a letter from British Foreign Secretary Arthur Balfour to Baron Lionel Walter Rothschild. It marks a watershed in the history of World Zionism as it unequivocally declares British support for a Jewish homeland in Palestine provided it does not interfere with the rights of non-Jewish communities in Palestine. The declaration was later made part of the Treaty of Sèvres,[100] and its language was incorporated into the preamble to the Mandate for Palestine confirmed by the League of Nations.[101]

Document 9: Hogarth Message to Sharif Hussein of Mecca (January 1918) [The Hogarth Message, 1939, Cmd. 5974, at 48–49]. This message to Sharif Hussein of Mecca from Commander D.G. Hogarth, C.M.G., R.N.V.R. of the Arab Bureau in Cairo reiterates Britain's support for Arab independence and calls for the establishment of a special regime to protect the Holy Places in Palestine. While the message expresses support for Jewish immigration to Palestine, it promises that such immigration would only be allowed if it does not threaten the political or economic freedom of the indigenous Arab population.

Document 10: British Declaration to the Seven Arab Spokesmen (June 1918) [Israel Cohen, *The Zionist Movement* 77 (1946), *reprinted in* 3 The Arab Israeli Conflict 36 (John Norton Moore ed., 1974)]. Written by the British high commissioner in Egypt, the Declaration to the Seven Arab Spokesmen affirms Britain's support for the complete and sovereign independence of Arabs in the region and pledges to assist the Arab population in achieving independence. Reportedly, based on these statements, the Arab spokesmen mistakenly assumed that the Balfour Declaration and other agreements between Britain and the Zionists that advocated the establishment of a Jewish homeland in Palestine were null.

---

[100] *See* Doc. 17. The Treaty of Sèvres gave way to the Treaty of Lausanne in 1923. *See* Doc. 29.

[101] *See* Doc. 24.

Document 11: Anglo-French Declaration (November 7, 1918) [145 Parl. Deb., H.C. (5th ser.) (1921) 36]. Fearing an Arab rebellion in Palestine, the British military occupation authority published this Anglo-French Joint Declaration, which calls for self-determination for Arabs in the region.

Document 12: Agreement between Emir Feisal and Dr. Chaim Weizmann (January 3, 1919) [3 David Hunter Miller, My Diary of the Peace Conference with Documents 188–89 (1928)]. Made between Emir Feisal, the Prince of the Hedjaz and the son of Sharif Hussein of Mecca, and Dr. Chaim Weizmann, head of the Zionist Commission to Palestine, this agreement was the first diplomatic effort by Arabs and Jews to find a joint solution to the growing conflict in Palestine. It proposes that Arabs and Jews work together to achieve their mutual national aspirations. Though there is no clear agreement on the makeup of a future government, the document refers to the creation of a separate Arab state in Palestine. Surprisingly, this agreement secured Arab assent though it explicitly advocates Jewish immigration, which was a major source of concern for indigenous Arab populations. The document concludes with a reservation by Emir Feisal that would allow him to terminate the agreement if an Arab state was not established.

Document 13: Correspondence between Emir Feisal and Felix Frankfurter (March 3–5, 1919) [*available at* http://course1.winona.msus.edu/aelafandi/polsci2870/documents.htm#frankfurter]. In these letters exchanged by Emir Feisal, the Hedjaz representative, and Felix Frankfurter,[102] president of the Zionist Organization of America, Feisal connects the Arab and Jewish struggles for independence from European powers, noting their similar oppression under foreign occupation. Frankfurter, in turn, expresses support for the Arab resistance movement and closes his letter by stating, "The Arabs and Jews are neighbors in territory; we cannot but live side by side as friends."

Document 14: Article 22 of the Covenant of the League of Nations (June 28, 1919) [League of Nations Covenant, June 28, 1919, art 22, 2 Bevans 48, 55–57]. Article 22 of the Covenant of the League of Nations defines the national status of all former colonial territories in Asia and Africa. It classifies territories according to three categories: (1) those closest to achieving national independence (*i.e,* "certain communities formerly belonging to the Turkish Empire"); (2) those requiring near-complete administration from a mandatory power (*i.e.*, territories in Central Africa); and (3) those to be permanently administered by a mandatory power (*i.e.*, "South-West Africa and certain of the South Pacific Islands"). It does not provide criteria for judging the progress of territories toward nationhood. This document paved the way for Britain to assume legitimate control over Palestine in 1922 as a mandatory power.[103] With its hierarchical system of European tutelage, the mandate system was a veiled form of colonial administration.

Document 15: Resolutions of the General Syrian Congress (Damascus Congress) (July 2, 1919) [*reprinted in* George Antonius, The Arab Awakening 440–42 (2000)]. The General Syrian Congress was an assembly of leaders from the Arab world who met in Damascus to decide the fate of formerly Ottoman territories after the breakup

---

[102] Felix Frankfurter became a Justice of the United States Supreme Court in 1939.

[103] *See* Doc. 24.

of the Ottoman Empire. In its resolutions, it calls for the complete independence of Greater Syria, which included Palestine and the area that would soon become Transjordan, argues for Lebanon's absorption into Syria, and rejects the Sykes-Picot Agreement, the Balfour Declaration, and the League of Nations' mandatory system. The Congress elected Emir Feisal the king of a united Syria. Britain did not recognize the congress as representative and rejected its resolutions.

Document 16: Excerpts from the Report of the American Section of the Inter-Allied Commission of Mandates in Turkey (King-Crane Commission Report) (August 28, 1919) [*available at* http://domino.un.org/Unispal.nsf/0/16e17fc18fab11d785256ced0075086e?Opendocument]. The King-Crane Commission of Inquiry was dispatched to Syria by U.S. President Woodrow Wilson in May 1919 to assess Arab national aspirations in light of the newly developed League of Nations mandatory system. Although Wilson had originally solicited the participation of France and Britain, the French refused to appoint representatives and the British representative withdrew. Consequently, two Americans, Henry C. King, president of Oberlin College, and Charles R. Crane, a Chicago businessman and trustee of Robert College in Constantinople, proceeded to Syria with their staff. In its report, the commission notes the increasing concern of Arabs in Palestine and Syria that Zionists will seize all of Palestine in establishing a Jewish homeland. The commission recommends "serious modification of the extreme Zionist program for Palestine."

Document 17: Excerpts from the Treaty of Peace between the Allied and Associated Powers and Turkey Signed at Sèvres (Treaty of Sèvres), (August 10, 1920) [*available at* http://www.lib.byu.edu/~rdh/wwi/versa/sevres1.html]. This treaty was concluded between the Turkish Ottoman Empire and the Allies (excluding Russia and the United States) at Sèvres, France, at the conclusion of World War I. It redraws the boundaries of the former Ottoman Empire and virtually abolishes Turkish sovereignty. The treaty was never adopted and was superseded by the Treaty of Lausanne in 1923.[104]

Document 18: Memorandum Submitted by Emir Feisal to the Conference of Allied Powers at the House of Commons (March 10, 1921) [*available at* http://domino.un.org/unispal.nsf/9a798adbf322aff38525617b006d88d7/14f06fe1edd50616852570c00058e77e!OpenDocument]. In this memorandum, Emir Feisal explains that Arabs joined the war on the side of the Allies because the British government had promised independence in return for their support. He writes, "My Father [Sharif Hussein of Mecca] considered that in view of the pledges given to him, the essential unity and independence of the Arab-speaking provinces of the Turkish Empire were secure in the event of the success of the Allies." He expresses his deep concern over decisions by the European powers to carve up the region into separate states irrespective of their cultural homogeneity and economic interdependence and requests that the Allied powers reconsider the Treaty of Sèvres as it would adversely affect the Arab region.[105]

Document 19: British Interim Report on the Civil Administration of Palestine during the Period July 1, 1920–June 30, 1921 by British High Commissioner Herbert Samuel (July 30, 1921) [*available at* http://domino.un.org/unispal.nsf/9a798adbf322aff38525617b006

[104] *See* Doc. 30.
[105] *See* Doc. 17.

d88d7/349b02280a930813052565e90048ed1c!OpenDocument]. Herbert Samuel, the high commissioner and commander-in-chief for the British Administration of Palestine, submitted this report to the League of Nations in fulfillment of British responsibilities as protector under the mandate system. It describes the political and financial situation in Palestine under British management and details the growing tensions between Arabs and Jews.

Document 20: Excerpts from the Haycraft Commission of Enquiry into the 1920–1921 Arab Riots (October 1921) [*available at* http://www.us-israel.org/jsource/history/haycraft.html]. The Haycraft Commission of Enquiry—named for its chairman, Sir Thomas Haycraft, chief justice of Palestine—was established by Samuel Herbert, the British high commissioner for Palestine, to investigate the causes of the 1920–21 Arab Riots. In its report, the commission concludes that the Jaffa riots and subsequent acts of violence were caused by Arab frustration with Jewish immigration and skepticism about Zionist policies in Palestine.

Document 21: Statement of British Policy in Palestine (Churchill White Paper) (June 3, 1922) [1922, Cmd. 17800, at 17–21, *available at* http://www.yale.edu/lawweb/Avalon/mideast/brwh1922.htm]. The Churchill White Paper, presented by Sir Winston Churchill to the British government in 1922, declares British support for the establishment of Arab sovereign independence in Palestine. It asserts that Britain's plan is not for Palestine as a whole to be converted into a Jewish national home and identifies territories on the east bank of the Jordan River as a distinct territory. It states that territories west of the Jordan River are excluded from Sir Henry McMahon's pledge of Arab independence. The Palestinian Arab community rejected this White Paper.

Document 22: Excerpts from the League of Nations Official Journal: Date on which the Question of the Draft Mandate for Palestine Should Be Placed on the Agenda of the Council (June 30, 1922) [*available at* http://domino.un.org/unispal.nsf/9a798adbf322aff38525617b006d88d7/b08168048e277b5a052565f70058cef3!OpenDocument]. This League of Nations document details the many difficulties faced by the Allied and associated powers in the execution of the Mandate for Palestine. It blames difficulties on the impact of the Treaty of Sèvres, Britain's inability to fully invest in the territory due to its war debt, and religious interests in the area.[106]

Document 23: Correspondence between the Colonial Office and the Palestine Arab Delegation and the Zionist Organisation (February 21–June 29, 1922) [*available at* http://domino.un.org/unispal.nsf/9a798adbf322aff38525617b006d88d7/48a7e5584ee1403485256cd8006c3fbe!OpenDocument]. This correspondence conducted by the Colonial Office and the two main representative bodies in Palestine—the Palestine Arab Delegation and the Zionist Organisation—discusses the planned implementation of the League of Nations Mandate for Palestine. In these letters, Arab and Jewish leaders react to the planned Mandate for Palestine. Letters from the Palestine Arab Delegation are a meticulous, line-by-line criticism of Britain's Palestine Order in Council, emphasizing the need for a representative

[106] *Id.*

government in Palestine.[107] They also complain that promises to establish a Jewish homeland in Palestine and the influx of "alien Jews" to the territory are threatening the prosperity of Palestinian national life. In contrast, the Zionist Organisation, represented by Chaim Weizmann, expresses its satisfaction with Britain's policies in Palestine, in particular the reiteration of the commitment to establishing a Jewish homeland.

2. Period of the League of Nations Mandate for Palestine: 1922–1948

This section contains forty-three documents covering the period of the League of Nations Mandate for Palestine, July 24, 1922, to May 15, 1948. These documents present the positions and recommendations of key political bodies at the time: Great Britain, the United States, Saudi Arabia, the League of Nations, the United Nations, the League of Arab States, and various Zionist organizations.

In 1919, following World War I and the break-up of the Turkish Ottoman Empire, the League of Nations established a system of mandates that allowed certain Western governments to administer former colonies and territories in Africa and Asia as "trusteeships."[108] This mandatory system was predicated on the theory that developed Europeans nations should assist less-developed African and Asian communities in governing their populations and in advancing toward national independence. The mandatory system was unprecedented in the history of international relations. It was a new form of colonialism that had the appearance of international legitimacy.

The League of Nations established mandates for three territories in the Middle East: Palestine, Lebanon, and Syria. On July 24, 1922, Britain was handed formal control over Palestine as a Class-A Mandate.[109] This designation meant that Palestine was deemed close to achieving independence and that all attempts should be made by the mandatory power to "encourage local autonomy" in the territory. The mandate also included a clear commitment to Zionist goals in Palestine as its preamble reproduced passages of the Balfour Declaration.[110]

The period of the mandate was fraught with conflicts between the indigenous Arab population and the increasing number of Jewish immigrants to Palestine, boosted by tragic events taking place on the world stage—first in Russia during the anti-Jewish Pogroms of 1821–1917 and then in Nazi-occupied Europe under the program of systematic, state-

---

[107] *See* Doc. 25.

[108] The League of Nations was formally dissolved on April 18, 1946, and its mission was transferred to the United Nations Trusteeship Council. Thus, international oversight of the mandatory system was maintained.

[109] *See* Doc. 24.

[110] *See* Doc. 24. In this document, Britain expresses its support for the establishment of a Jewish homeland in Palestine.

sponsored persecution and murder of Jews and "undesirables."[111] Persecution and political instability spurred Jews from numerous nations to immigrate to Palestine between 1939 and 1947. Some had entry visas, but most escaping the Holocaust did not.

Exacerbating tensions between local Arab and Jewish communities, the British Mandatory Power issued conflicting and inconsistent policy statements during this period. Policies regularly favored one side over the other depending on Britain's immediate political interests, routinely causing alarm and frustration among the newly disfavored group. Britain, thus, managed to alienate both sides of the conflict in Palestine.

Despite the backdrop of colonial occupation and unrest, Jews and Arabs in the region made progress toward their respective nationalist goals. The Jewish community in Palestine engaged in intense political development, forming the nucleus of an army (*haganah*) and establishing major social institutions such as the Hebrew University of Jerusalem (1925) and the Hadassah Hospital (1939). In 1944, the independent states of Egypt, Iraq, Saudi Arabia, Transjordan, Syria, and Lebanon joined together to form the League of Arab States, a regional multilateral organization for addressing Arab concerns.

Although Palestinian Arabs were the overwhelming majority in Palestine at the start of the mandate (representing 92 percent of inhabitants), their national goals were incoherent in comparison to those of the Zionists, their efforts to engage in political organization were consistently weak, and they were opposed by the British who had reservations about establishing an independent Arab state in Palestine. Dissatisfied with British policy and trying to stop further Jewish immigration, Palestinian Arabs in 1936 began a three-year struggle to effect governmental change. In response, Britain expelled the Palestinian leadership, leaving the primary Arab political role in Palestine to the Hashemites of Transjordan.

Divergent and competing interests in the region gradually engendered an unworkable political situation. British attempts to reign in the increasingly violent Arab and Jewish communities and stabilize Palestine had little or no lasting effect. In November 1947, thirty years after taking control of Palestine and after making little headway towards the creation of an independent state in Palestine as the Mandate for Palestine had required, Britain announced its decision to withdraw from Palestine and to leave the Question of Palestine to the United Nations Trusteeship Council.

Relevant documents in Section 6, Jerusalem and the Holy Sites, should be consulted.

Document 24: Mandate for Palestine Confirmed by the Council of the League of Nations (July 24, 1922) [*available at* http://domino.un.org/unispal.nsf/9a798adbf322aff38525617

[111] *See The "Final Solution": Nazi Extermination of European Jewry, in* Palestine and the Arab-Israeli Conflict: A History with Documents 213 (Charles D. Smith ed., 4th ed. 2001).

b006d88d7/2fca2c68106f11ab05256bcf007bf3cb! OpenDocument]. The League of Nations awarded Britain the Mandate for Palestine at the San Remo Conference in 1920; however, its terms of reference were not ratified until two years later. Drawing text directly from the 1917 Balfour Declaration,[112] the mandate determines that Britain is to be responsible for establishing a Jewish homeland in Palestine.

Document 25: Palestine Order in Council Issued by Great Britain (August 10, 1922) [THE LAWS OF PALESTINE 2569–89 (R.H. Drayton ed., 1934)]. The British government issued the Palestine Order in Council, which established a temporary government in Palestine under the Foreign Jurisdiction Act. It outlines the framework of a local government, constitutional development, and an election process.

Document 26: Memorandum by the British Representative on Article 25 of the Palestine Mandate (September 16, 1922) [1922, Cmd. 1785, at 11]. In this memorandum, the British government claims full responsibility as a mandatory power for Transjordan, the kingdom it created on the east bank of the Jordan River.

Document 27: Resolution of the U.S. Congress on Palestine (September 21, 1922) [Res. 73, 67th Cong., 42 Stat. 1012 (1922) (enacted)]. This congressional resolution, approved by the Senate and the House of Representatives, throws the political weight of the United States behind the establishment of a Jewish national home in Palestine. It also calls for respect for the civil and religious rights of Christians and "non-Jewish communities" in Palestine.

Document 28: Excerpts from the Report on Palestine Administration, Submitted by the United Kingdom to the League of Nations (December 31, 1922) [*available at* http://domino.un.org/unispal.nsf/9a798adbf322aff38525617b006d88d7/a682cabf739febaa052565e8006d907c!OpenDocument]. The United Kingdom presented this report to the League of Nations following its assumption of mandatory control of Palestine on July 24, 1922. The report details progress made in Palestine since the start of the mandate, including economic growth, agricultural recovery, railway improvements, increased tourism, and a program for opening new elementary schools. According to the report, 8,128 immigrants had entered the country in 1922, 7,844 of whom were Jews—and a consensus was taken in the month of October, showing a total population of 757,182, of whom 78 percent were Muslim, 11 percent Jewish, and 9.6 percent Christian.

Document 29: Mandate for Palestine Questionnaire Intended to Assist the Preparation of the Annual Reports of the Mandatory Powers (December 31, 1922) [*available at* http://domino.un.org/unispal.nsf/9a798adbf322aff38525617b006d88d7/73d84c3e3fce1f46052565f700573a64!OpenDocument]. The League of Nations drafted this questionnaire to assist Britain, as the mandatory power in Palestine, in preparing its annual reports on Palestine. It lays out the primary concerns and issues that should be reviewed and reported on each year.

Document 30: Excerpts from the Treaty of Lausanne (July 24, 1923) [Treaty of Lausanne, July 24, 1923, arts. 1, 16, 17, 19, 28 L.N.T.S 701, 13–113]. This treaty—signed by

[112] *See* Doc. 8.

the British Empire, France, Greece, Italy, Japan, Romania, the Serb-Croat-Slovene State, and Turkey in the ceremony hall of Lausanne University, Switzerland—was a revision of the Treaty of Sèvres.[113] It sets the boundaries of modern Turkey, drawing its borders with Iraq and Greece, following the Greco-Turkish War. It also sets Turkey's war capitulations and dictates how minority groups in the affected territories should be handled.

Document 31: Convention between the United States and Great Britain on Rights in Palestine (December 3, 1924) [U.S.-Gr. Brit., 44 Stat. 2184]. This convention, signed in London by U.S. Secretary of State Frank Kellog and British Foreign Secretary Austen Chamberlain, defines American rights with regard to Palestine. It provides that the United States will give its official approval to and recognition of the British mandate—this was necessary as the United States was a world power that was not a member of the League of Nations. In return, U.S. citizens would enjoy the privileges of the mandate. It also requires that the United States approve all proposed changes to the mandate. The convention was ratified by President Calvin Coolidge on December 5, 1925.

Document 32: Report by His Majesty's Government in the United Kingdom of Great Britain and Northern Ireland to the Council of the League of Nations on the Administration of Palestine and Transjordan for the Year 1929 (December 31, 1929) [*available at* http://domino.un.org/UNISPAL.NSF/181c4bf00c44e5fd85256cef0073c426/38bed104db074b49052565e70054eb22!OpenDocument]. Britain's 1929 Report to the League of Nations details the many disturbances that occurred between Arab and Jewish groups in Palestine. The so-called Wailing Wall Dispute is treated at length. The report includes a summary of the prosecution of cases arising out of the disturbances.

Document 33: Excerpts from the Statement of British Policy in Palestine (Passfield White Paper of 1930) (October 21, 1930) [1930, Cmd. 3692, at 12–23]. The Passfield White Paper, issued by the British government following two investigations of the Arab Riots of 1929 (*i.e.*, the Shaw Commission, led by Sir Walter Shaw, and the Hope-Simpson Expert Investigation of Land Capacity Issues), finds that riots occurred due to Arab disappointment of their political and national aspirations and fear for their economic future. It also finds that Arabs feared economic domination by a group that appeared to have unlimited funding from abroad. The commission further acknowledges the ambiguity of British statements to both Arabs and Jews: "a double undertaking is involved, to the Jewish people on the one hand and to the non-Jewish population of Palestine on the other." The White Paper sets limits to Jewish immigration.

Document 34: Letter from British Prime Minister James Ramsey MacDonald to Dr. Chaim Weizmann (February 13, 1931) [58 PARL. DEB., H.C. (5th ser.) (1931) 751–57]. After the Zionists mounted a well-organized campaign against the Passfield White Paper, British Prime Minister Ramsay MacDonald wrote Chaim Weizmann this letter effectively reversing its position.[114] Zionists regarded the letter as a restoration

---

[113] *See* Doc. 17.

[114] *See* Doc. 33.

of the *status quo*. Arabs, who had greeted the immigration limitations set by the Passfield White Paper with satisfaction, were disappointed.

Document 35: Conclusions and Recommendations of the Report of the Palestine Royal Commission (Peel Commission Report) (July 1937) [1937, Cmd. 5479, *reprinted in* 3 The Arab Israeli Conflict 150–183 (John Morton Moore ed., 1974)]. The Peel Commission—named for commission chairman the Honorable Earl Peel—was established by the British government to investigate the causes of the 1936 riots. Its report recommends both the termination of the British mandate in its present form and the partition of Palestine into two parts: a Jewish state and an Arab territory that would become a Palestinian state. It also proposed the massive transfer of Arabs from the territory of the Jewish state in order to make sense of the partition of Palestine into an Arab and a Jewish state. The commission also called for the creation, under Britain's control, of a special zone that would include Jerusalem, Bethlehem, Nazareth, the Sea of Galilee, and a corridor from Jerusalem to the Mediterranean. Upon its publication, the British government declared support for the report's conclusions and promised to take the necessary steps for its implementation. Arab Palestinians rejected the proposal.

Document 36: Political Resolution of the Twentieth Zionist Congress Concerning the Report of the Palestine Royal Commission (August 3, 1937) [The New Judea, August–September 1937, at 227]. The Twentieth Zionist Congress, held in Zurich, Switzerland, was called to discuss the political implications of the Peel Commission Report and its proposed partition of Palestine, with the creation of a British-controlled corridor from the coast to Jerusalem.[115] The resolution rejects the plan's proposed boundaries, but agrees in principle to partition.

Document 37: Resolution of the Assembly of the League of Nations Concerning Palestine (September 30, 1937) [League of Nations O.J. Spec. Supp.168, at 28 (1937)]. This League of Nations resolution expresses the Assembly's confidence in Britain's administration of the Mandate for Palestine and its conviction that the problem of Palestine will be equitably settled in the best interest of all involved parties.

Document 38: Statement by His Majesty's Government in the United Kingdom (November 1938) [*available at* http://domino.un.org/unispal.nsf/0/4941922311b4 e3c58525 6d17004bd2e2?OpenDocument]. Anticipating the Palestine Partition Commission Report (Woodhead Report), this statement considers the possible technical difficulties in the implementation of a partition plan and concludes that partition is not practicable. It proposes three alternatives, all of which leave Jerusalem under British mandatory control.

Document 39: Statement of British Policy in Palestine (MacDonald White Paper) (May 17, 1939) [1939, Cmd. 6019, *available at* http://domino.un.org/UNISPAL.NSF/ bc8b0c56b7bf621185256cbf005ac05f/eb5b88c94aba2ae585256d0b00555536!O penDocument]. The MacDonald White Paper of 1939 marks a significant shift in Britain's position on the creation of an independent Jewish state in Palestine. It proposes that Palestine become an independent, binational Arab-Jewish state, with Arabs dominating the national government. It limits Jewish immigration to

[115] *See* Doc. 35.

75,000 over five years, with further immigration subject to Arab "acquiescence." The decisions set forth in this paper were largely determined by British interests in World War II, as Britain needed the support of oil-rich Arab nations to win the war against Germany. Britain risked alienating the Jewish world community because it knew that Jews would not support Hitler over the Allies.

Document 40: Statement of the Jewish Agency Concerning the Statement of British Policy in Palestine (May 17, 1939) [THE NEW JUDAEA, May–June 1939, at 173–74]. The Jewish Agency issued this statement in reaction to the MacDonald White Paper, expressing anger and frustration with Britain's new position against Jewish immigration and the creation of an independent Jewish national homeland in Palestine.[116] The Jewish Agency regarded the White Paper as a "breach of faith."

Document 41: Excerpts from the Report of the League of Nations Permanent Mandates Commission to the League of Nations Council Concerning the Statement of British Policy in Palestine (June 29, 1939) [*reprinted in* 3 THE ARAB ISRAELI CONFLICT 225–29 (John Morton Moore ed., 1974)]. In this report, the League of Nations Permanent Mandates Commission asserts that the policy set out in the MacDonald White Paper[117] is not in accordance with the commission's interpretation of the League of Nations Mandate for Palestine.[118] It also notes that Britain's continuing policy shifts are undermining the effective functioning of the mandate. The commission concludes that the only relevant consideration is the establishment of two independent states in Palestine.

Document 42: Record of the Conversation between the Fürher and the Grand Mufti of Jerusalem on November 28, 1941, a Memorandum by an Official of the Foreign Minister's Secretariat (November 30, 1941) [*published in* 13 DOCUMENTS ON GERMAN FOREIGN POLICY 1918–1945: THE WAR YEARS, SERIES D 881 (United Nations Government Printing Office, 1964)]. In this record of the meeting in Germany between the Fürher and the Grand Mufti of Jerusalem during World War II, the Mufti thanks the Fürher for his support of Arab independence and the Palestinian cause. The Mufti expresses his belief that Germany would win the war and that the Arab cause would consequently benefit.

Document 43: Biltmore Declaration of the Extraordinary Zionist Conference (May 11, 1942) [JEWISH AGENCY FOR PALESTINE, BOOK OF DOCUMENTS SUBMITTED TO THE GENERAL ASSEMBLY OF THE UNITED NATIONS RELATING TO THE ESTABLISHMENT OF THE NATIONAL HOME FOR THE JEWISH PEOPLE 226–27 (1942)]. In this Declaration of the Extraordinary Zionist Conference, American Jewish organizations throw their weight behind the creation of an independent Jewish state in Palestine, given the severe persecution of Jews in Nazi occupied Europe. The declaration was signed in the Biltmore Hotel in New York by 800 delegations. The conference was dubbed "Extraordinary" because it substituted for the recurrent World Zionist Conference, which could not be held in Europe due to the state of war.

Document 44: Alexandria Protocol of the Pan-Arab Preliminary Conference (October 7, 1944) [16 DEP'T ST. BULL. 411 (1947), *available at* http://www.yale.edu/lawweb/avalon/

---

[116] *See* Doc. 39.

[117] *Id.*

[118] *See* Doc. 24.

mideast/alex.htm]. In the Alexandria Protocol, leaders from Syria, Transjordan, Iraq, Lebanon, and Egypt form a unified stance against the intervention of foreign powers in the Middle East. In particular, they express concern about Palestine becoming a Jewish homeland. This document became the basis for the formation of the League of Arab States.[119]

Document 45: Charter of the League of Arab States (March 22, 1945) [*available at* http://www.yale.edu/lawweb/ avalon/mideast/arableag.htm]. This charter creates the League of Arab States, a voluntary association of independent countries whose peoples are generally Arabic speaking. The league's stated purpose is to strengthen ties among member states, coordinate their policies, and promote their common interests. It was signed in Cairo by Egypt, Iraq, Lebanon, Saudi Arabia, Syria, Transjordan, and Yemen.

Document 46: Letter from U.S. President Franklin D. Roosevelt to King ibn Saud of Saudi Arabia (April 5, 1945) [A DECADE OF AMERICAN FOREIGN POLICY: BASIC DOCUMENTS (1941–1949) 623 (U.S. Government Printing Office, 1950)]. In this letter, U.S. President Franklin D. Roosevelt promises King ibn Saud that the United States will take no hostile action against the Arabs and that it will not change its basic policy toward Palestine without prior consultations with Arabs and Jews. This plan, made a week before Roosevelt's death, was reversed by Harry S. Truman, Roosevelt's successor.

Document 47: Excerpts from the Report of the Anglo-American Committee of Inquiry (April 20, 1946) [*available at* http://www.yale.edu/lawweb/avalon/anglo/angpre.htm]. The Report of the Anglo-American Commission of Inquiry is a review of the policies governing Jewish immigration to Palestine. Requested by U.S. President Harry S. Truman, the commission was created to examine the political, economic, and social conditions in Palestine as they affected Jewish immigration and the well-being of indigenous groups in Palestine. The report recommends the continuation of the mandate, the preservation of a unitary state in Palestine, the repeal of restrictions on land sales, and the immediate admission of 100,000 Jews into Palestine. The report also recommends that Zionist underground forces be disarmed. Members of the commission included Joseph C. Hutcheson, the American Chairman, Frank Aydelotte, Frank W. Buxton, Bartley C. Crum, James G. Mcdonald, and William Phillips.

Document 48: Statement of the Jewish Agency Concerning the Report of the Anglo-American Committee (May 1, 1946) [THE NEW JUDAEA, May 1946, at 149–50]. This statement by the Jewish Agency begins with a thankful acknowledgment of the Anglo-American Commission of Inquiry's recommendation that 100,000 Jews be immediately allowed entrance into Palestine.[120] It charges, however, that the commission's report does not adequately address the "homeless and stateless" condition of the Jewish people, given that, in its opinion, the establishment of a Jewish state is the only way to improve the condition of the Jewish people. It further contends that when Britain established Transjordan as an exclusively Arab state, it "precluded itself from denying to the other section the right to become a Jewish state."

Document 49: The Grady-Morrison Plan (July 24, 1946) [*reprinted in* A DOCUMENTARY HISTORY OF THE ARAB-ISRAELI CONFLICT (Charles L. Geddes ed., 1991)]. Through

[119] *See* Doc. 45.
[120] *See* Doc. 47.

examining recommendations by the Anglo-American Committee of Enquiry, the Grady-Morrison Plan offered solutions to the problems in Palestine and to issues surrounding Jewish immigration. The Grady-Morrison Plan begins with recognizing the resettlement in Europe and the emigration to countries outside of Europe as the two aspects of the problem of displaced persons and the position of European Jews. Because resettlement in Europe is deemed inevitable, one of the plan's objectives is to create conditions for resettling a substantial number of displaced persons, including many, but not limited to Jews.

The plan also states that although Jews can resettle in Europe, new homes must be found elsewhere, and Palestine cannot accommodate the number. Therefore, the plan encourages the British and U.S. governments to support the establishment of an international refugee organization to deal with problems of refugees and displaced persons. It further calls for the next General Assembly to ask all U.N. member states to take territories under their control for displaced persons. The plan states that even with Jewish immigration into Palestine the country cannot be a Jewish or Arab state and neither group should dominate the other. In securing self-government for the inhabitants it is important to maintain a form of government that protects the interests of Christianity, Judaism, and Islam in the Holy Land.

To achieve this, a plan for provincial autonomy was developed which divided Palestine into four administrative areas with local legislature: an Arab province, a Jewish province, a district of Jerusalem, and a district of the Negev. The provincial autonomy allows the Jewish province to regulate and control immigration into their designated area of Palestine and extinguishes, for the majority of Arabs, the fear of further Jewish immigration into the Arab province. This unitary binational plan attempts to segregate the two groups enough to reduce violence. Additionally, the Grady-Morrison Plan recommends methods for improving the economic and educational standards of Arabs. The plan recognizes that the proposed boundaries given to the Jewish area are superior in land and economic resources, but it explains the role of the central government to make grants to the provinces and whose general powers and aid will help overcome this disparity. This central government, with most of the powers over immigration, can allow any amount of Jewish immigrants into the country, implicitly recalling the 1939 White Paper.

Document 50: British Letter to the United Nations (April 2, 1947) [*reprinted in* A Documentary History of the Arab-Israeli Conflict (Charles L. Geddes ed., 1991)]. A letter was written to Dr. Victor Chi Tsai Hoo, the assistant secretary-general of the United Nations from Alexander Cadogan, the British ambassador to the United Nations. In it Sir Alexander Cadogan requested the United Kingdom government to add the issue of Palestine on the agenda for the following annual session of the General Assembly. In addition, a request was made that the secretary-general call for a special session of the General Assembly to create a specific committee that can prepare the issues and possible solutions for the Palestine Question before the discussion of the issue at the annual session.

Document 51: Statement by U.S. President Harry S. Truman Concerning Immigration into Palestine (October 4, 1946) [*available at* http://www.yale.edu/lawweb/avalon/decade/decad163.htm]. In this statement, U.S. President Harry S. Truman expresses his deep concern for the welfare of Jewish communities displaced by the war. Truman calls on Britain to approve the immediate immigration of 100,000 Jews into Palestine. He further argues that the immigration laws of other countries, including the United States, should be liberalized with a view to the admission of displaced persons.

Document 52: Cultural Treaty of the Arab League (November 20, 1946) [*available at* http://faculty.winthrop.edu/haynese/mlas/CulTreaty.html]. The Arab League's Cultural Treaty establishes a system of formal exchange and cultural cooperation between Arab states in order to create a close network of intellectually linked communities. The treaty calls on member states to take all necessary measures to approximate their legislative trends and to unify as far as possible their laws. The treaty lent itself to establishing a sphere of Arab influence and cultural homogeneity.

Document 53: United Nations General Assembly Resolution 106, Establishing the United Nations Special Committee on Palestine (UNSCOP) (May 15, 1947) [G.A. Res. 106, U.N. GAOR, U.N. Doc. A/RES/106 (S-1) (1947)]. United Nations General Assembly Resolution 106 establishes the UNSCOP, to be composed of delegates from Australia, Canada, Czechoslovakia, Guatemala, India, Iran, Netherlands, Peru, Sweden, Uruguay, and Yugoslavia. The General Assembly requests that the special committee prepare a report on the question of Palestine with proposals for a solution to the problem. It also decides that hearings should be granted to the Jewish Agency for Palestine and to the Arab Higher Committee.

Document 54: United Nations General Assembly Resolution 107, Calling on the Inhabitants of Palestine to Refrain from the Threat or Use of Force (May 15, 1947) [G.A. Res. 107, U.N. GAOR, U.N. Doc. A/RES/107 (S-1) (1947)]. In Resolution 107, the General Assembly calls on all governments and peoples, particularly the inhabitants of Palestine, to refrain from the threat or use of force or any other action that might create an atmosphere prejudicial to an early settlement of the question of Palestine.

Document 55: United Nations Special Committee on Palestine: Summary Report (August 31, 1947) [1947–48 U.N.Y.B., U.N. Sales No. 1949.I.13]. In its 1947 summary report, UNSCOP recommends the termination of the Mandate for Palestine. The majority proposal is for a "Plan of Partition with Economic Union." The minority proposal advocates the creation of an independent federal state.

Document 56: Memorandum by His Britannic Majesty's Government Presented in 1947 to the United Nations Special Committee on Palestine: Political History of Palestine under British Administration (July 1947) [G.A. Res. 107, U.N. GAOR, U.N. Doc. A/AC.14/8 (1947)]. This memorandum by the British government provides a thorough history of Palestine under British administration. It treats in depth: the attitude of Arabs and Jews, the attempt to create self-governing institutions (1922–23), the development of the country from 1922–29, and the disturbances that began in 1929.

Document 57: Excerpts from the Report of the United Nations Special Committee on Palestine (September 3, 1947) [U.N. GAOR, 2d Sess., Supp. No. 11, U.N. Doc. A/364 (1947)]. In this report, the Special Committee on Palestine resolves to terminate the Mandate for Palestine, but fails to reach a workable future settlement for Palestine. The majority recommends the partition of the territory into two states, with special international status for Jerusalem. The minority (India, Iran, and Yugoslavia) proposes the creation of a federal state with Jerusalem as the capital of the federation.

Document 58: U.S. Position on Palestine Question, Statement by U.S. Deputy Representative to the United Nations Herschel V. Johnson (October 11, 1947) [*available at* http://www.yale.edu/lawweb/avalon/decade/decad164.htm#1]. In this statement, the U.S. delegation to the United Nations supports the Plan for Partition in Palestine. It argues that certain amendments and geographical modifications will be required, however, to achieve the principles on which the plan is based (such as including Jaffa in the Arab state because of its predominantly Arab population). The United States pledges to assist both parties in implementing a revised partition plan.

Document 59: United Nations General Assembly Resolution 181, Recommending a Plan of Partition with Economic Union for Palestine (United Nations Partition Resolution) (November 29, 1947) [G.A. Res. 181 (II), U.N. GAOR, 128th plen. mtg., at 131–132, U.N. Doc. A/519 (1948)]. United Nations General Assembly Resolution 181 calls for the partition of Palestine into two independent states—one Arab and one Jewish—which would remain economically unified. Under this plan, Jerusalem and its environs are to be internationalized to form a *corpus separatum.* The plan also includes steps to be taken prior to independence and offers solutions for issues of citizenship, transit, economic union between the two states, access to Holy Places, and religious and minority rights. The United States played a decisive political role in marshalling the General Assembly's votes in favor of the partition, which passed with a vote of thirty-three in favor and thirteen against. Arabs were outraged by the plan because while they constituted a clear majority, they were granted only 45 percent of the land. Britain refused to forcefully implement the Partition Plan because it was not accepted by the Palestinians. Ironically, a two-state solution has now become the prevailing Palestinian national goal.

Document 60: United Nations Security Council Resolution 42, Appealing to Governments and Peoples to Prevent or Reduce Disorders in Palestine (March 5, 1948) [S.C. Res. 42, 3 U.N. SCOR, Nos. 36–51, at 43, U.N. Doc. S/691 (1948)]. As violence mounted between Arab and Jewish groups, the Security Council passed Resolution 42, appealing to governments and peoples in and around Palestine to take all possible measures to prevent or reduce disorders from occurring.

Document 61: Excerpts from the Statement by the U.S. Ambassador to the United Nations, Warren R. Austin, Recommending Placing Palestine under United Nations Trusteeship (March 19, 1948) [*available at* http://www.yale.edu/lawweb/avalon/decade/decad166.htm]. The United States was the first to endorse partition as expressed in Resolution 181. But, the war that was started by the Palestinian Arabs immediately after the General Assembly's vote, a war that developed into a bloody civil war between Arabs and Jews, put in jeopardy the two-state idea as manifested in Resolution 181. The Jewish side was seen at that stage as losing the war. It was at that crossroads that America seemed to change its position and withdrew its support for partition. The Zionists reacted in two ways. In the war front they moved to an offensive strategy to show to the Americans that partition can work because the Zionists were perfectly capable of securing the boundaries of the state they were offered by the international community. And in the diplomatic front, they lobbied President Truman until he thwarted the initiative of the State Department that, concerned with the violent opposition of the Arab world to partition, promoted the idea of placing Palestine under temporary international trusteeship. It was President Truman that made the difference, and reiterated America's support for the two-state idea. It asserts that a short-term solution would provide Arabs and Jews in Palestine with an opportunity to seek a long-term settlement. The United States also recommends that the Security Council suspend the Palestine Commission's efforts to implement the Partition Plan.[121]

Document 62: Statement by U.S. President Harry S. Truman, Concerning Palestine (March 25, 1948) [18 DEP'T ST. BULL. 451, 457 (1948)]. In this statement, U.S. President Harry Truman concedes that the partition plan is no longer a viable option.[122] He instead recommends establishing Palestine as a trusteeship, "not as a substitute for the partition plan but as an effort to fill the vacuum soon to be created by the termination of the mandate on May 15." Without this temporary measure, Truman predicts, "open warfare is just over the horizon."

Document 63: United Nations Security Council Resolution 43, Calling for a Truce between the Arab and Jewish Communities of Palestine (April 1, 1948) [S.C. Res. 43, U.N. SCOR, 3d Sess., Supp. No. 52, at 33–35, U.N. Doc. S/714 (1948)]. United Nations Security Council Resolution 43 calls for an immediate truce in Palestine and requests that the Jewish Agency for Palestine and the Arab Higher Committee send representatives to the Security Council to arrange it.

Document 64: United Nations Security Council Resolution 44, Requesting the Secretary-General to Convoke a Special Session of the General Assembly to Consider the Future Government of Palestine (April 1, 1948) [S.C. Res. 44, U.N. SCOR, 277th mtg., U.N. Doc. S/714 II (1948)]. United Nations Security Council Resolution 44 requests the secretary-general to convoke a special session of the General Assembly to consider the question of the future government of Palestine further.

Document 65: United Nations Security Council Resolution 46, Calling on Groups to End Military Activities and Build-Up (April 17, 1948) [S.C. Res. 46, U.N. SCOR, 3d Sess., Supp. No. 52, 283d mtg., at 7–8, U.N. Doc. S/723 (1948)]. United Nations Security Council Resolution 46 calls upon persons and organizations in Palestine to immediately cease all military activities, as well as acts of violence, terrorism, and sabotage. It demands that all groups refrain from any actions that might endanger the safety of the Holy Places in Palestine. The British government, as the mandatory power, is asked to supervise the execution of these measures and to keep the Security Council and the General Assembly informed on the situation.

Document 66: United Nations Security Council Resolution 48, Establishing a Truce Commission for Palestine (April 23, 1948) [S.C. Res. 48, U.N. SCOR, 287th mtg., U.N. Doc. S/727 (1948)]. In Resolution 48, the Security Council appoints a Truce Commission for Palestine following reports from the UNSCOP that it is unable to effect partition due to violence, the lack of cooperation from the mandatory power, and the disintegrating security situation. The Security Council requests that the Truce Commission assist in supervising the implementation of United Nations

---

[121] *See* Doc. 59.

[122] *Id.*

Security Council Resolution 46.[123] The Commission is composed of the Consuls of Belgium, France, and the United States in Jerusalem.

3. Arab-Israeli Wars: 1948–2007

Disputes over how to resolve the crisis of who would control Palestine after the withdrawal of the British Mandatory Power led in 1948 to the first of five major wars between the State of Israel and the forces of Arab states in the region and the Palestinians. Although armistice agreements were signed in 1949, legally the state of war persisted until the Arab-Israeli peace process produced treaties in 1979 and 1994. In the interim, four Arab-Israeli wars took place: the Suez War (1956), the June or Six-Day War (1967), the October, Ramadan, or Yom Kippur War (1973), and the War in Lebanon (1982).

To enable the reader to better follow the history of these conflicts, documents contained in this section are organized into five sections: (A) Palestine War or the War for Israeli Independence, containing related documents from 1948 to 1955; (B) Suez War, containing related documents from 1950 to 1964; (C) June War or Six-Day War, containing related documents from 1966 to 1972; (D) Yom Kippur War/Ramadan War/October War, containing related documents from 1973 to 1981; and (E) Lebanon War, containing related documents from 1978 to 2003.

A. Palestine War or the War for Israeli Independence: 1948

The first Arab-Israeli War began in November 1947 as a civil war between the Jewish and Arab community in Palestine that ended up drawing the Arab states to an invasion with the expiration of the Mandate for Palestine at midnight on May 14, 1948. The invasion precipitated the permanent departure of British administrative officers and military forces from the Port of Haifa in Palestine. With no plans in place for a post-mandate government, due in part to Britain's unwillingness to enforce the United Nations Partition Plan[124] without popular support, the withdrawal abandoned the country to a state of virtual anarchy. Almost immediately, the competing armies of Arabs and Zionists moved to make land gains and fill the power vacuum.

On May 14, David Ben-Gurion, as head of the provisional government, announced the establishment of the State of Israel in the Municipal Museum of Tel Aviv beginning on May 14, 1948, at 12:00 midnight Palestine time before the twenty-four-member Provisional Council (later to become the Knesset).[125] U.S. President Harry S. Truman gave *de facto*

---

[123] *See* Doc. 65.

[124] *See* Doc. 59.

[125] *See* Doc. 67. *See also* Timeline of the Jewish Agency for Israel, *available at* http://www.jafi.org.il/education/jafi75/timeline3i.html.

recognition of the state eleven minutes later.[126] The Soviet Union quickly followed suit. Egypt, Iraq, Lebanon, Syria, and Transjordan responded by sending their armies into Palestine.[127]

Israeli forces, despite their limited numbers and lack of military equipment, gained an early and decisive advantage in the war. Arab military forces were, in contrast, disorganized and largely ineffective. Israeli forces were able to reopen the road to Jerusalem, gain control of the Coastal Plain, secure the Upper Galilee, and make headway into the Negev. By the end of the war, Israel had secured 23 percent more land than was allotted to it under the 1947 Partition Plan.[128] The remainder of the Palestinian territory was occupied by Egypt and Jordan, with Egypt gaining the Gaza Strip and Transjordan acquiring the West Bank and East Jerusalem.[129] No independent Arab Palestinian state could be established in the area as envisioned by the Partition Plan. The major losers in this war were the Arab Palestinians, 700,000 of whom fled from the area out of fear, under increasing military pressure, and/or at the urging of their leaders and Arab governments.

Documents relevant to this period may also be found in: Section 5, Arms Control and Regional Security; Section 6, Jerusalem and the Holy Sites; and Section 8, Status of the Palestinians.

i. 1948 War

Document 67: Declaration of the Establishment of the State of Israel (May 14, 1948) [*available at* http://www.mfa.gov.il/MFA/Peace+Process/Guide+to+the +Peace+Process/Declaration+of+Establishment+of+State+of+Israel.htm]. David Ben-Gurion proclaimed the establishment of the State of Israel in Tel Aviv before members of the Provisional Council and others. The declaration, written in Hebrew, was signed by members of the Provisional Council, including such notables as Golda Meyerson (later known as Golda Meir). It went into effect at midnight (Tel Aviv time), when the Mandate for Palestine officially expired.

Document 68: Memo by President Harry S. Truman Recognizing the State of Israel on Behalf of the United States (May 14, 1948) [*available at* http://www.trumanlibrary.org/whistlestop/study_collections/israel/large/documents/index.php?documentdate=1948-05-14&documentid=48&collectionid=ROI&pagenumber=1]. In this memo from President Harry S. Truman, the U.S. government officially recognizes the State of Israel.

Document 69: United Nations General Assembly Resolution 186, Appointing a United Nations Mediator in Palestine (May 14, 1948) [G.A. Res. 186, U.N. GAOR, 2d Special Sess., Supp. No. 2, at 5–6, U.N. Doc. A/555 (1948)]. United Nations General

---

[126] *See* Doc. 68.

[127] *See* Doc. 70.

[128] *See supra* note 1.

[129] Subsequent to acquiring these additional lands, the Hashemite Kingdom of Transjordan changed its name to the Hashemite Kingdom of Jordan.

Assembly Resolution 186 affirms the General Assembly's support for the efforts of the Security Council to secure a truce in Palestine. The resolution relieves the Palestine Commission from further exercise of responsibilities under United Nations General Assembly Resolution 181 and appoints a United Nations mediator in Palestine, Count Folke Bernadotte, and describes his functions.[130] Bernadotte was assassinated by members of Leh'i or LYI, a Jewish militant group, in Jerusalem on September 17, 1948.

Document 70: Cablegram to the United Nations from the Secretary-General of the League of Arab States (May 15, 1948) [3 U.N. SCOR, Supp. May, at 83–88, U.N. Doc. S/745 (1948)]. Upon Israel's Declaration of Independence, the member states of the Arab League issued this statement declaring war on the State of Israel. The statement makes clear that the intent of the invasion is to destroy Israel and not just to defend the portions of Palestine allotted to the Palestinians under the United Nations Partition Plan.[131]

Document 71: National Radio Broadcast by Israeli Prime Minister David Ben-Gurion (May 15, 1948) [*available at* http://www.mfa.gov.il/ mfa/foreign+relations/ israels+foreign+relations+since+1947/1947-1974/6+broadcast+to+the+nation+by +prime+minister+ben-gu.htm]. In this radio address delivered the day after the establishment of the State of Israel, Prime Minister David Ben-Gurion calls on Israelis to devote their full strength to building and defending the nation in spite of the impending political and military struggles. Ben-Gurion notes the recognition of Israel by the United States and expresses the hope that other nations will soon follow suit. The address warns of the imminent attack by Arab states against Israel and urgently calls on Israelis to help create a military striking force.

Document 72: Cablegram Addressed to the Secretary-General by Foreign Minister of the Provisional Government of Israel (May 16, 1948) [S/747 of May 16, 1948]. In this cablegram from the foreign minister of the Provisional Government of Israel, Moshe Shertok, to the United Nations secretary-general, Israel proclaims its independence by virtue of the "natural and historic right" of the Jewish people and of General Assembly Resolution 181 (Partition Plan).[132] It conveys the State of Israel's willingness to formally sign and accept the Partition Plan and also requests admission to the United Nations.

Document 73: United Nations Security Council Resolution 49, Calling for a Cease-Fire in Palestine and a Truce in Jerusalem (May 22, 1948) [S.C. Res. 49, U.N. SCOR, Supp. May, at 97, U.N. Doc. S/773 (1948)]. In Resolution 49, the Security Council calls on concerned parties to implement a cease-fire and to give the highest priority to maintenance of the truce in Jerusalem.

Document 74: United Nations Security Council Resolution 50, Calling for a Cease-Fire (May 29, 1948) [S.C. Res. 50, U.N. SCOR, 3d Sess., Supp. May, at 103–04, U.N. Doc. S/801 (1948)]. In Resolution 50, the Security Council calls for a cessation of all military activities for four weeks, urges concerned governments and authorities to take precautions for the protection of the Holy Places and the city of Jerusalem,

---

[130] *See supra* note 1.

[131] *Id.*

[132] *See* Doc. 59.

instructs the United Nations mediator to supervise the observance of these provisions in concert with the Truce Commission, and decides that these groups should be provided with a sufficient number of military observers. Further, the Security Council decides that if either party rejects the resolution, the situation in Palestine will be considered with a view to action under Chapter VII of the United Nations Charter.[133] The observers mentioned in this resolution formed the basis of what later became the United Nations Truce Supervision Organization (UNTSO) in Palestine.

Document 75: United Nations Security Council Resolution 53, Appealing for a Prolongation of the Truce (July 7, 1948) [S.C. Res. 53, U.N. SCOR, 331st mtg., U.N. Doc. S/875 (1948)]. United Nations Security Council Resolution 53 is an appeal to concerned parties to accept in principle a prolongation of the truce as the existing truce, based on Security Council Resolution 50,[134] was due to expire in two days (on July 9, 1948).

Document 76: United Nations Security Council Resolution 56, Outlining Rules of the Truce (August 19, 1948) [S.C. Res. 56, U.N. SCOR, Supp. No. 107, 354th mtg., at 50–1, U.N. Doc. S/983 (1948)]. In Resolution 56, the Security Council outlines conditions for a truce between the concerned parties: each party will be responsible for the actions of both regular and irregular forces under its authority or in territory under its control; each party will have legal obligations with regard to arresting and prosecuting violators of the truce; the truce cannot be met with reprisals that further violate the truce; and no party may gain military or political advantage through a violation of the truce.

Document 77: Progress Report of the United Nations Mediator in Palestine (September 16, 1948) [U.N. GAOR, 3d Sess., Supp. No. 11, at 17–19, U.N. Doc. A/648 (1948)]. The United Nations mediator in Palestine, Count Folke Bernadotte, submitted this report detailing the many obstacles to negotiating for peace with Arab and Jewish authorities. Bernadotte outlines his "Seven Basic Premises," which are policy recommendations on the most divisive issues, including the Jewish state, boundary determinations, the right to repatriation, Jerusalem, and the international responsibility. Under Bernadotte's plan, Israel is to retain Galilee but surrender much of the Negev and Lydda and Ramle, Jerusalem is to be an international city, and Palestinian refugees are to have the right to return. The day after submitting this plan to the United Nations, Bernadotte was assassinated in Jerusalem.

Document 78: United Nations Security Council Resolution 57, Expressing Deep Shock at the Assassination of United Nations Mediator in Palestine Count Folke Bernadotte (September 18, 1948) [S.C. Res. 57, U.N. SCOR, 358th mtg., U.N. Doc. S/RES/57 (1948)]. In Resolution 57, the Security Council expresses deep shock at the assassination of Count Folke Bernadotte, the United Nations mediator for Palestine, by what was apparently a "criminal group of terrorists." The succeeding United Nations mediator, Ralph Bunche, in his September 28 report regarding the assassination, writes that the murders are believed to be members of the Lochamei Heruth Israel (LHY or Stern Group), a Jewish extremist group.[135]

---

[133] U.N. CHARTER Ch. VII, *available at* http://www.un.org/aboutun/charter/.

[134] Doc. 74.

[135] *See* U.N. SCOR, U.N. Doc. S/1018 (1948), *available at* http://domino.un.org/UNISPAL.NSF/0/45fc0c6e511ec0c5802564d400560ca0?OpenDocument.

Document 79: Law of the State of Israel: Area of Jurisdiction and Powers Ordinance (September 22, 1948) [1 LSI 64 (1948)]. This Israeli ordinance extends the application of Israeli law beyond the State of Israel to any part of Palestine that the Minister of Defense proclaims as being held by the Israeli Defense Army.

Document 80: Law of the State of Israel: Prevention of Terrorism Ordinance No. 33 (September 23, 1948) [1 LSI 76 (1948)]. Israel's Prevention of Terrorism Ordinance provides a legal definition of terrorism, terrorist organizations, and actions that support terrorism. The ordinance was aimed at stopping paramilitary organizations that were operating independently of the Israeli Army.

Document 81: Cablegram from the Premier and Acting Foreign Secretary of the All-Palestine Government to the Secretary-General Concerning the Constitution of the All-Palestine Government (September 28, 1948) [U.N. GAOR 1st Comm., 3d Sess., U.N. Doc. A/C.1/330 (1948)]. In this cablegram to the United Nations secretary-general, the premier of the All-Palestine government informs the United Nations that the Arabs of Palestine had declared an independent state. The cablegram identifies the borders of the state to be those that were established before the termination of the League of Nations Mandate.

Document 82: United Nations Press Release: Arabs, Jews Reject Mediator's Report on Palestine (October 7, 1948) [U.N. Press Release, U.N. Dep't of Public Info., U.N. Doc. PAL/328 (1948)]. In this press release, the United Nations notes the rejection by the six Arab states and Israel of Count Bernadotte's report on Palestine, with the Arab parties advocating a single sovereign state for Palestine and Israel condemning the proposal to give the Negev to the Arabs.

Document 83: United Nations Security Council Resolution 59, Noting with Concern that Israel Has Not Submitted a Report Concerning the Assassination of Count Folke Bernadotte (October 19, 1948) [S.C. Res. 59, U.N. SCOR, 367th mtg., U.N. Doc. S/1045 (1948)]. In light of the assassination of Count Folke Bernadotte a month prior, the Security Council in this resolution notes its concern that the State of Israel has not submitted a report on the progress of its investigation. The Security Council calls on governments to facilitate the freedom of movement and safety of the UNTSO personnel.

Document 84: Amended Version of Paragraph 18 of the Report of the Acting United Nations Mediator in Palestine (October 19, 1948) [U.N. SCOR, U.N. Doc. S/PV.367, S/INF/2/Rev. 1 (III) (1948)]. This report by the Acting United Nations mediator, Ralph Bunche, details problems in the Negev, including the failure to honor the demarcation lines, convoys to the Jewish settlements, and the large number of displaced Arabs and their inability to harvest their crops. The report recommends an immediate cease-fire to resolve the situation. Pursuant to the Security Council's adoption of the mediator's report, both sides accepted a cease-fire to be effective on October 22, 1948.

Document 85: Preliminary Report from the Acting United Nations Mediator in Palestine to the Secretary-General on Observance of the Truce in the Negeb and in the Lebanese Sector (October 25, 1948) [U.N. SCOR, U.N. Doc. S/1055 (1948)]. This preliminary report documents continued Israeli attacks in the Negev after the October 22 cease-fire date and the continued fighting in the Lebanese Sector following the Israeli rejection of the cease-fire.

Document 86: United Nations Security Council Resolution 61, Calling upon Interested Parties to Establish Permanent Truce Lines (November 4, 1948) [S.C. Res. 61, U.N. SCOR, 377th mtg., U.N. Doc. S/1070 (1948)]. In Resolution 61, the Security Council calls for the negotiation of a permanent truce until a peaceful adjustment of the future situation of Palestine is reached. It also authorizes the acting mediator to establish provisional lines beyond which troops are not to move.

Document 87: Law of the State of Israel: Emergency Regulations (Registration of Inhabitants) (Extension of Validity) Ordinance (November 5, 1948) [2 LSI 8–12 (1948–49)]. This enactment by Israel's Provisional Council mandates the registration of any person who resides in an area subject to Israeli law. Registration includes the reporting of biographical information and times of departure and return to those areas subject to the ordinance. Failure to register is punishable by imprisonment, fine, or both.

Document 88: United Nations Security Council Resolution 62, Deciding that an Armistice Shall Be Established in All Sectors of Palestine (November 16, 1948) [S.C. Res. 62, U.N. SCOR, 381st mtg., U.N. Doc. S/1080 (1948)]. In Resolution 62, the Security Council establishes an armistice in all of Palestine to facilitate the transition to a permanent peace. It calls on concerned parties to begin negotiations for the establishment of the armistice, including the establishment of demarcations lines and the withdrawal of forces.

Document 89: Law of the State of Israel: Emergency Regulations (Leaving the Country) Ordinance (November 19, 1948) [2 LSI 16 (1948–49)]. With this ordinance, Israel's Provisional Council extends restrictions on foreign travel until the state of emergency ceases to exist. The restrictions mandate that anyone leaving the country obtain an exit permit from the minister of immigration and provide immigration officers with the authority to board any vehicle in order to detain and question persons trying to leave without proper documentation.

Document 90: Letter from Israel's Foreign Minister to the United Nations Secretary-General Concerning Israel's Application for Admission to Membership of the United Nations and Declaration Accepting Obligations under the Charter (November 29, 1948) [U.N. SCOR, U.N. Doc. S/1093 (1948)]. In this letter, Israeli Foreign Minister Moshe Shertok requests the admission of Israel as a member of the United Nations. Along with the request for admission, the foreign minister encloses a declaration accepting the obligations of the United Nations Charter and a pledge to honor its obligations.[136]

Document 91: United Nations Press Release: New Cease-Fire Agreement between Israeli, Iraqi Forces (December 8, 1948) [U.N. Press Release, U.N. Dep't of Public Info., U.N. Doc. PAL/399 (1948)]. This United Nations press release announces that a cease-fire agreement ("Qalensuwa Agreement") was brokered between Iraqi and Israeli forces at meetings arranged by United Nations observers outside Tel Aviv. It also notes that progress was made on a potential agreement between Israel and Transjordan.

Document 92: United Nations Security Council Resolution 66, Calling for an Immediate Cease-Fire and Implementation of Security Council Resolution 61 (December 29, 1948) [S.C. Res. 66,

---

[136] *See generally* U.N. CHARTER, *available at* http://www.un.org/aboutun/charter/.

U.N. SCOR, 396th mtg., U.N. Doc. S/1169 (1948)]. United Nations Security Council Resolution 66 calls on concerned governments to declare an immediate cease-fire, to withdraw from positions taken since October 14 in accordance with Resolution 61, and to allow the supervision of the truce by United Nations observers.[137]

Document 93: General Armistice Agreement between Israel and Egypt (February 24, 1949) [42 U.N.T.S. 251]. Negotiations for the Israeli-Egyptian Armistice Agreement were held at Rhodes under the direction of Ralph Bunche, the United Nations mediator for Palestine. This was the first formal truce agreement concluded between an Arab state and Israel, setting the pattern for others with Lebanon, Jordan, and Syria.[138] Because this agreement is not a full peace settlement, however, its demarcation line is not meant to be a political or territorial boundary and is "delineated without prejudice to rights, claims and positions of either Party to the Armistice as regards ultimate settlement of the Palestine Problem." Colonel Mahmed Seif El Dine and M.K. El Raliniany signed for and on behalf of the government of Egypt. Walter Eytan, Yigael Yadin, and Elias Sasson signed for and on behalf of the government of Israel.

Document 94: General Armistice Agreement between Israel and Lebanon (March 23, 1949) [42 U.N.T.S. 287]. The Armistice Agreement between Israel and Lebanon, signed at Ras En Naqoura, provided guidelines for temporary demarcation lines, as well as the exchange of prisoners of war. Like the other three armistice agreements, it establishes a five-person Mixed Armistice Commission to oversee its implementation of the armistice.[139] Lieutenant-Colonel Mordechai Makleff, Yehoshua Pelman, and Shabtai Rosenne signed on behalf of Israel. Lieutenant-Colonel Toufic Salem and Commandant J. Harb signed on behalf of Lebanon.

Document 95: General Armistice Agreement between Israel and Jordan (April 3, 1949) [42 U.N.T.S. 304]. The Armistice Agreement between Israel and Jordan was signed at Rhodes, Greece, in the presence of the United Nations acting mediator on Palestine and the United Nations chief of staff of the UNTSO. A special committee, composed of two representatives of each party designated by the respective governments, was established for the purpose of formulating agreed plans and arrangements. Colonel Ahmed Sudki El-Jundi and Lieutenant-Colonel Mohamed Maayte signed on behalf of Jordan. Reuven Shiloah, and Lieutenant-Colonel Moshe Dayan signed on behalf of Israel. It is structured much like the other three armistice agreements.[140]

Document 96: General Armistice Agreement between Israel and Syria (July 20, 1949) [42 U.N.T.S. 327]. Syria was the last of the Arab states bordering Israel to sign an armistice agreement with Israel. This armistice agreement draws a demarcation line, provides for exchanges of prisoners of war, and establishes a five-person Mixed Armistice Commission to oversee the implementation of the agreement. It was signed near Mahanayim in the Upper Galilee by Lieutenant-Colonel Mordechai Makleff, Yehoshua Pelman, and Shabtai Rosenne on behalf of the Israeli government and by Colonel Fozi Selo, Lieutenant-Colonel Mohamed

---

137 *See* Doc. 87.

138 *See* Docs. 93–96.

139 *See* Docs. 93, 95, and 96.

140 *See* Docs. 93, 94, and 96.

Nasser, and Captain Afif Bizri on behalf of the Syrian government. It is structured much like the other three armistice agreements.[141]

ii. Post-War Developments

Document 97: United Nations Security Council Resolution 69, Recommending Israel's Admission to the United Nations (March 4, 1949) [S.C. Res. 69, U.N. SCOR, 409th mtg., U.N. Doc. S/1277 (1949)]. In Resolution 69, the Security Council recommends the admission of Israel to membership in the United Nations. The resolution is supported by nine members of the Security Council, with Egypt voting against it and Britain abstaining. The resolution was adopted despite objections raised on the basis that the draft resolution was not supported by all five permanent members of the Security Council (*i.e.*, Britain, China, France, United States, and USSR) given Britain's abstention. Such support is required to admit new members, as stipulated in Article 27, paragraph 3, of the United Nations Charter.[142]

Document 98: Report on the Assassination of Count Folke Bernadotte and Colonel André Serot Submitted to the Security Council by the Government of Israel (May 2, 1949) [U.N. SCOR, U.N. Doc. S/1315 (1949]. The government of Israel submitted this report on the assassination of Count Folke Bernadotte and his aid Colonel André Pierre Serot to the Security Council in accordance with Security Council Resolution 59.[143] It states that an organization calling itself Hazit Hamoledeth (Fatherland Front) had claimed responsibility for the assassination and that the provisional government of Israel had reason to believe that this group was connected to the LHY. On instructions from the government, LHY camps in Jerusalem were surrounded and occupied and, by October 23, 1948, 184 LHY members had been arrested in Jerusalem and another eighty-two members in Tel Aviv and other parts. Despite these efforts, no evidence sufficient to warrant a criminal prosecution was found. However, two leaders of LHY were brought before a special military court on charges of committing terrorist activities. The court found that due to the lack of direct evidence, it could not establish that LHY had ordered the assassination of Count Folk Bernadotte. Sections of the judgment of the court is included as an annex. The report emphasizes that Israel does not regard the case as closed.

Document 99: United Nations General Assembly Resolution 273, Admitting Israel to Membership in the United Nations (May 11, 1949) [G.A. Res. 273 (III), 3 U.N. GAOR, at 18, U.N. Doc. A/900 (1949)]. In Resolution 273, the General Assembly decides to admit Israel to membership in the United Nations, recognizing that Israel is a peace-loving state that accepts the obligations contained in the United Nations Charter.[144]

Document 100: Progress Report of the United Nations Conciliation Commission for Palestine (May 12, 1949) [U.N. GAOR Ad Hoc Political Comm., 4th Sess., Annex to the Summary Records of Meeting 2, at 5–9, U.N. Doc. A/927 (1949)]. Ralph Bunch,

---

[141] *See* Docs. 93–95.

[142] U.N. CHARTER, art. 27, para. 3, *available at* http://www.un.org/aboutun/charter/.

[143] *See* Doc. 83.

[144] *See supra* note 15.

the acting mediator for Palestine, presented this report to the president of the Security Council, detailing the situation in the Southern Negev as the result of an intensive investigation by UNTSO, undertaken since March 7, 1949. It states that both Transjordan and Israel have committed acts that constitute violations of their truce agreement.[145]

Document 101: Working Paper Prepared by the Secretariat, United Nations Conciliation Commission for Palestine: The Future of Arab Palestine and the Question of Partition (July 30, 1949) [U.N. Doc. A/AC.25/W.19 (1949)]. This working paper by the Secretariat traces the history of the many partition proposals for Palestine, including those advanced by Britain's Peel Commission[146] and Woodhead Commission,[147] and the General Assembly's Partition Plan (*i.e.*, United Nations General Assembly Resolution 181).[148] It highlights the concerned parties' positions on various proposals and describes the international community's role in attempting to broker a partition plan that would benefit all parties.

Document 102: United Nations Security Council Resolution 73, Relieving the Acting Mediator of any Further Responsibility in Palestine (August 11, 1949) [S.C. Res. 73, U.N. SCOR, 4th Sess., 437th mtg., at 8, U.N. Doc. S/1376 (1949)]. In Resolution 73, the Security Council finds that the General Armistice Agreements between Israel and Egypt, Lebanon, Syria, and Transjordan constitute a step towards permanent peace in Palestine The General Assembly assigns new functions to the UNTSO in Palestine and terminates the role of the United Nations mediator for Palestine.

Document 103: Tripartite Declaration of the United States, Britain, and France (May 25, 1950) [22 DEP'T ST. BULL. 886 (1950)]. This tripartite declaration presents the unified positions of the United States, Britain, and France with regard to questions affecting the peace and stability of the Arab states and Israel. The declaration outlines areas of agreement, including that the three governments will not sell arms to states that intend to undertake an act of aggression against another state. Later, in 1956, the United States bows out of this pact in response to Britain and France's role in the 1956 war.

Document 104: Exchange between the Minister for Foreign Affairs of the Government of Israel and the Secretary-General Concerning a Claim for Damage Caused to the United Nations by the Assassination of Count Folke Bernadotte (June 14–22, 1950) [U.N. SCOR, U.N. Doc. S/1506]. In this exchange, the committee appointed by the Israeli government to investigate the assassination of Count Folke Bernadotte finds that the assertion that there had been neglect on the part of the Israeli authorities was unjustified. In this letter from Israel's minister of foreign affairs, Israel stresses that its failure to find Bernadotte's assassins should be viewed in light of their status as a young nation with organizational deficiencies. Without admitting the validity of contentions, Israel agrees to pay a remittance of $54,628.00 as reparation to the United Nations. The foreign minister further states that although Israel does not consider the case closed, it is unwilling to reexamine the case.

---

[145] *See* Doc. 95.

[146] *See* Doc. 35.

[147] *See* Doc. 38.

[148] *See supra* note 1.

In his reply, the secretary-general acknowledges both payment to the United Nations and Israel's expression of regret. The secretary-general also expresses his disappointment that the investigation had failed to result in the apprehension of the assassins and expresses his hope that further investigations will be pursued.

Document 105: Treaty of Joint Defense and Economic Cooperation of the Arab League (June 17, 1950) [1 AMERICAN FOREIGN POLICY 1950–1955, BASIC DOCUMENTS (U.S. State Dep't ed., 1957)]. This Joint Defense and Economic Cooperation Treaty was signed by the Arab League member states Jordan, Syria, Iraq, Saudi Arabia, Lebanon, Egypt, and Yemen. It commits contracting states to consider any act of armed aggression made against any one or more of the members or their armed forces to be directed against all the members.

Document 106: Jerusalem Program Adopted at the Twenty-Third Zionist Congress (August 30, 1951) [*reprinted in* ARAB-ISRAELI CONFLICT AND CONCILIATION: A DOCUMENTARY HISTORY (Bernard Reich ed., 1995)]. At the twenty-third Zionist Congress, the status of the Zionist movement was a fundamental issue in need of adjustment after Israel gained its independence in 1948. The Jerusalem Program addressed this issue by defining the aims of Zionism. These goals included unifying the Jewish people, gathering them in the State of Israel and strengthening this state as heir historic homeland, promoting spiritual and cultural values and encouraging Hebrew education to preserve the identity of the Jewish people, and finally to protect the rights of Jews everywhere. More was added to the Jerusalem program in June of 1968 at the twenty-seventh Zionist Congress.

Document 107: General Progress Report and Supplementary Report of the United Nations Conciliation Commission for Palestine (Covering the Period from December 11, 1949 to October 23, 1950) (October 23, 1950) [U.N. GAOR, 5th Sess., Supp. No. 18, U.N. Doc. A/1367/Rev.1 (1950)]. This report of the United Nations Conciliation Commission for Palestine describes the conciliation efforts undertaken by the Commission from December 11, 1949, to October 23, 1950. It notes that the concerned Arab states have decided to negotiate with Israel as a single block, although Israel would prefer to negotiate individually with each state. The report also covers progress made in the area of ensuring access to the Holy Places and of refugees, consideration for which is guided by Security Council Resolution 194.[149]

Document 108: United Nations Security Council Resolution 89, Calling for the Handling of Complaints According to the Procedures of the Armistice Agreements (Egyptian Complaint on Expulsion of Palestinians by Israel) (November 17, 1950) [S.C. Res. 89, U.N. SCOR, 524th mtg., S/1907 (1950)]. In this resolution, the Security Council calls upon the involved parties to present complaints according to the procedures established in the Armistice Agreements, *i.e.*, by consulting the respective Mixed Armistice Commissions. The Security Council responds to Egypt's complaint about the expulsion of Palestinian Arabs by requesting both parties to implement the findings of the Egyptian-Israel Mixed Armistice Commission and by calling upon the concerned governments not to transfer persons across international borders or armistice lines without prior consultation through the Mixed Armistice Commissions.

---

[149] Doc. 503.

Document 109: United Nations Security Council Resolution 92, Calling for a Cease-Fire in the Demilitarized Zone on the Syrian-Israeli Armistice Line (May 8, 1951) [S.C. Res. 92, U.N. SCOR, 545th mtg., U.N. Doc. S/2130 (1951)]. Noting that fighting had broken out in a demilitarized zone established by the Israel-Syrian General Armistice Agreement, the Security Council calls on the parties to implement the cease-fire called for by the chief of staff of the UNTSO in Palestine.[150]

Document 110: Progress Report of the United Nations Conciliation Commission for Palestine (Paris Conference) (November 20, 1951) [U.N. GAOR, 6th Sess., Supp. No. 18, U.N. Doc. A/1985 (1951)]. Efforts were made at a conference in Paris September 13–November 19, 1951, by the United Nations Conciliation Commission for Palestine to advance relations between the governments of Egypt, Jordan, Lebanon, and Syria and the government of Israel following signature of the four armistice agreements. While these agreements promoted security, they did not provide solutions for contentious issues such as Jerusalem or refugees. Annex C provides the mostly critical comments of the Israeli, Egyptian, Jordanian, Lebanese, and Syrian delegations on the proposals. Based on their responses, the chairman of the commission concludes, "[The commission] has been unsuccessful in its endeavours, since neither party indicated a willingness substantially to recede from their rigid positions and to seek a solution through mediation along the lines spelled out in the Commission's pattern of proposals."

Document 111: Law of the State of Israel: World Zionist Organization-Jewish Agency (Status) Law (November 24, 1952) [7 LSI 3 (1952–53)]. Given the World Zionist Organization's important and historic role in aiding Jewish immigration and settlement in Israel, this Israeli law formalizes the close relationship and cooperation between the government of the State of Israel and that organization. Paragraph 4 reads, "The State of Israel recognises the World Zionist Organisation as the authorised agency which will continue to operate in the State of Israel for the development and settlement of the country, the absorption of immigrants from the Diaspora and the coordination of the activities in Israel of Jewish institutions and organisations active in those fields."

Document 112: United Nations Security Council Resolution 100, Asking Israel to Suspend Drainage Work in the Demilitarized Zone (Huleh) (October 27, 1953) [S.C. Res. 100, U.N. SCOR, 631st mtg., U.N. Doc. S/3128 (1953)]. In this resolution, the Security Council deems it desirable that the works started by Israel in the demilitarized zone near Jerusalem be suspended while the Security Council examines the issue. The resolution notes that the government of Israel has undertaken to suspend the works.

Document 113: Pact of Mutual Cooperation between Iraq, Turkey, Britain, Pakistan, and Iran (Baghdad Pact) (February 24, 1955) [233 U.N.T.S. 199]. The Baghdad Pact establishes a security network among Britain and four states in the region—Iran, Iraq, Pakistan, and Turkey. The pact commits these governments to mutual cooperation and protection, as well as nonintervention in each other's affairs. In part, the pact is meant to curb the rise of Arab nationalism and Soviet influence in the area. Iraq is the pact's only Arab member; but in 1958, when the Iraqi monarchy was overthrown by a military coup, Iraq withdrew from the pact.

---

[150] Doc. 96.

B. *Suez War: 1956*

On July 26, 1956, Egyptian President Gamal Abdel Nasser announced the nationalization of the Suez Canal, an important act that represented the close of the last stage of Western colonialism in Egypt.[151]

Britain and France, who both had serious stakes in the canal, however, were determined not to lose control of it. They devised a plan in a secret meeting that involved Israel attacking Egypt and then Britain and France engaging, as well, after delivering a twelve-hour ultimatum to the two parties to end the fighting, occupying the Suez Canal.[152] Britain and France were to invoke their rights under the 1888 Constantinople Convention, which established the international right of freedom of navigation through the Suez Canal.[153] Israel cooperated in part out of frustration over the blockade of the Suez Canal and the Gulf of Aqaba to its commercial shipping and *Fedayeen* attacks against Israeli civilians inside Israel originating from Gaza.

Israel launched the initial attack against Egypt on October 29, 1956, under Chief of Staff Moshe Dayan. The Israeli campaign was swift and effective. Within days of its first assault, the Gaza Strip and the entire Sinai Peninsula fell to Israel. As planned, on November 5, 1956, British and French forces began their invasion of Egypt, with British troops capturing Port Said and seeking to advance south in the direction of Suez City. A United Nations cease-fire stopped them.

The United States and the Soviet Union condemned the attacks and demanded that Israel return to its previous borders.[154] They also demanded that British and French forces withdraw from all Egyptian territory. After extensive negotiations, Israel complied with the demands, but only on the condition that the United Nations place a United Nations Emergency Force (UNEF) in the Sinai and at Sharm el-Sheikh to guarantee the free passage of Israeli ships through the Gulf of Aqaba.[155] Israeli withdrawal was carried out in phases from November 1956 to March 1957.

The unprecedented common stance of the United States and the Soviet Union during the 1956 war, at the height of the Cold War, owed to U.S. President Dwight D. Eisenhower's sense of betrayal at not having

---

[151] *See* Doc. 125.

[152] Britain and France dubbed the attack, "Operation Musketeer." Israel dubbed it "Operation Kadesh."

[153] *See* The Constantinople Convention Respecting the Free Navigation of the Suez Maritime Canal, *supra* note 77. *See also* http://www.mfa.gov.eg/mfa_portal/en-GB/foreign_policy/treaties/convention+repsecting+the+free+navigation+of+the+suez+maritime+canal.htm. Great Britain, Germany, Austria-Hungary, Spain, France, Italy, the Netherlands, Russia, and Turkey were parties to this treaty.

[154] *See* Docs. 133 and 129.

[155] *See* Doc. 141.

been informed of Britain and France's joint plan of attack ahead of time and the Soviet Union's strong ties to Egypt.

i. Pre-War Developments

Document 114: Decree on the Procedure of Ship and Airplane Searches and of Seizure of Contraband Goods in Connexion with the Palestine War (February 6, 1950) [published in Egyptian Official Gazette (No. 36), Apr. 8, 1950]. In this decree, Egyptian King Farouk authorizes the search of all ships and aircraft in order to ensure that no arms or other instruments of war would be shipped to Israeli forces in occupied areas of Palestine. The decree authorizes the use of force against any ship that attempts to avoid search and permits the seizure of any contraband found in violation of the order.

Document 115: Cablegram from the Chief of Staff of the UNTSO Transmitting a Report to the Security Council (June 12, 1951) [U.N. SCOR, U.N. Doc. S/2194 (1951)]. This cablegram resulted from a meeting of the Egyptian-Israel Special Committee meant to determine whether or not the Mixed Armistice Commission had the right to demand that Egypt not interfere with the passing of goods to Israel through the Suez Canal. Finding for Egypt, the chief of staff explains that, while such interference by Egypt is hostile, it is not technically an "aggressive action" under the definition provided by the General Armistice Agreement between Israel and Egypt, upon which the authority of the commission rests.[156] In the spirit of the agreement, however, the chief of staff requests that Egypt stop such interference. He further recommends that the question be referred to a higher authority such as the Security Council or the International Court of Justice (ICJ).

Document 116: United Nations Security Council Resolution 619, Concerning Restrictions on the Passage of Ships through the Suez Canal (September 1, 1951) [reprinted in THE ISRAEL-ARAB READER: A DOCUMENTARY HISTORY OF THE MIDDLE EAST CONFLICT (Walter Laqueur & Barry Rubin eds., 2001)]. The Security Council calls upon Egypt to cease improper interference with shipping in the Suez Canal. No legitimate reason to interfere with shipping is found.

Document 117: United Nations Security Council Resolution 95, Calling upon Egypt to Terminate Restrictions on Passage in the Suez Canal (September 1, 1951) [S.C. Res. 95, U.N. SCOR, 558th mtg., at 2–3, U.N. Doc. S/2322 (1951)]. Due to Egypt's policy of refusing Israeli cargo ships and ships bound for Israel to pass through the Suez Canal or the Straits of the Tiran, the Security Council passed Resolution 95, calling upon Egypt to terminate its restrictions on international commercial shipping.

Document 118: United Nations Security Council Resolution 101, Calling Israeli Attack at Qibya a Violation of Cease-Fire (November 24, 1953) [S.C. Res. 101, U.N. SCOR, U.N. Doc. S/3139/Rev.2 (1953)]. After Israeli forces attack Qibya, Jordan, on October 14 and 15, 1953, the Security Council adopts Resolution 101, which finds that the retaliatory action by Israel and all such actions constitute a violation of the cease-fire and are inconsistent with the parties' obligations under both the General Armistice Agreement between Israel and Jordan[157] and the Charter of the United

[156] *See* Doc. 93.

[157] *See* Doc. 95.

Nations.[158] The Security Council expresses the strongest censure of the action.

Document 119: United Nations Security Council Resolution 106, Condemning the Israeli Attack on Gaza of February 28, 1955 (March 29, 1955) [S.C. Res. 106, U.N. SCOR, U.N. Doc. S/3378 (1955)]. After Israeli forces attacked Egyptian troops in the Gaza Strip, the Security Council adopted Resolution 106, condemning the attack as a violation of the General Armistice Agreement between Egypt and Israel.[159] It calls upon Israel to refrain from any future actions that would further violate the agreement.

Document 120: United Nations Security Council Resolution 107, Calling on Egypt and Israel to Cooperate with the Chief of Staff of UNTSO in Preserving Security on the Armistice Demarcation Line (Gaza) (March 30, 1955) [S.C. Res. 107, U.N. SCOR, 696th mtg., U.N. Doc. S/3379 (1955)]. Due to tensions along the Egypt-Israel armistice demarcation line in February 1955, the Security Council issued Resolution 107, which calls upon both governments to cooperate with the proposals of the chief of staff of the UNTSO in Palestine for an unconditional cease-fire.

Document 121: United Nations Security Council Resolution 108, Calling on Egypt and Israel to Cooperate with the Chief of Staff of UNTSO in Preventing Violence on the Armistice Demarcation Line (Gaza) (September 8, 1955) [S.C. Res. 108, U.N. SCOR, 700th mtg., U.N. Doc. S/3435 (1955)]. United Nations Security Council Resolution 108 notes with approval Egypt and Britain's acceptance of the UNTSO chief of staff's appeal for an unconditional cease-fire. It calls upon both parties to appoint representatives to meet with the UNTSO chief of staff in order to implement his proposals.

Document 122: United Nations Security Council Resolution 111, Condemning the Israeli Attack on Syrian Territory of December 11, 1955 (January 19, 1956) [S.C. Res. 111, U.N. SCOR, 715th mtg., U.N. Doc. S/3538 (1956)]. Given reports from the chief of staff of the UNTSO in Palestine that Israeli forces had attacked Syrian forces on Syrian territory on December 11, 1955, and that Syrian authorities had interfered with Israeli activities on Lake Tiberias in violation of the provisions of the General Armistice Agreement between Israel and Syria, the Security Council in Resolution 111 calls upon both parties to cooperate with the chief of staff to carry out the provisions of the armistice agreement.[160] The Security Council calls upon both parties to arrange with the chief of staff for an immediate exchange of all military prisoners.

Document 123: United Nations Security Council Resolution 113, Calling for Measures to Reduce Tensions along the Armistice Demarcation Lines (April 4, 1956) [S.C. Res. 113, U.N. SCOR, 722d mtg., U.N. Doc. S/3575 (1956)]. In Resolution 113, the Security Council notes the failure of the parties to comply with Resolutions 107, 108, and 111, and with any of the proposals by the Chief of Staff of the UNTSO in Palestine.[161] In light of the persistent violence, the secretary-general is called on to arrange with the parties the adoption of measures that will reduce tension along the demarcation lines. The Security Council recommends the withdrawal of forces

---

158 *See generally* U.N. CHARTER, *available at* http://www.un.org/aboutun/charter/.

159 *See* Doc. 93.

160 *See* Doc. 96.

161 *See* Docs. 120–122.

from demarcation lines, full freedom of movement for United Nations observers, and the prevention of violations of the Armistice Agreements as measures to be discussed and adopted by the parties.

Document 124: United Nations Security Council Resolution 114, Calling on the Parties to the Armistice Agreements to Carry out the Measures Agreed upon with the Secretary-General (June 4, 1956) [S.C. Res. 114, U.N. SCOR, 728th mtg., U.N. Doc. S/3605 (1956)]. In Resolution 114, the Security Council commends the secretary-general and concerned parties on progress achieved following a mission by the secretary-general that garnered assurances from all parties to unconditionally observe the cease-fire. Believing that further progress should be made in consolidating these gains resulting, the Security Council declares that the parties should speedily carry out the measures agreed upon with the secretary-general.[162] The Security Council endorses the secretary-general's view that the reestablishment of full compliance with the armistice agreements represents a necessary stage before progress is possible on the main issues between the parties.

Document 125: Order of Egyptian President Gamal Abdel Nasser Nationalizing the Suez Canal Company (July 26, 1956) [American Foreign Policy, 1956, Current Documents 604–06 (U.S. Dep't of State ed., 1959)]. In a speech at Alexandria, Egyptian President Gamal Abdel Nasser announces the nationalization of the Suez Canal, transfering all of the canal's assets, rights, and obligations to Egypt and dissolves all of its previous management. The Suez Canal, Egypt's largest territorial asset, was run by the Paris-based Universal Company of the Suez Maritime Canal on a lease set to expire in 1968. This order stipulates that shareholders are to receive compensation, and commercial shipping in the canal is not to be disrupted.

Document 126: United Nations Security Council Resolution 118, Describing Requirements for a Settlement of the Suez Question (October 13, 1956) [S.C. Res. 118, U.N. SCOR, 11th Sess., Supp. for Oct.-Dec., 743d mtg., at 47–48, U.N. Doc. S/3675 (1956)]. In Resolution 118, the Security Council agrees that any settlement of the Suez question should meet the following requirements: (1) there should be free and open transit through the canal without discrimination, overt or covert; (2) the sovereignty of Egypt should be respected; (3) the operation of the canal should be insulated from the politics of any country; (4) the manner of fixing tolls and charges should be decided by agreement between Egypt and the users; (5) a fair proportion of the dues should be allotted to development; and (6) in the case of disputes, unresolved affairs between the Suez Canal Company and the Egyptian government should be settled by arbitration.

ii. 1956 War: October 29, 1956–March 6, 1957

Document 127: Statement by Israeli Ministry for Foreign Affairs on Reasons for the Military Operation in Sinai (October 29, 1956) [*available at* http://www.mfa.gov.il/MFA/Foreign%20Relations/Israels%20Foreign%20Relations%20since%201947/1947-1974/1%20Foreign%20Ministry%20Statement-%2029%20October%201956]. The Israeli Ministry for Foreign Affairs issued this statement on its military operations in Egypt after commencing its official attack. The Israeli Ministry for Foreign Affairs blames the assault on the situation created in Israel by *Fedayeen*

[162] *See* Docs. 93–96.

attacks and on Egypt's attempt to stifle the Israeli economy by preventing Israeli shipping through the Suez Canal. The ministry asserts that Israel's attempts to make peace with Egypt have been answered with "heightened propaganda" and "hostile activities against the very existence of Israel."

Document 128: Excerpts from the Speech by U.S. President Dwight D. Eisenhower, United States Rejects the Use of Force (October 31, 1956) [*published in* 28 DEP'T ST. BULL. 743 (1956)]. In this address, U.S. President Dwight D. Eisenhower assures the nation that the United States does not support the military actions undertaken by Israel, Britain, and France in the Middle East. The president notes that they are irreconcilable with the purposes of the United Nations and promises that the United States will not involve itself in the hostilities. Eisenhower expresses the United States' intention to bring a request to end hostilities before the General Assembly because Britain and France had vetoed such a resolution in the Security Council.

Document 129: United Nations Security Council Resolution 119, Calling an Emergency Special Session of the General Assembly to Consider the Invasion of Egypt (October 31, 1956) [S.C. Res. 119, U.N. SCOR, 751st mtg., U.N. Doc. S/3721 (1956)]. In Resolution 119, the Security Council, considering that a grave situation has been created by action undertaken against Egypt, decides to call an emergency special session of the General Assembly in order to make appropriate recommendations.

Document 130: United Nations General Assembly Resolution 997, Calling Israeli Invasion of Egypt a Violation of the General Armistice Agreement (November 2, 1956) [G.A. Res. 997 (ES-I), U.N. GAOR, 1st Emergency Special Sess., Supp. No. 1, at 2, U.N. Doc. A/3354 (1956)]. United Nations General Assembly Resolution 997 notes that Israeli armed forces have penetrated deeply into Egyptian territory in violation of the 1949 General Armistice Agreement between Egypt and Israel and that French and British armed forces are also conducting military operations against Egyptian territory. It urges all parties to agree to an immediate cease-fire and halt the movement of military forces and arms into the area. It also recommends that all member states refrain from introducing military goods in the area of hostilities. Finally, the secretary-general is requested to observe and report promptly on the compliance with this resolution. The United States submitted the draft of this resolution.

Document 131: United Nations General Assembly Resolution 998, Requesting the Secretary-General to Establish an Emergency International United Nations Force (November 4, 1956) [G.A. Res. 998 (ES-I), U.N. GAOR, 1st Emergency Special Sess., Supp. No. 1, at 2, U.N. Doc. A/3354 (1956)]. In Resolution 998 (ES-I), the General Assembly requests the secretary-general to submit a plan for establishing an emergency international United Nations force to secure and supervise the cessation of hostilities in accordance with United Nations General Assembly Resolution 997 (ES-I).[163] The United Nations subsequently stationed 3,300 troops in Gaza and along the Sinai border to act as a buffer between Israel and Egypt.

Document 132: United Nations General Assembly Resolution 999, Calling for a Cease-Fire (November 4, 1956) [A. Res. 999 (ES-1), U.N. GAOR, 1st Emergency Special Sess., U.N. Doc. A/Res/999 (1956)]. Passed on the same day as General Assembly

163 *See* Doc. 130.

Resolution 998 (ES-I),[164] this resolution authorizes the secretary-general to arrange with the concerned parties for the implementation of the cease-fire (pursuant to Resolution 997 (ES-I)[165]). It also requests that the Secretary-General and the UNTSO to obtain compliance of the withdrawal of all forces behind the armistice lines.

Document 133: Exchange between Soviet Premier Nikolai Bulganin and Israeli Prime Minister David Ben-Gurion (November 5–8, 1956) [*available at* http://www.mfa.gov.il/mfa/foreign+relations/israels+foreign+relations+since+1947/1947-1974/7+exchange+of+letters-+bulganin-+ben-gurion-+5+and.htm]. In his letter to Israeli Prime Minister David Ben-Gurion, Soviet Premier Nikolai Bulganin repeats the Soviet condemnation of Israel, Britain, and France's aggression against Egypt. Bulganin accuses the Israeli government of acting as a tool of foreign imperialist powers and appeals to Israel to stop the aggression and withdraw its troops from Egyptian territory. In response, Ben-Gurion explains that Israel acted out of self-defense, as Egypt had orchestrated *Fedayeen* attacks against Israeli citizens inside Israel and had established a blockade against Israel's freedom of navigation in the Suez Canal and the Straits of Eilat. Ben-Gurion assures Bulganin that Israel is a sovereign and peace-loving state.

Document 134: Exchange between U.S. President Dwight D. Eisenhower and Israeli Prime Minister David Ben-Gurion (November 5–8, 1956) [35 DEP'T ST. BULL. 797–98 (1956)]. In this letter to Israeli Prime Minister David Ben-Gurion, U.S. President Dwight D. Eisenhower indicates his strong disapproval of the tripartite invasion of Egypt. Eisenhower requests that Israel clarify its position with regard to its withdrawal from the Sinai given statements attributed to the Israeli government that it did not intend to comply with United Nations resolutions. Reminding Ben-Gurion of the United States' long-standing support for the Jewish state, Eisenhower makes it clear that Israel needs to comply with the United Nations resolutions. In response, Ben-Gurion assures Eisenhower that Israel would withdraw its forces upon conclusion of satisfactory arrangements with the United Nations in connection with an international force entering the Suez Canal area.

Document 135: United Nations General Assembly Resolution 1002, Noting the Establishment of a UNEF (November 7, 1956) [G.A. Res. 1002 (ES-I), U.N. GAOR, 1st Emergency Sess., Supp. No. 1, at 3–4, U.N. Doc. A/3354 (1956)]. In Resolution 1002, the General Assembly, recalling its previous resolutions, calls again upon Israel to immediately withdraw its forces behind the armistice lines and calls again upon the United Kingdom and France to immediately withdraw all their forces from Egyptian territory. The General Assembly urges the Secretary-General to communicate this resolution to the concerned parties and requests him to promptly report on compliance with this resolution.

Document 136: United Nations General Assembly Resolution 1120, Noting with Regret that Forces Have Not Been Withdrawn behind the Armistice Line (November 24, 1956) [G.A. Res. 1120, U.N. GAOR, U.N. Doc. A/RES/1120 (XI) (1956)]. In Resolution 1120, the General Assembly notes with regret that all the Israeli forces, all the British forces (though some arrangements are being made for the withdrawal of

[164] *See* Doc. 131.

[165] *See supra* note 95.

one British battalion), and two-thirds of the French forces remain in Egypt. The General Assembly reiterates its call to France, Israel, and Britain to comply with General Assembly Resolutions 997 and 1002.).[166]

Document 137: Special Message from U.S. President Dwight D. Eisenhower to Congress on the Situation in the Middle East (January 5, 1957) [*available at* http://www.eisenhower.utexas.edu/midleast.htm]. In this special message to a joint session of Congress, the newly reelected U.S. President Dwight D. Eisenhower requests that Congress and the president act together to protect Middle-Eastern nations against the communist threat. Eisenhower proposes authorizing the United States to cooperate with and assist any nation or group of nations in the Middle East in the development of economic strength dedicated to the maintenance of national independence. He also proposes authorizing the executive to undertake programs of military assistance and cooperation with any nation or group of nations in the region that desires such aid. Finally, he proposes authorizing assistance and cooperation to include the employment of the armed forces of the United States to secure and protect the territorial integrity and political independence of nations requesting aid against overt armed aggression from a communist nation. This message came to be known as the "Eisenhower Doctrine."

Document 138: United Nations General Assembly Resolution 1123, Noting with Regret and Concern the Failure of Israel to Comply with United Nations Terms (January 19, 1957) [G.A. Res. 1123, U.N. GAOR, U.N. Doc. A/RES/1123 (XI) (1957]. In Resolution 1123, the General Assembly notes with regret and concern Israel's failure to comply with Resolutions 997, 998, 999, 1002, and 1120, and requests that the Secretary-General continue efforts to secure Israel's withdrawal from Egypt.[167]

Document 139: United Nations General Assembly Resolution 1124, Deploring the Non-Compliance of Israel to Complete Its Withdrawal behind the Armistice Demarcation Line (February 2, 1957) [G.A. Res. 1124, U.N. GAOR, U.N. Doc. A/RES/1124 (XI) (1957)]. In Resolution 1124, the General Assembly deplores the non-compliance of Israel of withdrawal behind the armistice demarcation line. It calls upon Israel to do so without further delay.

Document 140: United States Aide Memoire to Israel (February 11, 1957) [36 DEP'T ST. BULL. 392–93 (1957)]. This *aide memoire* poses a diplomatic solution to Israel's continuing security concerns that have thus far prevented Israel from completely withdrawing from Egyptian territory. Although its position is that Israeli withdrawal from Gaza should be prompt and unconditional, the United States proposes posting the UNEF in the Gaza Strip and along the boundary between Israel and the Gaza Strip to minimize the threat of armed infiltration. The United States also proposes moving the UNEF into the Straits area to aid in guaranteeing the right of free and innocent passage to all parties. The *aide memoire* also gives notice that the United States is prepared to exercise the right of free and innocent passage in the Gulf and to join others to secure general recognition of this right.

Document 141: Statement by Israeli Foreign Minister Golda Meir to the United Nations General Assembly on Guaranteeing Navigation in the Suez Canal (March 1, 1957) [U.N. GAOR, 11th Sess., 666th plen. mtg., at 1275–76 (1957)]. In this statement to the

---

[166] *See* Docs. 130 and 135.

[167] *See* Docs. 130–132, 140, and 141.

General Assembly, Israeli Foreign Minister Golda Meir announces Israel's intention to carry out a full and prompt withdrawal behind the armistice demarcation line. Meir proposes a meeting between the chief of staff of the Israel Defense Army and the commander of the UNEF to discuss arrangements for the United Nations to take over security in Gaza. Meir also formulates Israel's policy with regard to the right of free passage in the Gulf of Aqaba and the Straits of Tiran following the withdrawal. Meir states that because they are international waters, no nation has the right to prevent free and innocent passage of Israeli ships in them. Meir warns that Israel will regard any such interference as an attack, thus prompting its right of self-defense.

Document 142: Excerpts of General Moshe Dayan's Eulogy in Ro'i Rothberg's Funeral [*reprinted in* BENNY MORRIS, RIGHTEOUS VICTIMS. A HISTORY OF THE ZIONIST-ARAB CONFLICT 1881–1999 287–88 (1999)]. On April 29, 1956, the security officer of Kibbutz Nahal-Oz, Ro'i Rothberg, was cut down by an Egyptian ambush on the border with the Gaza Strip. The eulogy delivered by the Israeli army's chief of staff, General Dayan, is one of the most frankest reflections on the nature of the Israeli-Palestinian conundrum that an Israeli leader has ever pronounced. An uncompromising warrior in the war against Israel's Arab enemies, Dayan was candid enough to appreciate how just was the cause of the disinherited Palestinians, and how justified was their hatred of the Israelis who settled on their confiscated lands. But, acknowledging the reason of the conflict did not make Dayan a preacher of peace and reconciliation; it only strengthened his conviction about the insolubility of the conflict and his understanding that this was a war for generations. "That is the fate of our generation," he said, "to be ready and armed, tough and harsh, or let the sword fall from our hands and our lives be cut short."

iii. Post-War Developments

Document 143: Declaration by the Government of Egypt Concerning the Suez Canal (April 24, 1957) [U.N. SCOR, Supp. for April–June, at 8, U.N. Doc. S/3818 (1957)]. This declaration by the government of Egypt begins with a statement by Egyptian Foreign Minister Mahmoud Fawzi announcing the Suez Canal is open for normal traffic. This declaration outlines the basic principles governing the Suez Canal and the arrangements for its operation. Article 3(a) guarantees "free and uninterrupted navigation for all nations within the limits of and in accordance with the provisions of the Constantinople Convention of 1888"; thus, implicitly recognizing Israel's right of passage through the canal.[168] It also stipulates that all disputes arising from operation of the Suez Canal should be referred to the ICJ.

Document 144: Aide Memoire Prepared by United Nations Secretary-General Dag Hammarskjöld on Conditions for the Withdrawal of UNEF (August 5, 1957) [*reprinted in* 6 I.L.M. 593–602 (1967). Following the 1956 war, United Nations Secretary-General Dag Hammarskjold prepared this *aide memoire* for his own files. It concerns the presence of the UNEF in Egypt and the circumstances under which it may be withdrawn. This document later plays a role in the 1967 war when United Nations Secretary-General U Thant withdraws UNEF from the Egypt-Israel demarcation line without consent from all parties.

---

[168] *See* Constantinople Convention, *supra* note 77.

Document 145: United Nations Security Council Resolution 127, Regarding the Status of the Zone between the Armistice Demarcation Lines (January 22, 1958) [S.C. Res. 127, U.N. SCOR, 810th mtg., U.N. Doc. S/3942 (1958)]. The Security Council adopted Resolution 127 after complaints were received from Jordan about activities conducted by Israel in the zone between the armistice demarcation lines, in the area of Government House in Jerusalem. The Security Council notes that the status of the zone is affected by the provisions of the Israel-Jordan General Armistice Agreement[169] and that neither Israel nor Jordan enjoys sovereignty over any part of the zone. The Security Council endorses the recommendations of the acting chief of staff, namely that: (1) the parties should discuss through the Mixed Armistice Commission civilian activities in the zone; (2) activities in the zone should be suspended until a survey has been completed and provisions made for their regulation; (3) discussions should be completed within two months; and (4) the Security Council should be advised of the result of the discussions. The Security Council calls upon the parties to cooperate with the chief of staff and the Mixed Armistice Commission in carrying out these recommendations.

Document 146: Excerpts from the Convention on the Territorial Sea and the Contiguous Zone (April 29, 1958) [15 U.S.T. 1606, 516 U.N.T.S. 205]. The Convention on the Territorial Sea and the Contiguous Zone protects innocent passage through territorial seas so long as it is done in observance of the laws of the coastal state. Coastal states are permitted to temporarily suspend passage when it is essential for the protection of the coastal state's security; but no suspension of innocent passage is allowed through straits used for navigation between high seas.

Document 147: United Nations Security Council Resolution 128, Complaint from Lebanon (June 11, 1958) [S.C. Res. 128, 825th mtg., U.N. Doc. S/4023 (1958)]. In Resolution 128, the Security Council, concerned about complaints of interference by the newly formed United Arab Republic[170] in Lebanon's internal affairs, decides to urgently dispatch to Lebanon an observation group to ensure that there is no illegal infiltration of personnel or supply of arms or other material across the Lebanese border. On July 15, U.S. President Dwight D. Eisenhower sends 5,000 U.S. marines to Lebanon to protect the pro-Western Lebanese government after a revolt in nearby Iraq results in the ousting of the Iraqi monarchy.

Document 148: United Nations Security Council Resolution 171, Calling on Israel to Scrupulously Refrain from Military Action in Violation of the General Armistice Agreement (April 9, 1962) [S.C. Res. 171, U.N. SCOR, 1006th mtg., U.N. Doc. S/5111 (1962)]. In Resolution 171, the Security Council deplores the hostile exchanges between Syria and Israel that began on March 8, 1962, and calls upon the two concerned governments to comply with their obligations under the United Nations Charter.[171] The Security Council determines that the Israeli attack of March 16–17, 1962, constitutes a flagrant violation of Security Council Resolution 111 (1956)[172] and calls upon

---

[169] *See* Doc. 95.

[170] The United Arab Republic was the political union of Egypt and Syria proclaimed on February 1, 1958. Despite the dissolution of the union with Syria's withdrawal in 1961, Egypt retained the name until September 2, 1971, when it took the name Arab Republic of Egypt.

[171] *See generally* U.N. CHARTER, *available at* http://www.un.org/aboutun/charter/.

[172] *See* Doc. 122.

Israel to scrupulously refrain from such action in the future. The Security Council endorses the measures recommended by the chief of staff of the UNTSO for the strengthening of that organization and calls upon the Israeli and Syrian authorities to assist the Chief of Staff in their early implementation.

Document 149: Arab League Summit in Cairo, Deciding to Divert Jordan River (January 13–17, 1964) [*available at* http://www.us-israel.org/jsource/History/watsum.html]. This declaration was issued at the first session of the Council of the Kings and Heads of State of the Arab League, held at the Arab League Headquarters in Cairo. In it, the council announces the adoption of practical resolutions to protect against threats posed by Israel that entail enabling the Palestinian people to participate in the "liberation of their country and attain[ment] of self-determination." The council further rallies the support and assistance of all parties to the Bandung Principles[173] and the Addis Ababa Charter[174] in the struggle against Israel.

Document 150: Declaration Issued by the Council of Kings and Heads of State of the Arab League at Its Second Session (September 5–11, 1964) [*available at* http://www.mideastweb.org/arabsummit1964.htm]. The Council of the Kings and Heads of State of the Arab League held its second meeting at Alexandria, Egypt. In its declaration, the council unanimously defines objectives for the liberation of Palestine from "Zionist colonialism" and calls upon all states to use their resources and capabilities to confront Israel. It also announces that the council has adopted resolutions for the implementation of an Arab plan to begin immediate work on projects for the exploitation of the waters of the River Jordan and its tributaries. The council further welcomes the establishment of the Palestine Liberation Organization (PLO) to consolidate a Palestinian entity.

C. *June War or Six-Day War: 1967*

Skirmishes broke out along Israel's borders with Syria and Jordan in March and June of 1967. In April, Syria informed Egypt as part of their five-year mutual defense pact that Israel was about to attack it. The Soviet Union confirmed the threat. As tensions escalated, Egypt requested that Secretary-General U Thant withdraw the UNEF from positions along the Egypt-Israel demarcation line.[175] Egypt also closed the Straits of Tiran and the Suez Canal to Israeli commercial navigation.[176]

Israel launched a preemptive attack against Egypt on June 6, 1967, destroying the Egyptian air force. Crippled by the blow, Egypt called on Jordan and Syria to join in fighting against Israel on the basis of the 1950 Treaty of Joint Defense and Economic Cooperation of the Arab

---

[173] Final Communique of the Asian-African (Bandung) Conference, Apr. 24, 1955, *reprinted in* SELECTED AGREEMENTS AND TREATIES AFFECTING SOUTH-EAST ASIA 31 (South-East Asia Treaty Organization ed., 1970). *See also* http://www.oup.co.uk/pdf/bt/cassese/cases/part3/ch18/1702.pdf.

[174] ADDIS ABABA (ORGANIZATIATION OF AFRICAN UNITY) CHARTER, May 25, 1963, 479 U.N.T.S. 39, 2 I.L.M. 766 (1963), available at http://www.africa-union.org/root/au/documents/treaties/text/ OAU_Charter_1963.pdf.

[175] *See* Doc. 141.

[176] *See* Doc. 152.

League.[177] The war engulfed Israel, Egypt, Syria, and Jordan—though Israel secretly urged Jordan not to join the war.

Between June 6 and 12, the Security Council passed multiple resolutions calling for a cease-fire.[178] Israel did not stop its offensive until it had secured all of its military objectives. At the end of fighting, Israel controlled the Sinai, the Golan Heights, the Gaza Strip, the West Bank, and, arguably the most important acquisition of all, East Jerusalem.[179]

For relevant documents on Jerusalem and the Occupied Territories, see Section 6, Jerusalem and the Holy Sites; and Section 8, Status of the Palestinians.

i. Pre-War Developments

Document 151: United Nations Security Council Resolution 228, Censuring Israeli Military Action in Hebron (November 25, 1966) [S.C. Res. 228, U.N. SCOR, 1328th mtg., U.N. Doc. S/RES/228 (1966)]. In Resolution 228, the Security Council deplores the loss of life and heavy damage to property resulting from the action of the Government of Israel in the southern Hebron area on November 13, 1966.

Document 152: Cable Containing Instructions for the Withdrawal of UNEF, Sent by the Secretary-General to the Commander of UNEF (May 8, 1967) [U.N. GAOR, U.N. Doc. A/6730, Add.1-3, A/6730/Add.3/Corr.1 (1967)]. After the United Arab Republic rescinded its consent to the presence of UNEF in the Sinai, United Nations Secretary-General U Thant relayed this cablegram to the Commander of UNEF, which includes procedures and instructions for the immediate withdrawal of UNEF forces. The withdrawal was carried out without the consent of the General Assembly, the Security Council, or the State of Israel.

Document 153: Statement by Egyptian President Gamal Abdel Nasser to Members of the National Assembly (May 29, 1967) [N.Y. Times, May 26, 1967, at 16, cols. 2–5]. In this statement to the Egyptian National Assembly, Egyptian President Gamal Abdel Nasser announces Egypt's plan to close the Strait of Tiran to Israeli shipping and all ships bound for Eilat. The blockade cut off Israel's only supply route with Asia and stopped the flow of oil from its main supplier, Iran. Israel considers the act a *casus belli.*

Document 154: Statement by U.S. President Lyndon B. Johnson Expressing U.S. Support for the Independence of All Nations in the Area (May 23, 1967) [*available at* http://www.presidency.ucsb.edu/ws/index.php?pid=28265&st=Israel&st1=thant]. In this statement, U.S. President Lyndon B. Johnson expresses the United States' commitment to the political independence and territorial integrity of all nations in the Middle East. Johnson expresses regret that the General Armistice Agreements of 1949 have failed to prevent hostilities and deplores the military buildup in the region.[180]

---

[177] *See* Doc. 105.

[178] *See* Docs. 156, 157, and 159.

[179] *See* Doc. 361.

[180] *See* Docs. 93–96.

Johnson also expresses dismay at the withdrawal of the UNEF from the Egypt-Israel armistice demarcation line.

Document 155: Exchange of Letters between Soviet Premier Alexei Kosygin and Israeli Prime Minister Levi Eshkol (May 26–June 1, 1967) [*available at* http://www.mfa.gov.il/MFA/Foreign%20Relations/Israels%20Foreign%20Relations%20since%201947/1947-1974/9%20Exchange%20of%20Letters%20Kosygin-Eshkol-%2026%20May%20and%201]. In this exchange of letters, Soviet Premier Aleksey Kosygin warns Israeli Prime Minister Levi Eshkol that Israel should not attack Syria or Egypt. Kosygin implicitly threatens intervention in such a conflict. In his reply, Eshkol calls on the Soviet Union to use its influence to achieve a lasting peace in the Middle East.

ii. 1967 War (June 5–11, 1967)

Document 156: United Nations Security Council Resolution 233, Concerning the Outbreak of Fighting and Calling for an Immediate Cease-Fire (June 6, 1967) [S.C. Res. 233, U.N. SCOR, 22d Sess., at 2, U.N. Doc. S/INF.22/Rev/2 (1968)]. The Security Council issued Resolution 233 at the outbreak of hostilities between Israel and Egypt, Jordan, Lebanon, and Syria. The resolution calls for an immediate cease-fire.

Document 157: Israel Military Order No. 2 Concerning Quarantine (June 7, 1967) [*reprinted in* Richard T. Drury & Robert C. Winn, Plowshares and Swords: The Economics of Occupation in the West Bank 139–40 (1992)]. With this military order, the commander of the Israeli Defence Forces (IDF) imposed a quarantine on the West Bank effective June 7, 1967, following Israel's occupation of the area. Any person violating the quarantine is to be punished by three years imprisonment.

Document 158: United Nations Security Council Resolution 234, Demanding a Cease-Fire (June 7, 1967) [S.C. Res. 234, U.N. SCOR, 1350th mtg., U.N. Doc. S/RES/234 (1967)]. In Resolution 234, the Security Council demands that all concerned governments should observe a cease-fire as a first step to ending hostilities. Israel announces that it will accept the cease-fire provided that Arab states do likewise. On June 7, the cease-fire goes into effect on the Jordanian front.

Document 159: Egyptian President Gamal Abdel Nasser's Resignation Broadcast (June 9, 1967) [*available at* http://www.usna.edu/Users/history/tucker/hh362/The%20Six-Day%20War.htm]. In this broadcast, President Gamal Abdel Nasser notes the "grave setback" suffered by the armies of the Arab states involved in the war and cites clear evidence of "imperialist collusion" with Israel in the form of American and British military support. Nasser accepts full responsibility for the defeat and announces his resignation from the presidency. He appoints Zakariya Muhiedin to succeed him. The following day, Nasser withdraws his resignation after a major show of public support for him in Egypt and throughout the Arab world.

Document 160: United Nations Security Council Resolution 236, Calling for the Prompt Return to the Cease-Fire Line (June 11, 1967) [S.C. Res. 236, U.N. SCOR, 1357th mtg., U.N. Doc. S/RES/236 (1967)]. In Resolution 235, the Security Council addresses the situation between Israel and Syria, calling for any troops that may have moved forward subsequent to the June 10 cease-fire to promptly return to their cease-fire positions.

iii. Post-War Developments

In the years following the 1967 war a new phase was inaugurated in the struggle for Palestine with Arafat's PLO definitely succeeding in dragging Israel into a total war on a global scale. Defeated and humiliated, the Arab states lost, for the moment, their will to fight the Zionist enemy. The PLO thus became the vanguard of the Arab struggle against the Jewish state. As soon as the war was over, the PLO started to stage guerrilla operations throughout the West Bank and Gaza. In July 1968, a new form of Palestinian terrorism was inaugurated with the hijacking of an El Al jet to Algiers. During the autumn and winter of that same year a car bomb exploded in Jerusalem, Tel-Aviv central bus station was stormed and El Al passengers were the target of a Palestinian terrorist squad at Athens airport. Israel retaliated. In March 1968, it conducted a massive incursion against PLO forces that had been using Jordanian territory for their war against Israel. The battle of Karameh would symbolize the rise of the PLO to prominence. Arafat became now a pan-Arab hero, and his picture occupied the front page of every major newspaper in the West. Jordan served as the battleground between Israel and the PLO until King Hussein ordered his army to break the power of the state within a state which Arafat had created on Jordanian territory. In the ensuing civil war, thousands of Palestinians were killed and many more left the country. The PLO moved now to Lebanon where it again established its own state within a state. Lebanon's territory became Arafat's playground, from which it conducted attacks on Israel, some, like the blowing of a bus packed with school children near Avivim in 1972, and the storming of the school Ma'a lot in 1974, remained carved in the Israelis collective memory to this day.

Document 161: Statement of United Nations Secretary-General U Thant on the 1957 Hammarskjöld Aide Memoire (June 19, 1967) [*reprinted in* 3 THE ARAB ISRAELI CONFLICT 746–49 (John Morton Moore ed., 1974)]. United Nations Secretary-General U Thant issued this statement to clarify the legal status of the 1957 Dag Hammarskjöld *aide memoire* regarding the UNEF in the Sinai.[181] U Thant stresses that the *aide memoire* is not an official United Nations document, but is rather of "a purely private character."

Document 162: Abba Eban's Speech at the General Assembly of the United Nations (June 19, 1967) [*reprinted in* THE ISRAEL-ARAB READER: A DOCUMENTARY HISTORY OF THE MIDDLE EAST CONFLICT (Walter Laqueur & Barry Rubin eds., 2001)]. Following the Six-Day War, Israeli Foreign Minister Abba Eban addressed the Special Assembly at the United Nations. Eban attributed the cause of the conflict to the aggression on Israel's right to exist and that the tension in the Middle East will continue as long as that cause remains. His speech follows with a narrative of the lead up to the Six-Day War from the Israeli perspective and ends with an indictment against the Soviet Union for its interference in Middle Eastern affairs.

---

[181] *See* Doc. 143.

Document 163: Speech by Yitzhak Rabin, Chief of Staff of the IDF: The Right of Israel (June 28, 1967) [*available at* http://www.usna.edu/Users/history/tucker/hh362/The%20Six-Day%20War.htm]. Upon accepting a Doctor of Philosophy from the Hebrew University of Jerusalem, Yitzhak Rabin gave this speech, which recalls his experiences as commander of the IDF. Rabin speaks of the spiritual resources that carried the Israeli army to victory in the recent war. This occasion marks the first time that Israelis could visit the Hebrew University campus (located in East Jerusalem) since the 1948 war.

Document 164: Statement by the President of the Security Council on Stationing United Nations Military Observers in the Suez Canal Sector (July 9, 1967) [U.N. SCOR, 1366th mtg., U.N. Doc. S/8053/Add.3 (1967)]. In this statement, the president of the Security Council determines that the chief of staff of the UNTSO should be requested to work with the United Arab Republic and Israel to station United Nations military observers in the Suez Canal under his supervision.

Document 165: The Yigal Allon Peace Plan (July 26, 1967). [*Documents on Palestine*, vol. 3, p. 91 (Mahdi Abdul Hadi ed., 2007)] Shortly following the 1967 war, Israeli Defense Minister Yigal Allon presented a plan to the Israeli prime minister to address the future of the Occupied Territories. The plan called for a partition of the West Bank that would effectively create a new security border between Israel and Jordan. The plan, however, was not implemented.

Document 166: Resolutions of the Arab Summit Conference (Khartoum Resolutions) (September 1, 1967) [*available at* http://www.yale.edu/lawweb/avalon/mideast/khartoum.htm]. Eight Arab heads of state attended an Arab summit conference in Khartoum, Sudan, from August 29 to September 1, 1967, which resulted in the formation of a common policy that was to underlay the decision making of most Arab states participating in the conflict until the early 1970s. The Khartoum Resolutions call for continued struggle against Israel, the creation of a fund to assist Egypt and Jordan financially, the lifting of an Arab oil boycott against the West, and an agreement to end the war in Yemen. But the most well-known resolutions are the "Three No's," which resolve that Arab states will follow the policy of no peace with Israel, no recognition of Israel, and no negotiations with Israel.

Document 167: United Nations Security Council Resolution 240, Condemning Violations of the Cease-Fire (October 25, 1967) [S.C. Res. 240, U.N. SCOR, 1371st mtg., U.N. Doc. S/RES/240 (1967)]. In Resolution 240, the Security Council condemns violations of the cease-fire without identifying which states had done so.

Document 168: United Nations Security Council Resolution 248, Condemning the Military Action Launched by Israel in Violation of the Cease-Fire Resolutions (March 24, 1968) [S.C. Res. 248, U.N. SCOR, 1407th mtg., U.N. Doc. S/RES/248 (1968)]. In Resolution 248, the Security Council observes that the military action by Israel against Jordan was both of a large scale and carefully planned. It condemns that action as a violation of the United Nations. Charter and cease-fires.

Document 169: United Nations Security Council Resolution 256, Condemning Massive Air Attacks by Israel on Jordanian Territory (August 16, 1968) [S.C. Res. 256, U.N. SCOR, 1440th mtg., U.N. Doc. S/RES/256 (1968)]. In Resolution 256, the Security

Council deplores the loss of life and heavy damage to property resulting from both massive air attacks by Israel on Jordanian territory and condemns the further military attacks by Israel in violation of the United Nations Charter and Security Council Resolution 248.[182]

Document 170: United Nations Security Council Resolution 258, Insisting on Respect for the Cease-Fire and Urging Cooperation with the Secretary-General's Special Representative (September 18, 1968) [S.C. Res. 258, U.N. SCOR, 1452d mtg., U.N. Doc. S/RES/258 (1968)]. In Resolution 258, the Security Council, gravely concerned about the deteriorating situation in the Middle East, insists that the cease-fire ordered by the Security Council in its resolutions be rigorously respected. Reaffirming United Nations Security Council Resolution 242, it urges all parties to extend full cooperation to the Special Representative of the Secretary-General in the fulfillment of the mandate entrusted to him under that resolution.[183]

Document 171: United Nations Security Council Resolution 262, Condemning the Israeli Attack on the International Airport of Beirut (December 31, 1968) [S.C. Res. 262, U.N. SCOR, 1462d mtg., U.N. Doc. S/RES/262 (1968)]. In Resolution 262, the Security Council observes that that the military action by Israeli forces against the International Airport of Beirut was premeditated, of a large scale, and of a carefully planned nature. The Security Council considers that Lebanon is entitled to appropriate redress for the violation.

Document 172: The Seven Points Declaration passed by the Central Committee of Fatah (January 1969) [*reprinted in* THE ISRAEL-ARAB READER: A DOCUMENTARY HISTORY OF THE MIDDLE EAST CONFLICT (Walter Laqueur & Barry Rubin 2001)]. Following the merging of the PLO and Fatah, the Central Committee of Fatah published a seven-point manifesto declaring its intentions. The points focus on the struggle against Israel and the intent to achieve self-determination for the Palestinian people.

Document 173: United Nations Security Council Resolution 265, Condemning the Recent Premeditated Air Attacks Launched by Israel on Jordanian Villages (April 1, 1969) [S.C. Res. 265, U.N. SCOR, 1473d mtg., U.N. Doc. S/RES/265 (1969)]. In Resolution 265, the Security Council expresses deep concern that recent air attacks on Jordanian villages and other populated areas are of a pre-planned nature and warns that if such attacks are repeated, it will have to consider further and more effective steps to curb such actions.

Document 174: United Nations Security Council Resolution 270, Condemning Israeli Air Attack on Villages in Southern Lebanon (August 26, 1969) [S.C. Res. 270, U.N. SCOR, 1504th mtg., U.N. Doc. S/RES/270 (1969)]. In Resolution 270, the Security Council condemns the premeditated air attack by Israel on villages in southern Lebanon in violation of its obligations under the United Nations Charter and previous Security Council resolutions.[184] The Security Council deplores all violent incidents in violation of the cease-fire and the extension of the area of fighting.

---

[182] *See generally* U. N. CHARTER, *available at* http://www.un.org/aboutun/charter/; *see also* Doc. 161.

[183] *See* Doc. 268.

[184] *See generally* U. N. CHARTER, *available at* http://www.un.org/aboutun/charter/; *see also* Doc. 276.

Document 175: United Nations Security Council Resolution 279, Demanding the Immediate Withdrawal of All Israeli Armed Forces from Lebanese Territory (May 12, 1970) [S.C. Res. 279, U.N. SCOR, U.N. Doc. S/RES/279 (1970)]. In this single-sentence resolution, the Security Council demands that Israeli armed forces immediately withdraw from Lebanese territory.

Document 176: United Nations Security Council Resolution 280, Condemning the Large-Scale and Premeditated Military Attack by Israel against Lebanon (May 19, 1970) [S.C. Res. 280, U.N. SCOR, 1542d mtg., U.N. Doc. S/RES/280 (1970)]. In Resolution 280, the Security Council condemns Israel for its attack on Lebanon and declares that if Israel repeats such armed attacks, the Security Council will consider further steps to give effect to its decisions.

Document 177: Cease-Fire Agreement between Israel and the United Arab Republic (August 7, 1970) [U.N. GAOR, 1851st mtg., at 66, U.N. Doc. A/PV 1851 (1970)]. This agreement between Israel and the United Arab Republic draws a cease-fire line to be effective immediately. Both sides agree to abide by the Geneva Convention of 1949 relative to the treatment of prisoners of war and to accept the assistance of the International Committee of the Red Cross (ICRC) in carrying out their obligations under that convention.[185]

Document 178: United Nations Security Council Resolution 285, Demanding Withdrawal of Israeli Armed Forces from Lebanon (September 5, 1970) [S.C. Res. 285, U.N. SCOR, 1551st mtg., U.N. Doc. S/RES/285 (1970)]. This one-sentence resolution demands the complete and immediate withdrawal of all Israeli armed forces from Lebanese territory.

Document 179: United Nations Security Council Resolution 286, Appealing to States to Take Steps to Prevent Hijackings (September 9, 1970) [S.C. Res. 286, U.N. SCOR, 1552d mtg., U.N. Doc. S/RES/286 (1970)]. In Resolution 286, the Security Council appeals to all parties for the immediate release of all passengers and crew held as a result of hijackings and calls on states to take all possible legal steps to prevent future hijackings.

Document 180: United Nations General Assembly Resolution 2645, Aerial Hijacking or Interference with Civil Air Travel (November 25, 1970) [G.A. Res. 2645, U.N. GAOR, 1920th plen. mtg., U.N. Doc. 2645 (XXV) (1970)]. In Resolution 2645, the General Assembly condemns all acts of aerial hijacking and calls upon states to take appropriate measures to deter such acts. The General Assembly also calls upon states to make every effort to adopt a convention on the unlawful seizure of aircraft.

Document 181: United Nations General Assembly Resolution 2628, Calling for Talks under the Auspices of the Secretary-General's Special Representative with a View to Implementing Resolution 242 (November 4, 1970) [G.A. Res. 2628, U.N. GAOR, 1896th plen. mtg., U.N. Doc. A/RES/2628 (1970)]. In Resolution 2628, the General Assembly

---

[185] *See generally* Geneva Convention Relative to the Treatment of Prisoners of War (Third Geneva Convention), *opened for signature* Aug. 12, 1949, 6 U.S.T. 3316, 75 U.N.T.S. 135 (entered into force Oct. 21, 1950), *available at* http://www.unhchr.ch/html/menu3/b/91.htm.

calls for talks to be held under the auspices of the Secretary-General's special representative with a view to implementing Security Council Resolution 242.[186]

Document 182: Report by United Nations Secretary-General U Thant on the Activities of the Special Representative to the Middle East, Gunnar V. Jarring (January 4, 1971) [U.N. SCOR, U.N. Doc. S/10070 (1971)]. In this report, United Nations Secretary-General U Thant describes the activities of Ambassador Gunnar V. Jarring, the newly appointed special representative to handle negotiations and diplomatic relations in the Middle East on behalf of the United Nations. The Secretary-General reports that Jarring had been in consultation with the representatives of Israel, Jordan, Lebanon, and the United Arab Republic[187] on the subject of the implementation of Security Council Resolution 242.[188] Syria, having rejected the resolution, is not involved in discussions. Annexes I and II are letters to Jarring from the concerned states presenting their unique positions on the subject.

Document 183: United Nations Security Council Resolution S/10070/Add.1, Further Report by the Secretary-General on the Activities of the Special Representative to the Middle East (February 1, 1971) [U.N. SCOR, U.N. Doc. S/10070/Add.1 (1967)]. This report by United Nations Secretary-General U Thant notes Ambassador Jarring's discussions with the involved parties and expresses the Secretary-General's optimism that the parties have resumed negotiations and progress has been made.

Document 184: Aide Memoire to Israel and the United Arab Republic by the United Nations Special Representative to the Middle East, Gunnar V. Jarring (February 8, 1971) [U.N. SCOR, Annex I, U.N. Doc. S/10403 (1971)]. In this report, Ambassador Gunnar V. Jarring, the United Nations Special Representative to the Middle East, concludes that the only possibility for breaking the deadlock between Israel and the United Arab Republic is to seek from each side parallel and simultaneous commitments that seem to be inevitable prerequisites of an eventual peace settlement. Jarring outlines the necessary steps to be taken by each side in order to proceed with negotiations.

Document 185: Reply of the United Arab Republic to the Jarring Aide Memoire (February 15, 1971) [*available at* http://domino.un.org/unispal.nsf/0/ab4e84c20927cc8185256a780064642f?OpenDocument]. This response from the United Arab Republic to the Jarring *aide memoire* emphasizes the need for the concerned parties to implement Security Council Resolution 242, which calls upon Israel to withdraw from the Sinai and the Gaza Strip immediately.[189]

Document 186: Reply of Israel to the Jarring Aide Memoire (February 26, 1971) [U.N. SCOR, Annex II, U.N. Doc. S/10403 (1971)]. In this response, Israel outlines provisions for a peace agreement with the United Arab Republic, without referencing Security Council Resolution 242.[190] Israel agrees to negotiate on the issue of refugees, but does not address the issue of withdrawing from the territories it has occupied.

---

[186] *See* Doc. 268.

[187] Despite the withdrawal of Syria from the binational United Arab Republic in 1961, Egypt continued to use the name until the death of Nasser in 1971.

[188] *See* Doc. 268.

[189] *Id.*

[190] *Id.*

Document 187: United Nations Security Council Resolution 313, Demanding that Israel Desist from All Military Action against Lebanon (February 28, 1972) [S.C. Res. 313, U.N. SCOR, 1644th mtg., U.N. Doc. S/RES/313 (1972)]. In this one-sentence resolution, the Security Council demands that Israel immediately desist and refrain from any ground and air military action against Lebanon and withdraw all its military forces from Lebanese territory.

Document 188: Consensus of the Members of the Security Council Concerning the Increase of the Number of Military Observers in the Lebanese-Israeli Sector (April 19, 1972) [U.N. SCOR, U.N. Doc. S/10611 (1972)]. In place of a formal meeting of the Security Council, which was considered unnecessary in this instance, the members of the Security Council issued this consensus on how to respond to the Lebanese government's request for additional United Nations observers to be stationed in the Israel-Lebanon sector. The Security Council president had informed the Secretary-General on March 31 that it was the members' view that the request should be met. In this consensus, the members of the Security Council invite the Secretary-General to consult with the Lebanese authorities on the implementation of these arrangements.

Document 189: United Nations Security Council Resolution 316, Calling for the Immediate Release of All Syrian and Lebanese Military Personnel Held by Israel (June 26, 1972) [S.C. Res. 316, U.N. SCOR, 1650th mtg., U.N. Doc. S/RES/316 (1972)]. In Resolution 316, the Security Council condemns all acts of violence and the repeated attacks of Israeli forces on Lebanese territory and population in violation of the principles of the United Nations Charter.[191] The Security Council expresses the strong desire that all Syrian and Lebanese military and security personnel abducted by Israeli armed forces on June 21, 1972, on Lebanese territory be released as soon as possible. In the event that such personnel are not released, the Security Council resolves to reconvene.

Document 190: United Nations Security Council Resolution 317, Deploring that Israel Has Not Released Abducted Syrian and Lebanese Military and Security Personnel (July 21, 1972) [S.C. Res. 317, U.N. SCOR, 1653d mtg., U.N. Doc. S/RES/317 (1972)]. In Resolution 317, the Security Council, deploring that Israel had not released Syrian and Lebanese military and security personnel abducted from Lebanese territory, calls upon Israel to return them without delay.[192]

Document 191: United Nations General Assembly Resolution 2949, Declaring Changes Carried Out by Israel in the Occupied Arab Territories Null and Void (December 8, 1972) [G.A. Res. 2949, U.N. GAOR, 2105th plen. mtg., U.N. Doc. A/RES/2429 (1972)]. In Resolution 2949, the General Assembly reaffirms that the territory of a state shall not be the object of occupation or acquisition by another state resulting from the threat or use of force. The General Assembly affirms that changes in the physical character or demographic composition of Occupied Territories are contrary to the purposes and principles of the Charter of the United Nations.[193]

---

[191] *See generally* U.N. CHARTER, *available at* http://www.un.org/aboutun/charter/.

[192] *See* Doc. 189.

[193] *See generally* U. N. CHARTER, *available at* http://www.un.org/aboutun/charter/.

D. *Yom Kippur War/Ramadan War/October War: 1973*[194]

The 1973 war began on October 6, 1973, with Egypt and Syria launching a surprise attack against Israel on the Jewish high holiday of Yom Kippur.[195] The holiday was strategically chosen as most Israeli soldiers would be engaged in religious observance and/or on leave from their military positions. In messages to the United States, Egyptian President Anwar al-Sadat explained that this war was not aimed at destroying Israel itself, but at driving Israel back to its pre-1967 position.

The bulk of combat was fought in the Suez Canal in the south and in the Golan Heights in the north between Israel and Egyptian-Syrian forces, with at least ten other Arab states symbolically aiding in the war effort with personnel, military equipment, or financial support.[196] Some Palestinian Arabs fought with the Egyptian-Syrian forces and shelled Israeli towns from Lebanon.

Initially, Israeli aircraft and tanks were destroyed at a high rate. By October 9, Israel grew increasingly concerned that the Arab armies would cross the 1967 borders in an attempt to destroy the state. Fearing that Israel might resort to using nuclear weapons to end the war, U.S. President Richard M. Nixon and Secretary of State Henry Kissinger decided that they could not refuse to provide assistance to Israel for defense. On October 14, the first American Galaxy transport aircraft arrived with supplies for Israel and other U.S. planes delivered military assistance to Israel in the Sinai.[197] This turned the tide of the war, as Israel broke through Egyptian positions in the Sinai.

On October 16, Israeli forces, under the command of General Ariel Sharon, crossed the Suez Canal and advanced south toward the City of Suez. That operation, in an area of the canal called the "*Deversoir*" (spillway), cut the supply line to Egypt's Third Army, east of the canal, while Sharon's division was behind it. This untenable situation precipitated Egypt's acceptance of a cease-fire agreement mediated by Kissinger, whereby both Egypt and Israel could claim victory and, thus, no one side was deemed defeated.

On the economic front, the Organization of Arab Petroleum Exporting Countries (OAPEC) announced on October 17 that it would reduce its

---

[194] This war is known in Israel as the Yom Kippur War and in the Arab world as the Ramadan War or the October War.

[195] Yom Kippur, "the Day of Atonement," is arguably the holiest day of the Jewish year. Most of the holiday is spent in the synagogue in prayer.

[196] Arab states included Algeria, Iraq, Jordan, Kuwait, Lebanon, Libya, Morocco, Saudi Arabia, Sudan, and Tunisia.

[197] *See* T.G. Fraser, The Arab-Israeli Conflict 99–101 (T.G. Fraser & J.O. Springhall eds., 1995).

oil production until Israel withdrew from the Arab territories occupied during the 1967 war. This was followed by a total oil embargo on the United States and the Netherlands. The prevailing Cold War atmosphere also complicated the war. Because the Soviet Union backed the Arab states and the United States backed Israel, it became increasingly possible that the two superpowers would clash over the Middle East.

Both Israel and Egypt accepted the United Nations cease-fire agreement laid out in Security Council Resolution 338 on October 22, but it was soon broken.[198] On October 23, the Security Council adopted Resolution 339, which confirms Resolution 338 and calls for the dispatch of United Nations observers to supervise a cease-fire.[199] Within two days, the Security Council established a UNEF, and on October 27, fighting officially ended. The primary lesson for Israel was Egypt's success in crossing the Suez Canal and briefly defeating Israeli forces.[200]

It is important to note that the United Nations issued virtually no formal resolutions or reports on the situation during the course of hostilities. The first United Nations decision to address the war, Security Council Resolution 338, was passed only when it was apparent that Egypt's offensive was stopped and Israel had moved its military from the defensive to the offensive. In adopting this strategy, the United Nations tacitly confirmed Egypt and Syria's right to reclaim their territories from Israel. More importantly, the Security Council wanted to avoid a confrontation between the United States and the USSR, and to reduce the tensions in the Middle East between the two superpowers.

i. Pre-War Developments

Document 192: United Nations Security Council Resolution 331, Requesting the Secretary-General to Submit a Comprehensive Report on the Efforts of the United Nations Pertaining to the Middle East Situation since June 1967 (April 20, 1973) [S.C. Res. 331, U.N. SCOR, 1710th mtg., U.N. Doc. S/RES/331 (1973)]. In Resolution 331, the Security Council requests a report from the Secretary-General with a full account of the efforts undertaken by the United Nations with regard to the Arab-Israeli conflict since June 1967. It also invites Mr. Gunnar Jarring, the special representative of the Secretary-General, to render assistance to the Security Council in the course of deliberations.

Document 193: United Nations Security Council Resolution 332, Condemning the Repeated Military Attacks Conducted by Israel against Lebanon (April 21, 1973) [S.C. Res. 332, U.N. SCOR, 1711th mtg., U.N. Doc. S/RES/332 (1973)]. In Resolution 332, the Security Council condemns the repeated military attacks conducted by Israel against Lebanon that result in the loss of life of innocent individuals.

---

198 *See* Doc. 288.

199 *See* Doc. 198.

200 *See* Doc. 200.

Document 194: Excerpts from the Report of the Secretary-General under Security Council Resolution 331 (May 18, 1973) [U.N. SCOR, U.N. Doc. S/10929 (1973)]. In compliance with Resolution 331, Secretary-General Kurt Waldheim submitted this report on United Nations efforts with regard to the Arab-Israeli conflict since June 1967.[201] The Secretary-General highlights the presence of monitors as a means of maintaining cease-fire agreements and notes the difficulty of implementing Security Council resolutions that address the monitoring of human rights abuses, the status of Jerusalem, and the problem of Palestinian refugees. The Secretary-General cites the lack of cooperation from both parties as a source of difficulty and hopes that over time the Security Council will be willing to once again consider the problem as a whole in order to find a way to implement a just and lasting settlement.

Document 195: U.S.-Vetoed Security Council Draft Resolution S/10974, First U.S. Veto of a Security Council Resolution Criticizing the Israeli Occupation (July 24, 1973) [S.C. Draft Res. S/10974, U.N. SCOR, U.N. Doc. S/10974 (1973)]. This vetoed draft resolution reiterates many of the statements and demands made in Security Council Resolution 242 (1967).[202] That it is the first resolution criticizing Israel to be vetoed by the United States is of particular historical interest.

Document 196: United Nations Security Council Resolution 337, Condemning Israel for Violating Lebanon's Sovereignty (August 15, 1973) [S.C. Res. 337, U.N. SCOR, 1740th mtg., U.N. Doc. S/RES/337 (1973)]. After receiving a report from Lebanon concerning the hijacking of a Lebanese civilian airliner on lease to Iraqi Airways by the Israeli air force, the Security Council, in Resolution 337, condemns Israel for the violation of Lebanon's sovereignty and territorial integrity and for the seizure. The Security Council considers these actions a violation of the Lebanese-Israeli Armistice Agreement of 1949 and the 1967 cease-fire resolutions.[203]

ii. 1973 War (October 6–24, 1973)

Document 197: Vetoed Security Council Draft Resolution S/11036, Calling upon All Parties to Cease All Firing and Terminate All Military Activity (October 21, 1973) [S.C. Draft Res. S/11036, U.N. SCOR, U.N. Doc. S/11036 (1973)]. This draft Security Council resolution, presented by the USSR and the United States, would have been the first United Nations resolution passed after fighting broke out in the 1973 war. It calls upon parties to immediately terminate all military activity—and, subsequent to that, to start implementing Security Council Resolution 242. It also decides that peace negotiations should start under appropriate auspices concurrently with the cease-fire.

Document 198: United Nations Security Council Resolution 339, Confirming Resolution 338 and Requesting the Dispatch of United Nations Observers to Supervise the Cease-Fire (October 23, 1973) [S.C. Res. 339, U.N. SCOR, 1748th mtg., U.N. Doc. S/RES/339 (1973)]. In Resolution 339, the Security Council confirms the cease-fire order of Security Council Resolution 338 and requests that United Nations observers be dispatched to monitor the truce between Israel and Egypt.

---

201 *See* Doc. 191.
202 *See* Doc. 289.
203 *See* Doc. 94.

Document 199: Speech by Israeli Prime Minister Golda Meier to the Knesset Regarding Israel's Acceptance of the Cease-Fire (October 23, 1973) [*available at* http://www.mfa.gov.il/nr/exeres/698608ed-49a0-4bd0-9c24-75b96b054c39.htm]. Prime Minister Golda Meir gave this statement before the Knesset the day after Israel and Egypt accepted a United Nations cease-fire, explaining Israel's reasons for doing so.

Document 200: United Nations Security Council Resolution 340, Deciding to Set Up a UNEF (October 25, 1973) [S.C. Res. 340, U.N. SCOR, U.N. Doc. S/RES/340 (1973)]. In Resolution 340, the Security Council, reiterating that the cease-fire is being continually violated, orders further military observers to be dispatched on both sides of the cease-fire line and decides to set up a UNEF.

Document 201: United Nations Security Council Resolution 341, Establishing a UNEF for Six Months (October 27, 1973) [S.C. Res. 341, U.N. SCOR, 1752d mtg., U.N. Doc. S/RES/341 (1973)]. In Resolution 341, the Security Council decides to establish a UNEF for six months, then for a longer period if necessary, in accordance with the Secretary-General's report on implementation of Security Council Resolution 340.

Document 202: Declaration of the European Community on the Middle East (November 6, 1973) [*reprinted in* 3 The Arab Israeli Conflict 1147–48 (John Morton Moore ed., 1974)]. In this statement, nine members of the European Community strongly urge both sides of the conflict to return to their previous positions in accordance with Security Council Resolutions 339 and 340.[204] The European Community also emphasizes the necessity of implementing Security Council Resolutions 242 and 338 if a permanent peace settlement is to be reached.[205]

Document 203: Cease-Fire Agreement between Israel and Egypt (November 11, 1973) [U.N. SCOR, U.N. Doc. S/11056 (1973)]. Israeli and Egyptian military representatives signed this cease-fire agreement at kilometer marker 101 on the Cairo-Suez road in the presence of the interim Force Commander of the UNEF. The agreement covers such topics as the return to the October 22 borders, humanitarian aid for the town of Suez, the transfer of the checkpoints on the Cairo-Suez road from Israeli control to UNEF control, and the exchange of prisoners of war.

iii. Post-War Developments

Document 204: Declaration of the Arab Summit Conference, Algiers (November 29, 1973) [*available at* http://www.us-israel.org/jsource/History/arabsum73.html]. The Arab Summit Conference issued this declaration, which states that the Egypt-Israel cease-fire agreement will only lead to peace when Israel evacuates all the occupied Arab territories and when Palestinians achieve full national rights. The conference also produced a set of secret resolutions that detail the military, economic, and political tools to be implemented by members in order to achieve the aims of the conference. These include the use of an oil embargo to strengthen support for the Arab cause.

Document 205: Separation of Forces Agreement between Israel and Egypt (January 18, 1974) [U.N. Doc. S/1198/Rev. 1/Add. 1 (1974)]. This separation of forces agreement

---

[204] *See* Docs. 198 and 200.

[205] *See* Docs. 289 and 293.

between Israel and Egypt defines demarcation lines, zones of disengagement, and the interpretive role of the UNEF. The implementation of the agreement is left to be worked out by Egyptian and Israeli military representatives, who will agree on the stages of the process. It is emphasized that the agreement does not constitute a final peace agreement, but represents a first step toward establishing peace according to the provisions of Security Council Resolution 338.

Document 206: United Nations Security Council Resolution 346, Extending the Mandate of the UNEF for a Further Six Months (April 8, 1974) [S.C. Res. 346, U.N. SCOR, 1765th mtg., U.N. Doc. S/RES/346 (1974)]. In Resolution 346, the Security Council decides to extend the mandate of the UNEF for another six months, viewing the Emergency Force as essential not only for the maintenance of quiet in the Egypt-Israel sector but also to assist if required in efforts for the establishment of a just and durable peace in the Middle East.

Document 207: Interim Report Issued by the Agranat Commission of Inquiry (April 1974) [*reprinted in* ARAB-ISRAELI CONFLICT AND CONCILIATION: A DOCUMENTARY HISTORY (Bernard Reich ed., 1995)]. This report is written by the five member Commission of Inquiry set up by the Israeli government to investigate and report to the cabinet on the matters of the enemy's intentions and decisions preceding the Yom Kippur War, the IDF's preparation preceding the war, and the IDF's actions to contain the enemy. The members of this commission were Supreme Court Chief Justice Shimon Agranat, Supreme Court Justice Moshe Landau, State Comptroller Yitzhak Nebenzahl, and former chiefs of staff of the IDF, Yagael Yadin and Haim Laskov. Their final report was released to the public in January of 1995.

The interim report primarily places the blame of misevaluations in the hours preceding the surprise attack from Egypt and Syria on the Director of Military Intelligence (DMI), who expected the attack to commence later in the day. The DMI and the Research Division of the Intelligence Branch also did not correctly evaluate warnings in the days preceding the war, falsely assuming that Egypt and Syria would not attack unless Egypt had sufficient air power against the Israeli air force. The conception that Egypt and Syria were incapable of starting total war resulted in troops not being mobilized properly and the reserves not called early enough.

The report maintains that among the three authorities that deal with security matters, the government and prime minister, the minister of defense, and the chief of staff who heads the IDF, there is no clear division of authority and responsibilities. This creates problems in the field of security, and impedes effectiveness of work. In the case of the Yom Kippur War, the General Staff's Intelligence Branch was detrimentally the only evaluation of the situation. The report finally concludes that despite the drawbacks, the IDF triumphed successfully against one of the most difficult confrontations an army can face.

Document 208: Report by the Agranat Commission (1974) [*reprinted in* THE ISRAEL-ARAB READER: A DOCUMENTARY HISTORY OF THE MIDDLE EAST CONFLICT (Walter Laqueur & Barry Rubin eds., 2001)]. The Israeli government appointed the Agranat Commission to investigate what led to the Yom Kippur War and the failures and successes seen during the conflict. It reports on disciplinary issues, the inability to read the progress of the battle, and how the failings of field intelligence resulted in unpreparedness for the surprise attack,

Document 209: Two-Phased Plan Issued by the PLO (June 1974) [*reprinted in* ARAB-ISRAELI CONFLICT AND CONCILIATION: A DOCUMENTARY HISTORY (Bernard Reich ed., 1995)]. After the Yom Kippur War, the PLO adopted a program to recover the national rights of Palestinians in order to establish a just and lasting peace. The Palestinian National Council stated that it would not accept Resolution 242, which treats their issues as a problem of refugees and ignores the national right of the people. The plan states that to establish the democratic Palestinian state, the PLO should work to liberate Palestinian territories by any means, including armed struggle. A national authority can thus be created over all of the liberated Palestinian land. In order achieve these national duties, the PLO should work to increase national unity and solidarity with other forces of liberation around the world to thwart the aims of Zionism and imperialism. In two stages, the PLO first wishes to create the Palestinian state in territory that is not occupied by Israel and then proceed with the military attack to gain back their land that is in Israel's control.

Document 210: United Nations Security Council Resolution 347, Condemning Israel for Violating Lebanon's Territorial Integrity (April 24, 1974) [S.C. Res. 347, U.N. SCOR, 1769th mtg., U.N. Doc. S/RES/347 (1974)]. The Security Council, in Resolution 347, condemns Israel's violation of Lebanon's territorial integrity and sovereignty and calls once more upon the government of Israel to refrain from further military actions and threats against Lebanon. It also calls upon Israel to release and return abducted Lebanese civilians to Lebanon.

Document 211: Separation of Forces Agreement between Israel and Syria (May 31, 1974) [U.N. Doc. S/11302/Add.1/Annex 1 (1974)]. Like the agreement between Israel and Egypt,[206] this separation of forces agreement between Israel and Syria defines demarcation lines, zones of disengagement, and the interpretive role of the UNEF. It allows for the exchange of wounded soldiers, as well as the exchange of the bodies of dead soldiers. It emphasizes that the agreement does not constitute a final peace agreement, but represents a first step toward establishing peace on the basis of Security Council Resolution 338.

Document 212: United Nations Security Council Resolution 350, Welcoming the Agreement on Disengagement between Israeli and Syrian Forces and Establishing the United Nations Disengagement Observer Force (May 31, 1974) [S.C. Res. 350, U.N. SCOR, 1774th mtg., U.N. Doc. S/RES/350 (1974)]. In Resolution 350, the Security Council welcomes the Israeli-Syrian Agreement on Disengagement[207] negotiated as part of the implementation of Security Council Resolution 338. The Security Council decides to set up a disengagement observer force for an initial period of six months, subject to renewal.

Document 213: Seventh Arab League Summit Conference, Resolution on Palestine, Rabat, *Morocco (October 28, 1974)* [*available at* http://www.mondediplo.com/focus/mideast/rabat74-en]. In this resolution, members of the League of Arab States

---

[206] *See* Doc. 205.

[207] *See* Doc. 211.

agree to use their collective resources to strengthen the Palestinian national entity in support of Palestinian sovereignty and national rights, despite the Israeli occupation and disenfranchisement. The Arab League agrees to five resolutions that outline this commitment, including to support the PLO in the exercise of its responsibility at the national and international levels. This resolution was issued two weeks after the United Nations General Assembly voted to acknowledge the PLO as the valid representative of the Palestinian people and invited its participation in the General Assembly on the Question of Palestine in plenary meetings.[208]

Document 214: U.S. Senate Resolution 214, Expressing Concern over Attempts to Expel Israel from the United Nations (July 18, 1975) [S. Res. 214, 94th Cong., 1st Sess. (July 18, 1975)]. Expressing concern over attempts to expel Israel from the United Nations, the U.S. Senate resolves in this Senate resolution that if such a measure is carried out, it will review all U.S. commitments to third world nations involved in the expulsion and consider the implication of continued membership in the United Nations.

Document 215: Memorandum of Understanding between Israel and the United States (September 1, 1975) [*available at* http://www.mfa.gov.il/MFA/Foreign%20Relations/Israels%20Foreign%20Relations%20since%201947/1974-1977/112%20Israel-United%20States%20Memorandum%20of%20Understandi]. In this memorandum of understanding, the United States pledges its assistance and support to Israel as a firm ally. The United States vows to make every effort to be responsive to Israel's military, energy, and economic needs within the limits of its resources and congressional authorization and appropriation. This memorandum was released on the same day as the interim agreement between Israel and Egypt was signed.[209]

Document 216: United Nations General Assembly Resolution 3379, Calling for the Elimination of All Forms of Racial Discrimination (November 10, 1975) [U.N. Doc. A/RES/3379 (1975)]. In Resolution 3379, the General Assembly determines that Zionism is a form of racism and racial discrimination, noting several relevant decisions by international bodies, including Resolution 77 (XII) of the Assembly of Heads of State and Government of the Organization of African Unity.

Document 217: Address by Israeli Ambassador to the United Nations Chaim Herzog to the General Assembly of the United Nations in Response to Zionism Is Racism Resolution (November 10, 1975) [*available at* http://www.jewishvirtuallibrary.org/jsource/UN/herzogsp.html]. Ambassador Herzog's speech draws the attention of the international community to the fact that the U.N. resolution comes on the thirty-seventh anniversary of Kristallnacht, the night that marked the beginning of the destruction of Germany's Jewry by Hitler. He defines the U.N. resolution as sheer anti-Semitism, and the General Assembly as stage where Hitler would have felt at home. Hatred and ignorance, the ambassador explains, is what stand behind this resolution, and he accuses its promoters for subverting U.N. institutions so that a resolution that was initially conceived as a condemnation of racism and colonialism turned, thanks to an automatic majority, into a contemptuous maneuver against Zionism. In his description of the history of Zionism, Ambassador Herzog points out at the support it had in the past from the Soviet Union, the same which now

---

[208] *See* Doc. 608.

[209] *See* Doc. 302.

leads this coalition of hatred and ignorance to a crusade against Zionism. He wonders how countries in the Soviet block and in the Arab world, where human rights are trampled daily and minorities are suppressed, dare talk of racism against a country, Israel, whose treatment of its Arab minority, however imperfect, is an example of co-existence. The issue is then, neither Zionism nor Israel. The issue is the fate of the United Nations that, by producing a resolution based on falsehood and arrogance, one that is devoid of any moral or legal value, has been dragged to its lowest point of discredit by a coalition of despots and racists.

Document 218: Basic Law of the State of Israel: The Army (March 31, 1976) [30 LSI 150 (1975–76)]. This Basic Law of the State of Israel passed by the Knesset defines the army of the State of Israel, its subordination to civil authority, and the power of the Chief of the General Staff in relation to the Minister of Defence.

Document 219: United Nations General Assembly Resolution 31/62, Peace Conference on the Middle East (December 9, 1976) [G.A. Res. 31/62, U.N. GAOR, U.N. Doc. A/RES/31/62 (1976)]. Gravely concerned at the lack of progress towards the achievement of peace in the Middle East, the General Assembly passed Resolution 31/62, requesting that the Secretary-General resume contacts with all parties to the conflict and the co-chairmen of the peace conference on the Middle East. It calls for the early convening of the peace conference under the auspices of the United Nations and the co-chairmanship of the Soviet Union and the United States, no later than the end of March 1977.

Document 220: Law of the State of Israel: No. 16 Emergency Regulations (Judea and Samaria, Gaza Region, Golan Heights, Sinai and Southern Sinai–Criminal Jurisdiction and Legal Assistance) Law (December 28, 1977) [32 LSI 58 (1977–78)]. The Knesset passed this law, extending the emergency regulations for another two years (until December 31, 1979). It defines the emergency regulations' area of jurisdiction as Judea and Samaria, the Gaza Region, the Golan Heights, and Sinai and Southern Sinai.

Document 221: Speech by Israeli Prime Minister Menachem Begin to the Knesset: Autonomy Plan for the West Bank and Gaza Strip (December 28, 1977) [*available at* http://www.knesset.gov.il/process/docs/autonomy1977_eng.htm]. In this speech to the Knesset, Prime Minister Menachem Begin announces that the military government in Judea, Samaria, and Gaza will be abolished and replaced by an administrative council consisting of eleven elected members to be based in Bethlehem. Begin also announces that residents of Judea, Samaria, and the Gaza district will be granted free choice of either Israeli or Jordanian citizenship and will be granted rights according to the laws of each state. Additionally, the prime minister reasserts Israel's claim of sovereignty over Judea, Samaria, and the Gaza region. In the knowledge that other claims exist, however, it proposes that the question of sovereignty in these areas be left open for the sake of peace. Begin also advocates the drawing of a proposal that would guarantee freedom of access to all Holy Places in Jerusalem.

Document 222: Statement by the Government of Israel on the Bombing of the Iraqi Nuclear Facility (June 8, 1981) [*available at* http://www.mfa.gov.il/MFA/Foreign%20Relations/Israels%20Foreign%20Relations%20since%201947/1981-1982/26%20Statement%20by%20the%20Government%20of%20Israel%20on%20the%20Bo]. In this statement, the Israeli government announces that reliable sources had informed Israel that the "Ossirac" reactor outside of Baghdad was designed to produce atomic weapons intended for use against Israel. Israel states that it was compelled to strike before such weapons were created.

Document 223: United Nations Security Council Resolution 487, Condemning Israeli Air Attack on Iraqi Nuclear Installations (June 19, 1981) [S.C. Res 487, U.N. SCOR, 2288th mtg., U.N. Doc. S/RES/487 (1981)]. Noting that Iraq was a member of the Treaty on the Non-Proliferation of Nuclear Weapons[210] and that Israel had not adhered to that treaty, the Security Council condemns the Israeli attack on the Iraqi nuclear installation as a violation of the United Nations Charter.[211] The Security Council finds the attack to be a serious threat to International Atomic Energy Agency (IAEA) safeguards. It also recognizes the right of Iraq to develop nuclear programs for peaceful purposes and considers that Iraq is entitled to redress from Israel.

Document 224: Memorandum of Understanding between Israel and the United States on Strategic Cooperation (November 30, 1981) [*available at* http://www.mfa.gov.il/MFA/Peace+Process/Guide+to+the+Peace+Process/US-Israel+Memorandum+of+Understanding.htm]. In this memorandum, Israel and the United States agree to protect their mutual interests. They also recognize the need to enhance their strategic cooperation in order to deter Soviet threats to the Middle East.

Document 225: Law of the State of Israel: The Golan Heights (December 14, 1981) [36 LSI 7 (1981–82)]. With this law, Israel extends its jurisdiction and administration to the Golan Heights, which was seized from Syria and occupied during the 1967 war.

Document 226: United Nations Security Council Resolution 497, Israeli Decision to Impose Its Laws, Jurisdiction, and Administration in the Occupied Syrian Golan Heights Is Null and Void (December 17, 1981) [S.C. Res. 497, U.N. SCOR, 2319th mtg., U.N. Doc. S/RES/497 (1981)]. In Resolution 497, the Security Council determines that the Israeli decision to impose its laws, jurisdiction, and administration in the occupied Syrian Golan Heights is null and void and without international legal effect and demands that Israel rescind its decision.[212] The Security Council further requests that the Secretary-General report on the implementation of this resolution within two weeks and decides that in the event of non-compliance the Security Council will meet urgently, and not later than January 5, 1982, to consider taking appropriate measures in accordance with the United Nations Charter.[213]

E. Lebanon War: 1978–2007

On March 11, 1978, a terrorist attack against two Israeli buses near Tel-Aviv by Palestinian groups based in Lebanon killed thirty-seven Israelis and injured an additional seventy-six. In response, the IDF launched a

---

[210] Treaty on the Non-Proliferation of Nuclear Weapons, *opened for signature* July 1, 1968, 21 U.S.T. 483, 729 U.N.T.S. 161 (entered into force Mar. 5, 1970), *available at* http://www.state.govt/ np/trty/16281.htm#treaty [hereinafter NPT].

[211] *See* U.N. CHARTER art. 2, para. 4, *available at* http://www.un.org/aboutun/charter/.

[212] *See* Doc. 226.

[213] *See generally* U.N. CHARTER, *available at* http://www.un.org/aboutun/charter/.

major military incursion into southern Lebanon (Operation Litani) seeking to eliminate the bases of these groups. Once Israel had moved into Lebanese territory and attacked its acknowledged targets, it did not immediately withdraw. The United Nations Security Council, backed by the United States, responded with Resolution 425, which secured an Israeli withdrawal by June and the creation of a United Nations Interim Force in Lebanon (UNIFIL).[214] However, attacks from Lebanon against Israeli towns persisted, frustrating attempts at the resumption of peaceful relations between the two states.

During this period, the large number of Palestinians in Lebanon had begun to function as a state within a state. Armed Palestinians operated outside the control of Lebanese authorities, threatening the stability of both Israel and Lebanon. War broke out between the two states on June 5, 1982, when Palestinian extremists led by Abu Nidal made an assassination attempt on Israeli Ambassador Shlomo Argov in London. This incident, combined with PLO shelling, became the pretext for Israel's "Operation Peace for Galilee," an invasion of Lebanon launched under the direction of Defense Minister Ariel Sharon. Its declared purpose was the creation of a forty-kilometer security zone in southern Lebanon. By June 13, however, Israeli forces had passed the forty-kilometer line and laid siege to the city of Beirut.

After intervention on the part of the United States, a cease-fire was accepted that came into effect on August 12, 1982. Subsequently, U.S. Ambassador Phillip Habib negotiated a peaceful PLO withdrawal from Lebanon under the supervision of a multinational force. On August 13, the PLO submitted a list of 7,100 fighters to be evacuated to Tunis and other Arab states, with a timetable for their evacuation. By September 9, the evacuation involved 8,144 PLO fighters by sea and 6,254 overland to Damascus. The supervising multinational force left Beirut on September 9. However, complicating the fragile situation, the newly elected Lebanese President Bashir Gemayel was assassinated on September 14, before he could take office.[215] Israeli troops then reentered West Beirut to maintain order.

On the evening of September 16, 1982, Lebanese Phalangists entered the Sabra and Shatila Palestinian refugee camps, killing an estimated 800 inhabitants.[216] Israeli Prime Minister Menachem Begin failed to acknowledge the significance of the incident until a large-scale demonstration in Tel Aviv demanded an independent inquiry into Israel's role in the massacre. Within days, Israeli troops left West Beirut. Subsequently, the specially formed Kahan Committee, chaired

---

[214] *See* Doc. 227.

[215] *See* Doc. 253.

[216] *See* Doc. 254.

by Israeli Supreme Court Chief Justice Yitzhak Kahan, issued a report on the massacre.[217] Defense Minister Ariel Sharon drew the principal condemnation for allowing Lebanese Phalangists operating under IDF control into the camps. As Sharon declined to resign, Begin was forced to dismiss him. Begin, who was also cited in the report, resigned in September 1983.

A month later, suicide car bombers attacked the bases of the multinational forces in Lebanon, killing seventy-eight French troops and 241 U.S. marines. On February 8, 1984, United States President Ronald Reagan announced the planned withdrawal of marines from Lebanon.[218]

In June 1985, Israeli Prime Minister Shimon Peres ordered a unilateral withdrawal of most Israeli troops from Lebanon, leaving only a small residual force and an Israeli-supported Lebanese militia in a "security zone." On May 22, 2000, Israeli Prime Minister Ehud Barak decided unilaterally to withdraw all Israeli troops from Lebanon, ending its twenty-two-year military presence.[219]

i. Pre-War Developments

Document 227: United Nations Security Council Resolution 425, Calling upon Israel to Immediately Cease Its Military Action against Lebanon (March 19, 1978) [S.C. Res. 425, U.N. SCOR, U.N. Doc. S/RES/425 (1978)]. In Resolution 425, the Security Council decides, in light of a request from the Lebanese government, to establish immediately an interim force in Lebanon for the purpose of confirming the withdrawal of Israeli forces, restoring international peace and security, and assisting the government of Lebanon in ensuring the return of its effective authority in the area.

Document 228: United Nations Security Council Resolution 426, Establishing a United Nations Interim Force for Southern Lebanon (March 19, 1978) [S.C. Res. 426, U.N. SCOR, U.N. Doc. S/RES/426 (1978)]. Passed on the same day as Security Council Resolution 425,[220] this resolution makes effective the establishment of the UNIFIL.

Document 229: United Nations Security Council Resolution 427, Approving the Increase in the Strength of the UNIFIL to Approximately 6,000 (May 3, 1978) [S.C. Res. 427, U.N. SCOR, 2076th mtg., U.N. Doc. S/RES/427 (1978)]. In Resolution 427, the Security Council approves the increase in the strength of the UNIFIL from 4,000 to approximately 6,000 troops. Taking note of the partial withdrawal of Israeli forces, the Security Council calls upon Israel to complete its withdrawal from all Lebanese territory without any further delay. Finally, the Security Council deplores attacks on the UNIFIL and demands full respect for the UNIFIL from all parties in Lebanon.

Document 230: United Nations Security Council Resolution 434, Expressing Grave Concern about the Situation in Lebanon (September 18, 1978) [S.C. Res. 434, U.N. SCOR, 2079th

---

[217] *See* Doc. 257.
[218] *See* Doc. 261.
[219] *See* Doc. 273.
[220] *See* Doc. 227.

mtg., U.N. Doc. S/RES/434 (1978)]. In this resolution, the Security Council expresses its grave concern at the serious conditions in Lebanon and commends the outstanding performance of the UNIFIL in carrying out its mandate. However, it notes with concern that UNIFIL has encountered obstacles in deploying freely throughout its area of operation.

Document 231: United Nations Security Council Resolution 436, Noting with Grave Concern the Deteriorating Situation in Beirut (October 6, 1978) [S.C. Res. 436, U.N. SCOR, 2089th mtg. U.N. Doc. S/RES/436 (1978)]. Security Council Resolution 436 notes with grave concern the deteriorating situation in Beirut and its environs and the consequent loss of life, human suffering, and physical destruction. It calls for an immediate and effective cease-fire and a cessation of hostilities. Further, it calls upon all concerned parties to allow units of the ICRC into the area of conflict to provide humanitarian assistance.

Document 232: United Nations Security Council Resolution 444, Deploring the Lack of Cooperation with UNIFIL Efforts (January 19, 1979) [S.C. Res. 444, U.N. SCOR, 2113th mtg. U.N. Doc. S/RES/444 (1979)]. Security Council Resolution 444 expresses concern over the grave situation in southern Lebanon and reiterates its conviction that its continuation poses a challenge to the authority of the Security Council. It deplores the lack of cooperation with the UNIFIL, in particular Israel's assistance to irregular armed groups operating in the area. It expresses its satisfaction with efforts by the Government of Lebanon to deploy in the south and encourages it to increase these efforts in coordination with UNIFIL. It also urges all United Nations member states to bring their influence to bear on those concerned so that UNIFIL can carry out its full responsibilities.

Document 233: United Nations Security Council Resolution 450, Calling upon Israel to Cease Its Acts against the Territorial Integrity, Unity, Sovereignty, and Political Independence of Lebanon (June 14, 1979) [S.C. Res. 450, U.N. SCOR, 2149th mtg., U.N. Doc. S/RES/450 (1979)]. Acting in response to a request from the Lebanese government and noting its concerns, the Security Council, in Resolution 450, affirms its call for respect for the territorial integrity, unity, sovereignty, and political independence of Lebanon within its internationally recognized boundaries. The Security Council calls upon Israel to cease acts against Lebanon, in particular its incursions into Lebanese territory and its assistance to irresponsible armed groups.

Document 234: United Nations Security Council Resolution 459, Expressing Anxiety about the Existence of Obstacles to the Full Deployment of UNIFIL (December 19, 1979) [S.C. Res. 459, U.N. SCOR, 2180th mtg., U.N. Doc. S/RES/459 (1979)]. In extending the mandate of the UNIFIL, the Security Council in Resolution 459 notes with concern the continued violations of the cease-fire, the attacks on UNIFIL, and the difficulty in implementing past resolutions. It also expresses its anxiety about threats to UNIFIL's existence, its freedom of movement, and the safety of its headquarters. The Security Council takes note of the government of Lebanon's determination to draft a program of action in consultation with the Secretary-General to promote the restoration of its authority.

Document 235: United Nations Security Council Resolution 467, Deploring All Acts of Interference with the UNTSO and All Acts of Hostility against UNIFIL (April 24, 1980) [S.C. Res. 467, U.N. SCOR, 2218th mtg., U.N. Doc. S/RES/467 (1979)]. In Resolution 467, the Security Council underscores its support for the work of the

UNIFIL and condemns all actions contrary to Security Council Resolutions 425, 426, and 459, including Israel's military intervention into Lebanon, violations of the Israel-Lebanon Armistice Agreement, interference with the UNTSO, and all acts of hostility against UNIFIL.[221] The Security Council condemns the deliberate shelling of UNIFIL's headquarters and commends the Secretary-General's efforts to bring about a cessation of hostilities.

Document 236: United Nations Security Council Resolution 488, Recalling the Terms of Reference and General Guidelines of UNIFIL (June 19, 1981) [S.C. Res. 488, U.N. SCOR, U.N. Doc. S/RES/488 (1981)]. Extending the mandate of the UNIFIL, the Security Council in Resolution 488 recalls the terms of reference and general guidelines for UNIFIL due to continued obstacles to its full deployment, "causing death, injury and destruction to the civilian population as well as among the peace-keeping force." The Security Council supports the efforts of the government of Lebanon to rehabilitate and reconstruct southern Lebanon, in particular the deployment of substantial contingents of the Lebanese Army in UNIFIL's area of operation.

Document 237: United Nations Security Council Resolution 490, Calling for the Immediate Cessation of All Armed Attacks (July 21, 1981) [S.C. Res. 490, U.N. SCOR, 2293d mtg., U.N. Doc. S/RES/490 (1981)]. Concerned at the heightened state of violence, the Security Council in Resolution 490 calls for an immediate cessation of all armed attacks and requests the Secretary-General to report back on the implementation of this resolution within forty-eight hours.

Document 238: United Nations Security Council Resolution 498, Calling upon Israel to Withdraw Its Forces from Lebanese Territory (December 18, 1981) [S.C. Res. 498, U.N. SCOR, 2320th mtg., U.N. Doc. S/RES/498 (1981)]. United Nations Security Council Resolution 498 reaffirms its previous calls for the territorial integrity of Lebanon, Israel's withdrawal from all Lebanese territory, and the need for an international peace-keeping force in the area to ensure the return of the government of Lebanon's authority. It calls upon all concerned parties to work toward the consolidation of a cease-fire. It also renews the mandate of the UNIFIL for another six months.

Document 239: United Nations Security Council Resolution 501, Approving the Immediate Increase in the Strength of UNIFIL (February 25, 1982) [S.C. Res. 501, U.N. SCOR, 2332d mtg., U.N. Doc. S/RES/501 (1982)]. In Resolution 501, the Security Council, gravely concerned at the deterioration of the situation in the Middle East and its consequences to the maintenance of international peace, decides to approve the immediate increase in the strength of the UNIFIL recommended by the Secretary-General from approximately 6,000 to approximately 7,000 troops. The Security Council also requests the Secretary-General to continue discussions with the government of Lebanon and other parties on a program of action for achieving further progress.

Document 240: United Nations Security Council Resolution 508, Calling for a Cease-Fire at the Lebanese-Israeli Border (June 5, 1982) [S.C. Res. 508, U.N. SCOR, 2374th mtg., U.N. Doc. S/RES/508 (1982)]. The Security Council adopted Resolution 508 in response to Israel's invasion of Lebanon. In it, the Security Council calls upon

---

[221] *See* Docs. 227, 228, and 234.

all parties to immediately and simultaneously cease all military activities within Lebanon and across the Lebanese-Israeli border.

ii. 1982 War (1982–1983)

Document 241: United Nations Security Council Resolution 509, Demanding that Israel Withdraw Its Forces from Lebanon (June 6, 1982) [S.C. Res. 509, U.N. SCOR, 2375th mtg., U.N. Doc. S/RES/508 (1982)]. In Resolution 509, the Security Council demands the withdrawal of Israeli forces from Lebanon and reaffirms the need for strict respect for the territorial integrity, sovereignty, and political independence of Lebanon within its internationally recognized boundaries.

Document 242: United Nations Security Council Resolution 511, Authorizing UNIFIL to Carry Out Interim Tasks (June 18, 1982) [S.C. Res. 511, U.N. SCOR, 2379th mtg., U.N. Doc. S/RES/511 (1982)]. In Resolution 511, the Security Council decides to extend the mandate of the UNIFIL for two months as an interim measure, bearing in mind the need to avoid developments that could aggravate the situation. The Security Council authorizes UNIFIL during that period to carry out interim tasks and calls on all concerned to fully cooperate with UNIFIL in the discharge of these duties.

Document 243: United Nations Security Council Resolution 512, Calling on All Parties to Respect the Rights of the Lebanese and Palestinian Civilian Populations and Facilitate Humanitarian Relief Efforts (June 19, 1982) [S.C. Res. 512, U.N. SCOR, 2380th mtg., U.N. Doc. S/RES/512 (1982)]. The Security Council in Resolution 512 calls upon all parties to the conflict to respect the rights of the civilian populations, refrain from violence, and take appropriate measures to alleviate suffering caused by the conflict. The Security Council further stresses the humanitarian responsibilities of the United Nations and its agencies.

Document 244: United Nations General Assembly Resolution ES-7/5, Condemning Israeli Invasion of Lebanon and Calling for Cessation of Military Activity (June 26, 1982) [S.C. Res. ES-7/5, U.N. SCOR, U.N. Doc. A/RES/ES-7/5 (1982)]. In Resolution ES-7/5, the General Assembly notes with regret that the Security Council has failed to take measures to ensure implementation of Resolutions 508 and 509 and demands that Israel withdraw unconditionally to the internationally recognized boundaries of Lebanon.

Document 245: United Nations Security Council Resolution 513, Calling for Respect for the Rights of Palestinians in West Beirut and South Lebanon (July 4, 1982) [S.C. Res. 513, U.N. SCOR, 2382d mtg., U.N. Doc. S/RES/513 (1982)]. In Resolution 513, the Security Council expresses alarm over the continued suffering of civilian populations in south Lebanon and in west Beirut. The Security Council calls for respect for the rights of the civilian populations without any discrimination and repudiates all acts of violence against these populations. The Security Council further calls for the restoration of the normal supply of vital facilities such as water, electricity, food, and medical provisions, particularly in Beirut.

Document 246: United Nations Security Council Resolution 515, Demanding that Israel Lift the Blockade of the City of Beirut (July 29, 1982) [S.C. Res. 515, U.N. SCOR, U.N. Doc. S/RES/515 (1982)]. In Resolution 515, the Security Council, deeply concerned at the situation of the civilian population of Beirut, demands that Israel immediately lift its blockade of Beirut to permit the dispatch of supplies to meet the urgent needs of the civilian population and allow the distribution of aid.

Document 247: United Nations Security Council Resolution 516, Authorizing the Secretary-General to Deploy a United Nations Observer to Monitor the Situation in and around Beirut (August 1, 1982) [S.C. Res. 516, U.N. SCOR, U.N. Doc. S/RES/516 (1982)]. In Resolution 516, the Security Council, alarmed by the continuation and intensification of military activities in and around Beirut, demands an immediate cease-fire and a cessation of all military activities within Lebanon and across the Lebanese-Israeli border. It also authorizes the Secretary-General to immediately deploy United Nations observers to monitor the situation in and around Beirut at the request of the Government of Lebanon.

Document 248: United Nations Security Council Resolution 517, Expressing Shock at the Israeli Invasion of Beirut and Calling for a Withdrawal (August 4, 1982) [S.C. Res. 517, U.N. SCOR, 2389th mtg., U.N. Doc. S/RES/517 (1982)]. In Resolution 517, the Security Council expresses its shock and alarm over the deplorable consequences of the Israeli invasion of Beirut and demands an immediate cease-fire and withdrawal of Israeli forces from Lebanon.

Document 249: U.S.-Vetoed Security Council Draft Resolution s/15347/Rev.1, Calling on Member States to Refrain from Military Aid to Israel Pending Withdrawal from Lebanon (August 6, 1982) [U.N. SCOR, U.N. Doc. s/15347/Rev.1 (1982)]. The United States vetoed this Security Council draft resolution submitted by the of Soviet Union, which decides that, in order to carry out the decisions of the Security Council, all state members of the United Nations should refrain from supplying Israel with weapons and from providing it with any military aid until the full withdrawal of Israeli forces from all Lebanese territory is effected. The final vote was eleven states in favor, United States veto, and three abstentions: Togo, United Kingdom, Zaire.

Document 250: Israeli Prime Minister Menachem Begin: The Wars of No Alternative and Operation Peace for the Galilee (August 8, 1982) [*reprinted in* THE ISRAEL-ARAB READER: A DOCUMENTARY HISTORY OF THE MIDDLE EAST CONFLICT (Walter Laqueur & Barry Rubin eds., 2001)]. Begin delivered this speech at the National Defense College in Israel to describe the manner in which Israel was justified in its attacks during the first Lebanon War. The speech focuses on how, unlike the Yom Kippur War, this was not a "war of no alternative," but Israel was still entitled to act in order to prevent a costlier war where Israel must fight for its very survival.

Document 251: United Nations Security Council Resolution 518, Demanding the Immediate Lifting of All Restrictions on the City of Beirut (August 12, 1982) [S.C. Res. 518, U.N. SCOR, 2392d mtg., U.N. Doc. S/RES/518 (1982)]. In its sixth resolution issued in two months on the Lebanon invasion, the Security Council demands that Israel and all parties to the conflict strictly observe the terms of Security Council resolutions relevant to the immediate cessation of all military activities within Lebanon and, particularly, in and around Beirut. It also demands the immediate lifting of all restrictions on the city of Beirut in order to permit the free entry of supplies to meet the urgent needs of the civilian population. In regard to United Nations observers in the area, the Security Council demands that Israel cooperate fully in securing their effective deployment, as requested by the Government of Lebanon, and in such a manner as to ensure their safety.

Document 252: Final Declaration of the Twelfth Arab Summit Conference, Adopted at Fez (September 9, 1982) [U.N. SCOR, 37th Sess., Annex, Agenda Items 31, 34, 58, and 134, U.N. Doc. A/37/696*-S/15510 (1982)]. In this text, the Twelfth Arab Summit Conference declares its strong condemnation of the Israeli aggression against the people and territory of Lebanon and against the Palestinian people. It draws the attention of international public opinion to the seriousness of the aggression and its consequences for the stability and security of the region. The member states reaffirm their solidarity with Lebanon and their readiness to provide any assistance requested by Lebanon.

Document 253: United Nations Security Council Resolution 520, Condemning the Murder of Lebanese President Bashir Gemayel (September 17, 1982) [S.C. Res. 520, U.N. SCOR, 2396th mtg., U.N. Doc. S/RES/520 (1982)]. In Resolution 520, the Security Council condemns the murder of Lebanon's president-elect, Bashir Gemayel, and efforts to disrupt the restoration of a strong, stable government in Lebanon.

Document 254: United Nations Security Council Resolution 521, Condemning the Massacre of Palestinian Civilians in Beirut (September 19, 1982) [S.C. Res. 521, U.N. SCOR, 2396th mtg., U.N. Doc. S/RES/521 (1982)]. In Resolution 521, the Security Council condemns the massacre of Palestinian civilians in Sabra and Shattila. The Security Council reaffirms Resolutions 512 and 513, which call for respect for the rights of civilian populations without any discrimination, and repudiates acts of violence against them. The Security Council requests the Secretary-General to initiate appropriate consultations, in particular with the government of Lebanon, on additional steps (including the possible deployment of United Nations forces) to assist in ensuring full protection for the civilian populations in and around Beirut.

Document 255: United Nations Security Council Resolution 523, Insisting UNIFIL Shall Have Full Freedom of Movement (October 18, 1982) [S.C. Res. 523, U.N. SCOR, 2400th mtg., U.N. Doc. S/RES/523 (1982)]. United Nations Security Council Resolution 523 insists that there will be no interference with the operations of the UNIFIL and that UNIFIL will have full freedom of movement in the discharge of its mandate. It extends the mandate for an interim period of three months.

Document 256: United Nations General Assembly Resolution 37/134, Condemning Israel for Its Invasion of Lebanon and Attempting to Secure Assistance to the Palestinian People (December 17, 1982) [G.A. Res. 37/134, U.N. GAOR, U.N. Doc. A/RES/37/134 (1982)]. Expressing its deep alarm at the Israeli invasion of Lebanon and horrified by the Sabra and Shatila massacre, the General Assembly, in Resolution 37/134, notes with concern the dire need of the victims for urgent humanitarian assistance and the need to provide economic and social assistance to the Palestinian people. The General Assembly calls upon governments and relevant United Nations bodies to provide such assistance to the victims.

Document 257: Report of the Commission of Inquiry into the Events at the Refugee Camps in Beirut (Kahan Report) (February 8, 1983) [*available at* http://www.mfa.gov.il/mfa/foreign+relations/israels+foreign+relations+since+1947/1982-1984/104+ report+ of+the+commission+of+inquiry+into+the+e.htm]. Following reports of massacres at Sabra and Shatila, the government of Israel established a Commission of Inquiry to investigate the facts and factors connected with the atrocity. Subsequently, the president of the Israeli Supreme Court appointed a commission to investigate the incident comprised of: Yitzhak Kahan, president of the Supreme Court (as chairman); Aharon Barak, justice of the Supreme Court; and Yona Efrat, major general (Res.). The Commission of Inquiry (later known as the Kahan Commission) found that the evidence indicated that the massacre was perpetrated by Lebanese forces known as Phalangists or Ketaib. Although it assigned direct responsibility for the events to the Phalangists, the commission reports that the danger of a massacre should have been foreseen if the Phalangists were to enter the camps without protective measures to guarantee the safety of the residents. The commission evaluates the relative responsibility of nine major Israeli authorities, including: the prime minister, Menachem Begin; the minister of defense, Ariel Sharon; and the foreign minister, Yitzhak Shamir. The commission recommends that the defense minister resign, the director of military intelligence not continue in his post, and other senior officers be removed.

Document 258: Draft Agreement between Israel and Lebanon (May 17, 1983) [*available at* http://www.mfa.gov.il/MFA/Foreign%20Relations/Israels%20Foreign%20Relations%20since%201947/1982-1984/114%20Agreement%20between%20Israel%20and%20Lebanon-%2017%20May%201]. Two separate ceremonies marked the signing of the Israel-Lebanon Draft Agreement. Arabic and French copies of the agreement were signed in Khalde, Lebanon, by Mr. Antoine Fattal for Lebanon and Dr. David Kimche for Israel, and witnessed by U.S. Ambassador Morris Draper. Later, Hebrew and English versions were signed in Kiryat Shmona, Israel. The agreement contains provisions for ending the state of war between Israel and Lebanon, supervising a treaty, Israel's withdrawal from Lebanon and security coordination, and establishing an Israeli mission in Beirut. The Lebanese government never ratified the agreement.

Document 259: Statements by Director General David Kimche of the Israeli Foreign Ministry Regarding the Israel-Lebanon Agreement (May 17, 1983) [*available at* http://www.mfa.gove.il/MFA/Israels%20Foreign%20Relations%20since%201947/1982-1984/115%20Statements%20by%20Director%20General%20Kimche%20at%20the%20t]. In this statement given after the signature of the draft agreement between Israel and Lebanon, Director General David Kimche declares that the agreement marks a new chapter in Israel and Lebanon's history, though there are still obstacles to overcome and groups who would like to render the agreement meaningless. Kimche declares that the Lebanese people are in favor of the agreement, as are Israelis. Kimche closes optimistically, saying, "Let us hope the work we have done together . . . will have laid the foundations of a strong and lasting bond of friendship between our two countries."

Document 260: United Nations Security Council Resolution 542, Deploring the Loss of Life Caused by Events Taking Place in Northern Lebanon (November 23, 1983) [S.C. Res. 542, U.N. SCOR, 2480th mtg., U.N. Doc. S/RES/542 (1983)]. In Resolution 542, the Security Council, deeply concerned by the intensification of fighting, deplores the loss of human life caused by events in northern Lebanon. It requests the concerned parties to immediately accept a cease-fire and to settle their differences exclusively by peaceful means.

Document 261: Statement by U.S. President Ronald Reagan on the Deployment of U.S. Marines in Lebanon (February 7, 1984) [*available at* http://www.reagan.utexas.edu/resource/speeches/1984/20784d.htm]. Following attacks on U.S. military camps in Beirut in October 1983 that killed 241 marines, the Reagan administration came under enormous congressional pressure to withdraw U.S. marines from Beirut. In this statement, U.S. President Ronald Reagan asks the secretary of defense to present him with a plan for the redeployment of marines from land to ships anchored offshore. The redeployment was completed by the end of February.

iii. Post-War Developments

Document 262: United Nations General Assembly Resolution 39/146, Calling on Member States to Isolate Israel until It Complies with Its International Obligations (December 14, 1984) [G.A. Res. 39/146, U.N. GAOR, U.N. Doc. 39/146 (1984)]. United Nations General Assembly Resolution 39/146 determines that Israel's record, policies, and actions confirm that it is not a peace-loving member state, and, therefore, calls upon member states to refrain from supplying Israel with any weapons and related equipment, to suspend economic, financial, and technological assistance to and cooperation with Israel, and to sever diplomatic, trade, and cultural relations with Israel so as to isolate it in all fields.

Document 263: United Nations Security Council Resolution 564, Expressing Deepest Concern at the Heavy Costs in Human Life in Lebanon (May 31, 1985) [S.C. Res. 564, U.N. SCOR, U.N. Doc. S/RES/564 (1985)]. Alarmed at the continued escalation of violence involving the civilian population in Lebanon, including Palestinians in refugee camps, the Security Council in Resolution 564 expresses its deepest concern at the heavy costs in human life and calls on all parties to take necessary measures to alleviate the suffering resulting from acts of violence.

Document 264: United Nations Security Council Resolution 573, Condemning Israeli Attack on Tunisia (October 4, 1985) [S.C. Res. 573, U.N. SCOR, 2615th mtg., U.N. Doc. S/RES/573 (1985)]. After Israel launched an air attack on PLO Headquarters in Hammam Al-Shut, Tunisia, the Security Council issued Resolution 573, vigorously condemning Israel's act of armed aggression against Tunisian territory, which violated of the United Nations Charter, international law, and norms of conduct.

Document 265: United Nations Security Council Resolution 587, Condemning Attacks against UNIFIL (September 23, 1986) [S.C. Res. 587, U.N. SCOR, U.N. Doc. S/RES/587 (1986)]. United Nations Security Council Resolution 587 condemns in the strongest terms the attacks against the UNIFIL and expresses indignation at the support that such criminal action may receive. It pays homage to the courage of the soldiers of UNIFIL and urges all concerned parties to cooperate with UNIFIL in the fulfillment of its mandate. Finally, it requests the Secretary-General to report on the application of this resolution within twenty-one days.

Document 266: Memorandum of Agreement between Israel and the United States (April 21, 1988) [*available at* http://www.mfa.gov.il/MFA/Foreign%20Relations/Israels%20Foreign%20Relations%20since%201947/1984-1988/355%20 Memorandum%20of%20Agreement%20between%20Israel%20and%20the]. Israel and the United States signed this memorandum regarding joint political, security, and economic cooperation, with Prime Minister Yitzhak Shamir signing for Israel and President Ronald Reagan signing for the United States. The agreement establishes a comprehensive framework for continued consultation and cooperation and appoints officials to meet regularly for joint discussions of current issues. The agreement is one of the most comprehensive ever signed between the two countries. It names Israel as a major non-NATO ally of the United States.

Document 267: League of Arab States Resolution 5544, Lebanese Hostages and Detainees Held in Israeli Camps and Prisons (March 21, 1996) [U.N. GAOR, 51st Sess., Annex, U.N. Doc. A/51/112 (1996)]. The League of Arab States in Resolution 5544 strongly condemns Israeli attacks and oppressive practices in the occupied Lebanese territories of southern Lebanon and the western Bekaa, in particular the kidnapping and detention of innocent citizens who were imprisoned without trial in Israel and in camps run by forces under Israeli control.

Document 268: United Nations Security Council Resolution 1052, Calling for an Immediate Cessation of Hostilities (April 18, 1996) [S.C. Res. 1052, U.N. SCOR, U.N. Doc. S/RES/1052 (1996)]. In Resolution 1052, the Security Council, gravely concerned at attacks on civilian targets and at the loss of life and suffering and stressing the need for all parties to respect the rules of international humanitarian law with regard to the protection of civilians, calls for an immediate cessation of hostilities and supports the ongoing diplomatic efforts to that end.

Document 269: United Nations General Assembly Resolution 50/22, Considering that Lebanon is Entitled to Appropriate Redress for Qana Bombings (April 25, 1996) [G.A. Res. 50/22, U.N. GAOR, 50th Sess., 117th plen. mtg., Agenda Item 44, U.N. Doc. A/RES/50/22 C (1996)]. In Resolution 50/22, the General Assembly expresses its grave concern over the accidental bombing of the UNIFIL base in the village of Qana on April 18, 1996, which resulted in the heavy loss of life among civilians. The General Assembly considers that Lebanon is entitled to appropriate redress from Israel.

Document 270: Cease-Fire Understanding between Israel and Lebanon (April 26, 1996) [*reprinted in Mideast Accord: Restricting the Violence in Lebanon,* N.Y. Times, April 27, 1996, at A8]. U.S. Secretary of State Warren Christopher was able to bring about an understanding between Israel, Lebanon, the Hezbollah, and Syria that effectively ended Israel's operations in Lebanon. The subsequent agreement between Israel and Lebanon establishes four conditions for a cease-fire: (1) armed groups in Lebanon will not carry out attacks into Israel; (2) Israel and those cooperating with it will not fire any kind of weapon at civilians or civilian targets in Lebanon; (3) the two parties will commit to ensuring that civilians are not the target of attack and that civilian-populated areas are not used as launching grounds for attacks; and (4) nothing in the agreement would preclude any party from exercising the right of self-defense. A monitoring group was also established consisting of the United States, France, Syria, Lebanon, and Israel. The agreement has been honored more in the breach than in the observance.

Document 271: Report of the Secretary-General's Military Advisor Concerning the Shelling of the United Nations Compound at Qana (May 7, 1996) [U.N. SCOR, U.N. Doc. S/1996/337 (1996)]. United Nations Secretary-General Boutros Boutros-Ghali prefaces the report of his military advisor, Major-General Franklin van Kappen, on the Qana bombing by considering the seriousness of the incident given that civilians, including women and children, had sought refuge in the Qana compound before it was bombed. The report presents the Israeli account of events, as well as a detailed sequence of events directly preceding the incident. The report finds that "it is unlikely that the shelling of the United Nations compound was the result of gross technical and/or procedural errors," as Israel had contended. To prevent a recurrence of the incident, van Kappen recommends that new precautions be adopted by Israeli forces with regard to firing at targets near United Nations positions.

Document 272: Commission on Human Rights Resolution 1998/62, Human Rights Situation in Southern Lebanon and Western Bekaa (April 21, 1998) [Res. 1998/62, U.N. High Comm. on Hum. Rts., 56th mtg., U.N. Doc. 1998/62 (1998)]. In Resolution 1998/62, the Commission on Human Rights censures repeated Israeli aggressions in southern Lebanon and western Bekaa, which had caused a large number of casualties, displacement of families, and destruction of property. The commission expresses its grave concern about Israel's detention of Lebanese citizens in the Khiyam and Marjayoun detention centers and also at the death of some detainees as a result of ill-treatment and torture. It also expresses its indignation at the Israeli Supreme Court ruling of March 4, 1998, which permits Israeli authorities to retain Lebanese detainees in Israeli prisons without trial and to hold them as hostages and as a bargaining card.

Document 273: Government of Israel Resolution to Deploy on the Border with Lebanon by July 2000 (March 5, 2000) [*available at* http://www.mfa.gov.il/MFA/ Government/ Communiques/2000/Government%20of%20Israel%20Resolution%20-%2005-Mar-2000]. In this resolution, the Israeli government announces that IDF will deploy on the border with Lebanon by July 2000. The government resolves to act to strengthen the frontline towns and villages in terms of security and socio-economics.

Document 274: Commission on Human Rights Resolution 2000/7, Human Rights in the Occupied Syrian Golan (April 17, 2000) [Res. 2000/7, U.N. Comm. on Hum. Rts., 52d mtg., U.N. Doc. 2000/7 (2000)]. In Resolution 2000/7, the Commission on Human Rights expresses its concern over the suffering of Syrian citizens in occupied Syrian Golan following review of a report by the Special Committee to Investigate Israeli Practices Affecting the Human Rights of the Palestinian People and Other Arabs of the Occupied Territories. The committee reaffirms Security Council Resolution 497, which determines that Israel's decision to impose its laws, jurisdiction, and administration in the Occupied Syrian Golan Heights are null and void. The commission calls upon Israel to desist from imposing Israeli citizenship and Israeli identity cards on Syrian citizens in the occupied Syrian Golan.

Document 275: Letter from the Secretary-General Addressed to the President of the Security Council Informing Him of Israel's Decision to Withdraw from Southern Lebanon (April 17, 2000) [U.N. SCOR, U.N. Doc. S/2000/322 (2000)]. In this letter to the president of the Security Council, United Nations Secretary-General Kofi Annan announces that the permanent representative of Israel, Ambassador Yehuda Lancry, had conveyed to him the formal notification of Israel's decision to withdraw its forces from Lebanon by July 2000. Annan reports that the withdrawal is to be carried out in full accordance with Security Council Resolutions 425 and 426 and that Israel intends to cooperate fully with the United Nations.

Document 276: Report of the Secretary-General on the Implementation of Security Council Resolutions 425 and 426, Announcing a Special Envoy to Monitor the Israeli Withdrawal from Lebanon (May 22, 2000) [U.N. SCOR, U.N. Doc. S/2000/460 (2000)]. In this report, the president of the Security Council details the mission of his special envoy, Terje Roed-Larsen, to Lebanon. The special envoy had, along with the force commander of the UNIFIL and a team of experts, met with the governments of Israel and Lebanon and other concerned member states in the region, including Egypt, Jordan, and the Syrian Arab Republic, to discuss Israel's withdrawal from Lebanon. The delegation also met with the PLO and the League of Arab States. The report presents the procedures and mechanism in place for confirming Israel's full withdrawal and assisting the Government of Lebanon in ensuring the return of its effective authority in the area.

Document 277: United Nations Security Council Resolution 1310, Endorsing the Understanding that UNIFIL Will Deploy throughout Its Area of Operations (July 27, 2000) [S.C. Res. 1310, U.N. SCOR, 4177th mtg., U.N. Doc. S/RES/1310 (2000)]. United Nations Security Council Resolution 1310 endorses the understanding that the UNIFIL will deploy and function fully throughout its area of operations and that the government of Lebanon will strengthen its presence in the area of operation. It welcomes the Secretary-General's statement that as of July 24, 2000, Israel had removed all violations of the withdrawal line. It also calls on the government of Lebanon to ensure the return of its effective authority and presence in the south and encourages it to ensure a calm environment.

Document 278: United Nations Security Council Resolution 1337, Calling on the Government of Lebanon to Ensure the Return of Its Effective Authority and Presence in the South (January 30, 2001) [S.C. Res. 1337, U.N. SCOR, 4267th mtg., U.N. Doc. S/RES/1337 (2001)]. In Resolution 1337, the Security Council extends the mandate of the UNIFIL for six months. It calls on the parties to fulfill their commitments to respect the withdrawal line identified by the United Nations, condemns all acts of violence, and expresses concern about serious breaches and violations of the withdrawal line. The Security Council welcomes the contribution of UNIFIL to operational demining, encourages further assistance in mine action by the United Nations to the government of Lebanon, and calls on donor countries to support these efforts through financial and in-kind donations.

Document 279: Commission on Human Rights Resolution 2001/6, Detailing the Human Rights Situation in Occupied Syrian Golan (April 18, 2001) [Res. 2001/6, U.N. Comm. on Hum. Rts., 61st mtg., U.N. Doc. 2001/6 (2001)]. In Resolution 2001/16, the Commission on Human Rights expresses its deep concern over the suffering of Syrian citizens in the occupied Syrian Golan due to the violation of their human rights occurring since the Israeli military occupation of 1967. The commission calls upon Israel to comply with relevant General Assembly and Security Council resolutions, particularly Security Council Resolution 497.

Document 280: Commission on Human Rights Resolution 2001/10, Human Rights Situation of Lebanese Detainees in Israel (April 18, 2001) [Res. 2001/10, U.N. Comm. on Hum. Rts., 62d mtg., U.N. Doc. 2001/10 (2001)]. In Resolution 2001/10, the Commission on Human Rights calls upon the government of Israel to refrain from holding detained Lebanese citizens as hostages for bargaining purposes and to release them immediately. It also affirms Israel's obligation to allow the ICRC and other international humanitarian organizations to visit the detainees regularly. Further, the commission calls upon the government of Israel to submit to UNIFIL maps of the landmine fields laid throughout civilian villages that obstruct the resumption of normal life.

Document 281: Report of the Secretary-General on the United Nations Interim Force in Lebanon (January 16, 2002) [*Report of the Secretary-General,* U.N. SCOR, U.N. Doc. S/2002/55 (2002)]. In this report, United Nations Secretary-General Kofi Annan recommends extending UNIFIL's mandate for six months (until July 31) in light of conditions in the area. However, he suggests that 1,700 troops be removed from the area. Annan also recommends that the government of Lebanese do more to reassert its authority over areas vacated by Israel twenty months previously.

Document 282: Commission on Human Rights Resolution 2002/10, Report on Human Rights Situation of Lebanese Detainees in Israel (April 19, 2002) [Res. 2002/10, U.N. Comm. on Hum. Rts., 47th mtg., Doc. 2002/10 (2002)]. In Resolution 2002/10, the Commission for Human Rights condemns the detention, ill-treatment, and torture by Israel of Lebanese civilians abducted and detained in Lebanon and subsequently transferred to prisons in Israel. The commission calls upon Israel to comply with the Geneva Conventions for the protection of victims of war and allow the ICRC to visit the detainees regularly.

Document 283: United Nations General Assembly Resolution 58/100, Occupied Syrian Golan (December 17, 2003) [G.A. Res. 58/100, U.N. GAOR, 58th Sess., Agenda Item 84, U.N. Doc. A/RES/58/100 (2003)]. In Resolution 58/100, the General Assembly, deeply concerned that the Syrian Golan has been under continued Israeli military occupation since 1967, calls upon Israel to comply with relevant resolutions.

iv. 2006 War

Document 284: United Nations Security Council Resolution 1655 (January 31, 2006) [S.C. Res. 1655, U.N. SCOR 5362d mtg., U.N. Doc. S/RES/1655 (2006)]. In response to Hezbollah's rocket fire attacks into Israeli territory, the Security Council urges Lebanon to assert its authority to prevent these attacks originating from its territory.

Document 285: United Nations Security Council Resolution 1697 (July 31, 2006) [S.C. Res. 1697, U.N. SCOR 5501st mtg., U.N. Doc. S/RES/1697 (2006)]. The Security Council expresses concern at the escalation of hostilities between Lebanon and Israel since July 12, 2006. In addition, it urges both sides of the conflict to respect the safety of UNIFIL and other United Nations personnel.

Document 286: United Nations Security Council Resolution 1701 (August 11, 2006) [S.C. Res. 1701, U.N. SCOR, 5511th mtg., U.N. Doc. S/RES/1701 (2006)]. In an attempt to bring an end to the conflict, the Security Council passed this resolution a month after the conflict began. It would serve as the template for the cease-fire agreement that Lebanon, Hezbollah, and Israel would sign in the following days.

Document 287: United Nations General Assembly Resolution 61/154, Human Rights Situation Arising from the Recent Israeli Military Operations in Lebanon (February 14, 2007). As an epilogue to the July war, the General Assembly deplores the civilian casualties that occurred during the conflict as a result of Israeli operations. The resolution notes the deaths of 1,100 civilians and destruction of vital civilian infrastructure in Lebanon.

Document 288: United Nations Security Council Resolution 1773 (August 24, 2007) [S.C. Res. 1773, U.N. SCOR, 5733d mtg., U.N. Doc. S/RES/1773 (2007)]. The Security Council emphasizes the need to rectify some of the causes to the July war conflict, including continued detention of Israeli soldiers and Lebanese prisoners in Israel. The Security Council also extends UNIFIL's mandate until August 31, 2008.

4. Arab-Israeli Peace Process: 1967–2008

On March 26, 1979, Egypt became the first Arab state to sign a formal peace treaty with the State of Israel.[222] This was a major step toward the normalization of relations between Israel and its neighbors after the League of Arab States formed a unified Arab stance against Israel with the Khartoum Resolution of 1967.[223] The treaty was the culmination of two years of groundbreaking diplomacy that saw Egyptian President Anwar al-Sadat address the Israeli Knesset in 1977 and President Jimmy Carter host Egyptian President Anwar al-Sadat and Israeli Prime Minister Menachem Begin at Camp David for the signing of the now famous Camp David Accords.[224] In 1994, the Hashemite Kingdom of Jordan became the second state to sign a peace treaty with Israel.[225] Since then, peace negotiations between Israel and the remaining Arab states have largely stalled.

The United States played a significant role in bringing about the existing Arab-Israeli peace deals, providing parties with both a sense of direction and a mechanism for dialogue. From 1973 to 1977, Secretary of State Henry Kissinger practiced what has been called "step-by-step" peace negotiations—meeting personally with Middle East leaders to secure gradual land and security concessions from each side. The U.S. policy was revised during the Carter administration to a more comprehensive approach that culminated in the first historic peace settlement. Under the presidency of Bill Clinton, the United States resumed its close involvement in the Arab-Israeli peace process.[226]

Other documents on related subjects may be found in: Section 3, Arab-Israeli Wars; Section 5, Arms Control and Regional Security; Section 6, Jerusalem and the Holy Sites; and Section 7, Israeli-Palestinian Peace Process.

---

[222] *See* Doc. 310. Egypt suffered significant political and economic fallout from its decision to become the first Arab state to sign a formal peace treaty with Israel. It was temporarily suspended from the League of Arab States, and the League moved its headquarters from Cairo to Tunis. In 1989, Egypt was readmitted into the Arab League and the league's headquarters was moved back to Cairo.

[223] *See* Doc. 165. This resolution and its famous "Three No's" stipulated that there would be no negotiations with Israel, no recognition of Israel, and no peace with Israel. This rendered Arab states in the region subject to a permanent state of war with Israel.

[224] *See* Doc. 308.

[225] *See* Doc. 320.

[226] *See* Dennis Ross, The Missing Peace: The Inside Story of the Fight for Middle East Peace (2004).

Document 289: United Nations Security Council Resolution 242, Demanding the Withdrawal of Israeli Armed Forces from Territories Occupied in the Recent Conflict (November 22, 1967) [S.C. Res. 242, U.N. SCOR, 22d Sess., 1382d mtg., at 8–9, U.N. Doc. S/RES/242 (1967)]. Emphasizing the inadmissibility of the acquisition of territory by war, United Nations Security Council Resolution 242 addresses key issues in the conflict: the recognition of Israel's right to exist; a just settlement of the refugee problem; and the withdrawal of Israeli troops from territories occupied in the 1967 war to "secure and recognized boundaries." Mention of Jerusalem, however, is conspicuously absent from this document. Resolution 242 has been the basis for all subsequent peace negotiations between Israel and neighboring Arab states.

Document 290: Statement by U.S. Secretary of State William P. Rogers (Rogers Plan) (December 9, 1969) [THE QUEST FOR PEACE: PRINCIPAL UNITED STATES PUBLIC STATEMENTS AND RELATED DOCUMENTS ON THE ARAB-ISRAELI PEACE PROCESS 1967–1983 23–29 (U.S. Dep't of State, 1984)]. United States Secretary of State William P. Rogers delivered this address before the 1969 Galaxy Conference on Adult Education in Washington. It reveals the U.S. government's thinking during discussions with the United Kingdom, France, and the Soviet Union in an effort to achieve an agreed interpretation of Resolution 242 for negotiations. On December 22, 1969, both Israel and Egypt rejected the Rogers plan, the former because of its resistance to the call for a withdrawal to the 1967 borders, and the latter because it was bound by the Khartoum principles. President Nasser would not accept a separate peace with Israel, nor the demilitarization of the Sinai Peninsula. He simply would not consider peace on the basis of a military defeat. In a vote in the U.S. Congress in 1970, seventy senators and 280 representatives rejected Secretary of State Rogers's peace plan as being too one-sided against Israel.

Document 291: Plan Issued by U.S. Secretary of State William P. Rogers (Rogers Plan B) (June 19, 1970) [*reprinted in* ARAB-ISRAELI CONFLICT AND CONCILIATION: A DOCUMENTARY HISTORY(Bernard Reich ed., 1995)]. U.S. Secretary of State, William P. Rogers, delineated the Rogers B Plan in similar letters to the foreign minister of the United Arab Republic, Mahmoud Riad, and the foreign minister of Jordan, Zaid Rifai. Violence in the Suez Canal increased during the spring of 1970 between Egypt and Israel so the United States became interested in encouraging a cease-fire agreement between the states.

The plan asked that Israel and the United Arab Republic adhere to a cease-fire and that the United Arab Republic, Jordan, and Israel agree to follow through with all parts of Resolution 242. It further states that discussions to carry this out must occur between the groups in order to create a fair and long-lasting peace agreement in which the groups recognize the sovereignty, territorial integrity, and political independence of one another. The plan also stated that Israel withdraw from the territories occupied after the 1967 conflict. Secretary of State Rogers writes that the parties must strictly follow the cease-fire resolution of the Security Council from July 1, 1970, to, at least, October 1, 1970. The United Arab Republic, Jordan, and Egypt accepted the plan, and the talks began on August 25, 1970. However, Egypt violated the cease-fire agreement and the United States was reluctant in supporting Israeli claims, so the Israeli ambassador to the United Nations refused to partake in continuing the talks.

Document 292: Plan Issued by U.S. Secretary of State William P. Rogers (Rogers Plan C) (October 4, 1971) [*reprinted in* ARAB-ISRAELI CONFLICT AND CONCILIATION: A DOCUMENTARY

HISTORY (Bernard Reich ed., 1995)]. In an effort to reach his ultimate goal of lasting peace, William P. Rogers, U.S. Secretary of State, posed the Rogers C Plan. Rogers' Six-Point Program, addressed to the United Nations General Assembly, remained within the framework of the U.N. Security Council Resolution 242.

The six points were meant to take into account the positions and concerns of both the Israeli and Egyptian side and call for further discussions between the parties. These points are as follows: to create an interim agreement, the Suez Canal agreement, as a step toward coming to a consensus for an overall settlement; the maintaining of a cease-fire; to institute a principle of withdrawal to make overall settlement a true possibility; to modify and reinforce supervisory mechanisms in the areas so each side can be confident the agreement will not be violated; to reach a compromise on the decision of an Egyptian military presence on the east of the Suez Canal; and finally, to open the passage of the Suez Canal for all nations.

Rogers claimed there was no alternative to arriving at an interim agreement, which would offer hope to their countries for progress and peace. Israel originally rejected the plan on October 12, 1971. On February 2, 1972, Israel reversed its decision and agreed to begin "close proximity" talks with Egypt, who rejected this method.

Document 293: United Nations Security Council Resolution 338, Calling for a Cease-Fire and Implementation of United Nations Resolution 242 (October 22, 1973) [S.C. Res. 338, U.N. SCOR, 1747th mtg., U.N. Doc. S/RES/338 (1979)]. At the height of the 1973 war, the United States and the Soviet Union worked jointly to present Resolution 338 to the Security Council, calling for an immediate ceasefire, implementation of Security Council Resolution 242, and the start of negotiations aimed at establishing a just and durable peace in the Middle East.[227] A cease-fire was soon arranged, achieved at least in part as a result of efforts by U.S. Secretary of State Henry Kissinger and his shuttle diplomacy. Resolutions 338 and 242 have since formed the basis of most peace negotiations.

Document 294: United Nations Security Council Resolution 344, Noting that a Peace Conference for the Implementation of Resolution 242 Is to Begin Shortly in Geneva (December 15, 1973) [S.C. Res. 344, U.N. SCOR, U.N. Doc. S/RES/344 (1973)]. In Resolution 344, the Security Council calls for the implementation of Security Council Resolutions 242 (1967) and 338 (1973) at an anticipated peace conference in Geneva to be held under the auspices of the United Nations.[228] The Security Council requests that the Secretary-General be integrally involved in the work of the conference, playing a full and effective role in accordance with relevant resolutions. The conference was convened on December 21, 1973, with Israel, Egypt, Jordan, the United States, the Soviet Union, and the United Nations attending and Syria boycotting.

Document 295: Memorandum of Agreement between the United States and Israel Regarding the Geneva Peace Conference (Sinai II Accords) (September 1, 1975) [*reprinted in* ARAB-ISRAELI CONFLICT AND CONCILIATION: A DOCUMENTARY HISTORY (Bernard Reich ed., 1995)]. An agreement was reached between the government of the Arab Republic of Egypt and the government of Israel that furthered the disengagement of military forces.

---

[227] *See* Doc. 289.

[228] *See* Docs. 289 and 293.

The leaders decided the conflict in the Middle East will be resolved by peaceful means rather than through military force. The parties agreed to strictly follow the cease-fire on land, sea, and air, and to refrain from using force or military blockades against one another. The agreement required a safe passage for all non-military cargoes headed for Israel through the Suez Canal.

The Sinai II Accords set up rules concerning the redeployment of military forces and their limitations in armament. It outlined the definitions of the lines, and created buffer zones. The provisions of the annex and map in the agreement include a partial pullback of Israel troops from the Mitla and Gidi passes in the Sinai Peninsula and a return of the Abu Rudeis oil fields. In addition, the United States was called to perform continual aerial surveillance missions of the areas covered by the agreement, with results readily available to Israel, Egypt, and the chief coordinator of the U.N. Peacekeeping Missions in the Middle East.

In memoranda agreements between Israel and the United States, the United States assured Israel it will support its best interests by aiding the government with military supplies and pursuing a final peace agreement between Israel and Egypt and Israel and Jordan. In the memorandum regarding the Geneva Conference, the United States reiterated its refusal to recognize or negotiate with the PLO until the PLO accepts Security Council Resolutions 242 and 338 and recognizes Israel's right to exist. In its final assurance to Israel, the U.S. government promised military and economic assistance to maintain Israel's defensive strength. In the United States' final assurance to Egypt, the United States offered to aid Egypt's economic development and stated it is prepared to discuss with Egypt the significance and remedial action required by the United States if Israel were to violate the terms of the agreement.

Document 296: Interim Agreement between Israel and Egypt (September 4, 1975) [*available at* http://www.knesset.gov.il/process/docs/egypt_interim_eng.htm]. This detailed interim agreement between Israel and Egypt covers such topics as the definitions of boundary lines and areas, buffer zones, terms for the process of implementation, and inspections by the UNEF. It also includes a proposal from the United States drafted by Secretary of State Henry Kissinger that describes the role that the United States could play in monitoring the border between Egypt and Israel.

Document 297: A Mideast Proposal by M. Cherif Bassiouni and Morton A. Kaplan (Revision) (1977) [M. CHERIF BASSIOUNI & MORTON A. KAPLAN, A MIDEAST PROPOSAL (2d ed. 1977)]. This Mideast proposal embodies the principle of land for peace, as later outlined in Sadat's speech and the Camp David agreement.[229] It recognizes both Israel's need for security within the region and the Palestinians' need for a homeland. It stresses that all involved parties must agree on certain principles in advance of the Geneva Conference for peace negotiations to succeed. It insists that the Arab states cannot make peace except on the condition of a return to the pre-1967 borders and a Palestinian settlement. It offers a fourteen-point protocol for peace, as well as commentary on such contentious issues as compensation, territorial access, and Jerusalem.

Document 298: United States-Union of Soviet Socialist Republics Joint Statement (Vance-Gromyko Communiqué) (October 1, 1977) [77 DEP'T ST. No. 2002, 639–40 (1977)].

---

[229] *See* Docs. 299 and 308.

U.S. Secretary of State Cyrus Vance and the Soviet Minister for Foreign Affairs A.A. Gromyko issued this joint statement as co-chairmen of the Geneva Peace Conference on the Middle East. The statement sets forth three major protocols: (1) a settlement that is comprehensive, incorporating all parties concerned and all questions, including such key issues as withdrawal of Israeli armed forces from territories occupied in the 1967 conflict; the resolution of the Palestine Question, including insuring the legitimate rights of the Palestinian people, and termination of the state of war and establishment of normal peaceful relations; (2) negotiations to be held within the framework of the Geneva Peace Conference; and (3) all the parties to the conflict must understand the necessity for careful consideration of each other's legitimate rights and interests. The United States and the Soviet Union express their readiness to participate in these guarantees.

Document 299: Excerpts from Egyptian President Anwar al-Sadat's Address to the Knesset (November 20, 1977) [*available at* http://www.knesset.gov.il/process/docs/sadatspeech_eng.htm]. In a bold move aimed at clearing the way for peace talks while still technically in a state of war, Egyptian President Anwar al-Sadat went to Jerusalem to speak directly to Israeli leaders in the Knesset and, through them, to the Israeli people. He began his speech by emphasizing the value of peace, as well as the common bond of Muslims, Christians, and Jews to the land of Jerusalem and to a shared monotheistic tradition. Sadat laments the internecine nature of war that harms Arabs and Israelis alike. He argues that a durable and just peace cannot be reached between Israel and Egypt or any other Arab nation without first finding a just solution to the Palestinian problem—which Sadat identifies as the crux of the issue. Sadat outlines the conditions for a lasting peace, one that is principally based on Security Council Resolution 242 and the "land for peace" model. He insists that Israel completely withdraw from the Occupied Territories, including Arab Jerusalem. Peace negotiations followed Sadat's address almost immediately.

Document 300: Address of Prime Minister Menahem Begin at the Knesset in Response to President Sadat's speech (November 20, 1977) [*available at* http://www.jewishvirtuallibrary.org/jsource/History/begintoknessetsadat.html]. The prime minister starts by dwelling on the common heritage of Islam and Judaism, both of which heralded the universal principle of the ban on human sacrifice. He praises the courage of President Sadat, but takes issue with him by insisting on the unique bond between the Jewish people and the Land of Israel, for "we took no foreign land, we returned to our homeland," and by claiming that it was Israel that had always extended its hand in peace and was turned down by the Arab side. He defines the meaning of the peace that needs to be made as a true reconciliation between the Jewish people and the Arab people. For this to be achieved, it would be necessary not to be daunted by the bitter memories of the past. Prime Minister Begin supports President Sadat's claim that his is not an initiative for a separate peace with Israel, for Israel wants peace with all its neighbors. The peace that would be negotiated with Egypt should usher not only in the end of the state of war between the two nations but also in normal diplomatic relations and economic cooperation, for, as King Hassan of Morocco has rightly said, the combination of Arab and Jewish genius can together convert the region into a paradise on earth. In the peace negotiations, Mr. Begin promises that" everything will be negotiable," but at the same time he dwells extensively on the unique bond between the Jewish people and Jerusalem. He also proposes to reconvene the Geneva Peace Conference to which he expects all Israel's Arab neighbors should be invited.

Document 301: Six-Point Program signed by the leaders of the PLO's Constituent Organizations in Tripoli, Libya (December 4, 1977) [*reprinted in* THE ISRAEL-ARAB READER: A DOCUMENTARY HISTORY OF THE MIDDLE EAST CONFLICT (Walter Laqueur & Barry Rubin eds., 2001)]. Following Sadat's visit to the Knesset, the PLO drafts the six-point program to protest Sadat's "treasonous visit." The program calls for the formation of the Steadfastness and Confrontation Front, continued striving toward a Palestinian state, and a boycott of the Sadat regime.

Document 302: Declaration of the Arab League Summit Conference in Tripoli, Libya (December 5, 1977) [*reprinted in* THE ISRAEL-ARAB READER: A DOCUMENTARY HISTORY OF THE MIDDLE EAST CONFLICT (Walter Laqueur & Barry Rubin eds., 2001)]. The Arab League's 1977 summit culminated in a declaration that served two major purposes. First, it complimented the PLO's six-point plan by condemning Anwar Sadat and going so far as to halting diplomatic relations with Egypt. Second, the declaration takes steps to applaud the PLO in its resistance against the Zionists.

Document 303: Statement by U.S. President Jimmy Carter (Aswan Formula) (January 4, 1978) [*reprinted in* ARAB-ISRAELI CONFLICT AND CONCILIATION: A DOCUMENTARY HISTORY (Bernard Reich ed., 1995)]. In the Aswan Declaration, or Aswan Formula, Jimmy Carter addressed Egyptian President Answar Sadat and the people of Egypt. Carter commended President Sadat's initiatives towards seeking peace with Israel. In his formula, some critical steps to peace were Israel's withdrawal from the territories it began occupying after 1967 and securing borders in regulation with United Nations Resolutions 242 and 338. He stressed the importance of recognizing the rights of the Palestinian people and resolving the Palestinian problem so that they are able to partake in the decisions affecting their own future. With this, he hoped to make 1978 the year that brings peace to the Middle East.

Document 304: Resolutions from the Arab Summit in Baghdad, Iraq (November 5, 1978) [*reprinted in* ARAB-ISRAELI CONFLICT AND CONCILIATION: A DOCUMENTARY HISTORY (Bernard Reich ed., 1995)]. Arab leaders held a summit in Baghdad, Iraq, after the signing of the Camp David Accords. At this summit the leaders discussed the importance of Pan-Arab responsibilities in their struggle against Zionist power and aggression against the interests of Arab nations. The summit affirmed the necessity of Arab nations to come together and make material and moral sacrifices for their common struggle for rights of the Arabs in Palestine and the Occupied Territories. The leaders resolved that a settlement regarding Palestine would not be acceptable unless it is agreed upon and adopted by a resolution of an Arab summit conference. The discussions from the summit deemed it important that no nation should take unilateral action in the Arab-Zionist conflict. The leaders concluded that the agreements signed by the Egyptian government at Camp David did not follow the resolutions of previous Arab summit conferences, specifically those at Algiers and Rabat. The agreements Egypt signed hurt the rights of Palestinians as well as the rights of the Arab nation in Palestine, so the summit called upon Egypt to end its unilateral action in these affairs.

Document 305: PLO Chairman Yasir Arafat: Interview on Camp David (November 19, 1979) [*reprinted in* THE ISRAEL-ARAB READER: A DOCUMENTARY HISTORY OF THE MIDDLE

East Conflict (Walter Laqueur & Barry Rubin eds., 2001)]. In his interview with the Algerian newspaper *Al-Sha'b,* Arafat addresses the Camp David Accords as a counterattack on the Palestinian people in response to the Steadfastness and Confrontation Front. Arafat describes Camp David as just one battlefront in the fight for Occupied Territories and Lebanon.

Document 306: The Baghdad Resolution issued by the League of Arab States (March 31, 1979) [*reprinted in* A Documentary History of the Arab-Israeli Conflict (Charles L. Geddes ed., 1991)]. The Baghdad Resolution condemned the Egyptian government for acting unilaterally and against the sixth, seventh, and ninth Arab summits, which prohibited Arab leaders from signing a peace treaty with the Zionists. In doing so, the Egyptian government hurt the interests of Arab solidarity, specifically by going against its national duty to help liberate the occupied Arab land and help the people of Palestine. To reprimand Egypt, the Arab foreign ministers resolved to withdraw Arab ambassadors from Egypt, end political and diplomatic relations, move the headquarters of the Arab League from Cairo to Tunis, and to only continue working with the Arab people in Egypt that were not involved in working with the Zionist enemy. Because these leaders felt that the peace treaty Egypt signed violates the rights of the Palestinian people, they decided to work to keep other countries from supporting the treaty. Through the foreign, economic, and finance ministers, the Council of the Arab League decided to stop giving loans or offering economic aid to Egypt, and to cease supplying oil to Egypt because the treaty obligates Egypt to sell oil to Israel. The resolution also banned any trade with Egyptian establishments that trade with their Zionist enemy. This resolution left Egypt cut off from the Arab world, but after signing the Egyptian-Israeli peace treaty, Egypt itself announced that it would freeze relations with the Arab League, so this result was predicted.

Document 307: Plan issued by Saudi Crown Prince Fahd ibn Abd al-Aziz (The Fahd Plan) (August 7, 1981) [*reprinted in* Arab-Israeli Conflict and Conciliation: A Documentary History (Bernard Reich ed., 1995)]. Crown Prince Fahd of Saudi Arabia outlined his plan for a settlement of the Palestinian process in an interview with the Saudi Press Agency. The principles he necessitated for a peaceful settlement included the following: Israel's withdrawal and removal of settlements from the territories occupied after 1967; the guarantee of freedom of worship for all religions; protection of the Palestinian people's rights, with the right to return to their homeland; placement of the West Bank and Gaza Strip under U.N. control for a few months; the establishment of an independent Palestinian state with Jerusalem as its capital; and finally, the guarantee of peace for all states in the region.

Document 308: Camp David Accords between Israel and Egypt (September 17, 1978) [17 I.L.M. 1466 (1978)]. The pivotal Camp David talks brought together Israeli Prime Minister Menachem Begin and Egyptian President Anwar al-Sadat and their advisors for the first time to conduct earnest peace negotiations. These ten-day talks took place at U.S. President Jimmy Carter's presidential retreat, Camp David, in Maryland. After an unsteady beginning, the parties agreed to the Framework for Conclusion of a Peace between Egypt and Israel, which sets out the terms for normal relations between the two countries in return for Israel's evacuation of the Sinai. It is agreed that a formal peace treaty will be signed within three months.

Document 309: Annex to the Framework Agreements: Exchange of Letters between U.S. President Jimmy Carter, Israeli Prime Minister Menachem Begin, and Egyptian President Anwar al-Sadat (September 17–22, 1978) [THE QUEST FOR PEACE: PRINCIPAL UNITED STATES PUBLIC STATEMENTS AND RELATED DOCUMENTS ON THE ARAB-ISRAELI PEACE PROCESS 1967–1983 83–87 (U.S. Dep't of State, 1984)]. In these letters, U.S. President Jimmy Carter serves as a secure conduit for Israeli Prime Minister Menachem Begin and Egyptian President Anwar al-Sadat to give notification of progress on the peace process and to express concerns. In the first letter, Begin reports that the Knesset will soon approve the removal of settlers from the Sinai. In response, Sadat affirms Egypt's position that all settlers must be withdrawn as a prerequisite to a final peace treaty and states that Arab sovereignty should be restored in Arab Jerusalem. In response, Begin states that a unified Jerusalem is the capital of the State of Israel. In transmitting this letter to Sadat, Carter assures him that the United States does not accept or recognize Israeli measures as altering the status of Jerusalem. Sadat presses the issues of the West Bank and Gaza and restoring the rights of the Palestinian people. In a final letter from Carter to Begin, Carter acknowledges that in each paragraph of the anticipated treaty, Israel will understand the terms "Palestinians" or "Palestinian People" as referring to "Palestinian Arabs" and the term "West Bank" as referring to "Judea and Samaria."

Document 310: Peace Treaty between Israel and Egypt (March 26, 1979) [18 I.L.M. 362]. Israeli Prime Minister Menachem Begin and Egyptian President Anwar al-Sadat signed this peace treaty on the front lawn of the White House in Washington, D.C. Thus, Egypt became the first Arab country to make peace with Israel. *It contains nine articles, a military annex, an annex on relations between the parties, agreed minutes interpreting the main articles of the treaty, a withdrawal schedule, and security arrangements.*

Document 311: Venice Declaration on the Middle East, Venice European Council (June 13, 1980) [6 E.C. BULL. 10 (1980)]. The Venice Declaration was issued in the wake of the U.S.-brokered peace treaty between Israel and Egypt to signal Europe's intention to play a more active role in future peace deals.[230] European Council members state that the traditional ties and common interests that link Europe to the Middle East oblige them to play a special role in securing regional peace. With the Venice Declaration, the nine member states of the European Community set the basis of their unified policy as follows: the inadmissibility of acquiring territory by force, the necessity of a negotiated solution, security for all states in the region, and respect for the inalienable rights of the Palestinian people, including self-determination. The declaration maintains that European Council member states will not recognize any unilateral initiatives aimed at changing the status of Jerusalem.

Document 312: Crown Prince Fahd's Eight-Point Peace Proposal (Fez Declaration) (August 8, 1981) [*reprinted in* A DOCUMENTARY HISTORY OF THE ARAB-ISRAELI CONFLICT (Charles L. Geddes ed., 1991)]. Crown Prince Fahd of Saudi Arabia created eight principles to bring a lasting and peaceful settlement to Palestine, which were brought before the twelfth Arab summit. Fahd declared that a true peace needs to recognize the rights of both groups. The Fez Declaration competed with the

---

[230] *See* Doc. 310.

Camp David Accord, so the U.S. Department of State declined to comment on it, and Ariel Sharon, then Israel's Defense Minister, declared that he would establish eight additional settlements for each of Fahd's principles. The heads of the Arab states at the summit adopted the plan after making slight changes. The leaders of the Arab states added the point that the Palestinian people's rights need to be recognized under leadership of the PLO, as their legitimate representative. The leaders also added that the Security Council should help guarantee peace in the region, including peace in an independent Palestinian state. The summit declared that the Security Council should guarantee respect of these principles.

Document 313: Proposal by the Soviet Union for a Middle East Settlement (July 29, 1984) [*reprinted in* ARAB-ISRAELI CONFLICT AND CONCILIATION: A DOCUMENTARY HISTORY (Bernard Reich ed., 1995)]. During the 1980s the Soviet Union and the United States put forth efforts to influence the Middle East. The USSR recommended proposals to finalize a settlement in the region. The Soviet Union maintained that all Israeli settlements set up after 1967 in Arab territories should be dismantled and the properties occupied by Israel after 1967 given back to the Arabs, resulting in fixed borders for the two groups. Agreeing with the declaration from the Arab Summit at Fez, the Soviet Union declared that the PLO should be recognized as the representative of the sovereign, independent, Palestinian state, and that the Palestinian territories should be supervised by the United Nations for the beginning months. The Palestinian state and other Arab states should likewise recognize the sovereignty of Israel. The USSR further agreed with the Fez Declaration that East Jerusalem should be returned to the Arabs and all religions must be able to freely worship. The proposal stressed the importance of all parties being involved in the agreement and settlement process in order to ensure lasting peace in the Middle East. All concerned and participating parties should therefore convene at an international conference on the Middle East that should end in the signing of treaties approved by all countries that follow the principals of USSR's proposal. The conference was meant to develop solutions to all other aspects of conflict in the region and establish an international guarantee that all parties maintain the settlement and allow for a lasting peace.

Document 314: Joint Statement Issued by Jordanian King Hassan II and Israeli Prime Minister Shimon Peres (July 23, 1986) [*reprinted in* ARAB-ISRAELI CONFLICT AND CONCILIATION: A DOCUMENTARY HISTORY (Bernard Reich ed., 1995)]. After a series of meetings, Israeli Prime Minister Shimon Peres and King Hassan of Morocco issued a joint statement. The meetings also included three of Peres' advisors and Rafi Edri, a Moroccan member of Israel's Knesset. By participating in these meetings Hassan became the second Arab leader to officially and openly meet with Israel's senior officials. The meeting was mostly devoted to discussing the Fez Declaration. The meeting was solely expletory, with no intentions to begin negotiations. King Hassan II reported back to the Arab leaders Mr. Peres' observations and conditions he finds necessary to establish peace. Likewise, Mr. Peres reported to the Israel government the explanations and viewpoint King Hassan offered with regards to each element of the Fez Declaration.

Document 315: The Peres-Hussein London Agreement (April 11, 1987) [*reprinted in* THE ISRAEL-ARAB READER: A DOCUMENTARY HISTORY OF THE MIDDLE EAST CONFLICT (Walter Laqueur & Barry Rubin eds., 2001)]. Negotiations between Israeli and

Jordanian leaders led to this document, which would serve as the guidelines for finding a political settlement between the two nations as well as with Palestinian representatives. However the intended conference failed to develop as planned due to hesitation on both sides.

Document 316: Madrid Declaration (June 27, 1989) [*reprinted in* ARAB-ISRAELI CONFLICT AND CONCILIATION: A DOCUMENTARY HISTORY (Bernard Reich ed., 1995)]. At the end of the semi-annual European Community Summit on June 26 and 27, 1989, the twelve heads of state released a formal statement on the situation in the Middle East. The Madrid Declaration says that through peaceful means a lasting settlement must be reached in which the PLO is involved and all states in the region, including Palestine and Israel, have secure and recognized borders. The European Council let known its appreciation of the decisions of the Palestinian National Council in Algiers to accept the Security Council Resolutions 242 and 338, recognizing Israel's right to exist and renouncing terrorism.

The declaration appealed to Israeli authorities to end its repressive measures in the Occupied Territories, where the number of dead and wounded was constantly increasing. Particularly it called for the reopening of educational facilities in the West Bank, but also asked Israel to follow the provisions of the Geneva Convention on the Protection of Civilian Populations in Times of War. The European Council also supported the idea of elections in the Occupied Territories to contribute to the peace process towards a just and lasting settlement.

Document 317: Egyptian President Hosni Mubarak's Ten-Point Plan (July 1989) [*reprinted in* ARAB-ISRAELI CONFLICT AND CONCILIATION: A DOCUMENTARY HISTORY (Bernard Reich ed., 1995)]. In order to facilitate the slow-moving process of Arab-Israeli negotiations, Egyptian President Hosni Mubarak offered a ten-point plan regarding an election process in the West Bank. The points included that all Palestinians in the West Bank should be allowed to vote and run for office, without interference from Israeli authorities. On Election Day the Israeli army would withdraw from the polling places and only Israelis that live or work in the Occupied Territories should be permitted to enter. Israel must agree in advance that it will accept the outcome of the election and negotiate for peace, while also protecting its security. Mubarak's ten-point plan also stated that both the United States and Israel should publicly accept and agree to adhere to the plan.

Document 318: Common Agenda between Israel and Jordan (September 14, 1993) [*available at* http://www.mfa.gov.il/MFA/Peace+Process/Guide+to+the+Peace+Process/Israel-Jordan+Common+Agenda.htm]. The Common Agenda between Israel and Jordan was the blueprint for the peace treaty between Israel and Jordan that soon followed.[231] It addresses key issues such as security, water, borders, territorial matters, and refugees and displaced persons.

Document 319: Washington Declaration by Israel, Jordan, and the United States (July 25, 1994) [*available at* http://www.kinghussein. gov.jo/wash_decl2.html]. The Washington Declaration was signed by Israeli Prime Minister Yitzhak Rabin and Jordan's King Hussein in Washington, D.C., during a formal ceremony hosted by U.S. President Bill Clinton. Its major achievement is a series of agreements and

---

[231] *See* Doc. 320.

concrete steps that terminate the state of belligerency between Jordan and Israel, with both states agreeing to seek a just, lasting, and comprehensive peace based on United Nations Security Council Resolutions 242 and 338.[232] The Washington Declaration further recognizes the special role of the Hashemite Kingdom with regard to Muslim Holy Shrines in Jerusalem. Ultimately, the declaration signals Israel and Jordan's intention to sign a formal peace treaty.

Document 320: Treaty of Peace between Israel and Jordan (October 26, 1994) [34 I.L.M. 43]. This treaty signed by Israeli Prime Minister Yitzhak Rabin and Jordanian Prime Minister Abdul Salam Majali establishes a solid framework for political, economic, and cultural cooperation between the State of Israel and the Hashemite Kingdom of Jordan. Among other arrangements, it includes provisions to control water usage from the Yarmouk and Jordan Rivers. This peace treaty was only the second of its kind to be made between Israel and one of its Arab neighbors.[233]

Document 321: Casablanca Declaration (November 1, 1994) [*reprinted in* ARAB-ISRAELI CONFLICT AND CONCILIATION: A DOCUMENTARY HISTORY (Bernard Reich ed., 1995)]. To bring new economic cooperation in the Middle East and North Africa, hundreds of Arab and Israeli government officials and corporate executives met in Casablanca, Morocco. The Casablanca Declaration outlined a plan for regional economic growth that was linked to bringing Arab-Israeli peace. The business leaders from around the world and the representatives from sixty-one countries recognized their mutual dependence and common goals. Peace agreements forged by the government leaders should be made to foster incentives for trade and investment for private sectors to further the peace process.

The Casablanca Declaration expressed a need in the West Bank and Gaza Strip for economic development that required international attention to support the Israel-PLO Declaration of Principles that is meant to enable the Palestinian people to participate at an equal level in the regional development. All attendees at the conference agreed to promote investment from inside and outside the region by overcoming obstacles to trade and investment, such as boycotts, and to play out the economic potential of the Middle East.

Document 322: Statement Issued at the Cairo Summit (February 2, 1995) [*reprinted in* ARAB-ISRAELI CONFLICT AND CONCILIATION: A DOCUMENTARY HISTORY (Bernard Reich ed., 1995)]. Leaders from Egypt, Jordan, Israel, and the Palestinian Authority met in their determination to facilitate the process towards a comprehensive peace in the Middle East. In this statement issued at the Cairo Summit, the parties agreed to move forward in concluding the negotiations of the interim agreement between Israel and the Palestinian Authority. The leaders further condemned the violence in the Middle East and stated their intentions to eliminate all weapons of mass destruction in the region. They also agreed to work towards educational improvements as well as economic enhancement through cooperation and a regional development bank.

Document 323: Speeches Given by U.S. President Bill Clinton, Israeli Prime Minister Ehud Barak, and Syrian Foreign Minister Faruk al-Shara at the Renewal of Syrian-Israeli

---

[232] *See supra* note 7.

[233] *See also* Doc. 310.

Negotiations (December 15, 1999) [*reprinted in* The Israel-Arab Reader: A Documentary History of the Middle East Conflict (Walter Laqueur & Barry Rubin eds., 2001)]. The speeches by President Clinton, Ehud Barak, and Farouk al-Shara in this document reflect the starting point for an attempt at a new round of aggressive negotiations between Israel and Syria. Within the following weeks, however, the negotiations grinded to a halt and did not result in any agreements.

Document 324: Draft Agreement between Israel and Syria, Prepared by the United States (January 13, 2000) [*available at* http://www.us-israel.org/jsource/Peace/syrdraft.html]. The Clinton administration presented this draft peace treaty to the State of Israel and the government of the Syrian Arab Republic before his departure from office. It was never signed as talks broke down between Israeli Prime Minister Ehud Barak and Syrian President Hafez Assad.

Document 325: Riyadh Declaration (March 29, 2007) [*available at* http://www.saudiembassy.net/2007News/Statements/StateDetail.asp?cIndex=703]. The two-day summit of the ninteenth session of the Council of the League of Arab States established a renewed roadmap for peace in the Middle East. The declaration called for solidarity among Arab states, renunciation of extremism, and a plan to reach a peace settlement in the Arab-Israeli conflict. The summit reiterated its support for the so-called Saudi Peace plan (that was endorsed by the 2002 Arab League Summit in Beirut) that called for Israel to withdraw to the 1967 borders with Syria and the Palestinians, resolve the refugees problem and the question of Jerusalem in exchange for full peace with the entire Arab world.

Document 326: Trip Report by Former U.S. President Jimmy Carter to Israel, Palestine, Egypt, Syria, Saudi Arabia, and Jordan (April 22, 2008) [*available at* http://www.cartercenter.org/news/trip_reports/middle_east_2008.html]. President Carter visited several Mid-East leaders, including those from Syria and Hamas, to discuss the challenges and options available in the ongoing peace process for the region. His synopsis recalls meetings with various leaders and organizations, discusses his role on the trip, and provides a summary of the results. The report's most substantive elements include Carter's reflection on his meetings with Syrian and Hamas leaders, specifically noting those states' concerns and peace process options to which they are most receptive.

5. Arms Control and Regional Security: 1948–2002

The process of demilitarization and arms control in the conflict began with the Agreement for the Demilitarization of Mount Scopus, signed by Arab and Jewish authorities on July 15, 1948.[234] Since then, there have been few cooperative attempts to address the issue of demilitarization, arms control, or the establishment of a regional security regime for the area. In fact, to the contrary, both the United States and the Soviet Union engaged in arms trade with states in the region throughout the period of the major Arab-Israeli wars.

The United Nations has consistently addressed the question of eliminating weapons of mass destruction from the Middle East in twenty-

[234] *See* Doc. 327.

nine similar resolutions passed since 1974 that reiterate the goal of creating a nuclear-weapons-free zone in the region.[235]

Nevertheless, Israel's official policy since 1961 has been "nuclear ambiguity," simply asserting that it would not be the first nation to introduce nuclear weapons into the region.[236] Israel has yet to sign the Nuclear Non-Proliferation Treaty, making it the only state in the Middle East not to do so.[237] It is presumed that Israel's nuclear weapons program dates back to the mid- to late-1950s and that, with initial French assistance and U.S. acquiescence, Israel has developed a relatively advanced nuclear arsenal.

One of the outcomes of the 1991 Madrid Peace Conference was the formation of the Arms Control and Regional Security working group, which consisted of representatives of thirteen Arab states, Israel, a Palestinian delegation, and a number of extra-regional entities. Expert-level meetings focused on confidence-building measures with regard to maritime issues, military exercises and information exchange, search and rescue coordination, and the establishment of Regional Security Centers in Jordan, Qatar, and Tunisia. After September 1995, complications in the peace process and an inability to reach agreement over a weapons-of-mass-destruction-free zone resulted in talks being suspended. However, several "Track II" efforts have been undertaken, including one coordinated by this editor between 1995 and 2004.[238]

Relevant documents in other chapters should be consulted, in particular those in: Section 4, Arab-Israeli Peace Process; and Section 7, Israeli-Palestinian Peace Process.

Document 327: Agreement for the Demilitarization of Mount Scopus (July 7, 1948) [*available at* http://www.mfa.gov.il/MFA/Foreign%20Relations/Israels%20Foreign%20Relations%20since%201947/1947-1974/14%20Agreement%20for%20the%20demilitarisation%20of%20Mount%20Sco]. This agreement, struck between Arab and Jewish military commanders and the chairman of the United Nations

---

[235] Resolutions 3263 (XXIX) of Dec. 9, 1974, 3474 (XXX) of Dec. 11, 1975, 31/71 of Dec. 10, 1976, 32/82 of Dec. 12, 1977, 33/64 of Dec. 14, 1978, 34/77 of Dec. 11, 1979, 35/147 of Dec. 12, 1980, 36/87 A and B of Dec. 9, 1981, 37/75 of Dec. 9, 1982, 38/64 of Dec. 15, 1983, 39/54 of Dec. 12, 1984, 40/82 of Dec. 12, 1985, 41/48 of Dec. 3, 1986, 42/28 of Nov. 30, 1987, 43/65 of Dec. 7 1988, 44/108 of Dec. 15, 1989, 45/52 of Dec. 4, 1990, 46/30 of Dec. 6, 1991, 47/48 of Dec. 9, 1992, 48/71 of Dec. 16, 1993, 49/71 of Dec. 15, 1994, 50/66 of Dec. 12, 1995, 51/41 of Dec. 10, 1996, 52/34 of Dec. 9, 1997, 53/74 of Dec. 4, 1998, 54/51 of Dec. 1, 1999, 55/30 of Nov. 20, 2000, 56/21 of Nov. 29, 2001, 57/55 of Nov. 22, 2002, and 58/34 of Dec. 19, 2003. *See* Doc. 329.

[236] Israel's jailing of Mordechai Vanunu, the nuclear whistleblower, in 1986 for publishing incriminating photographs of Israel's nuclear power plant at Dimona reveals the extent of Israel's nuclear gagging.

[237] *See* NPT, *supra* note 210. In 2003, with the fall of Saddam Hussein in Iraq and the end of Libya's weapons of mass destruction (WMD) program, the WMD threat facing Israel has largely diminished, though Iran and Pakistan still pose potential threats.

[238] *See* Doc. 340.

Truce Commission, protects the area known as Mount Scopus in Jerusalem until have hostilities ceased. Mount Scopus was home to important civic institutions such as the Hadassah Hospital, the Hebrew University, and the Augusta Victoria Hospital.

Document 328: Soviet-Egyptian Treaty of Friendship and Cooperation (May 27, 1971) [*reprinted in* ARAB-ISRAELI CONFLICT AND CONCILIATION: A DOCUMENTARY HISTORY (Bernard Reich ed., 1995)]. The newly elected president of Egypt, Anwar Sadat, brought strained relations between Egypt and the Soviet Union. Sadat brought many changes to government and Egypt's international relations, specifically Egypt's position on the Arab-Israel conflict. He and Soviet President Nikolai Podgornyi singed a fifteen-year Treaty of Friendship and Cooperation to strengthen their relations and promote universal peace. The treaty called for an unbreakable friendship and cooperation in the political, economic, scientific, technological, and cultural fields. As the first Soviet Treaty with an Arab country, Podgornyi was hoping to have influence of Sadat, but Sadat's main goal was to gain back the Egyptian territory occupied by Israel. The treaty did not last after Moscow refused to supply Sadat with aircraft and missiles. Just five years later Sadat officially decided to end the treaty.

Document 329: United Nations General Assembly Resolution 3263, Establishing a Nuclear-Weapon-Free Zone in the Region of the Middle East (December 9, 1974) [G.A. Res. 3263, U.N. GAOR, U.N. Doc. 3263 (XXIX) (1974)]. United Nations General Assembly Resolution 3263 calls for the establishment of a nuclear-weapon-free zone in the region of the Middle East. The same resolution has been adopted every year since.

Document 330: United Nations General Assembly Resolution 3474, Nuclear Proliferation in the Middle East (December 11, 1975) [G.A. Res. 3474, U.N. GAOR, 2437th plen. mtg., U.N. Doc. 3474 (1975)]. In Resolution 3474, the General Assembly recognizes that the establishment of a nuclear-weapon-free zone in the Middle East enjoys wide regional support and expresses the opinion that consulted member states should exert efforts towards the realization of that objective. It recommends that concerned member states proclaim their intention to refrain, on a reciprocal basis, from producing, acquiring, or in any other way possessing nuclear weapons and nuclear explosive devices and from permitting the stationing of nuclear weapons in their territory or the territory under their control by any third party.

Document 331: United Nations General Assembly Resolution 33/71 (A), Military and Nuclear Collaboration with Israel (December 14, 1978) [G.A. Res. 33/71(A), U.N. GAOR, 84th plen. mtg., U.N. Doc. A/RES/33/71(A) (1978)]. After expressing its grave concern over the continued and rapid Israeli military build-up, the General Assembly adopted this resolution requesting all states to refrain from military and nuclear collaboration with Israel and condemning the intensification of military collaboration between Israel and South Africa. The General Assembly calls upon all states: to refrain from any supply of arms, ammunition, military equipment or vehicles, or spare parts to Israel; to ensure that supplies do not reach Israel through other parties; and to end all transfer of nuclear equipment or fissionable material or technology to Israel.

Document 332: United Nations General Assembly Resolution 34/89, Israeli Nuclear Armament (December 11, 1979) [G.A. Res. 34/89, U.N. GAOR, 34th Sess., 97th plen.

mtg., U.N. Doc. A/RES/34/89 (1979)]. Alarmed by the increasing information and evidence of Israel's activities aimed at the acquisition and development of nuclear weapons, the General Assembly in Resolution 34/89 calls upon Israel to submit its nuclear facilities to inspection by the IAEA and strongly condemns any attempt by Israel to manufacture, acquire, store, or test nuclear weapons or introduce them into the Middle East.

Document 333: United Nations General Assembly Resolution 37/82, Israeli Nuclear Armament (December 9, 1982) [G.A. Res. 37/82, U.N. GAOR, U.N. Doc. A/RES/37/82 (1982)]. In Resolution 37/82, the General Assembly notes with grave concern Israel's persistent refusal to adhere to the Treaty on the Non-Proliferation of Nuclear Weapons.[239] Conscious of the consequences of Israel's nuclear-weapon capability and its collaboration with South Africa to develop nuclear weapons, the General Assembly reaffirms its demand that Israel renounce any possession of nuclear weapons and place all of its nuclear activities under international safeguards. It also requests that the Security Council investigate Israel's nuclear activities and the collaboration of other states, parties, and institutions in these activities. Finally, the resolution calls upon all states to submit to the Secretary-General all information concerning Israel's nuclear program.

Document 334: United Nations International Atomic Energy Agency Resolution 470, Demanding that Israel Place Its Nuclear Facilities under IAEA Safeguards (September 25, 1987) [U.N. Int'l Atomic Energy Agency Res. 470, U.N. Doc. GC(XXXI)/RES/470 (1987)]. In Resolution 470, the IAEA demands that Israel place its nuclear facilities under IAEA safeguards and requests the director general to report back on Israel's nuclear capabilities and threat and on the implementation of this resolution.

Document 335: Excerpts from the Report of the Secretary-General Regarding Israeli Nuclear Armament (October 16, 1987) [U.N. GAOR, 42d Sess., Agenda Item 68, U.N. Doc. A/42/581 (1987)]. The Secretary-General submitted this report to the General Assembly in pursuance of Resolution 41/93, which had requested that the Secretary-General follow closely Israel's nuclear activities and update the Study on Israeli Nuclear Armament (1981). It reviews and investigates Israel's nuclear capabilities.

Document 336: White House Fact Sheet on the Middle East Arms Control Initiative (May 29, 1991) [*available at* http://bushlibrary.tamu.edu/research/papers/1991/91052905.html]. On May 29, 1991, President Bush announced a comprehensive arms control proposal for the Middle East aimed at reducing the threat of conventional arms build-ups in the region. The proposal targets Iraq, Iran, Libya, Syria, Egypt, Lebanon, Israel, Jordan, Saudi Arabia, and the other states of the Maghreb and the Gulf Cooperation Council. The proposal calls on the five largest suppliers of arms to the region—China, France, the United Kingdom, the Soviet Union, and the United States, which are also the permanent members of the Security Council—to meet at senior levels to establish guidelines for transfers of conventional arms, as well as weapons of mass destruction (WMD) and associated technology to the region.

Document 337: Statement Issued after the Meeting of the Five on Arms Transfers and Non-Proliferation, Paris (July 9, 1991) [*available at* http://dosfan.lib.uic.edu/ERC/

[239] *See* NPT, *supra* note 210.

briefing/dispatch/1991/html/Dispatchv2no28.html]. U.S. President George Bush, French President François Mitterrand, and British Prime Minister John Major, along with representatives of the People's Republic of China and the USSR, met in Paris July 8–9, 1991, to review issues related to conventional arms transfers and the non-proliferation of weapons of mass destruction. In this joint statement, they note with concern the dangers posed by the excessive buildup of military capabilities in the region and confirm they will not transfer conventional weapons in circumstances that would undermine regional stability.

Document 338: Joint-Statement by Syrian President Hafiz al-Asad and U.S. President Bill Clinton (January 16, 1994) [*reprinted in* THE ISRAEL-ARAB READER: A DOCUMENTARY HISTORY OF THE MIDDLE EAST CONFLICT (Walter Laqueur & Barry Rubin eds., 2001)]. The January 1994 meeting between Asad and Clinton was the culmination of talks between the two men over the course of the preceding year. The meeting addressed both Arab-Israeli concerns as a well as the relationship between Syria and the United States.

Document 339: Syrian President Hafiz al-Asad and U.S.President Bill Clinton: Statement on Their Meeting (January 16, 1994) [*reprinted in* THE ISRAEL-ARAB READER: A DOCUMENTARY HISTORY OF THE MIDDLE EAST CONFLICT (Walter Laqueur & Barry Rubin eds., 2001)]. The January 1994 meeting between Asad and Clinton was the culmination of talks between the two men over the course of the preceding year. The meeting addressed both Arab-Israeli concerns as a well as the relationship between Syria and the United States.

Document 340: Group of Experts—Middle East Regional Security: A Strategic Overview (1996) [GROUP OF EXPERT ON MIDDLE EAST REGIONAL SECURITY WITH THE ELIMINATION OF WEAPONS OF MASS DESTRUCTION (IHRLI, 2003)]. This strategic overview of Middle East regional security was proposed by the Group of Experts on the Establishment of a Regional Security Regime in the Middle East, a Track II endeavor consisting of experts in the areas of the military, diplomacy, intelligence, science, and law. This document defines five principles for a regional security regime in the Middle East: states have the right to live in peace and security; each state has the right to self-defense; no state's security is enhanced by reducing another state's security; no state can intervene in the internal affairs of another state; and all conflicts should be resolved through peaceful means in accordance with international law. This text also calls for the establishment of institutional safeguards for security, such as a Middle East Security Council and a Middle East Disarmament and Arms Control Organization.

Document 341: United Nations General Assembly Resolution 52/41, the Risk of Nuclear Proliferation in the Middle East (December 31, 1997) [G.A. Res. 52/41, U.N. GAOR, U.N. Doc. A/RES/52/41 (1997)]. In Resolution 52/41, the General Assembly calls upon Israel as the only State in the Middle East not party to the Treaty on the Non-Proliferation of Nuclear Weapons to accede to it without delay and not to develop, produce, test, or otherwise acquire nuclear weapons and to place its nuclear facilities under IAEA safeguards as an important confidence-building measure.[240]

---

[240] *Id.*

Document 342: Report by the Director General to the Board of Governors and to the General Conference of the International Atomic Energy Agency, Application of IAEA Safeguards in the Middle East (August 17, 1999) [IAEA Doc. GOV/1999/51-GC(43)/17 (1999)]. In this report, the IAEA considers whether arms control and the establishment of a Nuclear-Weapons-Free Zone in the Middle East is a necessary precondition for the establishment of a comprehensive peace and security in the region—with Israel differing from all other states in the region on the issue. It determines that clarity about the views of Middle East states on such issues is indispensable to the preparation of model verification agreements. The director general adds that a future Middle East Nuclear Weapons Free Zone will require far-reaching, intrusive, and comprehensive verification arrangements, including mutual inspection by the parties. Annexes include letters from Iraqi, Israeli, and Jordanian heads of state on the topic.

Document 343: Report of the Secretary-General, Establishment of a Nuclear-Weapon-Free Zone in the Middle East (July 15, 2002) [U.N. GAOR, 57th Sess., Item 64, U.N. Doc. A/57/214 (2002)]. United Nations Secretary-General Koffi Annan submitted this report to the General Assembly pursuant to United Nations General Assembly Resolution 56/21, which requests a report on the establishment of a nuclear-weapon-free zone in the region of the Middle East. Annan reports that such a zone remains of considerable importance in the region and that he has consulted with concerned parties within and outside the region in order to explore ways of promoting one. The report contains the direct replies on the subject from the governments of Egypt, Israel, Lebanon, etc.

6. Jerusalem and the Holy Sites: 636–2008

The seventy-one documents contained in this section represent the key international treaties and laws devised for Jerusalem since the Early Arab Period. They are drawn from a range of sources: Umar ibn al Khattab, the Second Khalifa of Islam; the Turkish Ottoman Empire; the governments of Great Britain, Israel, and the United States; the United Nations; and the Holy See.

The City of Jerusalem is a center of faith for the three major monotheistic religions—Judaism, Christianity, and Islam—with each claiming a timeless connection to the city. Its special significance is reflected in the astonishing number of Jewish, Christian, and Muslim Holy Sites located within the small area of the Old City of Jerusalem, which covers a mere 220 acres (one square kilometer).

The ancient Israelites built two Holy Temples in Jerusalem on Mount Moriah, the purported site of Abraham's intended sacrifice of his son Isaac: Solomon's Temple, c. 965–931 B.C.E. to 586 B.C.E., and the Second Temple, 515 B.C.E. to 70 C.E. The Western Wall of the Second Temple (*kotel*) remains today and is a powerful symbol of Judaism's living legacy in the modern age. Christians have erected multiple shrines in Jerusalem owing to the city's important role in Jesus' life and death. The Church of the Holy Sepulchre in the Old City marks the site of Jesus' crucifixion and houses his purported tomb. Perhaps the most prominent edifice in Jerusalem's skyline is the Dome of the Rock mosque, part of the *Haram al Sharif* (Noble Sanctuary or Temple Mount), which includes the al-Aqsa mosque, extensive gardens, and several smaller structures. The Dome of the Rock marks the site from which, in tradition, the Prophet Mohamed made his night journey to the heavens in 613 C.E. (*al-Isra' wal-me'r j'*). Millions of religious pilgrims and travelers from around the globe have visited these Holy Sites. In 1981, the United Nations named the Old City of Jerusalem a World Heritage Site, acknowledging its extraordinary value and importance to the larger global community.

Jerusalem has long held a special status as a holy city and been treated in legal terms as a unique and separate entity. Special legal regimes have been devised for the area's Holy Sites to ensure free access and free exercise of worship to all religious followers—with sites placed under the control of respective faiths and denominations. This policy, known as the *status quo*, is based on a law promulgated by the Turkish Ottoman Empire in 1757.

Given the deep attachments that Jews, Christians, and Muslims have for Jerusalem, it is not surprising that disputes and hostilities continue to erupt over control of the city. In the modern period, several solutions have been offered, the most feasible of which are internationalization and partition.

Internationalization is a historically established approach, approved by the United Nations General Assembly in 1947 with Resolution 181.[241] Under the plan, Jerusalem would be established as a *Corpus Separatum*, an open city, under the control of a council of protection appointed by the United Nations. This was an improvement over proposals in the 1937 Peel Commission Report, which recommended partitioning Palestine into a Jewish and an Arab state and maintaining Jerusalem as part of a "special zone" administered by a British mandate.[242] For a variety of political reasons, internationalization did not succeed.[243] Nevertheless, it has remained the United Nations' overriding vision for Jerusalem since the approval of the Statute for the City of Jerusalem on April 4, 1950.[244]

---

241 *See* Doc. 59.

242 *See* Doc. 35.

243 Directly following the release of the United Nations internationalization plan, the Jewish resistance group *Leh'i* concentrated its activities in Jerusalem against members of the United Nations administration in order to prevent implementation of the United Nations Partition Plan and internationalization. *See supra* note 1.

244 *See* Doc. 372. Curiously, special provisions for Jerusalem are conspicuously absent from Security Council Resolutions 242 (1967) and 338 (1973), which have served as the legal framework for the peace process. Neither is Jerusalem mentioned in the Balfour Declaration (1917), nor in the Terms of the British Mandate for Palestine drafted by the Council of the League of Nations (1922).

The partition or division of Jerusalem into two distinct parts—one Arab and one Jewish—has been the less-favored though furthest realized of plans. The 1948 war produced a *de facto* partition of the city, separating Jerusalem into an Israeli-controlled western part of the city and a Jordanian-controlled eastern part, with Jordan controlling the Old City and most of the Holy Sites. The cultural integrity of the city and the *status quo* suffered considerably under the post-1948 conditions of virtual war.[245]

Following the 1967 war, the Jerusalem Question again became critical as the State of Israel unilaterally annexed the city.[246] No longer was there partition, but the cultural divide between east and west in Jerusalem persisted. In 1980, Israel named a united Jerusalem its capital, drawing criticism from the international community.[247] In 2000, following talks at Camp David II, Israeli negotiators again proposed dividing Jerusalem into two cities: a Jewish city to be known as Jerusalem, which would serve as Israel's capital; and an Arab city to be known as Al-Quds, which would serve as the capital of a new Palestinian Arab state.[248] Palestinian negotiators rejected the proposal, which would have relegated some Arab neighborhoods to Israel, while offering to the Palestinians a formula of only partial sovereignty on the *Haram al Sharif*. Six months later, however, a more generous peace formula was advanced by President Clinton in his "Peace Parameters" whereby Jerusalem was to be divided between Jewish and Arab neighborhoods and the *Haram* was to be placed under Palestinian sovereignty.

This section should be read in conjunction with all other section considering Jerusalem's pivotal role in the conflict.

Document 344: Covenant of Umar (Mu'aliadat Ahi Iliya') (636 or 638 C.E.) [available at http://www.mideastweb.org/covenantofomar.htm].[249] Umar ibn al Khattab, the Second Khalifa after Prophet Mohamed's death, issued this covenant, or *sulh*, for Jerusalem after taking control of the city from the Romans. Paying tribute to the unique cultural and religious status of Jerusalem, it goes far beyond the protection normally conferred upon conquered cities. The use of the word *Ilya* in reference to Jerusalem is a shortened version of *Aelia Capitolina*, the Roman name for the city.

Document 345: Jerusalem Peace Treaty of Jaffa (February 11, 1229) [reprinted in 9 ENCYCLOPEDIA BRITANNICA 824 (1969)]. The Peace Treaty of Jaffa, signed by the Holy Roman Emperor Frederick II (the Great) of Hohenstaufen and the Sultan

---

[245] During the nineteen years of Jordanian administration (1948–1967), Jordan failed to provide Jews with unhindered access to their Holy Places, such as the Western Wall, and barred them from entering the Old City.

[246] *See* Doc. 390.

[247] *See* Docs. 390–392.

[248] *See* Doc. 442.

[249] For text in original language, Arabic, see INTERNATIONAL INSTRUMENTS ON HUMAN RIGHTS: VOLS. 1 & 2 (M. Cherif Bassiouni ed., 2003).

of Babylon and Damascus Malik al-Kamel, allows the two parties to exercise provisional and joint sovereignty over Jerusalem. It continues the tradition of allowing Catholics and Sarrazin (*i.e.*, all non-Catholics, including Christian Orthodox, Copt, Jewish or Muslim, Arab, Egyptian, Kurd or Turk) free access to the city's Holy Sites.

Document 346: Imperial Firman Concerning the Christian Holy Places (February 1852) [W. ZANDER, ISRAEL AND THE HOLY PLACES OF CHRISTENDOM 178 (1971)]. The Ottoman government published multiple imperial firmans (*i.e.*, orders) for Jerusalem in order to regulate the status of the various churches and Holy Sites in the city.[250] The most important was this 1852 firman, which outlines with the powers and rights of the various denominations at specific sites. The arrangement, known generally as the *status quo*, was later applied to the Church of the Holy Sepulchre and its dependencies—the Convent of Deir al-Sultan, the Sanctuary of the Ascension, the Tomb of the Virgin Mary in Jerusalem, as well as the Church of the Nativity, the Milk Grotto, and the Shepherds' Field near Bethlehem.

Document 347: Imperial Firman-1311 (July 19, 1893) [U.N. SCOR, Appendix VII, U.N. Doc. S/8427/Add.1 (1968)]. Following the death of the Chief Rabbinate of Jerusalem, this firman appoints Yaco Shaoul Elyashar Effendi as his successor. It includes instructions from the Ottoman Government on the proper conduct toward the Jewish community, including a proscription on the oppression and fining of synagogues by officers and officials and a decree against interfering with the repairs and structural improvements of Jewish Holy Sites. It also prevents the confiscation of items from a synagogue in order to satisfy a debt and demands that any items taken from a synagogue be handed over to the authorities so that they can be returned.

Document 348: Decision Passed by the Majles Idarah of the Liwa (November 12, 1909) [United Nations Security Council Archives, February 23, 1968]. After members of the Jewish community began to sit in chairs at the Western Wall (the edge of the *Haram al-Sharif*) during prayer, the official trustee filed a petition to prevent the use of chairs out of concern for a possible future claim of ownership. The Administrative Council granted the petition, stating that no articles should be placed outside the site that might serve as an indication of ownership.

Document 349: Proclamation of Martial Law in Jerusalem (Declaration of General Allenby) (December 11, 1917) [*available at* http://www.mfa.gov.il/MFA/MFAArchive/1990_1999/1998/7/Jerusalem-s%20Municipal%20Archives]. British General Edmund Allenby, commander-in-chief of the Allied Egyptian Expeditionary Force, read this Proclamation of Martial Law outside the Citadel of King David in Jerusalem after occupying the City in December 1917. Jerusalem and Palestine thereby became an extension of the British colonial and military presence in the Middle East. The proclamation was printed in three languages: English, French, and Italian.

Document 350: Decree of the Surrender of Jerusalem into British Control (December 1917) [*available at* http://www.firstworldwar.com/source/ jerusalemdecree.htm]. In handing Jerusalem to the British, this decree expresses the concern that a continued British artillery attack would damage the city's Holy Sites.

[250] *See supra* Glossary of Terms.

Document 351: Palestine (Holy Places) Order in Council (July 25, 1924) [*available at* http://domino.un.org/UNISPAL.NSF/0/ c7aae196f41aa 055052565f50054e656?OpenDocument]. This Order in Council determines that no court in Palestine retains the judicial power to decide any matter in connection with the Holy Places in Palestine. The British high commissioner in Palestine is to decide all such issues.

Document 352: Report of the Commission Appointed by His Majesty's Government in the United Kingdom of Great Britain and Northern Ireland to Determine the Rights and Claims of Moslems and Jews in Connection with the Western or Wailing Wall at Jerusalem (December 1930) [*available at* http://domino.un.org/UNISPAL.NSF/0/59a92104ed00dc468525625b00527fea?OpenDocument]. After the Wailing Wall Riots of 1929, a commission was appointed to inquire into the rights and claims of Jewish and Arab groups to the Wailing Wall according to the judicial methods of the English courts.[251] The Jewish side was considered as the plaintiff and the Muslim side acted as the defendant.

Document 353: Palestine (Western or Wailing Wall) Order in Council (May 19, 1931) [*available at* http://domino.un.org/UNISPAL.NSF/a47250072a3dd7950525672400783bde/c2567d9c6f6ce5d8052565d9006efc72!OpenDocument]. Following a serious outbreak of violence over the Western Wall in August 1929, an international commission was appointed by the British government to determine the rights and claims of Muslims and Jews in connection with the Holy Site.[252] The commission—composed of experts from the Netherlands, Sweden, and Switzerland—spent a month in Jerusalem in 1930 interviewing witnesses on both sides. After failing to negotiate a settlement between the parties, the commission determined that Muslims own the Western Wall because it forms part of the *Haram al Sharif*, but that Jews should have free access to the wall. The commission's verdict also stipulates what types of objects may be brought to the wall and when.

Document 354: The Historical Connection of the Jewish People to Jerusalem: Memorandum Issued by the Jewish Agency (July 1, 1938) [*reprinted in* 3 The Arab Israeli Conflict 191–209 (John Morton Moore ed., 1974)]. The Executive Committee of the Jewish Agency submitted this detailed report to the twenty-first Zionist Congress and the sixth session of the Council of the Jewish Agency on the historical connection between Jerusalem and the Jewish people. It traces the Jews' connection to the city from the Biblical period through the nineteenth-century to the "New Jerusalem."

Document 355: United Nations Trusteeship Council Resolution 29, Resolving that the Working Committee on Jerusalem May Hear Interested Parties (December 11, 1947) [T.C. Res. 29, *reprinted in* 1 United Nations Resolutions on Palestine and the Arab-Israeli Conflict 1947–1974 175 (George Tomeh ed., 1975)]. In Resolution 29, the United Nations Trusteeship Council allows the Working Committee on Jerusalem to invite parties with a spiritual and religious interest in Jerusalem to present their views on the United Nations Statute for the City of Jerusalem.[253]

Document 356: United Nations Trusteeship Council Resolution 32, Deciding that the Draft Statute for the City of Jerusalem Is Now in Satisfactory Form (March 10, 1948) [T.C. Res. 32, U.N. TCOR, U.N. Doc. T/RES/32(II) (1948)]. In Resolution 32, the Trusteeship

---

[251] *See* Doc. 32.

[252] *Id.*

[253] *See* Doc. 358.

Council sets the deadline for approval of the completed statute and also determines that on the date of approval they will appoint a governor of Jerusalem.[254]

Document 357: United Nations Trusteeship Council Resolution 33, Requesting the Secretary-General to Provide Funds in Connection with the Draft Statute for the City of Jerusalem (March 10, 1948) [T.C. Res. 33, *reprinted in* 1 UNITED NATIONS RESOLUTIONS ON PALESTINE AND THE ARAB-ISRAELI CONFLICT 1947–1974 175 (George Tomeh ed., 1975)]. After receiving budget recommendations from the Committee on the Budgetary Implications of the Draft Statute, the Trusteeship Council in Resolution 33 requests that the Secretary-General provide those funds and prepare expenditure estimates for the United Nations' responsibilities in Jerusalem.[255]

Document 358: United Nations Draft Statute for the City of Jerusalem (April 21, 1948) [U.N. TCOR, 2d Sess., pt. 3, Annex, at 4–24, U.N. Doc. T/118/Rev. 2 (1948)]. The United Nations Trusteeship Council adopted the Statute for Jerusalem in fulfillment of United Nations Resolution 181, which called for Jerusalem to be established as a *corpus serparatum* (*i.e.*, separate entity/body) under a Special International Regime to be administered by the United Nations.[256] The statute outlines the territories to be included in the City of Jerusalem and defines who would be a resident and citizen. It also determines that the city will be demilitarized, with no paramilitary formations, exercises, or activities allowable within its borders.

Document 359: United Nations Trusteeship Council Resolution 34, Referring the Question of Approval of the Draft Statute for the City of Jerusalem to the General Assembly (April 21, 1948) [T.C. Res. 34, *reprinted in* 1 UNITED NATIONS RESOLUTIONS ON PALESTINE AND THE ARAB-ISRAELI CONFLICT 1947–1974 175 (George Tomeh ed., 1975)]. In Resolution 34, the Trusteeship Council refers the Statute for Jerusalem to the General Assembly for further instruction after finding it in satisfactory form.[257]

Document 360: United Nations General Assembly Resolution 185, Asking the Trusteeship Council to Study Measures for the Protection of Jerusalem and Its Inhabitants (April 26, 1948) [G.A. Res. 185, U.N. GAOR, U.N. Doc. A/RES/185 (S-2) (1948)]. In Resolution 185, the General Assembly instructs the United Nations Trusteeship Council to deliberate on suitable measures for the protection of Jerusalem and its populace and to submit those proposals to the General Assembly as quickly as possible.

Document 361: United Nations Security Council Resolution 54, Ordering Parties to Desist from Further Military Action and Instructing the Mediator to Continue His Efforts towards the Demilitarization of Jerusalem (July 15, 1948) [S.C. Res. 54, U.N. SCOR, 3d Sess., Supp. for July 1948, at 76–77, U.N. Doc. S/902 (1948)]. In this resolution, the Security Council determines that the situation in Palestine constitutes a threat to the peace within the meaning of Article 39 of the United Nations Charter.[258] It orders all concerned governments and authorities to desist from further military action and declares that failure to do so would lead to action under Chapter VIII. The Security Council instructs the mediator in Palestine to continue efforts towards the demilitarization of Jerusalem.[259]

---

[254] *Id.*
[255] *Id.*
[256] *See* Doc. 59.
[257] *See supra* note 15.
[258] *See* U.N. CHARTER, art. 39, *available at* http://www.un.org/aboutun/charter/.
[259] *See* Doc. 327.

Document 362: Cablegram from the United Nations Mediator Addressed to the Secretary-General Concerning Demilitarized Jerusalem (August 18, 1948) [U.N. SCOR, U.N. Doc. S/977 (1948)]. In this cablegram to the Secretary-General, the acting mediator in Palestine, Count Folke Bernadotte, expresses his deep concern over the situation in Jerusalem, noting that a cease-fire has not been implemented and that both parties "have come deliberately to ignore the authority of the United Nations." Bernadotte warns that the failure to demilitarize Jerusalem may lead to a general resumption of hostilities. He requests that the Security Council take prompt action to effect Security Council Resolution 54.[260]

Document 363: Cablegram from the Chairman of the Truce Commission Addressed to the President of the Security Council Concerning Violations of the Holy Places by Jewish and Arab Forces in Jerusalem (October 16, 1948) [U.N. Press Release, U.N. Dep't of Public Info., U.N. Doc. PAL/343 (1948)]. This cablegram from the chairman of the Truce Commission, Rene Neuville, describes the obstruction of free access to the Holy Sites by both Arabs and Jews. The chairman attributes these violations of the *status quo* to the "deliberate intention" of both parties.

Document 364: United Nations Conciliation Commission for Palestine, Working Paper Regarding the Control of Religious Properties (July 22, 1949) [U.N. GAOR, Conciliation Comm. for Palestine, U.N. Doc. A/AC.25/Com.Jer/W.28 (1949)]. In this document, the United Nations Conciliation Commission reports that the Arab delegations are generally prepared to accept the principle of an international regime for the Jerusalem area, subject to United Nations guarantees for its stability and permanence. Israel, while recognizing that the commission was bound by General Assembly Resolution 194, declared itself unable to accept the establishment of the international regime for the City of Jerusalem, although it accepted without reservation an international regime for the Holy Places.[261]

Document 365: United Nations General Assembly Resolution 303, Calling for the City of Jerusalem to be Established as a Corpus Separatum (December 9, 1949) [G.A. Res. 303, U.N. GAOR, 4th Sess., at 25, U.N. Doc. A/1251 (1950)]. In Resolution 303, the General Assembly proposes that Jerusalem be administered under United Nations sovereignty as an international city comprised of Jerusalem, Bethlehem, and other environs.

Document 366: Israeli Prime Minister David Ben-Gurion's Statement to the Knesset (December 13, 1949) [*available at* http://www.us-israel.org/jsource/Peace/bgjer.html]. In this statement, Israeli Prime Minister David Ben-Gurion announces to the Knesset in Tel Aviv that the City of Jerusalem is an inseparable part of the State of Israel and its eternal capital. This position was subsequently approved by the Knesset, and government agencies were established in the western part of the city.

Document 367: United Nations Trusteeship Council Resolution 426, Asking the President of the Council to Prepare a Working Paper on the Statute of Jerusalem (December 19, 1949) [T.C. Res. 426, U.N. TCOR, U.N. Doc. T/RES/426 (1949)]. In Resolution 426, the United Nations Trusteeship Council proposes that the president of the Trusteeship

[260] *See* Doc. 361.

[261] *See* Doc. 503.

Council prepare a working paper on the Statute of Jerusalem and that he receive suggestions from all interested parties on the subject.[262]

Document 368: United Nations Trusteeship Council Resolution 427, Removal to Jerusalem of Certain Ministries and Central Departments of the Government of Israel (December 21, 1949) [T.C. Res. 427, U.N. TCOR, U.N. Doc. T/RES/427 (1950)]. In Resolution 427, the United Nations Trusteeship Council asks its president to invite Israel to stop relocating its government offices to Jerusalem and asks the Secretary-General to inform all United Nations member states of the resolution. Israel's policy was incompatible with United Nations General Assembly Resolution 303, which calls for Jerusalem to be established as a *corpus separatum*.[263]

Document 369: United Nations Trusteeship Council Resolution 118, Inviting Israel and Jordan to Express Their Views on the Revision of the Draft Statute of Jerusalem (February 11, 1950) [*reprinted in* 1 UNITED NATIONS RESOLUTIONS ON PALESTINE AND THE ARAB-ISRAELI CONFLICT 1947–1974 177 (George Tomeh ed., 1975)]. The Trusteeship Council, in Resolution 118, decides to invite the State of Israel and the Hashemite Kingdom of Jordan, as the two states occupying the City of Jerusalem, to express their views on the revision of the Draft Statute for the City of Jerusalem and its implementation.

Document 370: Statement of the Committee for the Arab Property Owners in Jerusalem (February 14, 1950) [U.N. TCOR, 16th Sess., Agenda Item 19, U.N. Doc. T/519 (1950)]. This statement from the Arab Property Owners in Jerusalem, a committee consisting of Arab individuals whose property was brought under Jewish control following the 1948 war, demands restitution of properties and compensation for the loss of rent. The statement includes a constitution, a petition to King Abdallah of Jordan for assistance, and a telegram asking the Secretary-General to circulate these demands to all United Nations member states.

Document 371: Memorandum from the Council of the Ashkenasic Jewish Community, Jerusalem (February 21, 1950) [U.N. TCOR, 6th Sess., Agenda Item 19, U.N. Doc. T/520 (1950)]. In this memorandum, the Council of the Ashkenasic Jewish Community requests that the Orthodox community be recognized as religiously and politically independent. It also requests that the city of Jerusalem remain free of any political affiliation and governed by a municipal authority whose powers would be confined to domestic matters. The council advocates free access to the Jewish Holy Sites to all Jews.

Document 372: United Nations Statute for the City of Jerusalem (April 4, 1950) [*Question of an International Regime for the Jerusalem Area and Protection of the Holy Places, Special Report of the Trusteeship Council*, U.N. GAOR, 5th Sess., Supp. No. 9, at 19–27, U.N. Doc. A/1286 (1950)]. This second United Nations Statute for the City of Jerusalem was based on the provisions contained in the original partition plan, United Nations General Assembly Resolution 181 (1947), with the exception of those provisions regarding economic union. The Trusteeship Council requests that the governments of Israel and Jordan cooperate in the implementation of the statute.

Document 373: United Nations Trusteeship Council Resolution 234, Noting the Unwillingness of Jordan and Israel to Collaborate in the Implementation of the Statute of

---

[262] *See* Doc. 358.

[263] *See* Doc. 365.

Jerusalem (June 14, 1950) [T.C. Res. 234, U.N. TCOR (1950)]. After submitting the United Nations Statute for the City of Jerusalem to the governments of Israel and Jordan, the Trusteeship Council received no reply from Jordan and a reply from the government of Israel indicating their unwillingness to collaborate in implementing the Statute.[264]

Document 374: Special Report of the Trusteeship Council: Question of an International Regime for the Jerusalem Area and Protection of the Holy Places (June 14, 1950) [T.C. Res. 701, U.N. TCOR, 7th Sess., Agenda Item 10, U.N. Doc. T/RES/701 (1950)]. This special report was submitted to the General Assembly following the approval of the Statute for the City of Jerusalem.[265] The report traces the evolution of the statute, documenting the participation of all interested parties, the role of the Trusteeship Council, and the reservations of the Israeli and Jordanian governments into implementation. The report includes copies of the statute as approved by the council, the president's reports to the council, and the reply of the government of Israel.

Document 375: United Nations Security Council Resolution 127, Directing the Chief of Staff of UNTSO to Regulate Activities between the Demarcation Lines in Jerusalem (January 22, 1958) [S.C. Res. 127, U.N. SCOR, U.N. Doc. S/3942 (1958)]. After the government of Jordan complained about Israeli activity in the zone between the armistice demarcation lines in violation of the Israel-Jordan General Armistice Agreement, the Security Council, noting that neither Israel nor Jordan enjoys sovereignty over any part of the zone, directs the chief of staff of the UNTSO to regulate the zone in accordance with the principles of the agreement.[266] The chief of staff is directed to conduct a survey of property records to determine property ownership in the zone, ensuring that Israelis are not using Arab-owned properties and Arabs are not using Israeli-owned properties. The Security Council calls on Israel to suspend its activity in the zone until the survey is completed and for both parties to remove or destroy their respective military facilities and installations in the zone. It also recommends that Israel and Jordan discuss civilian activities within the zone through the Mixed Armistice Commission.

Document 376: United Nations Security Council Resolution 162, Urging Israel to Comply with the Decision of the Mixed Armistice Commission (Concerning Jerusalem) (April 11, 1961) [S.C. Res. 162, U.N. SCOR, U.N. Doc. S/4788 (1961)]. After the Mixed Armistice Commission found that Israel had breached its Armistice Agreement with Jordan by amassing more armaments than allowed for on the Israeli side of the Demarcation Line in Jerusalem, the Security Council in Resolution 162 endorses the commission's condemnation of the act and urges Israel to comply with the terms of the agreement by refraining from bringing any more equipment than that allowed for under the terms of the agreement.[267]

Document 377: Law of the State of Israel: Extending Jurisdiction to East Jerusalem (June 27, 1967) [21 LSI 75 (1967), *available at* http://www.mfa.gov.il/ MFA/Foreign%20Relations/Israels%20Foreign%20Relations%20since%201947/1947-1974/13%20Law%20and%20Administration%20Ordinance%20-Amendment%20No]. This Israeli law amends both the Law and Administration

[264] *See* Doc. 372.

[265] *Id.*

[266] *See* Doc. 95.

[267] *Id.*

Ordinance and the Municipalities Ordinance. The amending sections stipulate that Israeli law, jurisdiction, and administration shall be extended to any Israeli area designated by the government by order and that the minister of the interior may enlarge by proclamation the area of a particular municipality. Although the law makes no direct mention of Jerusalem, it provides the legal grounds for Israel to extend its jurisdiction into East Jerusalem.

Document 378: Law of the State of Israel: Protection of the Holy Places (June 27, 1967) [21 LSI 75 (1967)]. The Protection of the Holy Places Law ensures the protection of the Holy Places against desecration and guarantees freedom of access. It was passed by the Knesset after Prime Minister Levi Eshkol notified the Muslim leadership of its continued responsibility for the administration of the Temple Mount and mosques. Israeli security forces would be in charge of approaches to the site and the security and the maintenance of public order.

Document 379: United Nations General Assembly Resolution 2253, Requesting the Secretary-General to Report to the General Assembly on the Status of Jerusalem (July 4, 1967) [G.A. Res. 2253, U.N. GAOR, 5th Emergency Sess., Supp. No. 1, at 4, U.N. Doc. A/6798 (1967)]. In Resolution 2253, the General Assembly expresses its deep concern about Israel's attempts to change the status of Jerusalem.[268] It requests that the Secretary-General make a report to the General Assembly and the Security Council within the next week.

Document 380: Letter from Israel to the Secretary-General of the United Nations Concerning the Status of Jerusalem (July 10, 1967) [U.N. SCOR, 22d Sess., Supp. for July–Sept., at 73, U.N. Doc. S/8052 (1967)]. Following the adoption of multiple resolutions expressing concern about Israel's extension of its jurisdiction over East Jerusalem, United Nations Secretary-General U Thant requested that Israel give a reply. This letter from the Israeli government repeats earlier disclaimers on the subject and argues that the United Nations' conception of its new law is based on a fundamental misunderstanding as Israel had not annexed the city, but only integrated Jerusalem into its administrative and municipal spheres and furnished a legal basis for the protection of the Holy Places.

Document 381: Excerpts from the Statement by U.S. Representative to the United Nations Concerning the Status of Jerusalem (July 14, 1967) [57 DEP'T ST. BULL.148 (1967)]. On July 14, 1967, U.S. Ambassador Arthur J. Goldberg addressed the United Nations on the topic of U.S. policy on post-war and Israeli-occupied Jerusalem. In his statement, Goldberg insists that the status of Jerusalem cannot be decided unilaterally, but only through negotiations. The United States believes that the solution to the Jerusalem problem can only be found in the context of a larger solution to the war and the Israeli occupation of foreign territories.

Document 382: United Nations Security Council Resolution 250, Calling upon Israel to Refrain from Holding a Military Parade in Jerusalem (April 27, 1968) [S.C. Res. 250, U.N. SCOR, U.N. Doc. S/RES/250 (1968)]. In Resolution 250, the Security Council calls on Israel to refrain from holding a military parade in Jerusalem planned for May 2, 1968.

---

268 *See* Doc. 377.

Document 383: United Nations Security Council Resolution 251, Deploring the Military Parade Held by Israel in Jerusalem in Disregard of the United Nations' Unanimous Decision (May 2, 1968) [S.C. Res. 251, U.N. SCOR, U.N. Doc. S/RES/251 (1968)]. In Resolution 251, the Security Council deeply deplores Israel's decision to hold a military parade in Jerusalem despite the unanimous of the Security Council.[269]

Document 384: United Nations Security Council Resolution 252, Calling on Israel to Rescind All Measures to Change the Status of Jerusalem (May 21, 1968) [S.C. Res. 252, U.N. SCOR, 23d Sess., U.N. Doc. S/INF23 Rev.1 (1968)]. In Resolution 252, the Security Council condemns the demographic and physical changes that Israel introduced in Jerusalem. It declares that all legislative and administrative measures taken by Israel to change the status of Jerusalem are invalid. Canada and the United States both abstained from voting on this resolution.

Document 385: United Nations Security Council Resolution 267, Censuring Israeli Measures to Change the Status of Jerusalem (July 3, 1969) [S.C. Res. 267, U.N. SCOR, U.N. Doc. S/RES/267 (1969)]. In Resolution 362, the Security Council reaffirms the inadmissibility of the acquisition of territory by military conquest and strongly censures all measures taken to change the status of the city of Jerusalem.

Document 386: United Nations Security Council Resolution 271, Condemning the Extensive Damage Caused by Arson to the Holy al-Aqsa Mosque (September 15, 1969) [S.C. Res. 271, U.N. SCOR, U.N. Doc. S/RES/271 (1969)]. In Resolution 271, the Security Council grieves at the extensive damage caused by arson in al-Aqsa Mosque in Jerusalem on August 21, 1969, and recognizes that any act of destruction or profanation of Holy Places in Jerusalem, or any encouragement of such act, would seriously endanger international peace and security. It calls upon Israel to scrupulously observe the provisions of the Geneva Conventions and international law governing military occupation and to refrain from causing any hindrance to the discharge of the established functions of the Supreme Muslim Council of Jerusalem.[270]

Document 387: United Nations Security Council Resolution 298, Deploring the Failure of Israel to Respect United Nations Resolutions Concerning Measures to Change the Status of Jerusalem (September 25, 1971) [S.C. Res. 298, U.N. SCOR, U.N. Doc. S/RES/298 (1971)]. In Resolution 298, the Security Council again condemns the demographic and physical changes carried out by Israel in Jerusalem and reiterates the inadmissibility of territory gained by military conquest. It calls upon Israel to rescind all previous measures and to take no further steps in the occupied section of Jerusalem that may purport to change the status of the city or prejudice the rights of the inhabitants, the interests of the international community, or a just and lasting peace.

Document 388: UNESCO General Conference Resolution 3.422, Disapproving of the Continuation by Israel of Archaeological Excavations in Jerusalem (November 17, 1972) [*reprinted in* 1 United Nations Resolutions on Palestine and the Arab-Israeli Conflict 1947–1974 182 (George Tomeh ed., 1975)]. Noting that Israel's archaeological excavations in Jerusalem have made it difficult for the United Nations Educational, Scientific and Cultural Organization (UNESCO) to fulfill its mission, UNESCO in Resolution 3.422 calls on Israel to preserve all sites and cultural properties,

---

[269] *See* Doc. 382.

[270] There are four Geneva Conventions from 1949. *See supra* note 82.

especially in the Old City of Jerusalem, and to desist from alterations or excavations, particularly with regard to Christian and Islamic religious sites.

Document 389: United Nations Security Council Resolution 452, Deploring the Establishment of Settlements in Jerusalem (July 20, 1979) [S.C. Res. 452, U.N. SCOR, U.N. Doc. S/RES/452 (1979)]. In Resolution 452, the Security Council calls upon Israel to cease the establishment, construction, and planning of settlements in the Arab territories occupied since 1967, including Jerusalem. It notes the specific status of Jerusalem as a holy city and the need to protect and preserve the unique spiritual and religious dimension of the Holy Places in Jerusalem.

Document 390: United Nations Security Council Resolution 476, Deploring Israeli Attempts to Change the Status of the Holy City of Jerusalem (June 30, 1980) [S.C. Res. 476, U.N. SCOR, 2242d mtg., U.N. Doc. S/RES/476 (1980)]. Following steps taken by Israel to make a united Jerusalem its capital, the Security Council adopted Resolution 476, calling on Israel to desist from taking any measures affecting the character and status of Jerusalem.

Document 391: Basic Law of Israel: Jerusalem, Capital of Israel (July 30, 1980) [34 LSI 209 (1979–80)]. This Basic Law states that a complete and united Jerusalem is the capital of Israel. It also states that the Holy Places will be protected and that the government will provide for the development and prosperity of Jerusalem. The law was enacted in defiance of repeated United Nations admonitions against claiming Jerusalem as its official capital.[271]

Document 392: United Nations Security Council Resolution 478, Declaring All Measures Taken by Israel to Alter the Status of Jerusalem Are Null and Void (August 20, 1980) [S.C. Res. 478, U.N. SCOR, U.N. Doc. S/RES/478 (1980)]. In Resolution 478, the Security Council censures Israel's enactment of the Basic Law: Jerusalem, Capital of Israel, and affirms that its enactment constitutes a violation of international law.[272] The Security Council calls on member states to withdraw their diplomatic missions from Jerusalem. Subsequently, thirteen embassies left the city. In 1982, the Embassy of Costa Rica returned to West Jerusalem and was followed by El Salvador. The United States abstained from voting on this resolution.

Document 393: Statement Regarding Jerusalem by Israeli Foreign Minister Shimon Peres to the Knesset (September 9, 1993) [*available at* http://www.mfa.gov.il/MFA/MFAArchive/1990_1999/1993/9/FM%20PERES%20REMARKS%20IN%20KNESSET%20ON%20JERUSALEM%20-%2007-Sep-]. This letter from Israeli Foreign Minister Shimon Peres forms part of a three-letter exchange on divisive issues following the Israel-PLO Declaration of Principles on Interim Self-Government Arrangements (Oslo Accords).[273] In this letter, Peres confirms the significance of Jerusalem to all the monotheistic faiths and acknowledges Palestinian institutions in East Jerusalem. The letter, conveyed by Norwegian Minister of Foreign Affairs Johann Juergen Holst, was intended to remain secret because it carries certain Israeli commitments on the issue of Jerusalem. The letter was not delivered in due time either before or immediately following the signing of the Oslo Accords in

---

[271] *See, e.g.,* Docs. 381, 384, 385, 387, and 390.

[272] *See* Doc. 391.

[273] *See* Doc. 432.

Washington, D.C., on September 13, 1993. Israel's initial denial of the existence of the letter and then its subsequent late arrival caused some embarrassment to the Israeli government.

Document 394: Fundamental Agreement between the Holy See and the State of Israel (December 30, 1993) [33 I.L.M. 153 (1994)]. The Holy See and the State of Israel produced this Fundamental Agreement to further the efforts of the Bilateral Permanent Working Commission. It details the parties' commitment to religious freedom as set forth in the Universal Declaration of Human Rights, to maintaining the *status quo* for Christian Holy Sites, to encouraging pilgrimages to those sites, and to combating anti-Semitism.[274] The parties agree to negotiate any property disputes through the Bilateral Permanent Working Commission. The agreement also specifies the Holy See's commitment to remaining impartial to all territorial and border disputes regarding the State of Israel.

Document 395: The Washington Agreement between Israel and Jordan (July 26, 1994).[275] [*reprinted in* THE ISRAEL-ARAB READER: A DOCUMENTARY HISTORY OF THE MIDDLE EAST CONFLICT (Walter Laqueur & Barry Rubin eds., 2001)]. At the invitation of President Clinton, the leaders of Jordan and Israel met in Washington, D.C., to establish a new plan to develop peace negotiations between the two states. The agreement addressed issues regarding Jerusalem, state sovereignty, and plans to maintain communications between the two states.

Document 396: Agreement between the Holy See and the PLO (October 26, 1994) [*available at* http://www.jqf-jerusalem.org/2000/jqf8/pope.html#agreement]. The Holy See and the PLO having established official relations, issued this agreement, calling for an internationally guaranteed statute for Jerusalem and declaring that unilateral decisions that alter the character of Jerusalem are "morally and legally unacceptable." Drawing on the mission of the Bilateral Permanent Working Commission, this agreement reaffirms the parties' dedication to religious freedom as stated in the Universal Declaration of Human Rights, ensures the maintenance of the *status quo* for Christian Holy Places, and grants full effect in Palestinian Law to the legal personality of the Catholic Church.[276]

Document 397: Jerusalem Embassy Act of 1995, Providing for the Relocation of the U.S. Embassy in Israel to Jerusalem (November 8, 1995) [Pub. L. No. 104–45, 109 Stat. 398 (1995)]. The Jerusalem Embassy Act of 1995 was a bipartisan legislative initiative passed by the U.S. Congress in a ninety-three to five decision. It expresses U.S. support of Jerusalem as the undivided capital of Israel. It also states that the United States should relocate its embassy from Tel Aviv to Jerusalem by May 31, 1999. Several presidential determinations have suspended this act as it was passed in the promising years after the Oslo Accords with the expectation that a peaceful resolution to the Jerusalem issue was imminent.

---

[274] Universal Declaration of Human Rights, G.A. Res. 217A(III), art. 18, U.N. Doc. A/810, at 71 (1948) ("Everyone has the right to freedom of thought, conscience, and religion; this right includes freedom to change his religion or belief, and freedom, . . . to manifest his religion or belief in teaching, practice, worship and observance.").

[275] Date is one day off in The Israeli-Arab Reader than online sources.

[276] *Id.*

Document 398: United Nations Security Council Resolution 1073, Concerning the Israeli Plan to Open a Tunnel in the Vicinity of al-Aqsa Mosque (September 28, 1996) [S.C. Res. 1073, U.N. SCOR, U.N. Doc. S/RES/1073 (1996)]. Having received a letter from the League of Arab States that referred to the action by Israel to open an entrance to a tunnel in the vicinity of al-Aqsa Mosque and expressing concern about events in Jerusalem that resulted in a high number of deaths and injuries among Palestinian civilians, the Security Council passed Resolution 1073, calling for the immediate cessation and reversal of all acts that have resulted in the aggravation of the situation and that have negative implications for the Middle East peace process. The Security Council calls for the safety and protection of Palestinian civilians to be ensured.

Document 399: United States House of Representatives Concurrent Resolution 60: Jerusalem Must Remain the Undivided Capital of the State of Israel (June 10, 1997) [H.R. Con. Res. 60, 105th Cong. (1997)]. On the thirtieth anniversary of the 1967 war, the U.S. Congress passed this resolution, calling upon the president and the secretary of state to publicly affirm as U.S. policy that Jerusalem remains the undivided capital of Israel. The resolution traces the history of Jewish presence in Jerusalem and the city's change of status after the 1948 and 1967 wars.

Document 400: Status of Jerusalem, United Nations (1997) [U.N. Doc. 97-24262 (1997)]. This United Nations paper on the status of Jerusalem recounts the history of Jerusalem since the United Nations Partition Plan of 1947. It gives special treatment to Israel's occupation of East Jerusalem in 1967 and Israel's construction of settlements in East Jerusalem.

Document 401: United Nations Security Council Presidential Statement on Jerusalem (July 13, 1998) [U.N. Press Release, Dep't of Public Info., U.N. SCOR, 3904th mtg., U.N. Doc. SC/6546 (1998)]. Realizing that the United States would veto any United Nations resolution that might jeopardize the peace process between Israel and the PLO, the president of the Security Council, Danilo Türk, issued this statement on behalf of the Security Council, criticizing Israel's decision to broaden the jurisdiction of Jerusalem. It calls upon Israel not to proceed with its plan, nor to take any steps that would prejudice the outcome of peace negotiations.

Document 402: Holy See Non-Paper on Jerusalem (July 20, 1998) [*available at* http://www.christusrex.org/www1/ pope/non-paper.html]. The Holy See's Observer Mission to the United Nations published this single-page non-paper on Jerusalem, which criticizes Israel for its decision to broaden Jerusalem's jurisdiction. The Holy See calls for a peace settlement that would ensure a *status quo* policy for religious followers and the Holy Sites.

Document 403: Final Communiqué and Recommendations of the 17th Session of the Al-Quds Committee (July 30, 1998) [Al-Quds Comm., U.N. Doc. A/53/212 (1998)]. The 17th Session of the Al-Quds Committee took place in Morocco under the chairmanship of King Hassan II. The session was called to discuss Israel's attempts to change the demographic and geographic status of Jerusalem. In its Final Communiqué, the Al-Quds Committee makes sixteen recommendations, among them, asking the international community to stand against Israel's siege of Jerusalem, not to extend economic assistance to Israel that may be used for expansionist policies, and not to purchase goods from Jerusalem or any Jewish settlements.

Document 404: Rome Declaration on Bethlehem 2000 (February 19, 1999) [*available at* http://domino.un.org/unispal.nsf/0/da47f51cdf111a6c0525674c0077da82?OpenDocument]. The Bethlehem 2000 International Conference in Rome—organized by the Committee on the Exercise of the Inalienable Rights of the Palestinian People—issued this declaration in support of the Palestinian Authority's plan to celebrate the year 2000 in Bethlehem. The project was aimed at restoring historical, archaeological, and religious sites of unique significance.

Document 405: United Nations General Assembly Resolution 55/50, Deploring Transfer of Diplomatic Missions to Jerusalem (December 1, 2000) [G.A. Res. 55/50, U.N. GAOR, 55th Sess., Agenda Item 40, U.N. Doc. A/RES/55/50 (2000)]. The General Assembly in Resolution 55/50 deplores the transfer of some member states' diplomatic missions to Jerusalem.

Document 406: Council of the League of Arab States Resolution 115/6057, Attempts by Israel to Have a Number of Archaeological Sites in East Jerusalem Inscribed on the World Heritage List (March 12, 2001) [*available* at http://domino.un.org/UNISPAL.NSF/0/623676cf22954e5985256a56004e549c?OpenDocument]. The League of Arab States passed Resolution 115/6057 after receiving a report from the Permanent Mission of the State of Palestine detailing Israel's attempts to have a number of archaeological sites in East Jerusalem inscribed on the World Heritage List. The League decides to have member states establish connections with the World Heritage Committee to convey the Arab position. It also requests that the Secretary-General establish a special committee of legal experts to consider the question of Israel's action.

Document 407: United Nations General Assembly Resolution 55/254, Protection of Religious Sites (June 11, 2001) [G.A. Res. 55/254, U.N. GAOR, 55th Sess., Agenda Item 32, U.N. Doc. A/RES/55/254 (2001)]. In Resolution 55/254, the General Assembly calls for the protection of religious sites in conformity with international standards, recalling United Nations resolutions, declarations, and other international conventions that protect religious expression. This resolution encourages all states to promote a culture of tolerance and respect for the diversity of religion and for religious sites and requests the Secretary-General to devote attention to the protection of religious sites in the report on the United Nations Year of Dialogue among Civilizations.

Document 408: Law of the Palestinian Authority: Law of the Capital (October 5, 2002) [*available at* http://www.jmcc.org/documents/capitallaw.htm]. This law, ratified by the president of the State of Palestine, Yasser Arafat, declares *Al-Quds Al-Shareef* the capital of the Palestinian state. It also names *Al-Quds Al-Shareef* the permanent headquarters of Palestine's legislative, executive, and judicial authorities.

Document 409: HR1646 Foreign Relations Authorization Act, Maintaining the Commitment to Relocate the U.S. Embassy in Israel to Jerusalem (Fiscal Year 2003) [Foreign Relations Authorization Act, Fiscal Year 2003, § 214, Pub. L. No. 107–228, 116 Stat. 1365 (2002)]. The Foreign Relations Authorization Act establishes three provisions with respect to U.S. policy on Jerusalem as the capital of Israel: (1) it calls for the United States to immediately relocate its Embassy to Jerusalem; (2) it determines that no federal money will go to the U.S. consulate in Jerusalem unless it is under the supervision of the U.S. ambassador to Israel; and (3) it determines that U.S.

citizens born in the city of Jerusalem will record their place of birth as Israel.

Document 410: United Nations General Assembly Resolution 60/107, Israeli Practices Affecting the Human Rights of the Palestinian People in the Occupied Palestinian Territory, Including East Jerusalem (January 18, 2006) [G.A. Res. 60/107, U.N. GAOR, U.N. Doc. A/RES/60/107 (2006)]. Noting reports by the U.N. Commission on Human Rights and the Special Rapporteur of the Commission on Human Rights in Palestine, the General Assembly expresses concern regarding Israel's treatment of Palestinians in the Occupied Territories. Specifically, the General Assembly condemns use of excessive force, collective punishment, confiscation of land, and expansion of Israeli settlements.

Document 411: United Nations General Assembly Resolution 60/41, Jerusalem (February 10, 2006) [G.A. Res. 60/41, U.N. GAOR, U.N. Doc. A/RES/60/41 (2006)]. The General Assembly condemns Israel's continuation of illegal settlements and continued construction of a wall surrounding in East Jerusalem. The General Assembly then stresses the need for both Israeli and Palestinian concerns are addressed while also guaranteeing the freedom of movement and religion for Jerusalem's occupants.

Document 412: United Nations Report on the Mission to Israel Including Visit to Occupied Palestinian Territory, Submitted by Martin Scheinin, Special Rapporteur on the Promotion and Protection of Human Rights and Fundamental Freedoms while Countering Terrorism (November 16, 2007) [U.N. Doc. A/HRC/6/17/Add.4(2007)]. Scheinin's report addresses the challenges facing Israel in legislating security measures while providing for humanitarian needs and civil rights of Palestinians in the Occupied Territorries. The report also highlights the issues of security walls, terrorism, and counterterrorism.

Document 413: United Nations General Assembly Resolution 62/108, Israeli Settlements in the Occupied Palestinian Territory, Including East Jerusalem, and the Occupied Syrian Golan (January 10, 2008) [G.A. Res. 62/108, U.N. GAOR, U.N. Doc. A/RES/62/108 (2008)]. In Resolution 62/108, the General Assembly notes Israel's work in withdrawing from Gaza and the West Bank as well as dismantling settlements in those regions. However, the General Assembly continues to demand the same for East Jerusalem and Syrian Golan in which Israeli settlements continue to develop.

Document 414: United Nations General Assembly Resolution 62/109, Israeli Practices Affecting the Human Rights of the Palestinian People in the Occupied Palestinian Territory, Including East Jerusalem (January 10, 2008) [G.A. Res. 62/109, U.N. GAOR, U.N. Doc. A/RES/62/109 (2008)]. Citing reports by the Special Committee to Investigate Israeli Practices Affecting the Human Rights of the Palestinian People and Other Arabs of the Occupied Territories as well as the special rapporteur of the Human Rights Council, the General Assembly provides a veritable laundry list of concerns regarding the status of Palestinians in the Occupied Territories.

The General Assembly again expresses concern for the violation of human rights by Israel, such as collective punishment, closure of areas, construction of the wall inside the Occupied Territories, and destruction of property. In response, the General Assembly is convinced of the need for an international presence to monitor the situation.

7. Israeli-Palestinian Peace Process: 1982–2008

The eighty-seven documents in this section represent the many peace initiatives proposed since 1982 for resolving competing land claims and sovereignty disputes between Israel and the Palestinians. It is important to note that not every plan is a peace plan. Some initiatives were intended solely to be the basis for a peace plan or a method of arriving at a peace plan, but not solutions for the conflict in themselves.

The majority of initiatives are based on either the binational state model or the two-state solution. The binational model was first formally presented by the Anglo-American Commission in 1946.[277] It envisioned a democratic one-state system open to members of both communities. This model was favored by the early Jewish political party Mapam[278] and the Soviet Union, among others. It failed, however, to garner the support of the Palestinian leadership or Arab states. Since then, progressive thinkers and many among the Palestinian intelligentsia have called for a revival of the binational state model.[279]

The two-state solution, formally outlined in United Nations General Assembly Resolution 181 (Partition Plan), called for the creation of two sovereign states in Palestine—one Jewish and one Arab.[280] This proposal has become the prevailing model and serves as the basis for the present Israeli-Palestinian peace process. Thus far, no proposal based on either of these two models has been acceptable to both sides.

The fundamental issue of peace goes beyond the well-known issues of borders, security, arms control, right of return, compensation, Jerusalem, and water. Fundamentally, there can be no reasonable expectation of peace without reconciliation between the two communities. This in part may require the establishment of a truth and reconciliation commission, payment of compensation, and other mechanisms that are usually addressed in the context of confidence-building measures. Surprisingly, however, throughout the lengthy history of negotiations between Palestinians and Israelis, issues of justice, truth, and reconciliation have seldom been addressed. There is a lack of articulation of a vision of a shared future that is likely to provide a common basis of hope for the two communities' co-existence. There is no doubt that without a final status peace agreement between the State of Israel and the putative State of Palestine, instability will continue to prevail in the region with significant impact beyond the region.

---

[277] *See* Doc. 47.

[278] The socialist-Zionist party Mapam (United Workers' Party) was the second largest political party in the early years of the State of Israel.

[279] Modern proponents have included Meron Benvenisti, Noam Chomsky, Tony Judt, and Edward Said.

[280] *See* Doc. 59.

Other documents on related subjects may be found in: Section 3, Arab-Israeli Wars; Section 4, Arab-Israeli Peace Process; Section 5, Arms Control and Regional Security; Section 6, Jerusalem and the Holy Sites; and Section 8, Status of the Palestinians.

Document 415: U.S. President Ronald Reagan's Address to the Nation on U.S. Policy for Peace in the Middle East (Reagan Plan) (September 1, 1982) [*reprinted in* THE QUEST FOR PEACE 180–21 (U.S. Dep't of State ed., 1984)]. The Reagan administration prepared this diplomatic initiative for the Middle East to renew the peace process, deal with the Palestinian issue, improve Israel-Egypt relations, and provide an impetus for Jordan to join the peace process. President Reagan called his plan the next step in the process that was begun at Camp David to pave the way for autonomy for the Palestinian people.[281] In this address, Reagan identifies the legitimate rights of the Palestinian people and their just requirements, proposing a five-year transition period for transfer of domestic authority from Israel to the Palestinian inhabitants of the West Bank and Gaza and a freeze on new Jewish settlements during that time. The Reagan Plan was officially rejected by Jordan and the PLO in April 1983.

Document 416: Letter from Israeli Prime Minister Menachem Begin to U.S. President Ronald Reagan (September 5, 1982) [*available at* http://www.mfa.gov.il/MFA/Foreign%20Relations/Israels%20Foreign%0Relations%20since%201947/1982-1984/71%20Letter%20from%20Prime% 20Minister% 20Begin%20 to%20President%20R]. In this letter, Israeli Prime Minister Menachem Begin reacts very negatively to U.S. President Ronald Reagan's September 1 Address,[282] calling the plan "national suicide for Israel." Israel had not been notified by the U.S. administration of the content of the address until just before the speech was delivered. Conversely, Jordan, Saudi Arabia, Egypt, and the PLO had been consulted.

Document 417: Excerpts from the Final Declaration of the Twelfth Arab Summit Conference, Fez (Fez Arab Peace Plan) (September 9, 1982) [U.N. GAOR, 37th Sess., Agenda Items 31, 34, 58, and 134, Annex, U.N. Doc. A/37/696 (1982)]. The Fez Arab Peace Plan directly followed the public announcement of the Reagan Plan.[283] Before the summit, the Reagan administration had asked Saudi Arabia to work for a final resolution at Fez that would endorse the plan, but leaders at the Fez summit did not give Jordan the needed mandate to negotiate over the future of the Occupied Territories. Israel rejected the plan because it did not provide enough security guarantees. However, the plan is historic in that it represents a dramatic shift in Arab policy with regard to Israel, providing for both the implicit recognition of Israel and the possibility of negotiating a peace agreement with Israel. Thus, the plan overturns the "Three No's" of the Khartoum Resolution of 1967.[284]

Document 418: Speech Given by Leonid I. Brezhnev, General Secretary of the Central Committee of the Communist Party of the Soviet Union and President of the Presidium of the Supreme Soviet of the USSR, at a Kremlin Dinner (Brezhnev Plan) (September 15, 1982) [*available at* http://domino.un.org/unispal.nsf/0/52795e073a5079568525628100745892?

281 *See* Doc. 308.

282 Doc. 415.

283 *Id.*

284 Doc. 165.

OpenDocument]. The Brezhnev Plan was the third major peace initiative to be presented in September 1982. It was presented by General Secretary Leonid Ilich Brezhnev at a Kremlin dinner. Brezhnev died soon afterwards on November 10, 1982.

Document 419: Hussein-Arafat Accord (February 11, 1985) [*reprinted in* ARAB-ISRAELI CONFLICT AND CONCILIATION: A DOCUMENTARY HISTORY (Bernard Reich ed., 1995)]. Working within the framework of the 1982 Fez Plan as well as United Nations Resolutions, King Hussein, of Jordan, met with Yasser Arafat and developed five points for what they deemed a comprehensive peace plan to bring an end to the Palestinian issue. These five points included calling for the Palestinian's rights to self-determination, solving their refuge problem, and beginning peace negotiations in an international conference which would include the five U.N. Security Council permanent member states, all countries involved in the conflict, and a joint Jordan-Palestinian delegation. However, one year later King Hussein decided to stop all ties with the PLO and closed all PLO offices in Jordan. King Hussein took this action as he disapproved of the PLO's refusal to accept Resolutions 242 and 338 and its failure to truly progress towards a peaceful settlement. In April 1987 the PLO responded by renouncing their agreement.

Document 420: Statement Given by King Hussein of Jordan on Ending the Jordan-PLO Initiative (February 19, 1986) [*reprinted in* THE ISRAEL-ARAB READER: A DOCUMENTARY HISTORY OF THE MIDDLE EAST CONFLICT (Walter Laqueur & Barry Rubin eds., 2001)]. The Jordan-PLO initiative, formed only a year earlier, disintegrated with disputes over conflicting interests between the two parties. This was partially due to views on Resolution 242 and the PLO's power in the West Bank.

Document 421: Letter from U.S. Secretary of State George P. Shultz to Israeli Prime Minister Yitzhak Shamir (Shultz Initiative) (March 4, 1988) [N.Y. TIMES, Late City Final Edition, Mar. 10, 1988, at A10]. The outbreak of the first *Intifada* in December 1987 brought new urgency to United States efforts to broker a viable peace plan. Secretary of State George P. Shultz produced this initiative, which combines elements of the Camp David Accords, the Reagan Plan, proposals from Jordanian leader King Hussein, and ideas from Israeli Foreign Minister Shimon Peres. Shultz used Kissinger's "shuttle diplomacy" to promote his plan, traveling to the Middle East three times in five months. The basic elements of the Shultz plan call for: negotiations hosted by the five permanent United Nations Security Council members attended by all parties accepting Security Council Resolutions 242 and 338 and renouncing violence and terrorism; a joint Jordan-Palestinian delegation to represent Palestinians and negotiate the terms of a three-year transitional period for the territories; and international meetings to facilitate separate bilateral negotiations for a final settlement.[285] Egypt, Jordan, and Foreign Minister Peres supported the plan. Israeli Prime Minister Yitzhak Shamir questioned the land-for-peace formula. The PLO and Syria were very critical, with Palestinians of the West Bank and Gaza refusing to meet with Shultz.

Document 422: Stockholm Declaration (December 7, 1988) [*reprinted in* ARAB-ISRAELI CONFLICT AND CONCILIATION: A DOCUMENTARY HISTORY (Bernard Reich ed., 1995)]. The Palestinian National Council held a meeting in Algiers from November 12

---

[285] Docs. 289 and 293.

to November 15, 1988, after which it issued a political statement announcing the council's Declaration of Independence. Through this ceclaration the Palestinian National Council agreed to enter peace negotiations according to U.N. Resolutions 242 and 338 if the PLO was considered the legitimate representative for the Palestinian people. These negotiations should also include the Palestinian's right to an independent state, while also accepting the existence of the State of Israel. The declaration also condemned terrorism. In a discussion organized in Stockholm by the Swedish foreign minister, Sten Anderson, representatives of the PLO gave an explanation of the Declaration of Independence to American Jews. It was meant to show U.S. policy makers that it was possible to begin peace talks with the PLO. However, U.S. secretary of state, George Shultz, still insisted that the PLO did not meet the conditions necessary for such discussions with the United States to begin.

Document 423: Excerpts from Palestinian Chairman Yasser Arafat's Speech to the United Nations General Assembly (December 13, 1988) [U.N. GAOR, 43d Sess., Agenda Item 37, U.N. Doc. A/43/PV.78 (1989)]. A special General Assembly was organized in Geneva to discuss Palestinian issues after the United States refused to grant PLO Chairman Yasser Arafat a visa to travel to the United Nations headquarters in New York to speak before the General Assembly. Arafat gave this speech in Geneva before the United Nations, in which he details the injustices suffered by Palestinians and the Lebanese due to Israel's military policies. He offers a three-point Palestinian peace plan, which includes: (1) the formation of a preparatory commission of an international peace conference; (2) the United Nations' assumption of temporary supervision of Palestinian land; and (3) a peace settlement in accordance with Resolutions 242 and 338.[286]

Document 424: Letter from U.S. Secretary of State George P. Shultz to Swedish Foreign Minister Sten Andersson and Attachments (December 3, 1988) [*reprinted in* GEORGE SCHULTZ, TURMOIL AND TRIUMPH: MY YEARS AS SECRETARY OF STATE 1028–29 (1993)]. In this letter to Swedish Foreign Minister Sten Andersson, U.S. Secretary of State George Shultz presents the U.S. position on intended negotiations between the PLO and Israel. Shultz attached a Final Statement signed by PLO Chairman Yasser Arafat, which expresses the PLO's willingness to negotiate a comprehensive peace settlement with Israel on the basis of United Nations Security Council Resolutions 242 and 338[287] and to renounce terrorism.

Document 425: Israeli Peace Initiative (May 14, 1989) [*available at* http://www.usembassy-israel.org.il/publish/peace/may89.htm]. Formulated by Israeli Prime Minister Yitzhak Shamir and Defense Minister Yitzhak Rabin, the Israeli Peace Initiative of 1989 represents the consensus of Israeli policy in the National Unity government and attempts to resolve the final political status of the Palestinians within the framework of an overall Middle East peace settlement. This initiative is based on a proposal that was first presented by Israeli Prime Minister Menachem Begin in the framework of the Israeli-Egyptian Peace Treaty.[288] The initiative calls for elections in the Occupied Territories to select a Palestinian representative that

[286] *Id.*
[287] *Id.*
[288] Doc. 310.

would conduct negotiations for a transitional period of self-rule to last five years. It also proposes the convening of an international peace conference. Israel also outlines its four non-negotiable premises for peace, which include: (1) continuation of the political process based on the Camp David Accords; (2) opposition to the establishment of an additional Palestinian state in the Gaza district and in the area between Israel and Jordan; (3) a refusal to conduct negotiations with the PLO; and (4) no change in the status of Judea, Samaria, and Gaza that are not in accordance with Israeli designs. This initiative formed the basis of the Baker Plan,[289] which led to the 1991 Madrid Peace Conference.[290]

Document 426: Letter of Assurance from the United States to the Palestinians (October 18, 1991) [*reprinted in* THE ISRAEL-ARAB READER: A DOCUMENTARY HISTORY OF THE MIDDLE EAST CONFLICT (Walter Laqueur & Barry Rubin eds., 2001)]. In an attempt to bring Palestinian representatives to the table in a new round of peace negotiations, the United States expressed several assurances to ease Palestinians concerns regarding the talks. Chief among these were pledges that an agreement to talks would not prejudice Palestinians' claims to East Jerusalem, the Palestinians were free to choose their own delegates, and Security Council Resolution 242 would be a basis of negotiations.

Document 427: U.S. Secretary of State James Baker's Letter of Assurance to the Palestinians (October 18, 1991) [*available at* http://www.brook.edu/press/appendix/appen_m.htm]. In the months that followed the Persian Gulf War, U.S. Secretary of State James Baker carried out an intense round of "shuttle diplomacy," making eight separate trips to the Middle East in eight months. In this letter of assurance to the Palestinians written in the weeks leading up to the Madrid Peace Conference,[291] Baker restates the U.S. government's commitment to peace on the basis of United Nations Security Council Resolutions 242 and 338, the need for Palestinians to gain control over their political, economic, and other decisions, and the right of Palestinian negotiators to bring any issue to the table, including East Jerusalem.

Document 428: Israeli Prime Minister Yitzhak Shamir and Palestinian Delegation Leader Haydar Abd al-Shafi: Speeches at the Madrid Peace Conference (October 21, 1991) [*reprinted in* THE ISRAEL-ARAB READER: A DOCUMENTARY HISTORY OF THE MIDDLE EAST CONFLICT (Walter Laqueur & Barry Rubin eds., 2001)]. The speeches of the Israeli and Palestinian representatives develop a narrative of each parties' tribulations over the past sixty years in Israel. The speeches serve as condensed review of their arguments advocating their respective sides, accusations, aspirations for the conference, and hopes for peace.

Document 429: Letter of Invitation to the Madrid Peace Conference, Issued by the United States and the USSR (October 30, 1991) [*reprinted in* CHARLES D. SMITH, PALESTINE AND THE ARAB-ISRAEL CONFLICT 455–56 (4th ed. 2001)]. With this letter of invitation to the Madrid Peace Conference, the United States and the Soviet Union initiated the first conference of the Israeli-Palestinian peace process. One of the Madrid Conference's stated aims is to reach an interim self-governing arrangement,

---

[289] Doc. 427.
[290] *See* Docs. 429 and 430.
[291] *Id.*

followed by permanent status discussions based on United Nations Security Council Resolutions 242 and 338 after two years.[292]

Document 430: U.S. President George Bush's Opening Address to the Madrid Peace Conference (October 30, 1991) [*available at* http://www.presidency.ucsb.edu/ws/index.php?pid=20163&st=&st1=]. U.S. President George H.W. Bush's address opened the historic Madrid Peace Conference, marking the first time in forty-three years that Israeli and Palestinian leaders met together to discuss a permanent settlement.[293] In his address, Bush encourages Arabs and Israelis to lay down the past in favor of peace. The opening day of the conference was followed by one-on-one sessions between Israel and each of its neighbors and then wider discussions in the hope of finding a permanent solution.

Document 431: Letters Exchanged between PLO Chairman Yasser Arafat and Israeli Prime Minister Yitzhak Rabin Concerning Israel-PLO Recognition (September 9, 1993) [*available at* http://www.state.gov/ p/nea/rls/22579.htm]. In this letter to Israeli Prime Minister Yitzhak Rabin, PLO Chairman Yasser Arafat confirms four basic principles to lay the groundwork for anticipated peace negotiations: (1) the PLO's recognition of Israel's right to exist in peace and security, (2) its acceptance of Resolutions 242 and 338, (3) its commitment to the peace process, and (4) its renunciation of terror as a political tool. Rabin's letter to Arafat confirms Israel's commitment to recognize the PLO as the representative of the Palestinian people and commence negotiations with the PLO.

Document 432: Declaration of Principles on Interim Self-Government Arrangements between Israel and the PLO (September 13, 1993) [*available at* http://domino.un.org/unispal.nsf/0/71dc8c9d96d2f0ff85256117007cb6ca?OpenDocument]. The historic Declaration of Principles on Interim Self-Government (Oslo Accords) set the framework for subsequent Israeli-Palestinian negotiations and agreements. It declares the aim of negotiations as the establishment of a Palestinian Interim Self-Government Authority and an elected council to stand for a transitional period of no more than five years, followed by a permanent settlement based on Resolutions 242 and 338.[294] It declares Israel's intention to withdraw from the Gaza Strip and the Jericho area, adding that later permanent status negotiations will decide the issues of Jerusalem, refugees, settlements, security arrangements, borders, relations and cooperation, and other issues.

Document 433: Joint Statement following the First Meeting of the Israeli-Palestinian Economic Cooperation Committee (November 17, 1993) [*available at* http://www.mfa.gov.il/MFA/Foreign%20Relations/Israels%20Foreign%20Relations%20since%201947/1992-1994/136%20Joint%20Statement%20Following%20the%20First%20Meeting%20of]. Recognizing the importance of a healthy economy in the West Bank and the Gaza Strip to the peace process, this joint statement of the Israeli-Palestinian Economic Cooperation Committee, expresses the agreement to accelerate efforts in the areas of trade and labor, fiscal matters, finance, and banking.

---

[292] *Id.*

[293] *See* Doc. 429.

[294] *Id.*

Document 434: United Nations General Assembly Resolution 48/58 (December 14, 1993) [*reprinted in* ARAB-ISRAELI CONFLICT AND CONCILIATION: A DOCUMENTARY HISTORY (Bernard Reich ed., 1995)]. The United Nations General Assembly, on December 14, 1993, concluded that solving the issues in the Middle East would bring greater overall international peace and security. It therefore adopted a resolution supporting the peace process through the Israel-PLO Declaration of Principles on the Interim Self-Government Arrangements. It encouraged the development of a United Nations task force to aid economic, social, and technical development for the Palestinian people, during the interim period, partially through advocating for the assistance from member states. This resolution emphasized the need for immediate and quick progression towards peace, and found a United Nations presence in the Middle East necessary to support this process and to assist with the implementation of the Declaration of Principles.

Document 435: Protocol on Economic Relations between the Government of Israel and the PLO (April 29, 1994) [*available at* http://www.mfa.gov.il/MFA/Peace%20Process/Guide%20to%20the%20Peace%20Process/Gaza-Jericho%20Agreement%20Annex%20IV%20-%20Economic%20Protocol]. The Protocol on Economic Relations between the government of Israel and the PLO was to be instituted according to the timetable set out in the Declaration of Principles.[295] It stipulates that initially the agreement will apply only in the Gaza Strip and the Jericho area and then eventually to other areas. The protocol specifies which products can be imported into the West Bank and Gaza Strip, with the amounts being negotiable every six months. It also establishes a Palestinian Monetary Authority for areas under Palestinian sovereignty to act as the Palestinian Authority's advisor and to put into force a joint system of taxation in the territories. In the area of labor, both sides pledge to "maintain the normality of movement of labor between them." Finally, the protocol also provides for free movement of agricultural produce and industrial goods and cooperation in tourism.

Document 436: Agreement on the Gaza Strip and the Jericho Area between Israel and the PLO (May 4, 1994) [U.N. GAOR, 49th Sess., Annex, U.N. Doc. A/49/180 (1994)]. The Agreement on the Gaza Strip and the Jericho Area between Israel and the PLO establishes the process by which the first Israeli redeployment from occupied Palestinian territory would take place. It provides for transfer of authority from the Israeli military government and its Civil Administration to the new Palestinian National Authority (PNA) in the Jericho area of the West Bank and in Gaza and marks the beginning of the interim period as defined in the Declaration of Principles.[296]

Document 437: Letters Exchanged between PLO Chairman Yasser Arafat and Israeli Prime Minister Yitzhak Rabin following the Signing of the Gaza-Jericho Agreement (May 4, 1994) [*available at* http://www.pna.gov.ps/key_ documents/ISRAEL_PLO_Rec.asp]. These two formal letters were exchanged between PLO Chairman Yasser Arafat and Israeli Prime Minister Yitzhak Rabin to confirm their commitments to the Gaza-Jericho Agreement.[297] Arafat's letter to Rabin outlines the thirteen major

[295] Doc. 432.

[296] *Id.*

[297] Doc. 436.

points of the agreement. Rabin's letter confirms receipt of Arafat's letter and reiterates its contents. These letters were exchanged on the same day that the Agreement on the Gaza Strip and the Jericho Area was signed.

Document 438: Law of the State of Israel: Implementing the Agreement on the Gaza Strip and the Jericho Area, Restriction on Activity (May 4, 1994) [*available at* http://www.mfa.gov.il/MFA/MFAArchive/1990_1999/1994/12/Law%20Implementing%20the%20Agreement%20on%20the%20Gaza%20Strip%20a]. This Israeli law was passed on the same day that the Agreement on the Gaza Strip and the Jericho Area was signed, formalizing Israel's commitment to the plan.[298]

Document 439: Agreement on Preparatory Transfer of Powers and Responsibilities between Israel and the PLO (August 29, 1994) [*available at* http://domino.un.org/UNISPAL.NSF/0/fd15eca93fd9af2785257000005a5810?OpenDocument]. In the Agreement on Preparatory Transfer of Powers and Responsibilities between Israel and the PLO, Israel agrees to transfer powers and responsibilities to the PNA in the spheres of education and culture, health, social welfare, tourism, direct taxation and value added tax on local production. The PNA is to assume judicial power to appoint inspectors to ensure compliance in each of the spheres and to bring disciplinary proceedings against persons it employs.

Document 440: Oslo Declaration (September 13, 1994) [*reprinted in* ARAB-ISRAELI CONFLICT AND CONCILIATION: A DOCUMENTARY HISTORY (Bernard Reich ed., 1995)]. Norwegian Foreign Minister Bjorn Tore Godal, Israeli Foreign Minister Shimon Peres, and PLO Chairman Yasser Arafat met on September 13, 1994, and issued the Oslo Declaration. Meeting on the first anniversary of the signing of the Declaration of Principles, the leaders commended its gradual implementation. The Israeli and Palestinian sides further committed themselves to continue the peace process through fully executing the principles in the declaration, working harder to end acts of violence, and promoting their economic relationship and the economy of the Palestinian Authority.

Document 441: U.S. Executive Order 12947: Prohibiting Transactions with Terrorists Who Threaten to Disrupt the Middle East Peace Process (January 23, 1995) [Exec. Order No. 12,947, 60 Fed. Reg. 5079 (1995)]. Finding that foreign terrorists who disrupt the Middle East peace process constitute a threat to American national security, foreign policy and the economy, U.S. President Bill Clinton issued this executive order, declaring a national emergency to deal with such threats. He prohibits transactions by and contributions to individuals who commit or assist in acts of violence that disrupt the peace process. Among the blacklisted organizations are the Democratic Front for the Liberation of Palestine, Hezbollah, Islamic Resistance Movement (HAMAS), Jihad, Kahane Chai, and Popular Front for the Liberation of Palestine (PFLP).

Document 442: Interim Agreement on the West Bank and Gaza Strip between Israel and the PLO (September 28, 1995) [U.N. GAOR, 51st Sess., Agenda Item 10, Annex, U.N. Doc. A/51/889 (1997)]. Also known as "Oslo II," the Interim Agreement on the West Bank and Gaza Strip between Israel and the PLO was signed at Washington,

---

[298] *Id.*

D.C., on September 28, 1995, by Israeli Prime Minister Yitzhak Rabin and Israeli Foreign Minister Shimon Peres for the government of the State of Israel and Chairman Yasser Arafat for the PLO. The ceremony was witnessed by the United States of America, the Russian Federation, Egypt, Jordan, Norway, and the European Union. The interim agreement outlines future relations between Israel and the Palestinians and includes seven annexes, which cover in detail: security arrangements, elections, civil affairs, legal matters, economic relations, Israeli-Palestinian cooperation, and the release of Palestinian prisoners. This agreement marks the conclusion of the first stage in negotiations between Israel and the PLO. The main object of the Interim Agreement was to broaden Palestinian self-government in the West Bank by means of an elected self-governing authority—the Palestinian Council—for an interim period, while protecting Israel's security interests.

Document 443: Letter from Israeli Minister of Foreign Affairs Shimon Peres to His Counterparts on the Israeli-Palestinian Interim Agreement (September 28, 1995) [*available at* http://www.mfa.gov.il/MFA/Foreign%20Relations/Israels%20Foreign%20Relations%20since%201947/1995-1996/Letter%20from%20Foreign%20Minister%20Peres%20to%20his%20counterp]. In this letter to his counterparts, Israeli Minister of Foreign Affairs Shimon Peres speaks of the need for both sides to prevent violence against the other, as well as the desirability of economic links between Israel and Palestinian institutions and individuals. He calls the Interim Agreement on the West Bank and Gaza Strip "the result of a strategic decision taken by the Government of Israel to end its reluctant control of another people and further the opportunities for a lasting and comprehensive peace in the Middle East."[299]

Document 444: Framework for the Conclusion of a Final Status Agreement between Israel and the PLO (Beilin-Abu Mazen Document) (October 31, 1995) [*available at* http://domino.un.org/UNISPAL.NSF/0/7ba18696d92a8b6a85256cd3005a6e48?OpenDocument]. The Framework for the Conclusion of a Final Status Agreement between Israel and the PLO was negotiated in secret by a team of Palestinian and Israeli negotiators, under the supervision of Yossi Beilin for Israel and Abu Mazen (Mahmoud Abbas) for the Palestinians. Though it was never formally adopted by either side, many of the ideas on refugees, Jerusalem, settlements, and the principle of territorial exchange have been cited as potential solutions to outstanding issues.

Document 445: Israeli Prime Minister Yitzhak Rabin: Speech at Peace Rally (November 4, 1995) [*reprinted in* THE ISRAEL-ARAB READER: A DOCUMENTARY HISTORY OF THE MIDDLE EAST CONFLICT (Walter Laqueur & Barry Rubin eds., 2001)]. The prime minister of Israel delivered a speech supporting the strides towards peace that Israel had been making with its neighbors and decrying the effect of violence on democracy. In a moment of tragedy following the speech, however, a Jewish man associated with right-wing extremist groups assassinated the prime minister.

Document 446: Barcelona Declaration, Adopted at the Euro-Mediterranean Conference (November 27–28, 1995) [*available at* http://europa.eu.int/comm/external_relations/euromed/bd.htm]. The ministers of foreign affairs of the fifteen member states of

[299] Doc. 442.

the European Union[300] and twelve Mediterranean countries,[301] including the Palestinian Authority, met on November 27 and 28, 1995, in Barcelona at the Barcelona Conference to address: political partnership; economic partnership; and social, cultural and human partnership. Parties to the resultant declaration pledge to promote peace and stability in the region, to respect the right to self-determination, to settle their disputes by peaceful means, and to strengthen cooperation in preventing and combating terrorism.

Document 447: Presidential Determination Suspending Restrictions on U.S.-PLO Relations (January 4, 1996) [Pres. Determination No. 96–8, 3 C.F.R. pts. 100–102 (1996)]. In this memorandum, U.S. President Bill Clinton suspends restrictions on the United States' engagement with the PLO—with the justification for this change that relations with the PLO are in the "national interest." The implicit reason, however, is the perceived increased legitimacy of the PLO in view of its role as the official Palestinian representative in the peace process.

Document 448: Final Statement, Summit of the Peacemakers at Sharm el-Sheikh (March 13, 1996) [U.N. GAOR, 51st Sess., U.N. Doc. A/51/91 (1996)]. In this final statement, participants of the Summit of the Peacemakers at Sharm el-Sheikh express support for the peace process and vow to work together to ensure security in the region.

Document 449: Joint Statement by Israel and the United States (April 30, 1996) [*available at* http://clinton6.nara.gov/1996/04/1996-04-30-us-israel-joint-statement.html]. On April 30, Israeli Prime Minister Shimon Peres and U.S. President Bill Clinton signed a cooperation accord in Washington, D.C., to enhance their capabilities to deter, prevent, respond to, and investigate international terrorist acts or threats of international terrorist acts against Israel or the United States. Following meetings, Israel and the United States issued this joint statement, in which the two leaders agree on the importance of implementing present agreements and the need to expand the orbit of Arab-Israeli peacemaking with a view toward achieving normal, peaceful relations between Israel and its Arab neighbors. They also welcome the Palestinian National Council's decision to cancel all the provisions of the Palestinian National Covenant that deny Israel's right to exist.[302] Peres also met with Palestinian President Yasser Arafat during his visit.

Document 450: Amendment to the PLO Charter (May 4, 1996) [*U.N. Division for Palestinian Rights,* 7 DEVELOPMENTS RELATED TO THE MIDDLE EAST PEACE PROCESS 13 (1996)]. The Palestinian National Council—at its twenty-first session held in the city of Gaza—amended the Palestinian National Charter by canceling Articles 8–10, 15, and 19–23, which called for armed resistance against Israel.[303] Article 15 of the charter, for example, had stated that the liberation of Palestine "aims at the elimination of Zionism in Palestine." The amendment was passed with a vote of five hundred four to fifty-four, with fourteen abstentions.

---

[300] Austria, Belgium, Denmark, Finland, France, Germany, Greece, Ireland, Italy, Luxembourg, the Netherlands, Portugal, Spain, Sweden, and the United Kingdom.

[301] Algeria, Cyprus, Egypt, Israel, Jordan, Lebanon, Malta, Morocco, Syria, Tunisia, Turkey, and the Palestinian Authority.

[302] *See* Doc. 449.

[303] *See* Doc. 605.

Document 451: Agreement on Temporary International Presence in the City of Hebron between Israel and the PLO (May 9, 1996) [7 Developments Related to the Middle East Peace Process 16 (1996)]. This agreement enabled the Temporary International Presence in Hebron (TIPH) to immediately commence operation in the occupied territory. The TIPH continued its work until a new agreement superseded this one on January 17, 1997, as provided for in paragraph 1.

Document 452: Hebron Accords between Israel and Palestinian Authority (January 15, 1997) [*reprinted in* The Israel-Arab Reader: A Documentary History of the Middle East Conflict (Walter Laqueur & Barry Rubin eds., 2001)]. The long-awaited summit regarding the occupation of Hebron resulted in an agreement between Palestine and Israel in which the latter would redeploy its troops, thus transferring 80 percent of control to the Palestinians within a matter of days. The Hebron Accords also included a note for the records in which both parties agreed to additional terms that would prevent violence and facilitate future negotiations.

Document 453: Letter from U.S. Secretary of State Warren Christopher to Israeli Prime Minister Benjamin Netanyahu (January 15, 1997) [*reprinted in* The Israel-Arab Reader: A Documentary History of the Middle East Conflict (Walter Laqueur & Barry Rubin eds., 2001)]. Christopher's letter congratulates Netanyahu on the success of the Hebron Accords. It further emphasizes the United States' commitment to supporting the agreement as well as for the defense of Israel's borders.

Document 454: Protocol Concerning Redeployment in Hebron between Israel and the PLO (January 17, 1997) [Isr.-PLO, 36 I.L.M. 650]. The Protocol Concerning Redeployment in Hebron between Israel and the PLO signed by Israel and the PLO fulfills the provisions outlined in Article VII of Annex I of the Israeli-Palestinian Interim Agreement on the West Bank and the Gaza Strip, which called for the redeployment of Israeli military forces in the city of Hebron and provided for a TIPH. This agreement entered into force on February 1, 1997, and supersedes the Agreement on the Temporary International Presence in the City of Hebron, dated May 9, 1996.[304]

Document 455: Doha Declaration of the Fourth Middle East North Africa Economic Conference (November 19, 1997) [*available at* http://www.usembassy-israel.org.il/publish/peace/archives/1997/me1119b.html]. The Doha Declaration, released at the conclusion of the fourth Middle East North Africa Economic Conference, expresses the participants' strong commitment to the achievement of a just, lasting, and comprehensive peace in the Middle East, on the basis of the Madrid Peace Conference formula, *i.e.*, land for peace, and the United Nations Security Council Resolutions 242 and 338. The participants call for broadening and deepening progress on all outstanding issues and reaffirm their commitment to uphold the agreements already reached among the parties.

Document 456: Letter from Palestinian President Yasser Arafat to U.S. President Bill Clinton Announcing the Amendment of the Palestine National Charter (January 13, 1998) [*available at* http://www.mideastweb.org/arafatwye1998.htm]. Palestinian President Yasser Arafat sent this letter to U.S. President Bill Clinton clarifying the effect of the amendment to the Palestinian National Charter, which was intended

[304] *See* Doc. 451.

to fulfill the PLO's commitments as outlined in the mutual recognition letters exchanged between Israel and the PLO of September 9–10, 1993.[305] Arafat wrote, "Articles 6–10, 15, 19–23, and 30 have been nullified, and the parts in Articles 1–5, 11–14, 16–18, 25–27 and 29 that are inconsistent with [the Israel-PLO Letters of Recognition] have also been nullified. I can assure you on behalf of the PLO and the Palestinian Authority that all the provisions of the Covenant that were inconsistent with the commitments of September 9/10, 1993 to Prime Minister Rabin, have been nullified."

Document 457: Council of Europe Resolution 1156 (1998), Concerning the Palestine Refugee Situation in the Context of the Middle East Peace Process (April 23, 1998) [Res. 1156, EUR. PARL. ASS. DEB. 14th Sess. (April 23, 1998)]. In this resolution, the Council of Europe addresses the issue of Palestinian refugees in the context of the Middle East peace process. It states that the refugee situation must be resolved by resettlement to permanent accommodation, not only for humanitarian reasons but also as an essential step towards ending a major source of insecurity and tension in the region. It recognizes that resettlement will not be possible without the establishment of a viable Palestinian state that can provide refugees with citizenship and internationally recognized passports.

Document 458: Wye River Memorandum (October 23, 1998) [Isr.-P.L.O., 37 I.L.M. 1251]. Israeli Prime Minister Benjamin Netanyahu and Palestinian President Yasser Arafat met at the Wye River Plantation in Maryland in October 1998 to make progress toward compliance with signed agreements. The meeting resulted in the Wye River Memorandum, which details the steps needed to implement the Interim Agreement on the West Bank and Gaza Strip (Oslo II) and other related agreements so that Israel and the Palestinian Authority could carry out their reciprocal responsibilities more effectively, including those relating to further redeployments and security. Steps were to be carried out in a parallel phased approach in accordance with a clear timeline.

Document 459: U.S. President Bill Clinton: Speech to the Palestinian Leadership (December 14, 1998) [*reprinted in* THE ISRAEL-ARAB READER: A DOCUMENTARY HISTORY OF THE MIDDLE EAST CONFLICT (Walter Laqueur & Barry Rubin eds., 2001)]. On December 13, 1998, the Palestine National Council unanimously voted to remove clauses from the PLO charter that call for the destruction of Israel. It was during Clinton's trip to Israel and Gaza that this vote was made, as required by the Wye River accord. Clinton's speech reflects on the progress that Israel and Palestine had made in the five years since the Oslo Accords and looks to further commitment towards peace.

Document 460: Joint Declaration by the United States and the European Community on the Middle East Peace Process (December 18, 1998) [*available at* http://www.eurunion.org/partner/summit/Summit9812/mideast.htm]. This joint delcaration on the Middle East Peace Process was issued at the conclusion of the United States-European Union Summit, which took place December 18, 1998, at the White House. In noting the recent signature of the Wye River Memorandum—which broke a dangerous deadlock in the Peace Process—the United States and the European Community call on all parties to fully implement their remaining

[305] *See* Doc. 437.

obligations under existing agreements.[306] They pledge to work together to help parties move forward to a successful conclusion.

Document 461: Letter from U.S. President Bill Clinton to Palestinian President Yasser Arafat (April 26, 1999) [28(4) J. PALESTINE STUD. 145–68 (Summer 1999)]. In anticipation of a Palestinian Central Council special session on Palestinian statehood, U.S. President Bill Clinton sent this letter to Palestinian President Yasser Arafat pledging U.S. assistance to conclude a Mid-East peace deal within one year. The letter urges both sides to refrain from unilateral acts and calls for a three-way summit between Israeli, Palestinian, and United States leaders within six months of Israel's May 17 elections.

Document 462: Joint Statement by U.S. President Bill Clinton and Israeli Prime Minister Ehud Barak (July 19, 1999) [*available at* http://www.mfa.gov.il/MFA/MFAArchive/1990_1999/1999/7/Joint+Statement+by+President+Clinton+and+Prime+Min.htm]. U.S. President Bill Clinton and newly elected Israeli Prime Minister Ehud Barak released this joint statement addressing: the Middle East peace process; the restructuring of U.S. bilateral assistance to Israel; terrorism; and scientific cooperation. The two leaders pledge to make the Middle East peace process a top priority and affirm that their meetings have laid the groundwork for a vigorous effort to bring an end to the Arab-Israeli conflict.

Document 463: Sharm el-Sheikh Memorandum (September 4, 1999) [*available at* http://www.state.gov/p/nea/rls/22696.htm]. The Sharm el-Sheikh Memorandum was signed in Egypt by Israeli Prime Minister Ehud Barak and Palestinian President Yasser Arafat at a ceremony attended by Egyptian President Hosni Mubarak, Jordan's King Abdallah, and U.S. Secretary of State Madeleine Albright. The memorandum was needed after the failure of both sides to comply with the obligations and timeline outlined in agreements reached since September 1993, particularly the Wye River Memorandum (1998).[307] The memorandum reiterates these obligations and serves as a bridge between the completion of the interim period and the initiation of the permanent status.

Document 464: Protocol Concerning Safe Passage between the West Bank and the Gaza Strip between Israel and the PLO (October 5, 1999) [*available at* http://www.state.gov/p/nea/rls/22697.htm]. The Protocol Concerning Safe Passage between the West Bank and the Gaza Strip between Israel and the PLO establishes modalities for the use of safe passage between various areas—the West Bank and Israel, the Gaza Strip and Israel, and the West Bank and the Gaza Strip—with a view to implementing Article X and other related provisions of Annex I to the Israeli-Palestinian Interim Agreement on the West Bank and the Gaza Strip (Oslo II). The protocol was signed in Jerusalem by Minister Shlomo Ben-Ami from the Israeli side and Minister Gamil Tarifi from the Palestinian side.

Document 465: Israeli Prime Minister Ehud Barak : Leaving for the Camp David Talks (July 10, 2000) [*reprinted in* THE ISRAEL-ARAB READER: A DOCUMENTARY HISTORY OF THE MIDDLE EAST CONFLICT (Walter Laqueur & Barry Rubin eds., 2001)]. In anticipation of the Camp David Talks, Barak describes the challenges that he faces in continued

---

306 *See* Doc. 458.

307 *Id.*

negotiations for peace. Although he admits that there is no peace without a price, Barak maintains several principles from which he refuses to deviate.

Document 466: Trilateral Statement on the Middle East Peace Summit at Camp David (Camp David II) (July 25, 2000) [*available at* http://www.state.gov/p/nea/rls/22698.htm]. U.S. President Bill Clinton hosted Israeli Prime Minister Ehud Barak and Palestinian Authority Chairman Yasser Arafat at Camp David July 11–24, 2000, in an effort to reach a permanent status agreement. While Barak and Arafat did not sign an agreement, the two parties did agree on five basic principles to guide their negotiations, among which was the assertion that negotiations should be based on United Nations Security Council Resolutions 242 and 338.

Document 467: Israeli Prime Minister Ehud Barak: Statement After the Camp David Talks (July 25, 2000) [*reprinted in* THE ISRAEL-ARAB READER: A DOCUMENTARY HISTORY OF THE MIDDLE EAST CONFLICT (Walter Laqueur & Barry Rubin eds., 2001)]. Ehud Barak's took a regretful tone following the conclusion of the Camp David Talks. He determined that the lack of success is due to Israel's refusal to compromise its principles relating to Israeli security.

Document 468: Speech by Israeli Foreign Minister Shlomo Ben-Ami at the General Debate of the 55th General Assembly of the United Nations (September 18, 2000) [On file with author]. Delivered one month after the Camp David Summit for an Israeli-Palestinian Peace, this a conciliatory speech aimed at defining Israel's peace policy. The Israeli minister describes the historic relationship between Jews and the culture of Islam, and the respect that Israel has shown for the Holy Sites of Islam in Jerusalem, which he describes as "the very heart of the Jewish faith, identity and history." The solution of the refugee problem will have to be found within the State of Palestine once it is established, but Israel would be ready to admit a limited number of refuges within a scheme of family reunification. The Israeli government understands that no peace agreement can satisfy all the dreams of the parties, but it is also convinced that unless the wounds of years of confrontation are healed there would be no real peace. The Camp David negotiations allowed the parties to turn the sea that separated them into a river, and it is now up to the leaders to muster the necessary courage for the inevitable compromises. Prime Minister Barak's peace proposals so far have touched "the outer limits of his options as an Israeli and a Jew." Pecae, however, would still require a robust American involvement. The speaker believes that peace will have to be accompanied by regional economic cooperation, and also by an effective system of arms control. The minister also calls upon the countries of the Middle East to engage in direct negotiations with Israel with the aim of establishing a zone free of weapons of mass destruction in the region.

Document 469: Clinton Parameters to Palestinian and Israeli Negotiators (December 23, 2000) [*available at* http://www.peacelobby.org/clinton_parameters.htm]. In a last ditch effort to further the peace process before leaving office, U.S. President Bill Clinton offered these parameters to Israeli and Palestinian negotiators at a meeting in the White House. They are not the terms of a final deal, but guidelines for final accelerated negotiations that Clinton hoped would be concluded in the coming weeks. Clinton ended the parameters by warning the parties, "These are my ideas. If they are not accepted, they are not just off the table, they also go with me when I leave office." Palestinian President Yasser Arafat, after a delay, accepted the Clinton parameters, but with questions and reservations that for all practical purposes vacated his acceptance of much of the substance of what he supposedly agreed to. Israeli Prime Minister Ehud Barak accepted the parameters, but clearly intended to preserve elbow room whenever specific negotiations would take place. The parameters laid the foundation for the final negotiations that took place at Taba in January 2001.

Document 470: Official Palestinian Response to the Clinton Parameters (and Letter to the International Community) (January 1, 2001) [*available at* http://www.nad-plo.org/nclinton2.php]. Yasser Abed Rabbo, the Head of the Palestinian Negotiating Team, submitted this official response to the Clinton parameters,[308] which asserts that they fail to satisfy the conditions required for a permanent peace in their original state. Rabbo warns that the terms would divide a Palestinian state into three separate cantons connected and divided by Jewish-only and Arab-only roads and jeopardize the Palestinian state's viability. They would also divide Palestinian Jerusalem into a number of unconnected islands separate from each other and from the rest of Palestine and force Palestinians to surrender the right of return of Palestinian refugees. The following day, Arafat and Clinton met for four and a half hours in Washington to settle discrepancies.

Document 471: Israeli-Palestinian Joint Statement of the Status Negotiations between Israel and the Palestinian Authority at Taba (January 27, 2001) [*available at* http://domino.un.org/UNISPAL.NSF/0/badaa58661cc084f85256e37006fc44d?OpenDocument]. Soon-to-be-ousted Israeli Prime Minister Ehud Barak and Palestinian Authority Chairman Yasser Arafat sent their respective delegations to major peace negotiations at Taba, Egypt, January 22–28, 2001. Following talks on contentious issues such as refugees, security, borders, and Jerusalem that fell short of a permanent agreement, Israeli and Palestinian negotiators, Shlomo Ben-Ami and Abu-Ala, released this joint statement in which the parties blame circumstances and time constraints for their failure to reach understandings on all issues, but note that foundations have been laid for a future agreement. Taba arguably marks the end of the Oslo peace process that started in Madrid in 1991.

Document 472: European Union Non-Paper on the Taba Conference (2001) [*available at* http://www.europarl.eu.int/meetdocs/delegations/plco/20020325/04_fr.pdf]. This European Union Non-Paper was prepared by European Union Special Representative to the Middle East Process Ambassador Miguel Moratinos and his team following consultations with Israeli and Palestinian parties present at Taba in January 2001. Although the paper has no official status, it has been acknowledged by both parties as being a relatively fair description of the outcome of the negotiations.

Document 473: Jordanian-Egyptian Proposal (April 19, 2001) [*available at* http://domino.un.org/UNISPAL.NSF/0/b54aab90a80c526285256e370077a229?OpenDocument]. Jordan and Egypt, as the only Arab nations to sign peace treaties with Israel, presented this proposal aimed at ending the increased violence between Israel and the Palestinians and resuming negotiations. It focuses on three objectives: (1) steps to end the current crisis between Israel and the Palestinian

[308] *See* Doc. 469.

Authority, (2) confidence-building measures, and (3) rebuilding the negotiating process on the Palestinian track.

Document 474: Report of the Sharm el-Sheikh Fact Finding Committee (Mitchell Report) (April 30, 2001) [Doc. SN 3552/01 (2001), *available at* http://www.state.gov/p/nea/rls/rpt/3060.htm]. On October 17, 2000, at the conclusion of the Middle East Peace Summit at Sharm el-Sheikh, Egypt, U.S. President Bill Clinton stated that the United States, in conjunction with the Israelis and the Palestinians and in consultation with the United Nations Secretary-General, would develop a fact-finding committee to investigate the recent escalation of violence and find ways to prevent its recurrence. In its final report—"The Mitchell Report," named for Committee Chairman George J. Mitchell—the Sharm el-Sheikh Fact-Finding Committee emphasizes that it was not a tribunal and so was not intended to determine the guilt or innocence of individuals or the various parties. However, it concludes that there was no evidence that the Palestinian Authority had made a consistent effort to contain demonstrations and control the violence once it began or that the government of Israel had made a consistent effort to use non-lethal means to control demonstrations of unarmed Palestinians. The committee concludes that Likud leader Ariel Sharon's visit to *al-Haram al-Sharif* did not cause the "al-Aqsa *Intifada*" though it was "poorly timed and [its] provocative effect should have been foreseen." Their recommendations prioritize the need to end the violence, rebuild confidence, and resume negotiations. The Israelis and Palestinians were given until May 15 to respond to the report. The committee consisted of Suleyman Demirel, ninth president of the Republic of Turkey; Thorbjoern Jagland, minister of foreign affairs of Norway; Warren B. Rudman, former member of the U.S. Senate; and Javier Solana, high representative for the Common Foreign and Security Policy, European Union.

Document 475: Response of Israel to the Report of the Sharm el-Sheikh Fact Finding Committee (May 15, 2001) [*available at* http://www.mfa.gov.il/MFA/MFAArchive/2000_2009/2001/5/Israels+Comments+on+the+Mitchell+Committee+Report.htm]. In this official response to the Report of the Sharm el-Sheikh Fact Finding Committee, Israel welcomes the unqualified call for an unconditional cessation of violence, the establishment of a meaningful cooling-off period, and the resumption of negotiations.[309] It also asserts that Israeli security personnel acted according to the highest ethical standards, military orders, and a well-defined chain of command, all in the most difficult conditions.

Document 476: Response of the PLO to the Report of the Sharm el-Sheikh Fact Finding Committee (May 23, 2001) [*available at* http://www.pmo.gov.ps/peace/responsetomitchell.asp]. In its delayed response to the Report of the Sharm el-Sheikh Fact Finding Committee, the PLO expresses its belief that the report provided a balanced assessment of the facts and gives its full support for the immediate implementation of all of the committee's recommendations as a comprehensive package.[310] The PLO identifies as issues for further attention the creation of an international protection force and Israel's continuing assassination policy.

---

309 Doc. 474.

310 *Id.*

Document 477: Palestinian-Israeli Security Implementation Work Plan (Tenet Cease-Fire Plan) (June 14, 2001) [*available at* http://www.yale.edu/ awweb/avalon/mideast/ mid023.htm]. This work plan, advanced by U.S. Director of Central Intelligence George J. Tenet, details five mutually reinforcing steps for improving security between the government of Israel and the Palestinian Authority. The Tenet Plan, scheduled to start on June 13, 2001, was meant to lay the groundwork for the resumption of peace negotiations. At the request of Israeli Prime Minister Ariel Sharon, it specifies a period of seven days without attacks as a precondition for implementation. As this did not materialize, it was left unimplemented.

Document 478: United Nations Security Council Resolution 1397, Calling for Implementation of the Tenet Work Plan and Mitchell Report Recommendations (March 12, 2002) [S.C. Res. 1397, U.N. SCOR, 4489th mtg., U.N. Doc. S/Res/1397 (2002)]. The Security Council in Resolution 1397 calls upon the Israeli and Palestinian sides and their leaders to cooperate in the implementation of the Tenet Cease-Fire Plan[311] and recommendations of the Mitchell report with the aim of resuming negotiations on a political settlement. It also envisions a peaceful two-state solution.

Document 479: Arab Peace Initiative Established at the Arab League Summit (March 28, 2002) [*available at* http://saudiembassy.net/2002News/Statements/StateDetail.asp?cIndex=142]. This Saudi-initiated plan for a comprehensive peace calls for settlement of the Palestine-Israel conflict and other outstanding disputes that would be followed by a termination of the state of war between Israel and all Arab states and the formal recognition of Israel by those states. The plan calls for a solution to the refugees problem that is accepted by the parties, and it mentions U.N. Resolution 194 as a basis.

Document 480: Letter from the Secretary-General Containing a Joint Statement by the Quartet (April 10, 2002) [U.N. SCOR, U.N. Doc. S/2002/369 (2002)]. After a meeting in Madrid, representatives of the Quartet issued this joint statement, calling on the leaders of Israel and the Palestinian Authority to act in the interests of their own people, the region, and the international community and immediately end the violence.[312]

Document 481: Speech by U.S. President George W. Bush on Mid-East Peace (June 24, 2002) [*available at* http://www.whitehouse.gov/news/releases/2002/06/20020624-3.html]. In this speech, U.S. President George W. Bush disparages the existing Palestinian leadership for its alleged support of terrorism and its inability to participate with good faith in peace negotiations. Bush promises that when new leaders, new institutions, and new security arrangements are arranged, the United States will support the creation of a Palestinian state within the framework of a final settlement.

Document 482: Nusseibeh-Ayalon Agreement (August 6, 2002) [*available at* http://www.mifkad.org.il/en/principles.asp]. Sari Nusseibeh, president of Al Quds University, and Ami Ayalon, the former director of Israel's Domestic Security Service (*Shin*

---

[311] Doc. 477.

[312] The Secretary-General of the United Nations Kofi Annan, Minister of Foreign Affairs of the Russian Federation Igor Ivanov, Secretary of State of the United States Colin Powell, Minister for Foreign Affairs of Spain Josep Pique, and the High Representative for European Union Common Foreign and Security Policy Javier Solana.

Beth) and the former admiral of the Israeli navy, released these principles for an Israeli-Palestinian peace agreement. Promoting a two-state solution and Jerusalem as the capital of both states, the plan is largely consistent with the more detailed 2003 Geneva Accord.[313] Thus far, the agreement has not been accepted by official Israeli or Palestinian representatives.

Document 483: Communiqué Issued by the Quartet (September 17, 2002) [*available at* http://domino.un.org/UNISPAL.NSF/9a798adbf322aff38525617b006d88d7/54c9e0a5f8ccbd2b85256c3700653ea4!OpenDocument]. Representatives of the Quartet (*i.e.*, United Nations Secretary-General Kofi Annan, U.S. Secretary of State Colin Powell, Russian Foreign Minister Igor Ivanov, Danish Foreign Minister Per Stig Moeller, High Representative for European Common Foreign and Security Policy Javier Solana, and European Commissioner for External Affairs Chris Patten) released this joint Communiqué in New York, agreeing to intensify their efforts in support of achieving a final Israeli-Palestinian settlement based on the two-state solution.

Document 484: Elements of a Performance-Based Road Map to a Permanent Two-State Solution to the Israeli-Palestinian Conflict Issued by the United States and Welcomed by the European Union, Russia, and the United Nations (October 15, 2002) [U.N. SCOR, Annex, U.N. Doc. S/2003/529 (2003)]. The Elements of a Performance-based Road Map to a Permanent Two-State Solution to the Israeli-Palestinian Conflict Issued by the United States and Welcomed by the European Union, Russia, and the United Nations (Road Map), now endorsed by the United Nations, is not a final status plan, but a series of steps designed to calm the Israeli-Palestinian conflict, create a provisional Palestinian state, and allow for negotiations of a final status agreement. It calls for a three-phased implementation of proposals as set out in U.S. President George W. Bush's speech of June 24, 2002, making a two-state solution possible.[314] It does not specify the final borders of Palestine and Israel or any other details of the solution.

Document 485: Israel's Response to the Road Map (May 25, 2003) [*available at* http://www.knesset.gov.il/process/docs/roadmap_response_eng.htm]. The government of Israel presented this fourteen-point formal response to the Performance-based Road Map, which outlines conditions for progress, including the complete cessation of terror, violence, and incitement and the emergence of a new and different leadership in the Palestinian Authority.[315]

Document 486: Statement by the Quartet, Jordan (June 22, 2003) [*available at* http://www.state.gov/r/pa/prs/ps/2003/21808.htm]. Following their meeting at the Dead Sea in Jordan, representatives of the Quartet (*i.e.*, United Nations Secretary-General Kofi Annan, Russian Foreign Minister Igor Ivanov, Greek Foreign Minister George Papandreou, United States Secretary of State Colin Powell, High Representative for European Common Foreign and Security Policy Javier Solana, and European Commissioner for External Affairs Chris Patten) released this statement, welcoming U.S. President George W. Bush's decision to send a mission to the area to coordinate, monitor, and promote implementation of the parties'

---

[313] *See* Doc. 489.

[314] *See* Doc. 481.

[315] *See* Doc. 484.

commitments and responsibilities as laid out in the Road Map.[316] They detail progress made on Palestinian institutional reform and reaffirm their support for efforts to fulfill the reform goals set forth in the first phase of the Road Map.

Document 487: Statement by the Quartet, New York (September 26, 2003) [*available at* http://domino.un.org/unispal.nsf/0/a80bac3d1c9c285e85256db2004c77d6?OpenDocument]. After their meeting in New York, representatives of the Quartet released this statement, reminding all sides of their obligations and responsibilities to each other with regard to the Road Map.[317]

Document 488: Geneva Accord, Draft Permanent Status Agreement (October 2003) [*available at* http://www.haaretz.com/hasen/pages/ShArt.jhtml?itemNo=351461l]. A group of prominent Israelis and Palestinians[318] initialed this final status peace agreement in Geneva, now called the Geneva Accord. It is based on the Clinton parameters of December 2000, which were accepted by Israel and the Palestinian Authority as a basis for negotiations.

Document 489: United Nations Security Council Resolution 1515, Endorsing the Road Map Unanimously (November 19, 2003) [S.C. Res. 1515, U.N. SCOR, 4862d mtg., U.N. Doc. S/RES/1515 (2003)]. United Nations Security Council Resolution 1515 welcomes the diplomatic efforts of the international Quartet and endorses the Quartet's Performance-based Road Map to a Permanent Two-State Solution to the Israeli-Palestinian Conflict. It calls on the parties to fulfill their obligations under the Road Map in cooperation with the Quartet.

Document 490: Prime Minister Ariel Sharon's Speech at the Herzlia Conference, (December 18, 2003) [*available at* http://www.jewishvirtuallibrary.org/jsource/Peace/sharon_1203.html]. It was in this occasion that Prime Minister Sharon announced for the first time his plan for Israel's unilateral disengagement from the Gaza Strip. He spells out Israel's challenges in the field of economic and social improvement, education and science, and comes to the conclusion that Israel cannot wait for the Palestinians to be ripe for peace. Therefore, to be able to face its vital challenges, Israel must take unilateral steps. He reaffirms his commitment to the Road Map

---

[316] *Id.*

[317] *Id.*

[318] Israelis involved in negotiating and promoting the accord include: former Chief of Staff Amnon Lipkin-Shahak; Brigadier General (res.) Giora Inbar; Brigadier General (res.) Gideon Sheffer; Brigadier General (res.) Shlomo Brom; Colonel (res.) Shaul Arieli; former Justice Minister Yossi Beilin; Member of Knesset (Labor) Amram Mitzna, Member of Knesset (Labor) Avraham Burg; Member of Knesset (Labor) Yuli Tamir; Member of Knesset (Meretz) Haim Oron; Member of Knesset (Meretz) Yossi Sarid; Professor Aryeh Arnon (a leader of Peace Now); former Member of Knesset (Likud) Nehama Ronen; authors Amoz Oz, David Grossman, and Zvia Greenfield; Jerusalem expert Dr. Menachem Klein; and economist Yoram Gabay. Palestinians involved in negotiating and promoting the accord include: former Palestinian Minister of Information and Culture Yasser Abed Rabbo; former Minister of Tourism Nabil Qassis; Palestinian Legislative Council members Qadoura Fares and Mohamed Horani (associated with the Fatah/Tanzim); Samih al-Abed; Bashar Jum'a; Dr. Nazmi Shuabi; Gheith al-Omri; Jamal Zakut; Prisoners Affairs Minister Hisham Abdel Raziq; and General Zoheir Manasra (former governor of Jenin and head of Preventative Security in the West Bank).

and to the principle of two states—Israel and Palestine—living side by side in peace and security. Yet, he insists that without security, on which the Palestinians are still incapable to deliver, there can be no peace. Hence, his Disengagement Plan, which would entail the evacuation of all the Jewish settlers in Gaza, is aimed at increasing security as a step towards peace. The Disengagement Plan is a security measure, not a political one. He pledges that concurrent with the demand from the Palestinians to eliminate the terror organizations, Israel will persist in its policy of improving the living conditions of the Palestinian population. The aim, he states unequivocally, is that of establishing a "democratic Palestinian state with territorial contiguity . . . and economic viability."

Document 491: Statement by United Nations Secretary-General Kofi Annan at the 2004 Session of the Committee of the Exercise of the Inalienable Rights of the Palestinian People (March 12, 2004) [U.N. Press Release, U.N. Dep't of Public Info., U.N. Doc. SG/SM/9194 (2004)]. In this public statement delivered at the 2004 Session of the Committee of the Exercise of the Inalienable Rights of the Palestinian People, United Nations Secretary-General Kofi Annan calls on both parties to take immediate and specific steps to implement the Road Map without preconditions and notes the civilian death toll owing to the failure to make discernable progress.

Document 492: Exchange of Letters between U.S. President George W. Bush and Israeli Prime Minister Ariel Sharon (April 14, 2004) [*available at* http://www.pmo.gov.il/nr/exeres/D52EF985-40EE-4E58-8F6A-EBA088C917B7.htm,http://www.whitehouse.gov/news/releases/2004/04/20040414-3.html]. These letters exchanged by U.S. President George W. Bush and Israeli Prime Minister Ariel Sharon form an integral part of Sharon's Disengagement Plan.[319] In Bush's letter, the United States pledges support for the plan on the precondition that it is approved by the Israeli cabinet and the Knesset.

Document 493: Statement by U.S. President George W. Bush (April 14, 2004) [*available at* http://www.whitehouse.gov/news/releases/2004/04/20040414-2.html]. U.S. President George W. Bush issued this statement from the White House following a meeting with Israeli Prime Minister Ariel Sharon. In it, Bush expresses support for Israeli Prime Minister Ariel Sharon's Disengagement Plan, under which Israel would remove its military installations and settlements from Gaza and portions of the West Bank. Bush affirms the U.S. government's commitment to a two-state solution and the Road Map as the best means of realizing peace.

Document 494: Israeli Prime Minister Ariel Sharon's Disengagement Plan (April 18, 2004) [*available at* http://www.pmo.gov.il/nr/exeres/939E3D2E-1621-4AA9-A6DF-174AE7441DA2.htm]. Israeli Prime Minister Ariel Sharon presented this plan that calls for a unilateral Israeli withdrawal from all of Gaza and four settlements in the West Bank to take place in four stages by the end 2005. According to the proposal, Israel would redeploy military forces along new security lines and relocate some settlements, including nearly all of the settlements in the Gaza Strip. The plan also calls for accelerating the completion of the "separation barrier" between Israel and the West Bank. Arafat's top advisor, Nabil Abu Rudaina, stated that Sharon's plan violated the Road Map. This Disengagement Plan was the first serious diplomatic initiative undertaken by Sharon since he took office in 2001.

[319] Doc. 494.

Document 495: Letter from the Chief of the Israeli Prime Minister's Bureau, Dov Weissglas, to the U.S. National Security Advisor, Dr. Condoleezza Rice (April 18, 2004) [*available at* http://www.mfa.gov.il/MFA/Peace+Process/Reference+Documents/Letter+Weissglas-Rice+18-Apr-2004.htm]. The chief of Israeli Prime Minister's Bureau, Dov Weissglas, sent this letter to the U.S. National Security Advisor, Dr. Condoleeza Rice, to clarify Sharon's Disengagement Plan with regard to: (1) restrictions on settlement growth, (2) removal of unauthorized outposts, (3) mobility restrictions in Judea and Samaria,; and (4) legal attachments of Palestinian revenues. Weissglas presents strategies for resolving these issues and assures Rice that the Government of Israel remains committed to a two-state solution and to the Road Map—with the understanding that Sharon's Disengagement Plan is consistent with the Road Map.

Document 496: Government Resolution Regarding the Disengagement Plan (June 6, 2004) [*available at* http://www.pmo.gov.il/nr/exeres/C5E1ACE3-9834-414E-9512-8E5F509E9A4D.htm]. The Israeli cabinet approved this revised version of Sharon's Disengagement Plan, which coordinates the withdrawal of Israeli forces from the Gaza Strip and areas in the West Bank. It allows for the preparatory work necessary to evacuate settlements from these areas; however, it does not allow for their removal without further government approval. The vote carried fourteen to seven in favor after two Ministers, Avigdor Liberman and Benny Elon, were fired by Prime Minister Sharon and a compromise offered by Likud was accepted. On October 26, 2004, the Israeli Knesset voted to adopt the plan.

Document 497: Prime Minister Ariel Sharon's Statement on the Day of the Implementation of the Disengagement Plan (August 15, 2005) [*available at* http://www.mfa.gov.il/MFA/Government/Speeches+by+Israeli+leaders/2005/PM+Sharon+addresses+the+nation+15-Aug-2005.htm]. The prime minister expresses his sorrow at the mass evacuation of settlements he always believed should be part of the State of Israel. But, "the changing reality in this country, in this region, and in the world, required another assessment and changing of positions." Now, after the disengagement, the Palestinians bear the burden of proof, and he expects them to fight terror, and show sincere intentions of peace. He also consoles the settlers of Gaza in their sorrow by saying that theirs was a glorious chapter in the history of Israel.

Document 498: U.S.-Vetoed Security Council Draft Resolution (July 13, 2006) [*available at* http://domino.un.org/UNISPAL.NSF/22f431edb91c6f5 48525678a0051be1d/9d7e7d10afdd2a81852571ab004b106c!OpenDocument]. In response to rocket fire originating in Gaza and the abduction of Corporal Gilad Shalit, Israeli forces mobilized forces against Gaza. This proposed resolution called for immediate cessation of military action, as well as the release of Palestinian ministers and Shalit.

Document 499: Annapolis Summit Opening Remarks by Palestinian Authority Chairman Mahmoud Abbas and Israeli Prime Minister Ehud Olmert (November 27, 2007) [*available at* http://www.haaretz.com/hasen/spages/928669.html]. The United States organized the Annapolis Summit in order to lay the foundation for a roadmap to peace between Palestine and Israel. The plan also included aspirations to develop a bilateral agreement to develop a two-state plan. The conference ended with an agreed upon joint statement by both parties involved.

Document 500: Annapolis Summit Opening Remarks by President Bush Including Joint Statement (Novemeber 27, 2007) [*available at* http://www.haaretz.com/hasen/spages/928652.html]. Following a welcome to the attendees of the Annapolis Summit at the U.S. Naval Academy, President Bush read the joint statement agreed upon by both parties. The agreement establishes a joint goal for two states, Israel and Palestine. The joint statement also institutes a plan for vigorous negotiation that would conclude in an agreement by the end of 2008.

Document 501: Trip Report by Former U.S. President Jimmy Carter to Israel, Palestine, Egypt, Syria, Saudi Arabia, and Jordan (April 22, 2008) [*available at* http://www.cartercenter.org/news/trip_reports/middle_east_2008.html]. President Carter visited several Mid-East leaders, including those from Syria and Hamas, to discuss the challenges and options available in the ongoing peace process for the region. His synopsis recalls meetings with various leaders and organizations, discusses his role on the trip, and provides a summary of the results. The report's most substantive elements include Carter's reflection on his meetings with Syrian and Hamas leaders, specifically noting those states' concerns and peace process options to which they are most receptive.

8. Status of the Palestinians: 1948–2008

This section contains 134 documents relating to the effects of the Arab-Israeli conflict on the collective experience of Palestinian Arabs. Most documents are United Nations resolutions and reports, but others originate from Israel and the Arab states. They narrate the Palestinians' growing experience of national dispossession and repression resulting from Israeli policies and practices in the Occupied Palestinian Territories and in Israel.

It should be noted that from 1949 to 1969 the United Nations defined all non-Israeli Palestinians as legal refugees; however, characterization changed with the adoption of General Assembly Resolution 2535 (1969), which recognized Palestinians for the first time as a people with a national identity and collective rights.[320] Palestinians still retain a special status in refugee law, yet fall partially outside the protection of the 1951 Convention Relating to the Status of Refugees.[321] The recognition of Palestinian national identity was strengthened in 1974 after the United Nations granted observer status to the PLO and invited PLO Chairman Yasser Arafat to address the General Assembly as if he were a head of state.[322]

This section is divided into four separate though interrelated sections that reflect the evolution of the Palestinians' legal status from that of

---

[320] *See* Doc. 519.

[321] United Nations Convention Relating to the Status of Refugees, *opened for signature* July 28, 1951, 19 U.S.T. 6259, 189 U.N.T.S. 137 (entered into force Apr. 22, 1954), *available at* http://www.ufsia.ac.be/~dvanheul/migration/genconv.html. *See also* Protocol Relating to the Status of Refugees, Jan. 31, 1967, 19 U.S.T. 6223, 606 U.N.T.S. 267.

[322] *See* Docs. 608 and 609.

refugees (Section A) to that of a population under occupation in the West Bank and Gaza Strip (Section B) to their contemporary status as a nascent state (Section C) and, in some cases, as Arab citizens of Israel (Section D).

Documents in this section should be read in conjunction with relevant documents in other chapters, in particular those in: Section 3, Arab-Israeli Wars; Section 6, Jerusalem and the Holy Sites; and Section 7, Israeli-Palestinian Peace Process.

A. *Status of the Palestinians as Refugees: 1948–2003*

In late November 1947, serious conflict erupted when the Palestinians rose in arms against U.N. General Assembly Resolution 181 partitioning Palestine into a Jewish and an Arab state[323] which divided Palestine into two states and allotted a majority of the land in mandatory Palestine to the Jewish state despite the Jews' smaller numbers and significantly lower rate of landownership. Conditions escalated to a full-scale war in May 1948, after the British withdrew from Palestine and Israel declared its independence.[324] As a result, an estimated 700,000 Arab Palestinians fled or were expelled from their homes, becoming refugees in the West Bank, Gaza Strip, neighboring Arab states, and beyond.

In 1949, the United Nations General Assembly adopted Resolution 302, which established the United Nations Relief and Works Agency for Palestinian Refugees (UNRWA) with the mandate to provide humanitarian aid to displaced Palestinians. Reports issued by UNRWA describe the living conditions and human rights situation faced by Palestinians as refugees in Lebanon, Jordan, Syria, and in Israeli-controlled territory.

Following the 1948 war, Israel enacted several national laws that legalized the expropriation of Arab land and property and in effect blocked the return of Palestinian refugees to Palestine: the Emergency Land Requisition (Regulation) Law (1949), the Law of Return (1950), the Absentees' Property Law (1950), the Land Acquisition (Validation of Acts and Compensation) Law (1953), and the Prevention of Infiltration (Offences and Jurisdiction) Law (1954).[325]

Despite demands from the United Nations that Israel allow refugees to return in accordance with the right of everyone to leave and to return to his/her home state or territory as prescribed by the International Covenant on Civil and Political Rights (ICCPR), Israel has refused to recognize this right.[326] The issue of Palestinians' right of return remains

---

[323] *See* Doc. 59.

[324] *See* Doc. 67.

[325] *See* Doc. 505, 509, 507, 515, and 516.

[326] *See* International Covenant on Civil and Political Rights, *opened for signature* Dec. 16, 1966, art. 13, 999 U.N.T.S. 171 (entered into force Mar. 23, 1976) [hereinafter ICCPR]. *See also* First Optional Protocol to the International Covenant on Civil and

unresolved and is a major point of contention in Israeli-Palestinian peace negotiations.

Other documents on related subjects may be found in: Section 3, Arab-Israeli Wars; and Section 7, Israeli-Palestinian-Peace Process.

Document 502: United Nations General Assembly Resolution 212, Assistance to Palestine Refugees (November 19, 1948) [G.A. Res. 212, U.N. GAOR, U.N. Doc. A/RES/212 (III) (1948)]. United Nations General Assembly Resolution 212 urges all state members to make voluntary contributions to provide needed relief to Palestine refugees. It also authorizes the Secretary-General to establish a special fund into which contributions could be collected. It requests that the Secretary-General appoint a director of United Nations Relief for Palestine Refugees to oversee the planning and implementation of the relief program.

Document 503: United Nations General Assembly Resolution 194, Right of Return and Creation of a Conciliation Commission for Palestine (December 11, 1948) [S.C. Res. 194, U.N. GAOR, 3d Sess., 186th plen. mtg. at 21–25, U.N. Doc. A/810 (1948)]. United Nations General Assembly Resolution 194 establishes the Conciliation Commission for Palestine to be comprised of delegates from France, Turkey, and the United States and grants it the functions of the United Nations mediator for Palestine. It also resolves that refugees wishing to return to their homes and live at peace with their neighbors should be permitted to do so at the earliest practicable date, and compensation should be paid for the property of those choosing not to return. This is the first and most important United Nations resolution addressing Palestinian refugee rights. Resolution 194 also reaffirms the principle of internationalization of Jerusalem.

Document 504: Letter from Dr. Walter Eytan, Head of the Israeli Delegation, to the Chairman of the Conciliation Commission (May 7, 1949) [*available at* http://domino.un.org/pdfs/AAC25IS15.pdf]. In his letter to the chairman of the Conciliation Commission, Dr. Walter Eytan, the head of the Israeli delegation, states that Israel would be prepared to consider a plan for the reunion of families whose members were separated as a result of fighting. However, he stresses that family members to be reunited must be "genuine relatives of a close degree of consanguity." Eytan further states that Israel would be prepared to collect information from Arab residents in Israel concerning relatives of theirs who became refugees and who wish and are eligible to apply for repatriation.

Document 505: Law of the State of Israel: Emergency Land Requisition (Regulation) Law (November 14, 1949) [4 LSI 3, (1949–50)]. This law permits Israeli authorities to order the requisition of any type of owned property. Once a requisition order is put into effect, the original owner of the home or business is to be forced to surrender his or her home or business to the person specified in the requisition order. The law applies retrospectively to any person who has occupied the property before the law went into effect and also applies to citizens who forcefully enter a home under a billet order.

Political Rights, *opened for signature* Dec. 16, 1966, 999 U.N.T.S. 302 (entered into force Mar. 23, 1976) [hereinafter ICCPR First Optional Protocol]. *See also* Second Optional Protocol to the International Covenant on Civil and Political Rights, *opened for signature* Dec. 15, 1989, 1642 U.N.T.S. 414 [entered into force July 11, 1991].

The law authorizes the Israeli government to use force to carry out any order under this law.

Document 506: United Nations General Assembly Resolution 302, Establishing the UNRWA for Palestinian Refugees in the Near East (December 8, 1949) [G.A. Res. 302, U.N. GAOR, U.N. Doc. A/RES/302 (1949)]. This General Assembly Resolution creates the UNRWA to address the humanitarian needs of Palestinian refugees outside Israel.

Document 507: Law of the State of Israel: Absentees' Property Law (March 14, 1950) [S.H. 86, *reprinted in* 4 Laws of Israel 68–82]. This law establishes the Custodianship Council for Absentee's Property and empowers that office with wide-ranging controls over absentees' property, effectively transferring ownership of property from absentee owners to the State of Israel. This law defines an "absentee" as anyone who, from November 29, 1947, to May 19, 1948, has ceased to exist, has relocated to his or her homeland, or was a Palestinian citizen and left his or her ordinary place of residence in Palestine. The law also applies to those refugees who chose to remain inside Israel. Consequently, the law vests within the custodian the possession of all property and property rights in businesses, homes, and farms abandoned by those fleeing the conflict or the property Arab nationals of another state. Additionally, the custodian is granted the right to liquidate or demolish any property given to the Custodianship Council. The law allows no possibility for an absentee to claim that they were forced to abandon the property and stipulates that an absentee will be forced to pay remuneration in addition to any expenses incurred by the custodian in carrying out the law.

Document 508: United States: United Nations Palestine Refugee Aid Act of 1950: Title III of Public Law 535 (June 5, 1950) [64 Stat. 203, *repealed by* Act of Aug. 26, 1954, ch. 937, title V, § 542 (a)(6), 68 Stat. 861]. The Palestine Refugee Aid Act authorizes the U.S. Secretary of State to make contributions to the UNRWA for a period of one year. It stipulates that contributions are not to exceed $27.45 million.

Document 509: Law of the State of Israel: Law of Return (July 5, 1950) [4 LSI 114 (1950)]. On July 5, 1950, the Knesset unanimously adopted the Law of Return, giving Jews throughout the world the right to immigrate to Israel. The 1970 amendment accords the right to immigrate to Israel to those non-Jews who are either children or grandchildren of a Jew, the spouse of a Jew, or the spouse of a child or grandchild of a Jew on the condition that the person was not previously a Jew who knowingly converted to another faith. Subsequently, some 700,000 Jewish immigrants immigrated to Israel from Eastern and Central Europe and later from Yemen, Iraq, and Morocco.

Document 510: United Nations Security Council Resolution 89, Pledging to Look into Allegations of Expulsion of Arabs and Suggesting the Movement of Bedouins Be Controlled (November 17, 1950) [S.C. Res. 89, U.N. SCOR, 524th mtg., U.N. Doc. S/1907 (1950)]. United Nations Security Council Resolution 89 authorizes the chief of staff of the UNTSO to recommend to Israel, Egypt, and other Arab states steps needed to control the movement of nomadic Arabs across international frontiers or armistice lines by mutual agreement. It also calls upon these governments to stop transferring persons across international frontiers or armistice lines without prior consultation through the Mixed Armistice Commissions.

Document 511: United Nations General Assembly Resolution 393, Authorizing the Agency to Continue to Furnish Direct Relief to Refugees (December 2, 1950) [G.A. Res. 393, U.N. GAOR, 5th Sess., Supp. No. 20, at 22–23, U.N. Doc. A/1775 (1950)]. With Resolution 393, the General Assembly notes that United Nations member states had not yet made sufficient contributions to the UNRWA to accomplish its humanitarian mission. It states that repatriation or resettlement of refugees in Israel is essential and, in extending the mandate, makes funds available for the following year.

Document 512: Law of the State of Israel: State Property Law (February 6, 1951) [5 Laws of Israel 45–48]. This Israeli law grants any property or property rights owned by Palestinian authorities or any ownerless property within Israel to the Israeli government. This law also sets regulations over government land transactions.

Document 513: Progress Report of the United Nations Conciliation Commission for Palestine (November 20, 1951) [U.N. GAOR, 6th Sess., Supp. No. 18, U.N. Doc. A/1985 (1951)]. The United Nations Conciliation Commission for Palestine presented this progress report detailing its activities between January 23 and July 15, 1951. The Conciliation Commission's main concern during this period was the preparation of the newly constructed Refugee Office in Jerusalem and the arrival of its director, Mr. Holger Anderson. The commission describes its major proposals at the Paris Peace Conference (September 13–November 19, 1951), which addressed difficult issues such as war damages, the repatriation of refugees, and the question of blocked bank accounts. The report also includes the comments of the Israeli and Arab delegations on the commission's proposals. In conclusion, the Conciliation Commission complains of its failure to make substantial progress. Annex A to the report includes detailed figures on the evaluation of abandoned Arab properties prepared by the Refugee Office.

Document 514: Law of the State of Israel: Entry into Israel Law (August 26, 1952) [6 LSI 159 (1951–52)]. This Israeli law governs visitors' entry into Israel. Under the law, an individual who is not an Israeli citizen may only enter Israel according to a visa issued pursuant to the law, and visitors may enter Israel only at designated places of border control. Further, the minister of the interior may expel any person who enters Israel without being authorized to enter and any person who is not an Israeli citizen or a new immigrant under the Law of Return (1950) who is found in Israel without a residence permit.[327] This law, in combination with the aforementioned Law of Return, in effect privileged the entrance of Jews into Israel and barred the entrance or return of non-Jews.

Document 515: Law of the State of Israel: Land Acquisition (Validation of Acts and Compensation) Law (March 10, 1953) [7 LSI 43]. This law permits the government of the State of Israel to vest within the Development Authority any abandoned property essential for development, settlement, or security. These regulations are to be governed by certification by a government minister.

[327] *See* Doc. 509.

Document 516: Law of the State of Israel: Prevention of Infiltration (Offences and Jurisdiction) Law (August 16, 1954) [8 LSI 133 (1954)]. This Israeli law makes it a crime for persons who fled Israel during the conflict to return to their homes. Any person who attempts to return is to be brought before the Tribunal for the Prevention of Infiltration. The tribunal is to be operated under the Israeli Army Code and granted the authority to either imprison or deport any person attempting to return to their homes. All expenses for the deportation are to be paid with the property of the deportee.

Document 517: Basic Law of the State of Israel: Israel Lands (July 19, 1960) [14 LSI 48 (1960)]. This Israeli Basic Law prohibits the transfer of ownership of any land considered the territory of the State of Israel to another party.

Document 518: United Nations General Assembly Resolution 1725, Intensifying Work on Identification and Evaluation of Properties (December 20, 1961) [G.A. Res. 1725, U.N. GAOR, U.N. Doc. A/RES/1725 (XVI) (1961)]. In Resolution 1725, the General Assembly requests that the United Nations Conciliation Commission for Palestine intensify its work on the identification and evaluation of Arab refugee immovable properties in Palestine as of May 15, 1948, and complete its work by September 1, 1962.

Document 519: United Nations General Assembly Resolution 2535, Directing Attention to the Continuing Critical Financial Position of the UNRWA (December 10, 1969) [G.A. Res. 2535, U.N. GAOR, U.N. Doc. A/RES/2535(XXIV)A-C (1969)]. In Resolution 2535, the General Assembly expresses regret that repatriation or compensation of refugees pursuant to General Assembly Resolution 194 (1948) has not been achieved, nor has resettlement been implemented as a back-up measure.[328] This resolution highlights Israel's refusal to implement previous resolutions to this effect and requests that the Security Council take measures to ensure implementation. In this document, the General Assembly refers to Palestinians for the first time as a "people" with national rights. The continuing budgetary shortfalls of UNRWA are noted.

Document 520: United Nations General Assembly Resolution 2672, Repatriation or Compensation of the Refugees Has Not Been Effected (December 8, 1970) [G.A. Res. 2672, U.N. GAOR, U.N. Doc. A/RES/2672 (XXV) A-D (1970)]. General Assembly Resolution 2672 requests that the United Nations Conciliation Commission for Palestine find a means for implementing paragraph 11 of Resolution 194, which calls for the repatriation or compensation of refugees.[329] Resolution 2672 also declares that the principle of equal rights and self-determination for the Palestinian people is essential to the establishment of a lasting peace.

Document 521: Law of the State of Israel: Absentees' Property (Compensation) Law (June 27, 1973) [27 LSI 176 (1973)]. This Israeli law validates the transfer of absentees' property to the Israeli government through the payment of compensation, even when compensation is paid to the wrong person. This law prevents a refugee from seeking legal recourse to his or her property.

---

[328] *See* Doc. 503.

[329] *Id.*

Document 522: Replies by the Acting Observer of the PLO to Questions Put by Members of the Committee on the Exercise of the Inalienable Rights of the Palestinian People (March 17, 1976) [U.N. GAOR, Comm. on the Exercise of Inalienable Rts. of Palestinian People, U.N. Doc. A/AC.183/L.10 (1976)]. In this reply, the PLO clarifies its position on the "Right of Return" within the context of a possible peace settlement. The acting observer argues that sovereign independence for the Palestinian people is no substitute for the return of all Palestinians to their homes and property in any part of Palestine. The acting observer envisions a two-stage implementation of the Right of Return: the immediate return of Palestinians to territories occupied in 1967 and, subsequently, the return of all Palestinians displaced leading up to and during the 1948 war. Further, the acting observer argues that the right of return should not be made contingent upon Israel's compliance with the demand for withdrawal.

Document 523: United Nations Report: The Right of Return of the Palestinian People (November 1, 1978) [U.N. Doc. ST/SG/SER.F/2 (1978)]. This study, prepared by the Special Unit on Palestinian Rights for the Committee on the Exercise of the Inalienable Rights of the Palestinian People, reviews the historical and legal development of the concept of the "Right of Return" and discusses its application to the Palestinian people. Claims to international law, Israeli legislation, the Conciliation Commission, and the United Nations are discussed in detail.

Document 524: Report of the Secretary-General on Palestine Refugees in the Palestinian Territory Occupied by Israel since 1967 (September 11, 1990) [U.N. GAOR, 45th Sess., Agenda Item 76, U.N. Doc. A/45/464 (1990)]. This report, presented by United Nations Secretary-General Javier Pèrez de Cuèllar, provides information concerning Israel's compliance with General Assembly Resolution 44/47 E and is based on reports from the commissioner-general of the UNRWA. The Secretary-General reports that refugee shelters in the Gaza Strip and the West Bank have been demolished and sealed on punitive grounds by the Israeli authorities—and that the rehousing of refugees by Israeli Authorities had not yet been effected.

Document 525: PLO Chairman Yasir Arafat: The PLO and the Gulf Crisis (December 13, 1990) [*reprinted in* THE ISRAEL-ARAB READER: A DOCUMENTARY HISTORY OF THE MIDDLE EAST CONFLICT (Walter Laqueur & Barry Rubin eds., 2001)]. In an interview with Vjesnik, Yasir Arafat takes a critical stance against the United States, U.N. Security Council, and Israel in light of the early developments in the First Gulf War. He contends that the United States has created a declaration of war via the Security Council and that a war will bring collapse to order in the Arab world. Arafat then describes the inequitable treatment of Palestinians in relation to the events occurring in Kuwait.

Document 526: Elias Sanbar, Head of Palestinian Delegation to Multilateral Talks on Refugees (Ottawa, 1992) [*available at* http://www.pij.org/details.php?id=612]. Elias Sanbar's remarks in Ottawa discuss the need for the right of return of Palestinian refugees. He asserts that peace, stability, and justice can only be achieved by Israel's implementation of U.N. Security Council Resolution 242 and U.N. General Assembly Resolution 194.

Document 527: Middle East Peace Negotiations Multilateral Working Group on Refugees. Opening Remarks by Shlomo Ben Ami, Chairman of Israel's Delegation, Ottawa (November 11, 1992) [On file with author]. This is a call for an international effort to solve the problem of the Palestinian refugees as part of the peace process that was launched by the Madrid Peace Conference of October 1991. Professor Ben Ami describes the origins of the problem as stemming from the 1948 war that swept in its wake hundreds of thousand of refugees. The speaker acknowledges that the Israelis "assumed the inherent immorality of war," and was probably the first official Israeli representative to recognize that "the Palestinians were a major victim of the Arab/Israeli conflict." While recognizing that the state of the refugees living under Israeli administration is "a moral burden on our collective conscience," the Israeli head of delegation describes the many projects of rehabilitation and resettlement that his government has advanced in favor of the refugees. He also calls for a shift in the policy of international agencies, such as UNRWA, from welfare to rehabilitation and promises that his government views an agreed upon solution of the refugee problem as an essential component of the historical reconciliation between the Palestinian people and Israel. He, however, calls on the Arab side and the international community to remove the impediments for the emancipation of the refuges while the search for a political solution continues. For that purpose, the speaker advanced a plan of housing, infrastructure and basic services in refugee camps in Israel's administered territories while expressing the hope that similar projects will be carried out in the refugee camps in Arab countries as well.

Document 528: Excerpts from the Report of the Secretary-General on Cooperation between the United Nations and the League of Arab States and UNRWA (September 19, 1996) [U.N. Doc. A/51/380 (1996)]. In this report, United Nations Secretary-General Boutros Boutros-Ghali describes the prevailing close cooperation between the UNRWA and the League of Arab States. In addition to providing financial assistance to UNRWA, the League of Arab States is reported to have cooperated with UNRWA on workshops and topical meetings and providing education services to Palestine refugees in host countries.

Document 529: United Nations General Assembly Resolution 58/94, Palestine Refugees' Properties and Their Revenues (December 17, 2003) [G.A. Res. 58/94, U.N. GAOR, 58th Sess., Agenda Item 83, U.N. Doc. A/RES/58/94 (2003)]. In Resolution 58/94, the General Assembly notes the completion of the program of identification and evaluation of Arab property, as well as the Land Office's compilation of a schedule of Arab owners and a file of documents defining the location, area, and other particulars of Arab property. It expresses its appreciation of the work done to preserve and modernize the Conciliation Commission's existing records, including the land records, and its importance in securing a just resolution for Palestine refugees in conformity with General Assembly Resolution 194 (1948).[330] The General Assembly also urges Palestinians and Israelis to deal with the important issue of Palestine refugees' properties and their revenues in the framework of the final status negotiations.

[330] *Id.*

Document 530: UNRWA Report: Impact of the First Phase of Israel's Barrier on UNRWA-Registered Refugees (2003) [*available at* http://www.un.org/unrwa/emergency/barrier/f-phase.html]. This report evaluates the impact of the first phase of Israel's wall on refugees registered with the UNRWA. UNRWA determines that fourteen communities in the Qalqilya, Tulkarm, and Jenin Governorates, numbering 13,636 Palestinians—including 374 refugee families, or 1,870 individuals—will be most affected by the barrier, left isolated between the barrier and the pre-1967 borders (Green Line).

B. *Status of the Palestinians under Occupation: 1967–2008*

The United Nations reports and resolutions included in this chapter detail Israeli policies and their effects on Palestinian populations in the territories occupied by Israel as a result of the 1967 war.[331] Israeli occupational policies and practices have included collective punishment, the deportation and relocation of civilians, the destruction of villages and homes, the denial of the right of return to refugees, and torture. Issues arising from these policies relate to the legal status of Palestinians in accordance with international humanitarian law and, more particularly, the Fourth Geneva Convention of August 12, 1949, and the Hague Convention of 1907.[332] Israel, however, has claimed the inapplicability of these conventions to the Occupied Territories because it considers its conflict with the Palestinians to be of a non-international character. Moreover, Israel justifies its repressive practices on the basis of its inherent right to self-defense and by reason of military necessity. Israel has further discounted allegations of excessive use of force by labeling their occurrences as anomalous and unsanctioned.

As part of its post-1967 occupational policy, Israel has placed more than 400,000 people in Jewish-only settlements inside the West Bank, East Jerusalem, and Gaza Strip, an illegal practice under the Fourth Geneva Convention.[333] It was revealed recently that some of these settlements are also illegal under Israeli law. Israeli governments have for years turned a blind eye to the build-up of illegal settlements and used a variety of unofficial and even illegal methods to support them. According to the March 2005 Israeli report on illegal settlements prepared by former Chief State Prosecutor and Attorney Talia Sasson at the request of the state, local authorities disregarded the requirements of the law when they budgeted

[331] The territory under Israeli occupation—*i.e.*, the West Bank, East Jerusalem, Gaza Strip, Sinai, and the Golan Heights—is referred to in these documents as "Arab territories under military occupation since the hostilities of 6 June 1967," "Arab territories occupied since 1967," "Areas under Israeli occupation," "Occupied Territories," "Disputed Territories," and "Occupied Palestinian Territory(ies)."

[332] Hague Convention 1907 (IV), 36 Stat. 2277 (entered into force Jan. 26, 1910). Fourth Geneva Convention, *supra* note 82. There are three other Geneva Conventions from 1949. *See supra* note 82.

[333] *See* Doc. 481.

projects for illegal neighborhoods and settlements to establish mobile homes, connect communities to the waste and electricity infrastructure, and erect kindergartens, etc.

To date, Israel has complied with few of the decisions of the various United Nations bodies aimed at improving living conditions for Pale-stinians inside the Occupied Territories and at ending practices such as the construction and expansion of Jewish-only settlements and the separation barrier.

Additional documents on this subject may be found in: Section 9, Palestinian *Intifadas* (Uprisings); and Section 7, Israeli-Palestinian Peace Process: 1982–2004.

Document 531: United Nations Security Council Resolution 237, Calling on Israel to Ensure the Safety, Welfare, and Security of the Civil Population (June 14, 1967) [S.C. Res. 237, U.N. SCOR, 1361st mtg., U.N. Doc. S/RES/237 (1967)]. Security Council Resolution 237 calls upon the government of Israel to facilitate the return of those inhabitants who had fled the areas since the outbreak of hostilities.

Document 532: United Nations General Assembly Resolution 2252, Prisoners of War and Humanitarian Assistance to the Palestine Refugees (July 4, 1967) [G.A. Res. 2252, U.N. GAOR, 5th Emergency Sess., Supp. No. 1, at 3–4, U.N. Doc. A/6798 (1967)]. In Resolution 2252, the General Assembly welcomes with great satisfaction Security Council Resolution 237 and notes with gratitude the humanitarian assistance of various (NGOs) organizations in the area.[334]

Document 533: United Nations Security Council Resolution 259, Deploring the Delay in the Implementation of Resolution 237 as a Result of Israel's Imposition of Conditions for Receiving the Special Representative of the Secretary-General (September 27, 1968) [S.C. Res. 259, U.N. SCOR, 1454th mtg., U.N. Doc. S/RES/259 (1968)]. In this resolution, the Security Council expresses frustration with the conditions being set by Israel for receiving a special representative of the Secretary-General and requests the Secretary-General to urgently dispatch a special representative to the Arab territories under military occupation by Israel and to report on the implementation of Security Council Resolution 237.[335] This resolution requests that the government of Israel receive the special representative, cooperate with him, and facilitate his work.

Document 534: United Nations General Assembly Resolution 2443, Calling upon Israel to Stop Destroying the Homes of the Arab Civilian Population in the Territories Occupied by It (December 19, 1968) [G.A. Res. 2443, U.N. GAOR, 23d Sess., U.N. Doc. A/RES/2443 (1969)]. In Resolution 2443, the General Assembly calls upon Israel to stop destroying Arab homes in the Occupied Territories, echoing the concerns of other international bodies. It also establishes the Special Committee to Investigate Israeli Practices Affecting the Human Rights of the Population of the Occupied Territories and instructs it to report to the Secretary-General.

---

[334] *See* Doc. 533.

[335] *Id.*

Document 535: United Nations General Assembly Resolution 2546, Concerning Continued Reports of Collective Punishment and Deportation in the Territories Occupied by Israel (December 11, 1969) [G.A. Res. 2546, U.N. GAOR, U.N. Doc. A/RES/2546 (XXIV) (1969)]. In Resolution 2546, the General Assembly reaffirms its previous resolutions relating to the violations of human rights in the Occupied Territories given reports of collective punishments, mass imprisonment, indiscriminate destruction of homes, and other acts of oppression against the civilian population. The General Assembly calls upon the government of Israel to desist from its reported repressive practices and policies and to comply with its obligations under the Geneva Convention relative to the Protection of Civilian Persons in Time of War,[336] the Universal Declaration of Human Rights,[337] and the relevant resolutions adopted by various international organizations.

Document 536: Excerpts from the Report of the Special Working Group of Experts (February 11, 1970) [U.N. ESCOR, Hum. Rts. Comm., 26th Sess., Agenda Item 5, U.N. Doc. E/CN.4/1016/Add.2 (1970)]. This report from the Special Working Group of Experts determines that the Fourth Geneva Convention is applicable to the Occupied Territories.[338] The group states that while it is not able to verify alleged violations of the convention juridically, it is of the opinion that there are violations based on the evidence before it. In its recommendations, the working group calls upon Israel to apply the convention and investigate all alleged violations of it.

Document 537: Report of the United Nations Special Committee to Investigate Israeli Practices Affecting the Human Rights of the Population of the Occupied Territories (October 5, 1970) [U.N. GAOR, 25th Sess., Agenda Item 101, U.N. Doc. A/8089 (1970)]. In its first report, the special committee determines that the state of occupation itself constitutes a violation of human rights. It defines the areas under Israeli occupation as the Golan Heights, the West Bank (including East Jerusalem), the Gaza Strip, and the Sinai Peninsula. The report calls for an independent body to assist in the implementation of the Geneva Convention with the cooperation of concerned states.[339]

Document 538: Response of Israel to the Report of the Special Committee to Investigate Israeli Practices Affecting the Human Rights of the Population of the Occupied Territories (November 2, 1970) [U.N. Doc. A/8164 (1970)]. In this response to the Report of the Committee to Investigate Israeli Practices, the government of Israel accuses the special committee of bias.[340] It defends its practices, stating that its administration is humane, equitable, and constructive. Israel also asserts that the condition of the civilian population in the territories has improved and that the resident population enjoys freedom of movement, as well as satisfactory health care and services.

Document 539: United Nations General Assembly Resolution 2851, Report of the Special Committee to Investigate Israeli Practices Affecting the Human Rights of the Population of the Occupied Territories (December 20, 1971) [G. A. Res. 2851, U.N. GAOR, 26th

---

[336] *See* Fourth Geneva Convention, *supra* note 82.
[337] Universal Declaration of Human Rights, *supra* note 274.
[338] *See* Fourth Geneva Convention, *supra* note 82.
[339] *See* Fourth Geneva Convention, *supra* note 82.
[340] *See* Doc. 520.

Sess., at 42–44, U. N. Doc. GA/4548 (1971)]. In Resolution 2851, the General Assembly commends the special committee on its report and calls on the State of Israel to rescind and desist from practices that violate the human rights of the Palestinians.[341] The General Assembly also urges the special committee to continue its work and the government of Israel to cooperate with it.

Document 540: United Nations General Assembly Resolution 3175, Granting Permanent Sovereignty to the Arabs over Natural Resources in the Occupied Territories (December 17, 1973) [G.A. Res. 3175, U.N. GAOR, U.N. Doc. A/RES/3175 (XXVIII) (1973)]. General Assembly Resolution 3175 affirms the right of the Arab states and peoples whose territories were under foreign occupation to permanent sovereignty over all the natural resources in the lands under occupation. It also affirms the right of the Arab states and peoples to full compensation for the exploitation and looting of, and damages to, the natural resources, as well as the exploitation and manipulation of the human resources of the Occupied Territories. A similarly worded resolution has been adopted every year subsequently.

Document 541: United Nations Security Council Resolution 446, Declaring Israeli Settlements Are Illegal (March 22, 1979) [S.C. Res. 446, U.N. SCOR, 2134th mtg., U.N. Doc. S/RES/446 (1979)]. In Resolution 446, the Security Council determines that Israel's establishment of settlements in the Palestinian and other Arab territories occupied since 1967 has no legal validity and constitutes a serious obstruction to peace in the Middle East. The Security Council calls upon Israel to abide by the Fourth Geneva Convention, to rescind its previous measures, and to desist from taking any action that would result in changing the legal status and geographical nature or demographic composition of the Occupied Territories.[342] The resolution also establishes a commission to examine the situation relating to settlements.

Document 542: United Nations General Assembly Resolution 34/29, Calling on Israel to Rescind the Deportation Order for the Mayor of Nablus (November 16, 1979) [G.A. Res. 34/29, U.N. GAOR, U.N. Doc. A/RES/34/29 (1979)]. Concerned about Israel's ordered deportation of the mayor of Nablus and the resulting resignation of other mayors of cities and towns in the occupied territory, the General Assembly Resolution 34/29 calls upon Israel to rescind the order.

Document 543: Report of the Security Council Commission Established under Resolution 446 "to Examine the Situation Relating to Settlements in the Arab Territories Occupied since 1967, including Jerusalem" (December 4, 1979) [U.N. SCOR, U.N. Doc. S/13679 (1979)]. In this report, the Commission Established under Resolution 446 "to examine the situation relating to settlements in the Arab Territories Occupied since 1967, including Jerusalem" characterizes Israel's policy of non-cooperation with the commission as deplorable and notes that Israel is still pursuing its "colonization" of the Occupied Territories.[343] Given the grave consequences of the settlement program, the commission recommends that the Security Council keep the situation under constant review.

---

[341] *Id.*

[342] *See* Fourth Geneva Convention, *supra* note 82.

[343] *See* Doc. 537.

Document 544: United Nations Security Council Resolution 465, Declaring Israeli Settlements Are Illegal under the Fourth Geneva Convention (March 1, 1980) [S.C. Res. 465, U.N. SCOR, U.N. Doc. S/RES/465 (1980)]. Security Council Resolution 465 reaffirms the illegality of Israeli settlements under the Fourth Geneva Convention and calls upon Israel to cease the establishment, construction, and planning of such settlements.[344] It deplores the decision of Israel to prohibit the travel of Mayor Fahd Qawasmeh in order to appear before the Security Council and requests that Israel permit his free travel to the United Nations headquarters for that purpose. The Security Council further requests that no state provide Israel with assistance in connection with settlements in the Occupied Territories.

Document 545: United Nations Security Council Resolution 468, Calling on Israel to Return Expelled Palestinian Mayors (May 8, 1980) [S.C. Res. 468, U.N. SCOR, U.N. Doc. S/RES/471 (1980)]. The Security Council in Resolution 468 calls upon the State of Israel to rescind measures taken against three Palestinian leaders, the, mayors of Hebron and Halhoul and the sharia judge of Hebron, and to facilitate their immediate return.

Document 546: United Nations Security Council Resolution 471, Deploring that Jewish Settlers Are Allowed to Carry Arms and Deploring Assassination Attempts on Palestinian Mayors (June 5, 1980) [S.C. Res. 471, U.N. SCOR, U.N. Doc. S/RES/471 (1980)]. In Resolution 471, the Security Council expresses deep concern that Jewish settlers in the Occupied Territories are permitted to carry arms. The Security Council calls for the immediate apprehension and prosecution of the perpetrators of related crimes against civilians and condemns the assassination attempts on the lives of the mayors of Nablus, Ramallah, and Al-Bireh.

Document 547: Special Session Resolution ES-7/3, Requesting a Study of Reasons for Israel's Refusal to Comply with Resolutions (July 29, 1980) [U.N. GAOR, U.N. Doc. A/RES/ES-7/3 (1980)]. General Assembly Special Session Resolution ES-7/3 commends the Committee on the Exercise of the Inalienable Rights of the Palestinian People for its studies on various aspects of the Question of Palestine and requests it to thoroughly study the reasons for the refusal of Israel to comply with relevant United Nations resolutions, particularly the General Assembly resolution demanding the withdrawal of Israel from the Occupied Territories, including Jerusalem.

Document 548: Report of the Secretary-General on the Living Conditions of the Palestinian People in the Occupied Arab Territories (October 17, 1980) [U.N. GAOR, 35th Sess., Agenda Item 61(e), U.N. Doc. A/35/533 (1980)]. This report from United Nations Secretary-General Kurt Waldheim details the social and economic impact of the Israeli occupation on the Palestinian people. In preparing the report, the Secretary-General relied on the services of three experts, who, despite official requests, were not granted permission by the Israeli government to visit the Occupied Territories and so relied largely on secondary sources of information from organizations such as the International Labor Organization, UNESCO, and the World Health Organization. The report details the conditions of trade and investment, land and water, and the social characteristics and employment that affect the quality of life of Arabs in the Occupied Territories. It also examines the impact of Jewish settlements in the Occupied Territories. The report finds that

---

344 *See* Fourth Geneva Convention, *supra* note 82.

current policies do not ensure the equitable allocation of conventional resources among Israeli settlements and other communities in the Occupied Territories.

Document 549: United Nations Economic and Social Council Resolution 1982/18, Situation of Women and Children in the Occupied Arab Territories (May 4, 1982) [E.S.C. Res. 1982/18, U.N. ESCOR, U.N. Doc. E/RES/1982/18 (1982)]. In Resolution 1982/18, the Economic and Social Council expresses grave concern that Palestinian women continue to be denied their rights in the Occupied Territories, such as the right of return, the right to self determination, and the right to national independence. The council appeals to all women to declare their solidarity with Palestinian women and to aid in securing the release of thousands of prisoners held by Israeli occupying forces. It further appeals to all states and international organizations to extend their support to Palestinian women and requests the United Nations do the same.

Document 550: Report of the Secretary-General on the Living Conditions of the Palestinian People in the Occupied Territories (June 14, 1985) [U.N. GAOR, 40th Sess., U.N. Doc. A/40/373 (1985)]. This report from United Nations Secretary-General Javier Pèrez de Cuèllar on the living conditions of the Palestinian people in the Occupied Territories describes the state of the economy and obstacles to growth. The Secretary-General notes Israel's seizure of portions of land and water resources, hampering local agricultural development as well as inhibiting opportunities to obtain funds and technical support to modernize operations.

Document 551: United Nations Security Council Resolution 592, Deploring the Killing and Wounding of Students at Birzeit University (December 8, 1986) [S.C. Res. 592, U.N. SCOR, 2727th mtg., U.N. Doc. S/RES/592 (1986)]. In Resolution 592, the Security Council strongly deplores the Israeli army's opening fire at Birzeit University, which resulted in the death and wounding of students. It calls upon Israel to release any person or persons detained as a result of recent events at the university.

Document 552: Report on the Human Rights Situation in the Palestinian Territories Occupied since 1967, Submitted by Mr. René Felber, Special Rapporteur, Pursuant to Commission on Human Rights Resolution 1993/2 A (January 28, 1994) [U.N. ESCOR, Comm. on Hum. Rts., 50th Sess., U.N. Doc. E/CN.4/1994/14 (1994)]. This report from the special rapporteur, Mr. Rene Felber, summarizes the fundamental human rights concerns within the Occupied Territories since the signing of the Declaration of Principles on Interim Self-Government Arrangements in September of 1993 (Oslo Accords).[345] The special rapporteur notes the decline of the standard of living during more than twenty-five years of occupation. Condemning the violent behavior on both sides and insisting on a review of conditions, the Special Rapporteur concedes that the report is only preliminary.

Document 553: Cairo Agreement between Israel and PLO (March 4, 1994) [*reprinted in* THE ISRAEL-ARAB READER: A DOCUMENTARY HISTORY OF THE MIDDLE EAST CONFLICT (Walter Laqueur & Barry Rubin eds., 2001)]. Following the Oslo Accords, the Cairo Agreement initiates steps towards greater autonomy of Palestinians in Gaza and the Jericho region. It specifies withdrawal of Israeli military forces from the

---

[345] *See* Doc. 432.

regions and settles on the terms of the transfer of civil and military authority to the Palestinian Authority.

Document 554: Report on the Human Rights Situation in the Palestinian Territories Occupied since 1967, Submitted by Mr. René Felber, Special Rapporteur, Pursuant to Commission on Human Rights Resolution 1993/2 A (December 13, 1994) [U.N. ESCOR, 51st Sess., Agenda Item 4, U.N. Doc. E/CN.4/1995/19 (1994)]. This report by the special rapporteur, Mr. René Felber, submitted subsequent to his twelve-day visit to the area, considers the consequences of the Israeli policy of collective punishment on the daily lives of Palestinians as well as the situation of prisoners in the military detention camp at Ketziot. It focuses on Israel's confiscation of Palestinian land and the situation in Gaza. The special rapporteur acknowledges that the General Assembly and the commission have not been successful in enforcing human rights in the Occupied Territories through the reporting of facts and concludes that only states are in a position to influence the government of Israel.

Document 555: Report of the Secretary-General on the Situation of and Assistance to Palestinian Women (March 13, 1995) [U.N. ESCOR, 39th Sess., U.N. Doc. E/CN.6/1995/8 (1995)]. In this report, submitted pursuant to the request of the Commission on the Status of Women, United Nations Secretary-General Boutros Boutros-Ghali notes the emergence of Palestinian women's organizations and committees in the sphere of self-governance as well as a new "feminist consciousness" as a result of women's increased involvement in political demonstrations and social reform. The report documents a rise in the number of female students and the growing number of women in leadership positions; however, it also expresses concern over the prevalence of political and domestic violence in the lives of women and children in the Occupied Territories. The report calls for support for Palestinian women working to achieve equal rights.

Document 556: Report on the Situation of Human Rights in the Palestinian Territories Occupied since 1967, Submitted by Mr. Hannu Halinen, Special Rapporteur, Pursuant to Commission on Human Rights Resolution 1993/2 A (March 15, 1996) [U.N. ESCOR, Comm. on Hum. Rts., 52d Sess., U.N. Doc. E/CN.4/1996/18 (1996)]. In this report, the special rapporteur, Mr. Hannu Halinen, expresses regret that his findings remain incomplete as most are based on one brief visit to Gaza, given Israel's unwillingness to receive him. While condemning acts of terrorism by the Palestinians, the special rapporteur expresses deep concern over Israel's response to security incidents, such as sealing off the West Bank, Gaza, and East Jerusalem, instituting severe curfews, and engaging in the demolition of homes of suspected terrorists. The special rapporteur calls for the establishment of a new human rights culture instituted with the aid of appropriate bodies and partners to ensure the success of the peace process.

Document 557: Excerpts from the Report on the Extrajudicial, Summary, or Arbitrary Executions in the Occupied Arab Territories (January 25, 1996) [U.N. ESCOR, 52d Sess., U.N. Doc. E/CN.4/1996/4 (1996)]. In this report, the special rapporteur reviews the conditions of detention in Al-Khyam Prison, which, according to its findings, appears to be under Israeli control. Additionally, the special rapporteur also addresses two allegations submitted on behalf of individuals against the Palestinian Authority.

Document 558: Council of the League of Arab States Resolution 107, Regarding Settler Colonialism in the Occupied Palestinian Territory (March 31, 1997) [*See* U.N. GAOR, 51st Sess., Agenda Items 33, 35, 85, U.N. Doc. A/51/859 (1997)]. In this resolution, the Council of the League of Arab States reaffirms the legitimacy of Security Council Resolution 465,[346] which declares Israeli settlements illegal under the Fourth Geneva Convention.[347] The council warns that "colonialist" settlement activity impinges upon the peace process and reaffirms the need to conduct an international seminar on settlement activity.

Document 559: Excerpts from the Report of the Secretary-General Following the Fourth World Conference on Women, Addendum II (January 26, 1998) [*See* U.N. ESCOR, Comm. on Women, 42d Sess., U.N. Doc. E/CN.6/1998/2/Add.2 (1998)]. In this report, United Nations Secretary-General Kofi Annan concludes that much effort is being made by Palestinians and the international community following the Fourth World Conference on Women held in Bejing, September 4-15, 1995, to improve the economic and social conditions facing Palestinian women. However, the Secretary-General notes the continued injury to Palestinian women as a result of the military occupation.

Document 560: United Nations Economic and Social Council Resolution 1998/1, Continued Violation of Human Rights in the Occupied Territories (March 27, 1998) [E.S.C. Res. 1998/1, U.N. ESCOR, Comm. on Hum. Rts., U.N. Doc. E/CN.4/RES/1998/1 (1998)]. In Resolution 1998/1, the Economic and Social Council expresses grave concern over Israel's refusal to abide by previous resolutions set forth by United Nations bodies. In noting the stagnation of the peace process, the Economic and Social Council also expresses grave concern about the Government of Israel's attitude toward the principles upon which the process was based. The council condemns the Israeli practice of firing on civilians, the opening of a tunnel under the al Aqsa Mosque, and the use of torture during interrogations. Israel is called upon to halt all activities associated with collective punishment and to withdraw from all territories occupied since 1967.

Document 561: United Nations Commission on Human Rights Resolution 1998/3, Calling upon Israel to Prevent Any New Installation of Settlers in the Occupied Territories (March 27, 1998) [Res. 1998/3, U.N. Comm. on Hum. Rts., U.N. Doc. E/CN.4/RES/1998/3 (1998)]. In Resolution 1998/3, the Commission on Human Rights expresses grave concern over Israeli settlement activities, including the construction of bypass roads, the expulsion of local residents, and other violations of the Geneva Convention.[348] The commission characterizes such activities as an obstacle to peace in the region. It calls upon the government of Israel to implement concrete actions to supplement its commitment to the peace process and to cease settlement activity while preventing new installations.

Document 562: United Nations Economic and Social Council Resolution 1998/10, Recognizing Israeli Occupation as Main Obstacle to the Advancement of Palestinian Women (July 28, 1998) [E.S.C. Res. 1998/10, U.N. ESCOR, 44th plen. mtg., U.N. Doc. 1998/10 (1998)]. In Resolution 358, the Economic and Social Council expresses concern about the stalemate in the peace process and stresses its support for the process.

---

[346] *See* Doc. 544.

[347] *See* Fourth Geneva Convention, *supra* note 82.

[348] *Id.*

It calls on Israel to facilitate the return of all refugees and displaced women and children to their homes in compliance with United Nations resolutions and in the interest of improving the socioeconomic situation of the Palestinian people. Requests are made for a continuation of monitoring by the Commission on the Status of Women and for the Secretary-General's continued review of the situation.

Document 563: United Nations Economic and Social Council Resolution 1998/32, Economic and Social Repercussions of the Israeli Occupation on the Living Conditions of the Palestinian People (July 29, 1998) [E.S.C. Res. 1998/32, U.N. ESCOR, U.N. Doc. E/RES/1998/32 (1998)]. In Resolution 1998/32, the Economic and Social Council declares that the Israeli occupation impedes efforts to achieve sustainable development and a sound economic environment in the Occupied Territories. It criticizes particularly the restrictions placed on freedom of movement and stresses the importance of territorial contiguity. It calls on Israel to stop exploiting the resources of the Syrian Golan. Finally, it identifies economic stability as an essential facet to long-term peace.

Document 564: Concluding Observations of the United Nations Human Rights Committee on Israel Regarding the ICCPR (August 18, 1998) [Human Rts. Comm., 63d Sess., U.N. Doc. CCPR/C/79/Add.93 (1998)]. In these observations, the United Nations Human Rights Committee comments on the lack of substantive data regarding the implementation of the ICCPR in Israel's periodic report.[349] Among the concerns raised by the committee are the failure of the government of Israel to incorporate the covenant fully into Israeli law and the numerous injuries sustained by the Palestinian people under occupation. The committee recommends that Israel ratify the Optional Protocol to the ICCPR and requests the submission of a second periodic report.[350]

Document 565: Report on the Situation of Human Rights in the Palestinian Territories Occupied since 1967, Submitted by Mr. Hannu Halinen, Special Rapporteur, Pursuant to Commission on Human Rights Resolution 1993/2 A (January 20, 1999) [U.N. ESCOR, 55th Sess., U.N. Doc. E/CN.4/1999/24 (1999)]. The special rapporteur, Mr. Hannu Halinen, prefaces this detailed report on human rights violations in the Occupied Territories by noting that current violations remain largely the same as those recorded in previous United Nations resolutions. Halinen reports that during his visit to the area he was informed by Palestinians that human rights violations had become more collective in nature and had increased in scope since the outset of the peace process. Halinen also notes that almost all provisions of the Universal Declaration of Human Rights are being violated in the Occupied Territories.[351]

Document 566: Excerpts from the Report of the Working Group on Indigenous Populations on Its Seventeenth Session (Bedouins) (August 12, 1999) [U.N. ESCOR, Comm. on Hum. Rts., 51st Sess., Agenda Item 7, U.N. Doc. E/CN.4/Sub.2/1999/19 (1999)]. Although this report does not exclusively focus on the situation of Palestinians, it does record a representative of the Palestinian Bedouins' notification of Israel's

---

[349] *See* ICCPR, *supra* note 326.

[350] *See* ICCPR First Optional Protocol, *supra* note 326.

[351] *See* Universal Declaration of Human Rights, *supra* note 274.

practice of displacing Bedouin tribes by confiscating their land and demolishing their homes.

Document 567: Israeli Supreme Court Judgment on the Interrogation Methods Applied by the General Security Service (September 6, 1999) [H.C. 5100/94, Public Committee Against Torture in Israel and Others v. The State of Israel]. In this judgment, the Israeli Supreme Court considers two public and five individual petitions contending that Israel's General Security Service (GSS; *i.e.*, Israel's secret service apparatus) does not have the authority to use severe methods when interrogating suspected Palestinian terrorists. The court holds that the defense of necessity did not grant the GSS the authority to engage in these practices, but it did not preclude use of the defense in deciding whether to prosecute or bring criminal charges against GSS investigators.

Document 568: United Nations General Assembly Resolution 55/132, Demanding Complete Cessation of Construction of Israeli Settlements in the Occupied Territories (December 8, 2000) [G.A. Res. 55/132, U.N. GAOR, U.N. Doc. A/RES/55/132 (2000)]. In Resolution 55/132, the General Assembly reaffirms that settlements are illegal and an obstacle to peace. It calls for a total cessation of Israel's settlement activities in the occupied areas, in Jerusalem, and in the Golan Heights.

Document 569: United Nations Commission on Human Rights Resolution 2002/3, Report on the Situation in Occupied Palestine (April 12, 2002) [E.S.C. Res. 2002/3, U.N. ESCOR, U.N. Doc. E/CN.4/RES/2002/3 (2002)]. In Resolution 2002/3, the Commission on Human Rights recalls its previous resolutions that confirm the inalienable rights of the Palestinian people and endorses the Arab peace initiative.[352] It also decides to include further consideration of the rights of peoples under foreign occupation as an agenda item for the fifty-ninth session of the commission.

Document 570: The Impact of Israel's Separation Barrier on Affected West Bank Communities, Report of the Mission of the Humanitarian and Emergency Policy Group of the Local Aid Coordination Committee (May 4, 2003) [*available at* http://www.reliefweb.int/library/documents/2003/hepglacc-opt-04may.pdf]. Concerned over the harmful effects of Israel's wall on Palestinian communities, the Local Aid Coordination Committee issued this report, providing details of the socio-economic and civil consequences of the wall on Palestinian communities. The committee notes that parts of the wall extend beyond the pre-1967 borders (Green Line) and expresses concern that such a path will render thousands of Palestinians isolated from the rest of the West Bank. The committee also expresses concern over how the wall will impact access to some of the most abundant wells in the West Bank.

Document 571: Report of the Special Rapporteur of the Commission on Human Rights on the Situation of Human Rights in the Palestinian Territories Occupied by Israel since 1967 (Dugard Report) (September 8, 2003) [U.N. ESCOR, Comm. on Hum. Rts., 60th Sess., U.N. Doc. E/CN.4/2004/6 (2003)]. Following a one-week visit to the Occupied Territories, the special rapporteur, Mr. John Dugard, issued this report on Israel's response to terror. It finds Israel's actions disproportionate and in violation of human rights and international humanitarian law. It expresses concern over Israel's practice of restricting freedom of movement, instituting curfews, increasing the

[352] *See* Doc. 479.

number of checkpoints, demolishing homes, and creating more settlements and calls for an independent inquiry into allegations of torture in Israeli prisons.

Document 572: Letter from the Permanent Representative of Israel to the Chairperson of the Commission on Human Rights Regarding the Ziegler Report (September 18, 2003) [*available at* http://www.unhchr.ch/Huridocda/ Huridoca.nsf/(Symbol)/E.CN.4.2004.G.9.En?Opendocument]. In this letter, the Permanent Representative of Israel accuses Jean Ziegler, the United Nations Special Rapporteur on the Right to Food, of contravening standard protocol by failing to submit a copy of his report to Israel prior to releasing it to the press.[353] The Permanent Mission of Israel strongly protests such conduct and requests that the special rapporteur be sanctioned for disregarding procedure.

Document 573: Letter from the Permanent Observer for Palestine to the Chairperson of the Commission on Human Rights Regarding the Ziegler Report (September 30, 2003) [U.N. ESCOR, Human Rts. Comm, 60th Sess., U.N. Doc. E/CN.4/2004/G/10 (2003)]. This letter from the Permanent Observer for Palestine extends appreciation to the United Nations Special Rapporteur on the Right to Food, John Ziegler, for his effort and objectivity in preparing his report.[354] The permanent observer also objects to the permanent representative of Israel's use of the term "Disputed Territories" in his letter to the chairperson of the commission.[355]

Document 574: Letter from the Permanent Observer for Palestine to the Acting High Commissioner for Human Rights on Massacres in Rafah and the Yubna Refugee Camp (October 14, 2003) [U.N. ESCOR, Human Rts. Comm., 60th Sess., U.N. Doc. E/CN.4/2004/G/11 (2003)]. This letter from the Permanent Observer for Palestine catalogues the casualties and human rights violations that occurred during the recent Israeli incursions into Gaza. It expresses concern over the total closure of both the Gaza Strip and all cities within the West Bank. The letter also notes the violation of international law inherent in Israel's new checkpoint policy and the continued construction of the wall. The permanent observer requests the aid of the high commissioner in stopping Israeli policies that violate international law.

Document 575: U.S.-Vetoed Security Council Draft Resolution, Declaring Israel's Separation Wall Illegal (October 14, 2003) [U.N. Doc. A/2003/980 (2003)]. This draft Security Council resolution, presented by Guinea, Malaysia, Pakistan, and the Syrian Arab Republic, would have declared Israel's construction of a wall departing from the 1949 Armistice Line illegal and ordered that construction be ceased and reversed.[356]

Document 576: Letter from the Permanent Observer for Palestine to the Chairperson of the Commission on Human Rights, Regarding Israel's Response to the Ziegler Report (October 23, 2003) [U.N. ESCOR, Human Rts. Comm., 60th Sess., U.N. Doc. E/CN.4/2004/G/13 (2003)]. In this letter to the chairperson of the Commission on Human Rights, the permanent observer and ambassador for Palestine, Mr. Nabil Ramlawi, expresses his frustration with Israel's criticism of the Ziegler Report.

---

[353] *See* Doc. 578.
[354] *Id.*
[355] *See* Doc. 572.
[356] *See* Docs. 93–96.

Document 577: United Nations General Assembly Resolution ES-10/13, Demanding that Israel Stop and Reverse Construction of the Wall in the West Bank (October 27, 2003) [G.A. Res. ES-10/13, U.N. GAOR, 10th Emergency Special Sess., Agenda Item 5, U.N. Doc. A/RES/ES-10/13 (2003)]. In Resolution ES-10/13, the General Assembly demands that Israel stop and reverse the construction of the wall in the Occupied Territories, including East Jerusalem. It also calls upon both parties to fulfill their obligations under relevant provisions of the Road Map and requests the Secretary-General to report on compliance with this resolution periodically.[357]

Document 578: United Nations Economic, Social, and Cultural Rights Report by the Special Rapporteur on the Right to Food, Concerning His Mission to the Occupied Palestinian Territories (Ziegler Report) (October 31, 2003) [U.N. ESCOR, Comm. on Hum. Rts., 60th Sess., U.N. Doc. E/CN.4/2004/10/Add.2 (2003)]. United Nations Special Rapporteur on the Right to Food, Jean Ziegler, visited Israel and the Occupied Territories in July 2003, marking the first time a United Nations rapporteur was allowed to investigate first-hand the situation in the Occupied Territories. Ziegler reports that the growing hunger and malnutrition are a direct result of Israel's military policies and that the situation has worsened since the outbreak of the Second *Intifada* to the extent that the Occupied Territories are facing a humanitarian catastrophe. Ziegler expresses concern over the inability of Palestinians to access food, water, and humanitarian aid due to road closures, the imposition of curfews, and the construction of the wall. Ziegler strongly recommends that the government of Israel respect its obligations under international human rights and humanitarian law, specifically by ending the occupation.

Document 579: Report of the Secretary-General Prepared Pursuant to General Assembly Resolution ES-10/13, Concluding that Israel Is Not in Compliance with the Assembly's Demand that It Stop and Reverse Construction of the Wall (November 24, 2003) [U.N. GAOR, 10th Emergency Special Sess., Agenda Item 5, U.N. Doc. A/ES-10/248 (2003)]. This report was issued by United Nations Secretary-General Kofi Annan at the request of the General Assembly following Israel's refusal to comply with General Assembly Resolution ES-10/13, which demanded that Israel stop and reverse its construction of the wall.[358] The Secretary-General includes in his report the legal positions regarding the wall of both Israel and the PLO and requests the support of the international community in achieving a two-state solution.

Document 580: United Nations General Assembly Resolution ES-10/14, Requesting an ICJ Advisory Opinion on the Separation Wall (December 8, 2003) [G.A. Res. ES-10/14, U.N. GAOR, 10th Emergency Special Sess., U.N. Doc. A/RES/ES-10/14 (2003)]. In Resolution ES-10/14, the General Assembly decides to request the ICJ to render an advisory opinion on the following question: "What are the legal consequences arising from the construction of the wall being built by Israel, the occupying power, in the Occupied Palestinian Territory, including in and around East Jerusalem, as described in the report of the Secretary-General, considering the rules and principles of international law, including the Fourth Geneva Convention of 1949, and relevant Security Council and General Assembly resolutions?"

---

[357] *See* Doc. 484.

[358] *See* Doc. 577.

Document 581: United Nations Office for the Coordination of Humanitarian Affairs, Preliminary Analysis of the Humanitarian Consequences of the Wall on Palestinians in the West Bank (December 15, 2003) [*available at* http://domino.un.org/unispal.nsf/9a798adbf322aff38525617b006d88d7/7c15cf1a7ca6780a85256e16006eb529!OpenDocument]. This report was issued by the United Nations Office for the Coordination of Humanitarian Affairs in response to the government of Israel's approval of a new route for the wall that would result in a final wall four times longer than the initial size. The office expresses its solemn concern at the lack of consideration given to the Palestinian population, whose lives would be affected by restrictions on freedom of movement and isolation from the rest of the community.

Document 582: United Nations General Assembly Resolution A/RES/58/155, Situation of and Assistance to Palestinian Children (February 26, 2004) [G.A. Res. 58/155, U.N. GAOR, U.N. Doc. (2004)]. The General Assembly expresses concern in Resolution 58/155 that Palestinian children living under Israeli occupation are being deprived of many basic rights. It demands that Israel comply with the Convention on the Rights of the Child[359] and the Geneva Convention[360] to ensure that Palestinian children lead a life free from the fear that occupation engenders. The General Assembly also calls upon the international community to provide urgently needed assistance.

Document 583: Report of the Special Rapporteur of the Commission on Human Rights, John Dugard, on the Situation of Human Rights in the Palestinian Territories (Addendum to the Dugard Report) (February 27, 2004) [U.N. ESCOR, 60th Sess., U.N. Doc. E/CN.4/2004/6/Add.1 (2003)]. This report by the special rapporteur of the Commission on Human Rights, John Dugard, charges Israel with the use of excessive force against Palestinians including restrictions on mobility, the inhumane treatment of children, destruction of property through home demolitions, and "territorial expansion." The special rapporteur acknowledges the security concerns of the government of Israel but characterizes Israel's actions as "so remote from the interest of security that it assumes the character of punishment, humiliation, and conquest."

Document 584: Note Verbale from the Permanent Mission of Israel to the Secretariat of the Commission on Human Rights (Regarding the Dugard Report) (March 16, 2004) [U.N. ESCOR, Comm. on Hum. Rts., 60th Sess., U.N. Doc. E/CN.4/2004/G/24 (2004)]. In this response to the Dugard report, the government of Israel accuses the special rapporteur of using his position as a platform for advancing a political agenda.[361] It takes issue with the omission of facts attesting to Israel's efforts to deal with Palestinians in an evenhanded manner. Further, Israel defends its construction of the wall as a necessary security measure and accuses the special rapporteur of being ambivalent to the terrorist threats facing Israel and its citizens. It also claims that the one-sided nature of the report puts the credibility of the Commission on Human Rights into question.

---

[359] Convention on the Rights of the Child, Nov. 20, 1989, 1577 U.N.T.S. 3, 28 I.L.M. 1448 (entered into force Sept. 2, 1990).

[360] *See* Fourth Geneva Convention, *supra* note 82.

[361] *See* Doc. 571.

Document 585: Note Verbale from the Permanent Mission of Israel to the United Nations High Commissioner for Human Rights (Regarding the Addendum to the Dugard Report) (April 2, 2004) [U.N. ESCOR, Comm. on Hum. Rts., 60th Sess., U.N. Doc. E/CN.4/2004/G/42 (2004)]. In this note verbale, the Permanent Mission of Israel denounces the addendum to the Dugard report as "one sided, highly politicized and biased."[362] Specifically, Israel condemns the special rapporteur for failing to find any Israeli security measures to be legitimate or proportionate. It further accuses the special rapporteur of being ambivalent towards acts of terrorism perpetrated by Palestinians against Israelis.

Document 586: United Nations Commission on Human Rights Resolution 2003/7, Israeli Settlements in the Occupied Arab Territories (April 15, 2004) [Res. 2003/7, U.N. Comm. on Hum. Rts., U.N. Doc. E.CN.4.RES/2003/7 (2004)]. Recalling the illegality of Israeli settlements in the Occupied Territories, the Commission on Human Rights in Resolution 2003/7 expresses grave concern about the continued expansion of settlements, the escalation in violence, and the construction of the wall. The commission urges Israel to comply with previous commission resolutions on the subject and cease all settlement activity.

Document 587: Report Prepared by the Economic and Social Commission for Western Asia on the Economic and Social Repercussions of the Israeli Occupation on the Living Conditions of the Palestinian People (June 12, 2004) [U.N. ESCOR, U.N. Doc. E/2004/21 (2004), U.N. GAOR, 59th Sess., U.N. Doc. A/59/89 (2004)]. This report from the Economic and Social Commission for Western Asia draws on the annual report of the UNRWA. It attributes the rise in unemployment and the increase in health problems afflicting Palestinians in the Occupied Territories and the Syrian Golan to key factors such as extrajudicial killings, arbitrary arrests and detentions, population displacement, mobility restrictions, and the existence of the wall. The commission concludes that the Occupied Territories assume a "war-torn economy status," which humanitarian assistance alone cannot rectify. The commission calls for the lifting of the occupation as the only sustainable solution to the economic and social deprivations affecting the Palestinian population.

Document 588: Israeli Supreme Court Decision: HCJ 2056/04—Beit Sourik Village Council et al. v. The Government of Israel et al. (June 30, 2004) [H.C. 2056/04, Beit Sourik Village Council v. Israel]. The question before the Israeli Supreme Court in this case was whether Israel's confiscation of land in Judea and Samaria to erect a "separation fence" is legal and whether the "fence" itself is illegal. The court uses the principle of proportionality in making its judgment, determining whether the security objective necessitating the erection of the fence was proportionate to the harm inflicted upon the Palestinian landowners. The court holds that it is not proportionate because the farmers will be cut off from their land with limited access across the fence and that these injuries are in violation of international humanitarian law. The Court notes that such injuries could be substantially decreased by creating an alternate route. Given the disproportionate nature of the injuries to local inhabitants, the court nullifies the confiscation orders.

---

[362] *See* Doc. 583.

Document 589: ICJ Decision: Legal Consequences of the Construction of a Wall in the Occupied Palestinian Territory (July 9, 2004) [2004 I.C.J. 131]. The ICJ rendered this advisory opinion pursuant to a request by General Assembly Resolution ES-10/14.[363] The court expresses the opinion that the construction of the wall is contrary to international law. Accordingly, Israel is obligated to stop its construction and dismantle already existing portions. Further, Israel is under obligation to pay reparations for any damage incurred by its construction. The court observes that all state parties to the Geneva Convention have an obligation to ensure Israel's compliance with international humanitarian law.[364] Thus, the United Nations should give further consideration to what action is required to stop the illegal consequences of the wall's construction.

Document 590: United Nations General Assembly Resolution ES-10/15, Calling on Israel to Comply with Its Legal Obligations as Identified in the Advisory Opinion (August 2, 2004) [U.N. GAOR, 10th Emergency Sess., Agenda Item 5, U.N. Doc. A/ES-10/L.18/Rev.1 (2004)]. In Resolution ES-10/15, the General Assembly demands that Israel comply with its legal obligations as set forth in theICJ's advisory opinion.[365] It calls upon all state members to comply with their legal obligations to ensure that Israel respects the Geneva Convention.[366] It also requests that the Secretary-General establish a "register of damage." Finally, it calls upon both parties to immediately implement their obligations under the Road Map.

Document 591: Report of the Special Rapporteur of the Commission on Human Rights on the Situation of Human Rights in the Palestinian Territories Occupied by Israel since 1967 (August 12, 2004) [U.N. ESCOR, 59th Sess., U.N. Doc. A/59/256 (2004)]. This report by the special rapporteur of the Commission on Human Rights, Mr. John Dugard, focuses on Israeli military incursions into the Gaza Strip, the construction of the wall, and restrictions on the freedom of movement. Findings stem from the special rapporteur's visit to the Occupied Territories, including both Gaza Strip and the West Bank, June 18–25, 2004. With regard to incursions into Gaza, Dugard reports that Israel has engaged in a massive destruction of property and charges that Israel does not plan to relinquish control of Gaza, but plans to continue its control of Gaza's borders, sea, and airspace. With regard to the wall, Dugard charges that Israel is using it to incorporate settlers within Israel, confiscate Palestinian land, and encourage Palestinians to leave their lands and home. He challenges the view that the wall is primarily intended to stop suicide bombings as constructing the wall along the pre-1967 Border (Green Line) would have had the same effect. Further, Dugard finds that the inhabitants of Gaza are effectively imprisoned by a combination of the wall, fence, and sea. Further, he compares the restrictions to the "pass laws" of apartheid South Africa.

On October 28, 2004, the Israeli government issued a formal statement in response to this report criticizing the nature of the mandate of the special rapporteur that it believes only examines one side of the conflict and prejudges

[363] *See* Doc. 580.

[364] *See* Geneva Conventions, *supra* note 82.

[365] *See* Doc. 589.

[366] *See* Geneva Conventions, *supra* note 82.

key issues. The Israeli statement defends Israel's construction of the wall and refutes the special rapporteur's allegations that Israel intends to use it to confiscate Palestinian lands.

Document 592: Report on the Human Rights Situation in the Palestinian Territories Occupied since 1967, submitted by John Dugard, Special Rapporteur (March 5, 2005) [U.N. ESCOR, U.N. Doc. E/CN.4/2005/29/Add.1]. This report from the special rapporteur, Mr. John Dugard, provides an updated summary of the fundamental human rights concerns within the Occupied Territories. This addendum is based on Dugard's visit to the Occupied Territories in February of 2005. The document reviews the status of the Second *Intifada,* the then current ceasefire between Israel and the Palestinian Authority, Israel's construction of a wall in the Occupied Territories, and human rights issues affecting the citizens of those areas region, including Jerusalem.

Document 593: Israeli Supreme Court Opinion—International Legality of the Security Fence and Sections Near Alfei Menashe (September 15, 2005). The Israeli Supreme Court rules that disputed parts of Israel's security wall route are illegal and that a new route must be developed instead.

Document 594: United Nations General Assembly Resolution 60/107, Israeli Practices Affecting the Human Rights of the Palestinian People in the Occupied Palestinian Territory, Including East Jerusalem (January 18, 2006) [U.N. ESCOR, U.N. Doc. E/CN.4/2006/29 (2006)]. Noting reports by the U.N. Commission on Human Rights and the special rapporteur of the Commission on Human Rights in Palestine, the General Assembly expresses concern regarding Israel's treatment of Palestinians in the Occupied Territories. Specifically, the General Assembly condemns use of excessive force, collective punishment, confiscation of land, and expansion of Israeli settlements.

Document 595: United Nations General Assembly Resolution 60/41, Jerusalem (February 10, 2006) [G.A. Res. 60/41, U.N. GAOR, U.N. Doc. A/RES/60/41 (2006)]. The General Assembly condemns Israel's continuation of illegal settlements and continued construction of a wall surrounding in East Jerusalem. The General Assembly then stresses the need for both Israeli and Palestinian concerns are addressed while also guaranteeing the freedom of movement and religion for Jerusalem's occupants.

Document 596: United Nations General Assembly Resolution 60/39, Peaceful Settlement of the Question of Palestine (February 16, 2006) [G.A. Res. 60/39, U.N. GAOR, U.N. Doc. A/RES/60/39 (2006)]. In Resolution 60/39, the General Assembly expresses continued concern for the military actions Israel has taken in the Occupied Palestinian Territories. It also notes the ICJ's advisory opinion, which demands that Israel comply with its obligations under international law.

Document 597: Report on the Human Rights Situation in the Palestinian Territories Occupied since 1967, Submitted by John Dugard, Special Rapporteur (September 27, 2006) [U.N. ESCOR, U.N. Doc. A/HRC/5/11 (2007)]. Special Rapporteur Dugard's report categorically addresses Israel's military and security measures taken against Palestinians in the Occupied Territories. The report emphasizes the nature of various security walls Israel has constructed in these territories.

Document 598: Report on the Human Rights Situation in the Palestinian Territories Occupied since 1967, Submitted by John Dugard, Special Rapporteur (January 29, 2007) [U.N. ESCOR, U.N. Doc. A/HRC/5/11 (2007)] Dugard's report again addresses Israel's incursions in the Occupied Territories, humanitarian concerns, and issues surrounding construction of security walls. Most notably the report goes on to describe Israel's practices as an apartheid.

Document 599: United Nations Report on the Mission to Israel Including Visit to Occupied Palestinian Territory, Submitted by Martin Scheinin, Special Rapporteur on the Promotion and Protection of Human Rights and Fundamental Freedoms while Countering Terrorism (November 16, 2007) [U.N. Doc. A/HRC/6/17/Add.4 (2007)]. Scheinin's report addresses the challenges facing Israel in legislating security measures while providing for humanitarian needs and civil rights of Palestinians in the Occupied Territorries. The report also highlights the issues of security walls, terrorism, and counterterrorism.

Document 600: United Nations General Assembly Resolution 62/108, Israeli Settlements in the Occupied Palestinian Territory, Including East Jerusalem, and the Occupied Syrian Golan (January 10, 2008) [G.A. Res. 62/108, U.N. GAOR, U.N. Doc. A/RES/62/108 (2008)]. In Resolution 62/108, the General Assembly notes Israel's work in withdrawing from Gaza and the West Bank as well as dismantling settlements in those reasons. However, the General Assembly continues to demand the same for East Jerusalem and Syrian Golan in which Israeli settlements continue to develop.

Document 601: United Nations General Assembly Resolution 62/109, Israeli Practices Affecting the Human Rights of the Palestinian People in the Occupied Palestinian Territory, Including East Jerusalem (January 10, 2008) [G.A. Res. 62/109, U.N. GAOR, U.N. Doc. A/RES/62/109 (2008)]. Citing reports by the Special Committee to Investigate Israeli Practices Affecting the Human Rights of the Palestinian People and Other Arabs of the Occupied Territories as well as the special rapporteur of the Human Rights Council, the General Assembly provides a veritable laundry list of concerns regarding the status of Palestinians in the Occupied Territories.

The General Assembly again expresses concern for the violation of human rights by Israel, such as collective punishment, closure of areas, construction of the wall inside the Occupied Territories, and destruction of property. In response, the General Assembly is convinced of the need for an international presence to monitor the situation.

Document 602: Report on the Human Rights Situation in the Palestinian Territories Occupied since 1967, Submitted by John Dugard, Special Rapporteur (January 21, 2008) [U.N. ESCOR, U.N. Doc. A/HRC/7/17 (2008)]. Dugard's 2008 report initially addresses criticism of the special rapporteur's prior reports on the Occupied Palestinian Territories, specifically the reports' repetitiveness and focus only on Israel's actions. The report goes on to report on Israel's military incursions into the Occupied Territories and the humanitarian concerns in Gaza and the West Bank. Dugard rebukes the Security Council's disregard of the ICJ's advisory opinion on Israel's wall in the Occupied Territories. The report concludes with a critical appraisal of the Annapolis Summit.

C. *Palestinians' Emergence as a National Entity: 1963–2007*

After the 1948 war, active Palestinian nationalism did not reemerge until the formation of the *Fatah*[367] group in 1959 and the PLOin 1964.[368] The new movement borrowed from earlier ones the same rootedness in land and the same political symbols; however, the new Palestinian leadership was composed of young men from lower to middle-class backgrounds who circumvented the pre-1948 leadership, which was largely drawn from the Palestinian elite. The first meeting of the PLO was held in East Jerusalem, signaling the relocation of the Palestinian nationalist movement to the original nerve center of the Palestinian body politic.

Israel's victory over Arab forces in the 1967 war dramatically changed the landscape of Palestinian politics, as control of the West Bank, the Gaza Strip, and East Jerusalem shifted from the Hashemite Kingdom of Jordan to the State of Israel. Subsequently, groups like the PLO that emphasized Palestinian identity over Pan-Arabism gained strength. This period also saw the formation of the PFLP, which was among the first Palestinian militant groups to use terrorism as a means to win attention to its cause, carrying out numerous terrorist attacks in the international arena, in particular hijacking civilian airliners.

In 1974, the question of Palestine and the right of the Palestinian people to self-determination was reintroduced in the General Assembly following PLO Chairman Yasser Arafat's speech to the General Assembly on November 13, 1974.[369] Soon after, the United Nations General Assembly passed Resolution 3236,[370] which reaffirmed the inalienable rights of the Palestinian people, and Resolution 3237,[371] which granted the PLO observer status.

With major political and military setbacks in the 1970s and 1980s that sent the Palestinian political leadership into exile in Jordan, Lebanon, and then Tunisia, popular support for the resistance movement waned until the outbreak of the *Intifada* in December 1987. This was a crucial phase of the movement as it returned the nexus of Palestinian political energy to the former Palestine. Yet, during this period, the PLO's popular leadership was challenged by rival groups that stressed Islam over Pan-Arabism, such as the Islamic Resistance Movement (*Hamas*) and Islamic Jihad.[372]

---

[367] The word *Fatah* is derived from the inverted acronym for *Harakat al-Tahrir al-Watani al-Filastini*, which translates to "The Palestine National Liberation Movement."

[368] *See* Docs. 604.

[369] *See* Doc. 609.

[370] *See* Doc. 610.

[371] *See* Doc. 611.

[372] *See* Doc. 639.

In 1988, King Hussein of Jordan relinquished Jordanian responsibility for the West Bank,[373] enabling the PLO to declare the establishment of an independent Palestinian state in the West Bank and Gaza Strip in November 1988.[374] Since then, at least 114 states have formally granted *de jure* recognition to the state.

In 1996, the PNA was established and, on January 20, 1996, general elections were held, bringing Arafat to the presidency. Arafat's name has since become synonymous with the PLO and the PNA and symbolic of the Palestinian nationalist movement.

Other documents on related subjects may be found in: Section 6, Jerusalem and the Holy Sites; Section 9, Palestinian *Intifadas* (Uprisings); and Section 7, Israeli-Palestinian Peace Process.

Document 603: Draft Constitution of the PLO (1963) [*available at* http://www.pna.gov.ps/Government/gov/The_Draft_Constitution_of_the_PLO.asp]. This draft Constitution establishes the PLO, with all Palestinians as its "natural members." It sets up the structure of a National Assembly to be a representative body meeting every two years to issue resolutions, with its venue rotating between Jerusalem and Gaza. The first meeting is set for May 14, 1964, in Jerusalem. It also proposes the establishment of a fifteen-member executive committee of the National Assembly and the appointment of a president who will represent the Palestinians at the Arab League and be situated in Cairo. The text also provides for raising money for "The National Palestinian Fund" through taxation, financial donations, the issuance of "Liberation Stamps," and loans to finance the operations of the Executive Committee.

Document 604: Proclamation of the Establishment of the PLO (May 28, 1964) [*available at* http://www.palestine-un.org/plo/doc_three.html]. This document proclaims the establishment of the PLO in Jerusalem to serve the Palestinian Arab people in "waging the battle of liberation."

Document 605: Palestinian National Charter Issued by the PLO (July 17, 1968) [*available at* http://www.state.gov/p/nea/rls/22573.htm]. The Palestinian National Charter sets out the PLO's key political assertions, such as what comprises the original territory of Palestine, who rightfully owns the land in former Palestine, and who are legitimate Palestinians. According to the charter, Jews who lived in Palestine before the 1948 war are Palestinians, and Jews, as a group, do not constitute a single nation with an identity. The charter calls for unified international opposition to Israel. Further, Article 9 claims that armed struggle is the only way to liberate Palestine.

Document 606: Proposal Issued by King Hussein of Jordan for a United Arab Kingdom (March 15, 1972) [*reprinted in* ARAB-ISRAELI CONFLICT AND CONCILIATION: A DOCUMENTARY HISTORY (Bernard Reich ed., 1995)]. King Hussein of Jordan declared his proposed formula for the establishment of a United Arab Kingdom. In the United Arab

---

[373] On July 31, 1988, King Hussein announced the severance of all administrative and legal ties with the occupied West Bank. *See* Doc. 597.

[374] *See* Doc. 615.

Kingdom, King Hussein foresaw the inclusion of the Hashemite Kingdom of Jordan with two regions: the Palestinian region including the West Bank and all other liberated territories with citizens that desire to join the kingdom, and the Jordan region formed by the East Bank. Both regions would be represented in an elected national assembly that governs over the region along with the king.

Document 607: Political Program Adopted at the Twelfth Session of the Palestine National Council, Cairo (June 8, 1974) [*available at* http://www.mfa.gov.il/MFA/Foreign%20Relations/Israels%20Foreign%20Relations%20since%201947/1974-1977/3%2012th%20Palestinian%20National%20Council%20Political%20Prog]. The Palestine National Council proclaims in this Political Program that a lasting peace is only achievable once the Palestinian people have recovered their national rights and begun the process of self-determination. It reaffirms the PLO's rejection of Security Council Resolution 242 on the basis that "it obliterates the national right of [the Palestinian] people and deals with the cause of people as a problem of refugees."[375] The council also details its plans for the full liberation of Palestinian territory and the establishment of a democratic Palestinian state.

Document 608: United Nations General Assembly Resolution 3210, Recognizing the PLO as the Representative of the Palestinian People (October 14, 1974) [G.A. Res. 3210, U.N. GAOR, U.N. Doc. A/RES/3210 (XXIX) (1974)]. In Resolution 3210, the General Assembly recognizes the PLO as the sole representative of the Palestinian people and invites it to participate in the deliberations of the General Assembly on the Question of Palestine in plenary meetings.

Document 609: Speech Given by PLO Chairman Yasser Arafat at the United Nations General Assembly Meeting (November 13, 1974) [*available at* http://domino.un.org/UNISPAL.NSF/9a798adbf322aff38525617b006d88d7/a238ec7a3e13eed18525624a007697ec!OpenDocument]. This speech, delivered by PLO Chairman Yasser Arafat, followed the passage of Assembly Resolution 3210, which gave the PLO observer status in the General Assembly.[376] With this speech, Arafat became the first representative of a group other than a member state to directly address the General Assembly (with the exception of the ceremonial address of Pope Paul IV). Arafat begins his speech by congratulating the United Nations on its ever-increasing membership base, which gives it validity as a world body and on its reenergized mission to assist nations in Asia, Africa, and Latin America in their pursuit of peace and independence. Referring to Israel as the "Zionist entity," Arafat identifies the state as a persistent imperialist force in the Middle East. He further casts the Palestinian national struggle against Israel in the mold of other struggles against oppressive imperialist nations. Arafat calls on the United Nations to intervene, famously declaring, "Today I have come bearing an olive branch and a freedom-fighter's gun. Do not let the olive branch fall from my hand. I repeat: Do not let the olive branch fall from my hand."

Document 610: United Nations General Assembly Resolution 3236, Reaffirming the Inalienable Rights of the Palestinian People in Palestine (November 22, 1974) [G.A. Res. 3236, U.N. GAOR, U.N. Doc. A/RES/3236 (XXIX) (1974)]. General Assembly

[375] *See* Doc. 289.

[376] *See* Doc. 608.

Resolution 3236 reaffirms the inalienable rights of the Palestinian people to self-determination, national independence, and sovereignty, and the right to return to their homes and property. The resolution also requests that the Secretary-General confer with the PLO on all future matters concerning the Question of Palestine.

Document 611: United Nations General Assembly Resolution 3237, Inviting the PLO to Participate in General Assembly Conferences as an Observer (November 22, 1974) [G.A. Res. 3237, U.N. GAOR, U.N. Doc. A/RES/3237 (XXIX) (1974)]. General Assembly Resolution 3237 grants the PLO observer status in the United Nations, enabling it to participate in the sessions and work of the General Assembly, as well as in all international conferences convened under the auspices of the General Assembly and other United Nations bodies.

Document 612: United Nations General Assembly Resolution 3376, Establishing the Committee on the Exercise of the Inalienable Rights of the Palestinian People (November 10, 1975) [G.A. Res. 3376, U.N. GAOR, U.N. Doc. A/RES/3376 (XXX) (1975)]. In Resolution 3376, the General Assembly establishes the Committee on the Exercise of the Inalienable Rights of the Palestinian People. Composed of twenty member states, the committee is given the task of developing a program for the implementation of the rights of the Palestinian people. A similar resolution is adopted annually under the agenda item "Question of Palestine."

Document 613: United Nations Economic and Social Council Resolution 36, Approving the Application by the PLO for Full Membership of the Economic Commission for Western Asia (April 26, 1977) [ESCOR Res. 36, U.N. ESCOR, U.N. Doc. ECWA/RES/36 (IV) (1977)]. After noting the growing importance of the economic and social role of the Palestinian people, the Economic Commission for Western Asia grants the PLO observer membership status similar to that of a state member.

Document 614: His Majesty King Hussein of Jordan's Address to the Nation Concerning Disengagement from the West Bank (July 31, 1988) [*available at* http://www.kinghussein.gov.jo/88_july31.html]. In this address, King Hussein of Jordan announces the decision to disengage from the West Bank and hand it over to the Palestinian people in anticipation of the establishment of an independent Palestinian state. King Hussein identifies Arab unity and respect for the Palestinians' right to self-determination as key factors in Jordan's decision. He assures Palestinians living in Jordan of their continued right to full Jordanian citizenship and pledges to support development projects in the West Bank by working with foreign governments and international institutions to encourage contributions.

Document 615: Declaration of Palestinian Independence Issued by the PLO (November 15, 1988) [*available at* http://www.pna.gov.ps/Government/gov/Declaration_of_Independence.asp]. The Declaration of Palestinian Independence begins with an overview of the history of the land of Palestine and its inhabitants. It details the hardships faced by Palestinian Arabs in their pursuit of national independence, beginning with Article 22 of the Covenant of the League of Nations, which established Palestine as a mandate.[377] Issued at the beginning of the first *Intifada*,

[377] *See* Doc. 14.

the declaration notes the movement's ability to bring worldwide attention to the plight of the Palestinians. It names Jerusalem as the capital of the State of Palestine.

Document 616: United Nations General Assembly Resolution 423/160 A, Granting Observer Status to the PLO (December 9, 1988) [G.A. Res. 423/160, U.N. GAOR, U.N. Doc. A/RES/43/160 (1988)]. In Resolution 423/160, the General Assembly grants the PLO and the South West Africa People's Organization the ability to issue and circulate its communications directly as official documents of the General Assembly.

Document 617: United Nations General Assembly Resolution 43/177, Acknowledging the Proclamation of the State of Palestine (December 15, 1988) [G.A. Res. 43/177, U.N. GAOR, U.N. Doc. A/RES/43/177 (1988)]. General Assembly Resolution 43/177 acknowledges the proclamation of the State of Palestine by the Palestine National Council on November 15, 1988, and decides that the designation "Palestine" should be used instead of "Palestine Liberation Organization" in the United Nations system.[378]

Document 618: United Nations General Assembly Resolutions Acknowledging the State of Palestine (December 15, 1989) [*reprinted in* A Documentary History of the Arab-Israeli Conflict Charles L. Geddes ed., 1991)]. On December 15, 1989, the United Nations General Assembly Convened in Geneva to discuss the Palestine Question. They issued two resolutions in which they were mindful to work to achieve a just, peaceful, and comprehensive solution to the problem. In these resolutions, the General Assembly acknowledged the claim to the State of Palestine made by the Palestinian National Council. They further called for Israel to withdraw from the territories occupied after 1967, for the resolution of the problems for Palestinian refugees, and for access to the Holy Sites to people of all faiths. The first resolution was adopted by the General Assembly by 138 in favor, two (Israel and the United States) opposed, and two (Canada and Costa Rica) abstentions. The second resolution, which specifically acknowledged the declaration of the Palestinian state, was also only opposed by Israel and the United States, however, thirty-six states (much of Western Europe) abstained.

Document 619: Speech Given by Israeli Prime Minister Yitzhak Rabin to Knesset (September 21, 1993) [*reprinted in* The Israel-Arab Reader: A Documentary History of the Middle East Conflict (Walter Laqueur & Barry Rubin eds., 2001)]. Following negotiations in Oslo, Norway, Israeli Prime Minister Yitzhak Rabin addressed the Knesset prior to its vote of confidence on the principles agreed to. Rabin emphasizes that all the terms have been divulged and that steps must be made towards peace. His speech recognizes that the Israelis cannot choose their neighbors or enemies and therefore must deal with what they have: the PLO. Two days following the speech, the Knesset would vote in favor of the agreement sixty-one to fifty.

Document 620: Hani al-Hassan: Opposition to the Israel-PLO Accord (October 9, 1993) [*reprinted in* The Israel-Arab Reader: A Documentary History of the Middle East Conflict (Walter Laqueur & Barry Rubin eds., 2001)]. Not all Palestinians welcomed the results of the Oslo Accords. Both Hamas and some members of

[378] *See* Doc. 615.

Fatah rejected the agreement, arguing that the accords are an anathema of the PLO's purpose and that Israel's intentions are not trustworthy.

Document 621: Agreement between the Government of the State of Israel and the PLO (Cairo Agreement) (May 4, 1994) [*reprinted in* ARAB-ISRAELI CONFLICT AND CONCILIATION: A DOCUMENTARY HISTORY (Bernard Reich ed., 1995)]. Israel formally began its withdrawal from the Gaza Strip and Jericho area after the Cairo agreement was made between PLO Chairman Yasser Arafat and Israeli Prime Minister Yitzhak Rabin. This agreement allowed the Palestinians in this region some self-rule with a partial transfer of authority to the Palestinian Authority. This was done in an effort to carry out the Declaration of Principles on Interim Self-Government Arrangements. The Cairo Agreement additionally covered economic relations between Israel and the Palestinian Authority, issues with human rights and preventing hostilities, and the specifics of the Palestinian Authority, their rights and responsibilities, and over what aspects it should hold power.

Document 622: Agreement on Preparatory Transfer of Powers and Responsibilities (August 29, 1994) [*reprinted in* ARAB-ISRAELI CONFLICT AND CONCILIATION: A DOCUMENTARY HISTORY (Bernard Reich ed., 1995)]. The Agreement on Preparatory Transfer of Powers and Responsibilities worked towards the Israel-Palestinian Declaration of Principles. The transfer of power in the West Bank and Gaza Strip from Israel to the Palestinian Authority gave the Palestinian Authority responsibilities over five specified spheres. These are the educational and cultural, health, social welfare, tourism, and taxation domains. The transfer of power was gradual over the following months. The Palestinian Authority gained authority over the educational system on August 28, 1994, the welfare and tourism spheres on November 15, 1994, and finally the health and taxation spheres on December 1, 1994.

Document 623: Statement by the Central Council of the PLO (April 29, 1999) [*available at* http://www.palestine-un.org/plo/cc.html]. In this statement, the Central Council of the PLO declares its intention to continue steps toward completing the elements and institutions of a Palestinian state and reiterates the importance of Jerusalem as its capital. The council notes the broad international support it has received for the right of self-determination and calls upon all Palestinians to confront Israeli policies hostile to statehood, including the building of settlements and bypass roads, violations of human rights, and the destruction of Palestinian homes.

Document 624: Report of the Special Rapporteur on Civil and Political Rights, Including the Independence of Judges and Lawyers (January 21, 2000) [U.N. ESCOR, Human Rts. Comm., 56th Sess., U.N. Doc. E/CN.4/2000/61 (2000)]. This report by the special rapporteur details the independence of judges and lawyers in Palestine. It notes that the Palestinian Bar Association has protested a lack of judicial independence and has demanded judicial reform.

Document 625: Program of Reform as Prepared by the Ministerial Reform Committee and Approved by President Yasser Arafat (June 23, 2002) [*available at* http://www.pna.gov.ps/key_decuments/100day.asp]. This Program of Reform for the Government of the PNA, approved by Palestinian President Yasser Arafat, proposes sweeping reforms for all aspects of the Palestinian government, including the reinforcement of the separation of powers, preparation for holding municipal, legislative and presidential elections, activation apparatuses in the enforcement of court rulings, and development of internal auditing. It proposes a 100-day schedule for implementing thirteen of the most critical reforms.

Document 626: Palestinian Legislative Council: The Basic Law (March 18, 2003) [12 Palestine Y.B. Int'l L. 2002/2003 377–403 (2005)]. This Basic Law, issued by the Palestinian Legislative Council, establishes the basic legal framework for the State of Palestine. It determines that Jerusalem is the capital, Islam the official religion, the principles of Islamic *Shari'a* the main source of legislation, and Arabic the official language of the state. The law defines: public rights and freedoms; legislative, executive, and judicial authority; rules in the case of a state of emergency; and general and transitional provisions—all of which are to be instituted in accordance with the basic principles of human rights.

Document 627: Constitution of the State of Palestine, Third Draft (May 14, 2003) [*available at* http://www.mopic.gov.ps/constitution/english%20constitution.asp]. The Constitution of the State of Palestine outlines the general foundations of the state and the general rights, liberties, and duties of its citizens. Article 12 of Chapter I affirms that nationality shall not be affected by an individual's refugee status, but shall be based on heredity. Article 13 provides that refugees will have the right of return, as well as the right to compensation in accordance with United Nations Security Council Resolution 194 (1948).[379] Chapter II provides for basic civil rights, including equality without distinction, freedom of speech, freedom of assembly, freedom of the press, freedom of religion, including free access to holy shrines, and the right to privacy, etc. Chapter III addresses legislative authority invested in the House of Representatives and executive authority invested in the president of the state. Chapter IV outlines procedures for the formal adoption of the Constitution.

Document 628: The Mecca Agreement (February 9, 2007) [*available at* http://www.jmcc.org/documents/meccaagree.htm]. Following clashes between Fatah and Hamas in Gaza, members of both parties met in Mecca to sign this ceasefire agreement and form a national unity government.

Document 629: Speech given by President of the Palestinian Authority Mahmoud Abbas following the Dissolution of the Unity Party (June 20, 2007) [*available at* http://www.jmcc.org/documents/abbasspeechjun07.htm]. Through early 2007, fighting continued between Hamas and Fatah in the Gaza strip despite the signing of the Mecca Agreement. By June, Mahmoud Abbas declared a state of emergency in Gaza and dissolved the Unity Party that had been formed during the Mecca Agreement.

D. Status of Palestinian-Israelis:[380] 1952–2003

After the four major armistice agreements of 1949 were concluded, approximately 150,000 Arabs remained in Israel to become Israeli

[379] *See* Doc. 494.

[380] In this book, the term "Palestinian Israelis" will be used to refer to those Arabs currently residing within the State of Israel. This term is used with an understanding of the complexity of identity distinctions within the region.

citizens.[381] Some Arab Palestinians remained in their native villages, while others were internally displaced by Israeli authorities to other parts of the state. In large measure, Palestinian Israelis were left disconnected both geographically and culturally from their Arab neighbors and from members of their community who had fled during the war.

Presently, there are approximately 1.3 million Palestinian Israeli citizens in Israel, constituting nearly 20 percent of the country's total population.[382] The status of this group remains ambiguous, as an Arab minority within a Jewish state. Given this circumstance, the very terms that are used in reference to this group are politically charged. The Israeli National Security Council refers to members of this group as "Arab citizens of Israel," while members of this group often use the word "Palestinian" in their self-descriptions, with many adopting the term "Palestinian citizen of Israel" or "Palestinian Arab citizen of Israel." Palestinian nationalists, on the other hand, refer to this group as "Arabs of the inside." This term implies that the State of Palestine still exists and that some Palestinians are outside of Palestine, while others are still inside. The implications of this term cause Israel to doubt the allegiance of its Arab Palestinian minority.

Palestinian Israelis are often discriminated against in official policy and administrative practices, and their communities are often denied the services and financial support provided to Jewish Israeli communities.[383] Discriminatory Israeli legislation and Israel's treatment of Palestinians in the Occupied Palestinian Territories add to these tensions. This situation was improved somewhat in the early 1990s when Palestinian Israeli parties entered into a coalition agreement with Yitzhak Rabin's Labor Party, helping it to win a parliamentary majority, which resulted in better social services for Palestinian Israeli communities. But, in comparison with Jewish communities, Palestinian Arabs are still behind in receiving public services and financial support from the government.

With statistics estimating a continued increase in the number of Arab Palestinian citizens of Israel, this group will likely have a larger impact on Israeli elections and politics in the future.

The documents collected in this chapter are illustrative of this situation, but not exhaustive.[384]

---

[381] *See* Docs. 93–96.

[382] Approximately 82 percent of Palestinian Israelis are Sunni Muslims; the rest are divided equally between Christians and Druze.

[383] IDENTITY CRISIS: ISRAEL AND ITS ARAB CITIZENS (International Crisis Group ed., 2004).

[384] This section does not include a number of judicial and administrative decisions relating to the rights of Palestinian Israelis. To have included them would have dramatically expanded the scope of this compilation.

Document 630: Law of the State of Israel: Nationality Law (April 1, 1952) [6 LSI 50 (1951–52)]. This Israeli law bars the return of Palestinians who previously resided in areas that became part of Israel as a result of the 1948 war. It also allows the deportation of those individuals who subsequently reentered without formal permission. Further, it outlines the various ways that Israeli citizenship may be gained. In the case of Jews seeking citizenship, it reaffirms the Law of Return.[385] For non-Jews, it states that citizenship may be gained by residence, birth, or naturalization, or through service in the Israeli Army, marriage, or one's parents.

Document 631: Basic Law of the State of Israel: Human Dignity and Liberty (March 17, 1992) [*available at* http://www.knesset.gov.il/laws/special/ eng/basic3_eng.htm]. This Basic Law declares that no violation of body, life, dignity, property, liberty of movement—including freedom of a citizen to come and go from Israel—or privacy could be perpetrated by the IDF, the police, prison administration, government officials, or emergency regulations, except in the case of a "proper purpose." The list of protected rights provides Constitution-like protections for some civil liberties and human rights. The right to equality is not addressed. This Basic Law, like the Freedom of Occupation Basic Law, declares its supra-legal constitutional status.[386]

Document 632: Basic Law of the State of Israel: Freedom of Occupation (March 9, 1994) [*available at* http://www.knesset.gov.il/ laws/special/eng/ basic4_eng.htm]. This Basic Law declares that all Israeli citizens have a right to engage in any occupation. It further states that this right cannot be compromised by another law or by an emergency regulation and, like the Human Dignity and Liberty Basic Law, declares its supra-legal constitutional status.[387]

Document 633: Law of the State of Israel: Citizenship and Entry into Israel Law—Temporary Order (July 31, 2003) [*reprinted in* 12 PALESTINE Y.B. INT'L L. 2002/2003 413–16 (2005)]. This Israeli law prohibits the granting of citizenship, residence, or stay in Israel to any resident of the "region" (*i.e.*, West Bank and Gaza Strip), with the exception of workers, patients, or those with other temporary purposes, or for a period that would not exceed six months. In effect, this law prevents Israeli citizens who marry Palestinians from the West Bank or Gaza Strip from having their spouses acquire residency permits. The law was approved for one year, subject to extension.

Document 634: United Nations Committee on the Elimination of Racial Discrimination Decision 2 (63), Expressing Concern about Israel's Enactment of the Nationality and Entry into Israel Law (August 14, 2003) [CERD Decision 2(63), U.N. GAOR, U.N. Doc. CERD/C/63/Dec.2 (2003), 1599th meeting, 63d Sess.]. In Decision 2 (63), the United Nations Committee on the Elimination of Racial Discrimination calls on Israel to revoke the Nationality and Entry into Israel Law (Temporary Order) in order to facilitate family unification on a nondiscriminatory basis.[388]

Document 635: Official Summation of the Or Commission Report (September 1, 2003) [*available at* http://www.haaretz.com/hasen/pages/ShArtjhtml?itemNo=335594]. The Or Legal Commission of Inquiry (COI), headed by Israeli Supreme Court

---

[385] *See* Doc. 507.
[386] *See* Doc. 632.
[387] *See* Doc. 631.
[388] *See* Doc. 633.

Justice Theodor Or, was established to investigate the October 2000 clashes between Israeli police and Palestinian Israeli citizens at the start of the Second *Intifada*. An official report was requested after thirteen Palestinian Israeli citizens were killed by Israeli police during violent protest demonstrations. In the report, the Or Commission condemns nine members of the Israeli police, including former national police chief Yehuda Wilk and former commander of the northern force, Alik Ron, for eleven decisions, most relating to the use of snipers and live ammunition against unarmed demonstrators. The Or Commission notes that the Jewish majority in Israel must take into account that Israel is not exclusively Jewish, but democratic. Further, it stresses that equality is a primary element of the constitutional structure of Israel and the prohibition against discrimination applies to all citizens of the state.

9. Palestinian *Intifadas* (Uprisings): 1987–2004

This section contains fifty-five documents pertaining to the two Palestinian *Intifadas*, or uprisings, that began in 1987 and 2000. Although these conflicts are part of the escalating state of conflict in the region over control of former Palestinian territory, from a legal perspective, they differ from the five major Arab-Israeli wars in that international law defines them as non-international in character—they have not occurred between states. Yet the right of an occupied people to resist a belligerent occupation applies.

Many of the primary contentions over issues of sovereignty and self-determination that initially led to war in 1948 persist.

This section is divided into two sections: A. First Palestinian *Intifada*, containing *Intifada* and post-*Intifada* documents from 1987 to 1999; and B. Second Palestinian *Intifada* or *Intifadet al-Aqsa*, containing related documents from 2000 to 2004.

A. *First Palestinian* Intifada*: 1987–1999*

On December 8, 1987, an Israeli army vehicle crashed into a truck carrying Palestinian workers in the Gaza Strip, causing the death of four passengers. The incident sparked protests in the West Bank and Gaza Strip that escalated into full-blown riots.[389] Tensions again mounted in July 1988 when the Israeli government approved a plan to build a tunnel adjacent to the *Haram al Sharif*, the most Holy Muslim Site in Jerusalem—causing Palestinian civilians to clash with Israeli police in and around the al-Aqsa Mosque. Palestinians from all walks of life—merchants, laborers, men, women, and children—participated in the *Intifada*, as the movement came to be known, which involved massive demonstrations, economic boycotts, tax resistance, and strikes. These efforts were aimed at ending the military occupation of the West Bank and Gaza Strip and achieving national independence for Palestinians.

[389] Rumors had circulated that the incident was a deliberate retaliation for the fatal stabbing of an Israeli in Gaza two days before.

The *Intifada* was not headed by the established Palestinian leadership, but by a younger generation of Palestinians born and raised under Israeli occupation. They formed small local neighborhood groups and took command of the local resistance.[390]

As violence escalated, the United Nations followed the situation closely, primarily through the Committee on the Exercise of the Inalienable Rights of the Palestinian People and the Special Committee to Investigate Israeli Practices Affecting the Human Rights of the Palestinian People and Other Arabs of the Occupied Territories. These committees submitted reports on measures used by the Israeli armed forces to end Palestinian protests, such as the use of live ammunition against demonstrators and punitive beatings. According to reports, Israel also resorted to various forms of collective punishment, such as the demolition of houses, the imposition of prolonged curfews, and restrictive economic measures. These policies worsened the already difficult living conditions inside the Occupied Territories.

The human, social, and economic costs of the Intifada were high. In the first two years, approximately 50,000 Palestinians were arrested (about half of whom were under the age of eighteen), 7,000 were wounded, and 500 killed.[391] For Israel, the political fallout was significant as images of the IDF's often aggressive responses to Palestinian protesters were broadcast across Israel and around the world. The Intifada's most salient images were of Arab children throwing stones at Israeli tanks and soldiers.

The *Intifada* lasted for nearly five years, until roughly the signing of the Declaration of Principles (Oslo Accord) in 1993.[392] This agreement led to Israel's decision to relinquish limited control over parts of the Occupied Territories to the PNA, established in 1988. The *Intifada* waned as Palestinians began to build hope for a better future.

Documents in relevant chapters should be consulted, in particular those in: Section 8, Status of the Palestinians; and Section 7, Israeli-Palestinian Peace Process.

i. First Palestinian Intifada

Document 636: United Nations Security Council Resolution 605, Deploring Policies and Practices of Israel that Violate the Human Rights of the Palestinian People (December 22, 1987) [S.C. Res. 605, U.N. SCOR, 2777th mtg., U.N. Doc. S/RES/605 (1987)]. United Nations Security Council Resolution 605 expresses concern that Israeli practices in the Occupied Territories present major obstacles to achieving peace.

---

390 *See, e.g., Communiqué No. 1 of the Intifada Issued by the Unified National Leadership, reprinted in* CHARLES D. SMITH, PALESTINE AND THE ARAB-ISRAELI CONFLICT: A HISTORY WITH DOCUMENTS 296 (4th ed. 2001).

391 PETER MANSFIELD, A HISTORY OF THE MIDDLE EAST 317 (1991).

392 *See* Doc. 432.

It deplores the Israeli practice of opening fire on civilians and reaffirms the applicability of the Geneva Convention to the Occupied Territories.[393]

Document 637: United Nations Security Council Resolution 607, Deploring Israel's Decision to Continue Deporting Civilians (January 5, 1988) [S.C. Res. 607, U.N. SCOR, 2780th mtg., U.N. Doc. S/RES/607 (1988)]. Following Israel's announcement that it would continue to deport Palestinian civilians from the Occupied Territories, the Security Council adopted Resolution 607, calling on Israel to refrain from deportation and requesting that Israel follow the Fourth Geneva Convention, in particular Articles 47 and 49.[394]

Document 638: Final Declaration of the Extraordinary Arab Summit Conference, Algiers (June 7–9, 1988) [U.N. GAOR, 43d Sess., U.N. Doc. A/43/407 (1988)]. The Final Declaration of the Extraordinary Arab Summit Conference held in Algiers addresses foremost the uprising of the Palestinian people. It hails the movement as "a link in the chain of its struggle that has continued for more than half a century" and discusses measures to support the uprising.

Document 639: Covenant of the Islamic Resistance Movement (Hamas) (August 18, 1988) [*available at* http://www.hamasonline.com/indexx.php?page=Hamas/hamas_convenant]. Drawing heavily upon *Qur'an*ic verses, the Covenant of the Islamic Resistance Movement (Hamas) declares the establishment of Hamas, states its position and goals, and calls on all Arabs and Muslims and their institutions to join its struggle. It emphasizes the deeply Islamic base of the movement, which differentiates it from the more secular PLO. Hamas' declared objective is to reclaim the Palestinian homeland–which it believes to be an Islamic *Waqf* consecrated for all future Muslim generations–and to facilitate the return of refugees. It calls on Muslims from all walks of life to join the *Jihad* as an individual duty and criticizes Israeli policies in the Occupied Territories using deeply anti-Semitic rhetoric. Hamas claims to be a humane movement that only attacks when it is attacked—and rejects the peace process, charging that *Jihad* is the only way to liberate all of Palestine.

Document 640: United Nations Security Council Resolution 672, Expressing Alarm at the Violence that Took Place at Al Haram al Shareef (October 12, 1990) [S.C. Res. 672, U.N. SCOR, 2948th mtg., U.N. Doc. S/RES/672 (1990)]. In Resolution 672, the Security Council expresses alarm at the violence that took place at *Al Haram al Shareef* in Jerusalem, which resulted in the death of over twenty Palestinian and the injury of more than 150 people, including civilians. It condemns the acts of violence committed by Israeli security forces and asks the Secretary-General to send a mission to the region and submit a report containing findings and conclusions.

Subsequently, Israel rejected what it deemed the one-sidedness of the resolution and its reference to Jerusalem as "occupied territory." The Israeli cabinet announced it will not receive the Secretary-General's mission because it has already appointed an independent commission of inquiry to investigate the incident.

---

[393] *See generally* Fourth Geneva Convention, *supra* note 82.

[394] *Id.*

Document 641: United Nations Security Council Resolution 673, Expressing Alarm at the Rejection of Resolution 672 by the Israeli Government (October 24, 1990) [S.C. Res. 673, U.N. SCOR, 2949th mtg., U.N. Doc. S/RES/673 (1990)]. In Resolution 673, the Security Council expresses alarm at Israel's rejection of Resolution 672 and its refusal to accept the mission of the Secretary-General.[395] It urges the government of Israel to reconsider its decision and permit the mission to proceed in keeping with its purpose.

Document 642: Report Submitted to the Security Council by the Secretary-General in Accordance with Security Council Resolution 672 (October 31, 1990) [U.N. SCOR, U.N. Doc. S/21919 (1990)]. The United Nations Secretary-General, Javier Pèrez de Cuèllar, submitted this report to the Security Council in compliance with Resolution 672.[396] In it, Cuèllar details his unsuccessful attempt to arrange a mission to the region with the permission of the Acting Permanent Representative of Israel. Cuèllar enumerates the resolutions and statements issued by the United Nations in October addressing the issue of the safety and protection of Palestinian civilians in the Occupied Territories and reaffirming the applicability of the Fourth Geneva Convention and reiterates Israel's position that the Fourth Geneva Convention does not apply to the Occupied Territories.

Document 643: United Nations Security Council Resolution 681, Expressing Concern over the Dangerous Deterioration of the Situation in the Occupied Territories (December 20, 1990) [S.C. Res. 681, U.N. SCOR, 2907th mtg., U.N. Doc. S/RES/681 (1990)]. In Resolution 681, the Security Council expresses grave concern over the dangerous deterioration of the situation in the Occupied Territories and at the violence and rising tension in Israel. The Security Council expresses alarm at Israel's decision to deport four Palestinians from the Occupied Territories in contravention of its obligations under the Fourth Geneva Convention.[397] Taking note of Israel's recent invitation of the Secretary-General to visit the region, the Security Council requests him to proceed with his mission.

Document 644: Report Submitted to the Security Council by the Secretary-General on the Deterioration of the Situation in the Occupied Territories (April 9, 1991) [U.N. SCOR, U.N. Doc. S/22472 (1991)]. This report by United Nations Secretary-General Javier Pèrez de Cuèllar examines the situation regarding Palestinian civilians under Israeli occupation from December 20 to February 28, 1990. Cuèllar notes that Security Council Resolution 681 was adopted at a time of great tension in the region, given Iraq's invasion of Kuwait and the prospect of serious military hostilities.[398] In particular, Iraq had threatened to use conventional and non-conventional weapons against Israel. In response, Israel had distributed gas masks to its citizens and Palestinian residents of Jerusalem, but had not distributed equipment to the Palestinian population in the Occupied Territories. This prompted United Nations officials to express concern about the needs of this group. A ruling by the Israeli High Court of Justice on January 14, 1991, demanded that the Israeli military commander exercise equality and not discriminate against residents. The Secretary-General also notes that Israel had imposed curfews on the Occupied Territories during the war due to security concerns, which Cuèllar

---

[395] Doc. 640.

[396] *Id.*

[397] *Id.*

[398] Doc. 643.

determines Israel had a right to do to defend itself. The Secretary-General weighs this consideration against Israel's obligation to protect the Palestinian civilian populations, who suffered undue hardship as a result of curfews.

Document 645: United Nations General Assembly Resolution 46/82, Calling for Israel's Immediate Unconditional Withdrawal from Occupied Territory (December 16, 1991) [G.A. Res. 46/82, U.N. GAOR, 73d plen. mtg., U.N. Doc. A/RES/64/82 (1991)]. In Resolution 46/82 (A), the General Assembly reiterates many of the calls and affirmations of previous resolutions, including its support for the PLO as the sole legitimate representative of the Palestinian people. It again claims the applicability of the Fourth Geneva Convention (1949) to the Palestinian territory occupied since 1967 and the inadmissibility of the acquisition of territory by force.[399] It expresses its concern over Israeli policies that threaten to escalate and expand the conflict in the region. Part B deals exclusively with Jerusalem, determining that Israel's decision to impose its laws, jurisdiction, and administration on the city is illegal and therefore null and void.

Document 646: United Nations General Assembly Resolution 46/86, Revoking Resolution 3379, which Called Zionism a Form of Racial Discrimination (December 16, 1991) [G.A. Res. 46/86, U.N. GAOR, 74th plen. mtg., U.N. Doc. A/RES/46/86 (1991)]. In this one-sentence resolution, the General Assembly decides to revoke General Assembly Resolution 3379, which had deemed Zionism a form of racial discrimination.[400] Thirteen of the nineteen Arab state members—including Syria, Lebanon, and Jordan who were engaged in potential peace negotiations with Israel—voted to retain the resolution. Six states, including Egypt, were absent. No Arab country voted for repeal, and the PLO denounced the vote.

*ii. Post-*Intifada *Developments*

Document 647: United Nations Security Council Resolution 904, Massacre of Palestinian Worshippers at the Mosque of Ibrahim in Hebron (March 18, 1994) [S.C. Res. 904, U.N. SCOR, 3351st mtg., U.N. Doc. S/RES/904 (1994)]. In Resolution 904, the Security Council strongly condemns the massacre of Palestinian worshipers in the Mosque of Ibrahim in Hebron. It calls upon Israel to implement measures to prevent acts of violence by Israeli settlers and requests the cosponsors of the Madrid Peace Conference (*i.e.*, the United States and the Russian Federation) to continue their efforts to invigorate the peace process.[401]

Document 648: Shamgar Commission Report (June 26, 1994) [*available at* http://www.mfa.gov.il/MFA/Government/Law/Legal%20Issues%20and%20Rulings/COMMISSION%20OF%20INQUIRY-%20MASSACRE%20AT%20THE%20TOMB%20OF%20THE]. Following the Hebron massacre, Israel's government established a commission of inquiry headed by president of the Supreme Court, Justice Meir Shamgar. The commission found that the massacre was carried out by Dr. Baruch Goldstein who acted alone in the attack. In addition, the Shamgar Commission recommended installation of electronic security devices, a specially trained security force that could handle the unique tensions of worshipping

---

[399] *See* Fourth Geneva Convention, *supra* note 82.

[400] Doc. 216.

[401] *See* Doc. 429.

Muslims and Jews, and a method for separating Jewish and Muslim worshippers completely with the intent of protecting both groups from further violence.

Document 649: Council of the League of Arab States, Arab Charter on Human Rights (September 15, 1994) [18 HUM. RTS. L.J. 151 (1997)]. The Arab Charter of Human Rights was adopted in Cairo by members of the League of Arab States. Article 1(b) states that racism, Zionism, occupation, and foreign domination constitute fundamental obstacles to the realization of the basic rights of peoples. The charter declares that there is a need to "condemn and endeavor to eliminate all such practices." It was never ratified and remains in a process of revision.

Document 650: Letter from Israeli Ambassador Gad Yaacobi to the United Nations Regarding Measures to Eliminate International Terrorism (April 10, 1995) [U.N. GAOR, 50th Sess., U.N. Doc. A/50/133 (1995)]. In this letter to United Nations Secretary-General Boutros Boutros-Ghali, Israeli Ambassador Gad Yaacobi stresses that since the signing of the Declaration of Principles (Oslo Accords), 125 Israelis had been killed in fifty-two separate terrorist attacks, most of them committed by Islamic Fundamentalist organizations.[402]

Document 651: Statement by United Nations Secretary-General Boutros Boutros-Ghali Condemning the Bus Bombing in Gaza that Killed Israelis (April 10, 1995) [U.N. Press Release, U.N. Dep't of Public Info., U.N. Doc. SG/SM/5608 (1995)]. This statement from United Nations Secretary-General Boutros Boutros-Ghali strongly condemns the April 9 attacks in the Gaza Strip that killed eight people and wounded sixty-one others. It marks the first time that the United Nations condemned a terrorist attack against Israelis that was carried out in the Occupied Territories.

Document 652: Excerpts of the Final Communiqué of the Arab Summit Conference, Cairo (June 23, 1996) [U.N. GAOR, 50th Sess., Agenda Items 42, 44, 66 and 73, Appendix, U.N. Doc. A/50/986 (1996)]. This final communiqué of the Arab Summit Conference held in Cairo focuses nearly exclusively on the Palestinian-Israeli peace process following the Madrid Conference. It reaffirms the commitment of Arab states to securing a just resolution to the conflict and calls on Israel to unequivocally commit to the peace process so as to restore Palestinian rights and return the Occupied Territories, as well as to ensure balanced and equal security in the region in keeping with the principle of land-for-peace.

Document 653: United Nations General Assembly Resolution 51/26, Peaceful Settlement of the Question of Palestine (December 4, 1996) [G.A. Res. 51/26, U.N. GAOR, 72d plen. mtg., U.N. Doc. A/RES/51/26 (1996)]. In Resolution 51/26, the General Assembly responds positively to advancements made toward peace between Israel and the Palestinians. It acknowledges the mutual recognition between the Government of the State of Israel and the PLO,[403] notes with satisfaction the withdrawal of the Israeli army that took place in the Gaza Strip and Jericho area in accordance with agreements,[404] notes with satisfaction the successful holding of the first Palestinian general elections, and notes the establishment of the Office of the United Nations Special Coordinator in the Occupied Territories. The General

[402] *See* Doc. 432.
[403] *See* Doc. 431.
[404] *See* Docs. 436–437.

Assembly emphasizes its commitment to reestablishing the 1967 borders (Green Line) and pursuing the issue of refugees. Additionally, it emphasizes the need for the United Nations to play a more active and expanded role in the peace process and in the implementation of the Declaration of Principles (Oslo Accords).[405]

Document 654: Excerpts from the Report of the Secretary-General, Pursuant to General Assembly Resolution 51/26 (November 6, 1997) [U.N. GAOR, 52d Sess., Agenda Items 36, and 37, U.N. Doc. A/52/581 (1997)]. In this report, United Nations Secretary-General Kofi Annan notes the stagnation of the Peace Process during the past year. Annan reports on the "horrifying terrorist bombings in Israel, which took the lives of innocent people" and shook the confidence between Israelis and Palestinians. Annan calls on both sides to do everything possible to restore mutual trust, revitalize peace negotiations, and ensure steady progress through the transitional period.

Document 655: Excerpts from the United Nations International NGO Meeting on the Question of Palestine, Cairo (April 26, 1998) [*available at* http://domino.un.org/UNISPAL.NSF/85255e950050831085255e95004fa9c3/03359a8fde96a60e052566c00053cd24!OpenDocument]. In this text, the NGOs participating in the United Nations International NGO Meeting on the Question of Palestine in Cairo April 25–26, 1998, note with satisfaction that the meeting was convened in the region for the first time. They affirm that the question of Palestine is fundamentally about the struggle for land and the fulfillment of the inalienable Palestinian rights to establish an independent state alongside Israel with Al-Quds or East Jerusalem as its capital. The NGOs state that Israeli policies have undermined confidence in the current peace process, and they call on Israel to implement the Oslo Agreement.[406] They further assert that cooperation between Palestinians and Israeli NGOs is important to securing the rights of Palestinians.

Document 656: Memorandum of Agreement between Israel and the United States (October 30, 1998) [*available at* http://www.usembassy-israel.org.il/publish/peace/archives/1998/october/memo_of_agreement.html]. This memorandum was the first strategic cooperation agreement between Israel and the United States to be signed at the highest offices of each government—by U.S. President Bill Clinton and Israeli Prime Minister Binyamin Netanyahu. Previously, such memoranda were signed at a ministerial level. It states that, in view of the long-term commitment by the United States to the maintenance of Israel's qualitative edge, the two states would work together to enhance Israel's defensive and deterrent capabilities and to upgrade the framework of their military relationship.

Document 657: Excerpts from the Report of the Working Group on Arbitrary Detention (Al-Khiam Prison) (December 28, 1999) [U.N. ESCOR, U.N. Comm. on Hum. Rts., 56th Sess., U.N. Doc. E/CN.4/2000/4 (1999)]. Given confusion over what state or entity was in authority at Al-Khaim Prison in southern Lebanon, the Commission on Human Rights Working Group on Arbitrary Detention determines in this report that it is justified in addressing communications and urgent appeals concerning Al-Khiam to the Israeli Government "inasmuch as it has been sufficiently demonstrated that the SLA [Southern Lebanon Army] is acting on behalf of the IDF."

---

405 *See* Oslo Accords, *supra* Doc 432.

406 *Id.*

B. Second Palestinian Intifada *or* Intifadat al-Aqsa: *2000–2004*

On September 28, 2000, violent protests erupted on the *Haram al Sharif,* the most sacred Muslim Holy Site in Jerusalem, following a visit to the site by Likud leader Ariel Sharon. Palestinians, who recalled Sharon's uncompromising rhetoric toward Arabs as well as his role in the massacre of Palestinians in the Sabra and Shatila camps in Beirut (1982), regarded the visit as a deliberate provocation and an attempt to assert Israeli sovereignty over the site.[407] Between September 28 and October 6, 2000, more than seventy Palestinians were killed and 1,900 injured in clashes with Israeli police. The twelve-year-old Palestinian Muhammad al-Dura became a symbol of the new *Intifada* after he was shot to death on September 30, 2000, at Netzarim Junction in Gaza by Israeli bullets as he hid beside his father. The incident was filmed and broadcast worldwide. By mid-October, the unrest was being referred to as "*Intifadet al-Aqsa,*" the al-Aqsa *Intifada.*

Many observers of the Palestinian-Israeli conflict viewed these events as the logical outcome of the floundering peace process. The Sharm El-Sheikh Fact-Finding Commission—known as the "Mitchell Commission"—established at the Sharm el-Sheikh Conference (October 17, 2000) to determine the cause of the unrest found that Israel's settlement activity in Palestinian territories was a root cause. The Israelis were, however, obviously happy with the report's conclusion that Sharon's visit to the Temple Mount was not the reason for the outbreak of violence, a conclusion the Palestinians were understandably not happy about. The Mitchell report was a carefully balanced document that more than dealing with the root causes of the problem tried to establish the premises for a return to negotiations. Indeed, the Mitchell report was later endorsed by both the Palestinians and the Sharon government, together with the Tenet plan, as the basis for a possible shift from violence to political negotiations.

The situation escalated on March 29, 2002, when Israel launched Operation Defensive Shield, sending its forces into the West Bank and the Gaza Strip to arrest terrorists, find and confiscate weapons, and destroy facilities where, according to Israeli intelligence, explosives were being manufactured. Simultaneously, Israeli troops occupied and surrounded the West Bank city of Ramallah and laid siege to Palestinian Authority Chairman Yasser Arafat's compound for five weeks with Arafat inside.[408] In part, this was result of the growing belief that Arafat was shirking his role as partner in the peace process and not doing enough to stop Palestinian armed resistance groups from attacking Israeli civilians inside Israel.[409]

---

[407] *See* Docs. 254 and 257.

[408] *See* Doc. 670.

[409] Israel and the United States had formed a hard-line position against Arafat

After fighting broke out in Bethlehem on April 3, 2002, Israeli forces laid siege to the Church of the Nativity—built on the purported site of Jesus' birth—with more than one hundred armed Palestinians inside. The siege lasted for five weeks, until a deal was brokered that allowed remaining fighters to be evacuated from the church unharmed and relocated to various European Union states and Cyprus.[410] On April 4, Israeli forces reoccupied all but two of the major West Bank towns and, on April 17, Israeli forces reoccupied sections of the Gaza Strip, undoing much of the work of the peace process. After concluding operations, the government of Israel on June 16, 2002, authorized a plan to build a "Security Wall" running the full length of the West Bank at an estimated cost of $1m per kilometer.

Since that time, the Security Council and General Assembly have passed several resolutions condemning Israeli policies in the Occupied Territories, including extrajudicial execution, the construction of Jewish-only settlements, the use of force against civilians, and the construction of the wall inside the pre-1967 borders (the Green Line). International criticism of the wall was bolstered by the ICJ's Advisory Opinion of July 9, 2004, which found the wall in violation of international law.[411]

Since the start of the Second Palestinian *Intifada*, at least 3,070 Palestinians and 940 Israelis have been killed. Approximately 2,778 Palestinians were killed by security forces in the West Bank and Gaza, including 557 who were under the age of eighteen, and 424 Israeli civilians were killed in Israel, including seventy-six under the age of eighteen.[412] There have been 138 suicide bombings conducted by Palestinian terrorist groups against Israelis inside Israel and the Occupied Territories between September 29, 2000, and September 26, 2004.[413]

Relevant documents may also be found in: Section 8, Status of the Palestinians; and Section 7, Israeli-Palestinian Peace Process.

Document 658: United Nations Security Council Resolution 1322, Condemning Acts of Violence, Especially the Excessive Use of Force against Palestinians (October 7, 2000) [S.C. Res. 1322, U.N. SCOR, 4205th mtg., U.N. Doc. S/RES/1322 (2000)]. The Security Council in Resolution 1322 deplores the provocation of Prime Minister Ariel Sharon's visit to the *Al-Haram Al-Sharif* in Jerusalem on September 28, 2000, and

---

after talks at Camp David II (2000) failed to produce a peace settlement. *See* Doc. 442.

[410] *See* Doc. 674.

[411] *See* Doc. 589.

[412] Figures taken from B'Tselem's record of Fatalities in the al-Aqsa *Intifada*, Data by Month *available at* http://www.btselem.org/English/Statistics/casualties.asp. There are no figures to show the proportion of Palestinians who were combatants and those who were civilians.

[413] Figures taken from BBC News, "*Intifada* Death Toll," *available at* http://news.bbc.co.uk/1/hi/world/middle_east/3694350.stm.

the subsequent violence, which resulted in the death of over eighty Palestinians and many other casualties. It reaffirms the need for full respect for the Holy Places of Jerusalem and condemns acts of violence, especially the excessive use of force against Palestinians.

Document 659: Mission Report on Israel's Violations of Human Rights in the Palestinian Territories Occupied since 1967, Submitted by Mr. Giorgio Giacomelli, Special Rapporteur (October 17, 2000) [U.N. ESCOR, Comm. on Hum. Rts., 5th Special Sess., U.N. Doc. E/CN.4/S-5/3 (2000)]. In this report, the United Nations Special Rapporteur on the Occupied Palestinian Territories, Giorgio Giacomelli, describes his mission to the region in October 2000. Giacomelli addresses the subject of military occupation and Israeli actions during the start of the *Intifada* from late September until October 17, 2000, in particular, the upsurge in the number of human rights violations. He outlines human rights concerns in the Occupied Territories, such as right to life, means of force used by the IDF, right to health, freedom of movement, and collective punishment.

Document 660: Commission on Human Rights Resolution S-5/1, Commission on Human Rights Report on Grave and Massive Violations of the Human Rights of the Palestinian People by Israel (October 19, 2000) [Res. S/5-1, Comm. for Hum. Rts., 6th Sess., Doc. S/5-1 (2000)]. In Resolution S-5/1, the Commission on Human Rights condemns Ariel Sharon's provocative visit to *Al-Haram al-Sharif* on September 28, 2000, which they blame for triggering the events that followed. It expresses grave concern about the "widespread, systematic and gross violations of human rights perpetrated by the Israeli occupying power" and decides to establish a human rights inquiry commission to gather and compile information on violations. It also requests the high commissioner for human rights to undertake an urgent visit to the Occupied Territories to evaluate violations.

Document 661: Israel's Response to the Report Submitted by the Special Rapporteur, Mr. Giacomeli (October 19, 2000) [U.N. ESCOR, Human Rts. Comm., Agenda Item 3, Annex, U.N. Doc. E/CN.4/S-5/4 (2000)]. In this official response to the report submitted by the United Nations Special Rapporteur on the Occupied Palestinian Territories, Israel expresses concern about its content and perceived one-sidedness, calling much of it "a series of unsubstantiated allegations."[414] Israel further questions the wisdom of conducting a mission to the Occupied Territories when the Secretary-General was in the region attempting to resolve the crisis.

Document 662: Final Communiqué of the Extraordinary Arab Summit Conference, Cairo (October 22, 2000) [U.N. GAOR, 55th Sess., Agenda Items 40 and 41, Annex, U.N. Doc. A/55/513 (2000)]. The final communiqué of the Arab Summit Conference accuses Israel of having transformed the peace process into a war against the Palestinian people in which military force is used to blockade and isolate Palestinians and hold them hostage within the West Bank and the Gaza Strip. It calls for the formation of an impartial international commission of inquiry to report to the Security Council and the Commission on Human Rights on the causes of the recent deterioration of the situation in the Occupied Territories.

---

[414] *See* Doc. 659.

Document 663: Excerpts from the Report of the Commission on Human Rights on Its Fifth Special Session, Administrative Implications of Commission on Human Rights Resolution S-5/1 (November 9, 2000) [U.N. ESCOR, Comm. on Hum. Rts., 5th Special Sess., U.N. Doc. E/CN.4/S-5/5/Add.1 (2000)]. In these excerpts from its report, the Commission on Human Rights dedicates itself to creating a commission of inquiry comprised of human rights investigators and forensic experts to investigate the situation in the Occupied Territories. It pledges the high commissioner for human rights will undertake a five-day mission to the Occupied Territories, as would the six special rapporteurs, the representative of the Secretary-General on internally displaced persons, and two members of the Working Group on Enforced or Involuntary Disappearances.

Document 664: Report of the United Nations High Commissioner on Human Rights on the Question of the Violation of Human Rights in the Occupied Arab Territories, Including Palestine (November 29, 2000) [U.N. ESCOR, Comm. on Hum. Rts., 57th Sess., U.N. Doc. E/CN.4/2001/114 (2000)]. Following her mission to the region in November 2000, Mary Robinson, the high commissioner for human rights, submitted this report detailing her visits to the Occupied Territories, Israel, Egypt, and Jordan. Robinson reports that the human rights situation in the Occupied Territories is bleak, with the civilian population feeling besieged by a stronger power that is prepared to use superior force against demonstrators. She details actions by Israeli military authorities that caused the death and serious injury of Palestinians, such as the use of live ammunition, rubber-coated steel bullets, and tear gas. Robinson details the impact of the escalating violence on children, the medical situation, the destruction of property, the Jewish settlements, curfews, freedom of movement, the economic impact, and the humanitarian access inside the Occupied Territories. The high commissioner also reports that IDF officers believe that the current *Intifada* was launched as a deliberate strategy of the Palestinian leadership. The report concludes with the recommendation that an international monitoring presence be established in the Occupied Territories to ensure international protection.

Document 665: United Nations General Assembly Resolution 55/131, Applicability of the Geneva Convention to the Occupied Palestinian Territory (December 8, 2000) [G.A. Res. 55/131, U.N. GAOR, U.N. Doc. A/RES/55/131 (2000)]. In Resolution 55/131, the General Assembly reaffirms the applicability of the Geneva Convention to the Occupied Territories, including Jerusalem, and demands that Israel accept its *de jure* applicability.[415] It also notes the convening on July 15, 1999, of a Conference of High Contracting Parties to the Geneva Convention on measures to enforce the convention in the Occupied Territories and Jerusalem.

Document 666: United Nations General Assembly Resolution 55/133, Israeli Practices Affecting the Human Rights of the Palestinian People in the Occupied Territory (December 8, 2000) [G.A. Res. 55/133, U.N. GAOR, 55th Sess., Agenda Item 85, U.N. Doc. A/RES/55/133 (2000)]. In Resolution 55/133, the General Assembly stresses the need for compliance with existing Israeli-Palestinian agreements and notes that the third phase of redeployment in the Gaza Strip and the Jericho area had not been implemented. It expresses its support for the summit held at Sharm el-

---

[415] *See* Fourth Geneva Convention, *supra* note 82.

Sheikh, Egypt, and its appreciation to countries that participated in the Temporary International Presence in Hebron for their positive contribution.

Document 667: Draft United Nations Security Council Resolution Calling for the Establishment of an International Protection Force for the Occupied Territories (December 18, 2000) [Draft Res., U.N. SCOR, U.N. Doc. S/2000/1171 (2000)]. The Security Council failed to adopt this draft resolution—sponsored by Bangladesh, Jamaica, Malaysia, Mali, Namibia and Tunisia—to establish a United Nations force of military and police observers in the Occupied Territories. Argentina, Canada, France, Netherlands, Russian Federation, United Kingdom, and the United States abstained from the vote. Representatives from several states indicated during the discussion that while an observer force may be useful at some stage, it was not timely in view of negotiations being resumed.

Document 668: Letter from the Chairperson of the Committee on Economic, Social, and Cultural Rights to the Permanent Representative of Israel to the United Nations (May 11, 2001) [U.N. ESCOR, U.N. Doc. E/2001/77 (2001)]. In this letter, the chairperson of the Committee on Economic, Social, and Cultural Rights informs the permanent representative of Israel to the United Nations that Israel's international treaty obligations apply to territories under its jurisdiction and effective control, including Jerusalem, the West Bank, and Gaza Strip. Further, the committee chairperson asserts that the Israeli view that jurisdiction was transferred to other parties is not valid because Israel is currently "besieging" these territories. The committee expresses its concern for the lack of protection for Palestinian civilians in these areas.

Document 669: Final Communiqué of the Extraordinary Ministerial Meeting of the Council of the League of Arab States Regarding the Palestinian Issue, the Arab Israeli Conflict, Cairo (December 20, 2001) [*available at* http://www.arableagueonline.org/arableague/english/details_en.jsp?art_id=675&level_id=219]. The Foreign Ministerial Council of the League of Arab States held an extraordinary meeting on December 20, 2001, at the request of the PNA, to discuss the deteriorating situation in the Occupied Territories. In its Final Communiqué, the council agrees to nine points of action, including: renewing its commitment to a just and comprehensive peace based on United Nations resolutions; condemning Israel's decision to suspend contacts with the legitimate Palestinian leadership; and calling on the United States to implement the guidelines offered by Secretary of State Colin Powell regarding the framework for a peaceful settlement. Further, the council calls Israel's attempt to link its assassination policy and its oppression of the Palestinian people to the events of September 11, 2001, as a ploy to mislead international public opinion.

Document 670: United Nations Security Council Resolution 1402, Calling for a Cease-Fire and an Israeli Withdrawal from Palestinian Cities (March 30, 2002) [S.C. Res. 1402, U.N. SCOR, 4506th mtg., U.N. Doc. S/RES/1402 (2002)]. In Resolution 1402, the Security Council expresses its grave concern at the further deterioration of the situation, including the recent suicide bombings in Israel and the military attack against Palestinian Authority President Yasser Arafat's headquarters in Ramallah. It calls upon both parties to implement a meaningful cease-fire, Israel to withdraw its troops from Palestinian cities, including Ramallah, and the parties to implement the Tenet security work plan[416] as a first step towards implementation of the Mitchell Committee recommendations.[417] The Security Council also reiterates its demand for an immediate cessation of all acts of violence.

Document 671: United Nations Security Council Resolution 1403, Welcoming the Mission of the U.S. Secretary of State to the Region (April 4, 2002) [U.N. SCOR, 4506th mtg., U.N. Doc. S/RES/1403 (2002)]. In Resolution 1403, the Security Council expresses its grave concern over the further deterioration of the situation and notes that Security Council Resolution 1402 was not implemented.[418] It welcomes the mission of U.S. Secretary of State Colin Powell to the region, as well as the efforts by others, including the United States, the Russian Federation, the European Union, and the United Nations Special Coordinator, to bring about a comprehensive, just, and lasting peace in the Middle East.

Document 672: United Nations Security Council Resolution 1405, Calling for the Lifting of Restrictions Imposed on the Operations of Humanitarian Organizations in the Occupied Territories (April 19, 2002) [S.C. Res. 1405, U.N. SCOR, 4506th mtg., U.N. Doc. S/RES/1405 (2002)]. In Resolution 1405, the Security Council calls for the lifting of restrictions imposed on the operations of humanitarian organizations, including the ICRC and the UNRWA, in the Occupied Territories and in particular in Jenin. The Security Council emphasizes the urgency of access for medical and humanitarian organizations to the Palestinian civilian population. It also welcomes the initiative of the Secretary-General to develop accurate information regarding recent events in the Jenin refugee camp through a fact-finding team.

Document 673: United Nations General Assembly Resolution ES-10/10, Requesting a Report on the Violence in Jenin (May 7, 2002) [G.A. Res. ES-10/10, U.N. GAOR, 17th plen. mtg, U.N. Doc. A/RES/ES-10/10 (2002)]. Gravely concerned at the reports of breaches of international humanitarian law committed in the Jenin refugee camp and other Palestinian cities by the Israeli forces, the General Assembly in Resolution ES-10/10 condemns the attacks against the Palestinian people and requests the Secretary-General to present a report on the recent events in Jenin and other Palestinian cities. It also demands that Israel cease all hindrances and obstacles to the work of humanitarian organizations and United Nations agencies in the Occupied Territories. Finally, it calls upon all concerned parties to redouble their efforts to assist in ending the current crisis and resuming negotiations towards a final settlement.

Document 674: Council of the European Union: Common Position Concerning the Temporary Reception by Member States of the European Union of Certain Palestinians (May 21, 2002) [2002 O.J. (L 138) 33–44]. In this text, the Council of the European Union decides that thirteen Palestinians that will be evacuated from the Church of the Nativity in Bethlehem may be transferred abroad, ending Israel's April 2002 siege. It agrees that while one Palestinian is to remain in the Republic of Cyprus, the other twelve

---

[416] Doc. 477.

[417] *See* Sharm el-Sheik, Fact-finding Committee Report (April 30, 2001, *available at* http://www.globalpolicy.org/security/issues/israel-palestine/document/mitchell043001.pdf.

[418] Doc. 670.

are to be received on a temporary basis and exclusively on humanitarian grounds by Belgium, Greece, Ireland, Italy, Portugal, and Spain.

Document 675: Report of the Secretary-General Prepared Pursuant to General Assembly Resolution ES-10/10 on the Violence in Jenin (July 30, 2002) [U.N. GAOR, 10th Emergency Special Sess., Agenda Item 5, U.N. Doc. A/ES-10/186 (2002)]. United Nations Secretary-General Kofi Annan prepared this report in fulfillment of General Assembly Resolution ES 10/10.[419] It details Israel's incursions into the Palestinian cities of Jenin, Ramallah, Bethlehem, and Nablus and their environs from March 29 to April 21, 2002. Annan observes that Israel justified the incursions as being necessary to destroy the infrastructure of Palestinian militant groups based in these cities that were conducting suicide bombings against Israeli civilians. Annan reports that the effects of the incursions on the Palestinian population were considerable, with the civilian population suffering under IDF-imposed curfews, internal and external closures, detention, and demolitions. Further, 497 Palestinians were killed and 1,447 injured during the violence. The Secretary-General concedes that it is difficult to determine how many civilians were among the Palestinian dead, given Israel's contention that many had died while fighting against Israeli forces. In his concluding observations, the Secretary-General recognizes that his report is limited as it was prepared without the full cooperation of both parties or a visit to the area. He contends that the deteriorating situation demonstrates the urgent need for both parties to resume the peace process.

Document 676: United Nations General Assembly Resolution ES-10/11, Demanding the Immediate Withdrawal of Israeli Forces from Palestinian Population Centers (September 10, 2002) [G.A. Res. ES-10/11, U.N. GAOR, 10th Emergency Special Sess., Agenda Item 5, U.N. Doc. A/RES/ES-10/11 (2002)]. In Resolution ES-10/11, the General Assembly, gravely concerned at the reoccupation of Palestinian cities, demands the immediate cessation of Israel's military incursions and all acts of violence, terror, provocation, incitement, and destruction. It demands the immediate withdrawal of Israeli forces from Palestinian population centers to a return to positions held prior to September 2000 and calls for urgently needed assistance and service to alleviate the dire humanitarian situation facing the Palestinian people.

Document 677: Fatah-Tanzim Statement: A Declaration to the Peaceful and Progressive People of Israel and the World (September 10, 2002) [*available at* http://archives.cnn.com/2002/WORLD/meast/09/10/fatah.text/]. In this statement to the "the Peaceful and Progressive People of Israel and the World," Fatah-Tanzim (a loosely organized *Fatah* militia) argues for the right of Palestinians to resist Israeli occupation and restates the Palestinians' nationalistic goals. The group calls for an immediate return to negotiations to resolve the Palestinian problem in accordance with international norms.

Document 678: United Nations Security Council Resolution 1435, Condemning Terrorist Acts of Both Sides and Supporting the Efforts of the Quartet (September 24, 2002) [S.C. Res. 1435, U.N. SCOR, 4614th mtg., U.N. Doc. A/RES/1435 (2002)]. In Resolution 1435, the Security Council reiterates its demand for the complete cessation of all acts of violence, including all acts of terror, provocation, incitement, and destruction. It demands that Israel immediately cease measures in and around Ramallah

[419] Doc. 673.

including the destruction of Palestinian civilian and security infrastructures and calls upon the Palestinian Authority to ensure that those responsible for terrorist acts are brought to justice. Finally, the Security Council expresses its full support for the efforts of the Quartet and calls upon all parties to cooperate with these efforts.[420]

Document 679: United Nations Report of the Secretary-General to the Security Council on the Peaceful Settlement of the Question of Palestine (November 26, 2002) [U.N. Doc. A/57/621–S/2002/1268]. The Secretary-General reports on the events of 2002 in regard to the situation in Israel and the Occupied Territories. Most notably, it addresses the Jenin Conflict and the challenges that peace process faces going forward.

Document 680: United Nations Security Council Resolution 1456, Adopting a Declaration on the Issue of Combating Terrorism (January 20, 2003) [S.C. Res. 1456, U.N. SCOR, 4688th mtg., U.N. Doc. S/RES/1456 (2003)]. Following a high-level meeting, the Security Council adopted this declaration, reaffirming that terrorism constitutes one of the most serious threats to peace and security and that any acts of terrorism are criminal and unjustifiable, regardless of their motivation. It calls for all states to take urgent action to prevent and suppress support for terrorism and to become party to all relevant international conventions and protocols relating to terrorism.

Document 681: Statement by United Nations Secretary-General Kofi Annan Urging Israel to Reconsider Expulsion Decision (September 12, 2003) [U.N. Press Release, U.N. Dep't of Public Info., U.N. Doc. SG/SM/8868 (2003)]. After the Israeli security cabinet passed a decision to expel Palestinian Authority President Yasser Arafat from the Occupied Territories, United Nations Secretary-General Kofi Annan issued this statement strongly urging the Israeli Government to reconsider.

Document 682: U.S.-Vetoed Security Council Draft Resolution Demanding that Israel Desist from Deporting Palestinian Authority President Yasser Arafat (September 16, 2003) [S.C. Draft Res., U.N. SCOR, 4828th mtg., U.N. Doc. S/2003/891 (2003)]. The Security Council failed to adopt this draft resolution demanding that Israel desist from any act of deportation and cease any threat to the safety of the elected president of the Palestinian Authority. The United States vetoed the resolution, explaining it "[would] not support any resolution that evades the explicit threat to Middle East peace process posed by Hamas and other such terrorist groups."[421]

Document 683: United Nations General Assembly Resolution ES-10/12, Illegal Israeli Actions in Occupied East Jerusalem and the Rest of the Occupied Palestinian Territory (September 25, 2003) [G.A. Res. ES-10/12, U.N. GAOR, 10th Emergency Special Sess., Agenda Item 5, U.N. Doc. A/RES/ES-10/12 (2003)]. In Resolution ES-10/12, the General Assembly reiterates its grave concern at the tragic and violent events that had taken place since September 2000. It condemns the suicide bombings and their

---

[420] *See* Doc. 484.

[421] *See* Press Release, U.S. Mission to the U.N., Explanation of Vote by Ambassador John D. Negroponte on the Resolution Addressing the Situation in the Middle East in the Security Council (Sept. 16, 2003), *available at* http://www.un.int/usa/03_141.htm.

recent intensification and calls on the Palestinian Authority to take all necessary measures to end violence and terror. It also deplores the extrajudicial killings and their recent escalation, underlining that they violate international law and international humanitarian law. Finally, it expresses full support for the efforts of the Quartet and demands that both sides fully implement their obligations in accordance with the Road Map.

Document 684: Statement by Israeli Ambassador Dan Gillerman to the United Nations, Tenth Emergency Special Session of the General Assembly (October 20, 2003) [U.N. GAOR, 21st mtg., 10th Emergency Special Sess., U.N. Doc. A/ES-10/PV.21 (2003)]. This statement to the Tenth Emergency Special Session of the General Assembly by Israeli Ambassador Dan Gillerman begins by criticizing the call for another emergency special session as it violates the conditions set out in the Uniting for Peace procedure. Gillerman criticizes the General Assembly and the Security Council for not referring expressly and forcefully in that day's resolutions to the Palestinians' obligation to end terrorism. Gillerman further outlines why Israel was compelled to build a "security fence" and reiterates that the fence has no political significance. He also criticizes the Palestinian observer for exploiting the ICJ by asking for an advisory opinion on the security fence.

Document 685: Statement by Dr. Nasser Al-Kidwa, Ambassador of Palestine to the United Nations, Tenth Emergency Special Session of the General Assembly (October 20, 2003) [U.N. GAOR, 21st mtg., 10th Emergency Special Sess., U.N. Doc. A/ES-10/PV.21 (2003)]. In his statement before the Tenth Emergency Session of the General Assembly, the Ambassador of Palestine to the United Nations, Dr. Nasser Al-Kidwa, addresses the issue of Israel's construction of a wall in the Occupied Territories, including East Jerusalem, calling it "expansionist." He criticizes the October 14 veto of a Security Council resolution that would have declared the wall illegal under relevant provisions of international law. Al-Kidwa describes Israel's wall as exemplifying a hybrid of colonization and an apartheid system that attempts to negate the national existence of the indigenous people. He further calls for the formulation of a clearly stated and unanimous international position in opposition to the wall.

Document 686: United Nations General Assembly Resolution 58/97, Applicability of the Geneva Convention Relative to the Protection of Civilian Persons in Time of War to the Occupied Palestinian Territory (December 17, 2003) [G.A. Res. 58/97, U.N. GAOR, 58th Sess., Agenda Item 84, U.N. Doc. A/RES/58/97 (2003)]. In Resolution 58/97, the General Assembly welcomes and encourages the initiatives of states parties to the Fourth Geneva Convention aimed at ensuring respect for the convention. It also demands that Israel accept the *de jure* applicability of the convention in the Occupied Territories, including East Jerusalem, and comply scrupulously with the convention's provisions.

Document 687: United Nations General Assembly Resolution 58/99, Israeli Practices Affecting the Human Rights of Palestinian People in the Occupied Palestinian Territory (December 17, 2003) [G.A. Res. 58/99, U.N. GAOR, 58th Sess., Agenda Item 84, U.N. Doc. A/RES/58/99 (2003)]. In Resolution 58/99, the General Assembly stresses the need for full compliance with existing Israeli-Palestinian agreements and the implementation of the Quartet Road Map.[422] It expresses grave concern over the use of suicide bombing attacks against Israeli civilians and the extensive destruction caused by the Israeli occupying forces in Palestinian cities, towns, villages, and refugee camps. It also expresses deep concern about the Israeli policy of closure and severe restrictions, including curfews, throughout the Occupied Territories. Finally, it condemns the events that occurred in the Jenin refugee camp in April 2002 that resulted in the loss of life, injury, destruction, and the displacement of persons.

Document 688: U.S.-Vetoed United Nations Security Council Draft Resolution, Condemning the Extrajudicial Execution Committed by Israel that Killed Sheikh Ahmed Yassin (March 24, 2004) [S.C. Draft Res., U.N. SCOR, U.N. Doc. S/2004/240 (2003)]. The United States vetoed this Security Council draft resolution condemning Israel's extrajudicial execution of Hamas leader Sheikh Ahmed Yassin. The U.S. representative stressed that it was important to remember that Yassin was the leader of a terrorist organization that had proudly taken credit for attacks on innocent civilians.[423]

Document 689: United Nations Security Council Resolution 1544, Condemning the Killing of Palestinian Civilians that Took Place in the Rafah Area (May 19, 2004) [S.C. Res. 1544, U.N. SCOR, U.N. Doc. S/RES/1544 (2004)]. In Resolution 1544, the Security Council calls on Israel to address its security needs within the boundaries of international law and condemns the killing of Palestinian civilians that took place in the Rafah area. It expresses grave concern over the humanitarian situation facing Palestinians made homeless in the Rafah area and calls for the provision of emergency assistance to them.

Document 690: Excerpts of Declaration Issued at the Sixteenth Session of the Arab Summit, Tunis (May 23, 2004) [*available at* http://www.arabsummit.tn/en/tunis-declaration.htm]. In the Tunis Declaration, the League of Arab States declares the commitment of all international parties to materialize the principles of international legality and the United Nations resolutions pertaining to the Arab-Israeli conflict, in accordance with the Arab peace initiative[424] and in implementation of the Road Map. It also addresses the situations in Iraq and Sudan.

---

[422] *See* Fourth Geneva Convention, *supra* note 82.

[423] *See* S.C. Press Release, U.N. Dep't of Public Info., 4929th mtg., U.N. Doc. SC/8034 (2004), *available at* http://domino.un.org/UNISPAL.NSF/0/b3ed1ea25fdcccf085256e6100568cf8?OpenDocument.

[424] *See* Doc. 479.

About the Authors

M. Cherif Bassiouni is a Distinguished Research Professor of Law at DePaul University and is President Emeritus of its International Human Rights Law Institute. He served as counsel to President Sadat in connection with the 1978 *Camp David Accords*. Between 1996–2003 he chaired a Track II Committee of Experts on the "Elimination of Weapons of Mass Destruction," which consisted of some 40 experts from Egypt, Israel, Jordan, and the United States.

Shlomo Ben Ami is Vice-President of the Toledo International Centre for Peace. He is a former Israeli foreign minister (2000–2001) who headed the Israeli delegation at the 1993 multilateral talks on refugees, participated at the Camp David summit (July 2000), and led the Israeli team at the Taba peace negotiations with the Palestinians (January 2001).

Both have been active in the Arab-Israeli peace process for many years which has brought them together in producing this book.

www.ingramcontent.com/pod-product-compliance
Lightning Source LLC
Chambersburg PA
CBHW072242240926
51846CB00012B/141